S0-ADD-750

Nell Irvin Painter
Route 9
Boothe Hill 15
Chapel Hill, NC 27514

MAIN CURRENTS IN MODERN AMERICAN HISTORY

Also by Gabriel Kolko

The Limits of Power: The World and United States Foreign Policy, 1945–1954 *with Joyce Kolko*

The Roots of American Foreign Policy

The Politics of War: The World and United States Foreign Policy, 1943–1945

Railroads and Regulation, 1877–1916

The Triumph of Conservatism: A Reinterpretation of American History, 1900–1916

Wealth and Power in America: An Analysis of Social Class and Income Distribution

GABRIEL KOLKO

MAIN CURRENTS IN MODERN AMERICAN HISTORY

PANTHEON BOOKS, NEW YORK

Copyright © 1976, 1984 by Gabriel Kolko

All rights reserved under International and Pan-American Copyright Conventions. Published in the United States by Pantheon Books, a division of Random House, Inc., New York, and simultaneously in Canada by Random House of Canada Limited, Toronto. Originally published by Harper & Row, Publishers, Inc., New York, and Fitzhenry & Whiteside Limited, Toronto, in 1976.

Library of Congress Cataloging in Publication Data

Kolko, Gabriel.
Main currents in modern American history.
Reprint. Originally published: New York : Harper & Row, c1976. With new epilogue.
Includes bibliographical references and index.
1. United States—History—20th century.
2. United States—History—1865–1898. I. Title.
E741.K64 1984 973.9 84-42662
ISBN 0-394-72512-3 (pbk.)

Manufactured in the United States of America

First Pantheon Paperback Edition

Contents

To the Vietnamese Revolution
and the heroic people who made it

Preface

The United States from its inception has been a nation blind to itself—its past, its present, and its future. Intellectually and culturally underdeveloped, it has left it to a handful of European commentators and rare, alienated mavericks to produce some of the more penetrating assessments of American life and society. No industrialized people confronts reality so ill-prepared in terms of ideas and insights to cope with the problems before it.

In a critical sense, this myopia is the consequence of the pervasive self-satisfied chauvinism which characterized the United States during its first modern century after the Civil War, and optimism is virtually the national ideology. Until the traumatic experience of Vietnam, which undermined the illusions of an unprecedented number of Americans, vaingloriousness or the absence of a critical vision was virtually unanimous among those who wrote about their own nation. Even occasional critics thought that reforms which were, in the scale of things, essentially minor could redeem the society. Vietnam temporarily and quite superficially broke that consensus, but how long this skeptical mood among some will continue remains to be seen. America yet marches into a future with its eyes turned toward the past, remaining astonishingly indulgent of its own tragedies and foibles, and as menacing to itself and the world as ever. The large majority of its writers and scholars continue to reinforce its optimism, mindlessness, and banality, even if they no longer celebrate the nation as during the great euphoria of the first two decades of the postwar epoch. And they nevertheless persist in avoiding the fundamental questions of the causes of the United States' growing, even inexhaustible, problems at home and the dangers it poses abroad. The consequence of this aversion to fundamentals is that there still exists, even today after the Korean and Vietnam holocausts, an only minor dissenting tradition in American thought—one which leaves unchallenged the far larger and influential mood of national optimism and self-satisfaction, to say nothing of the dissociation between reality and the definition of it. Absent is a critical alternative overview of the American historical process and system.

No academic discipline is more ill-equipped than history to analytically or intellectually explain the origins of the crises which have plagued the United States and the world with increasing intensity over the past half-century. Empiricism without insight has produced fine monographs, of which there have been an increasingly large number dealing with various phases of modern American history, but it cannot by itself create vital linkages which lead to a more comprehensive vision. Historians since World War Two have avoided the main questions and the exceedingly difficult basic problems, partially out of conservatism for some but largely because the murky reflective banalities of conventional liberal thought have encouraged myopia. Moreover, it is also a fact that the United States is a nation so complex and distinctive that existing general theories, most of which were formulated in Europe, tend to be too irrelevant or incomplete to offer much help in filling the conceptual void. The result is that, for all of these and other reasons, American scholarship has largely been immune to the dominant experiences of its age: the violence and deepening crises at home, the capacity for unlimited savagery and ruthlessness of United States foreign policy abroad, and the clear trend of the nation toward greater difficulties without resolutions for any of them. The gap between acceptable intellectual mystifications and social reality and experience grows wider with time, notwithstanding the appearance after 1960 of critical and valuable writings on various quite specific dimensions of the general American malaise.

The main purpose of this book is to describe historically the nature and purpose of power and its institutions in the United States, and its evolution over the century since the 1870s—the period of modern capitalism. That century witnessed numerous changes in the political and economic order as well as among classes. In a vital sense, these altering domestic configurations touch such fundamental issues as which groups held power, how they exercised it, and the consequences of their actions. But history involves, as well, the question of the powerless: workers and farmers above all. American capitalism during its first century was a system that was quite consistent at the level of its ultimate functions, but its structure and problems evolved in ways we must consider here in a manner which gives due respect to both continuity and change in American history.

Ideally, written history should assess the main institutional and social forces in a society over time and show how they interacted. Suffice it to say, scholarship has not served the United States or many other nations well in this regard. The integration of American history both in its domestic and international dimensions is a challenge that will demand the attention of many writers, and in this book I am merely offering a synthesis which will surely require many improvements and further development. In addition to attempting to describe the main economic and political institutional attributes of an all-subsuming capitalism over the past century, and especially its expressions in terms of foreign policy and national economic issues, I have tried to deal with the challenges before the social order which it solved as well as those it was unable to master.

It is this increasing failure that I find to be a main trend in modern American history, for problems and crises have multiplied faster than solutions, and this gap has grown with time. Capitalism's structural dilemmas and contradictions allow us to concentrate on historical dynamics which are meaningful, even if such a focus is perhaps not all-inclusive. But whatever the deficiencies of descriptive history, it seems quite clear that the main drift in modern American history illustrates the limits of capitalism and its social order in dealing with its emerging difficulties. The weaknesses and tensions of the system, therefore, we must move to the fore, with the growing inability of the directors of the society to control or rationalize it being the central institutional phenomenon over the past century. In the end we find confirmation of this trend in a society in protracted crisis, adrift, and with its redemption in the form of concrete, much less general, answers increasingly elusive. The constraints that circumstances and structural dilemmas impose on the numerous efforts to overcome problems thereby become a way of defining and understanding the character of the social order in specific terms, and designating precisely which institutions and factors cause challenges to emerge in the first place.

Immediately after the Civil War the American economy was qualitatively transmuted into modern industrial capitalism, setting the context for the first national efforts at economic and political integration during the decades after 1887. In a sense, all such attempts, then and thereafter, proved tentative and often abortive, and what was more significant than concrete approaches to the economic and political problems of an era were the very conditions and causes which prompted such actions in the first place. Means were less important than ends, and individual methods were often discarded after their ineffectuality became apparent. But it was during the first generation after the Civil War that the main problems of the economic structure were to arise, and eventually to require political reactions that have continued until this day. During the late nineteenth century the quite complex economic structure evoked state measures which for the most part were tentative, even experimental, and failed to accomplish their objectives because of the very difficulty of the tasks, the changing nature of the economic institutions requiring political assistance, and the increasing importance of war and foreign affairs in defining the direction of American society.

Dealing with the historical nature and purpose of power requires analyses of structural attributes of the United States as they evolve over time in addition to those aspects of the society which remain constant. And this logically necessitates a discussion of efforts to resolve the problems of a capitalist economy as well as the indispensable political framework at home and abroad in which all such efforts proceeded. In the following pages I try both to focus on key institutions—economic, political, and the social relations of power and powerlessness—as well as the vital contextual events. Foreign, national, and structural issues are interspersed because that rather more accurately captures the context and dynamics of a history too complex, in the last analysis, to be described in a wholly satisfactory manner within any format. I have, in short, juxtaposed historical and structural approaches to the analysis of American society, often within the same chapter. The chapters are grouped chronologically, but those on the working class, power, and the political structure overlap all the rest.

Readers will note a certain variability in detail between different chapters, and my coverage is relatively more general of any topic I have examined in six of my earlier books as well as articles. In fact, all I have done here is treat such issues quite broadly, revising and sharpening a number of analytic themes on the period 1876–1916 which I have documented at much greater length elsewhere. Subjects on which I have not hitherto published, such as the period 1920–1940 or the working class, include some additional details not readily found elsewhere and essential to my overall interpretation. This volume, therefore, is both a revision and synthesis of my earlier work as well as an attempt to move well beyond it and thereby encompass the main currents of modern American history.

Initial research and analysis for this book was greatly assisted by the American Council of Learned Societies, which in 1971 kindly awarded me a fellowship. The Killam Program of The Canada Council made it possible for me to write and finally complete the book with a senior research scholarship during 1974–1975, and I am especially indebted to it for its generosity as well as creating those ideal conditions essential for writing. To both these organizations my appreciation, and, needless to say, neither assumes any responsibility whatsoever for the contents of this book. I wish to thank Stanley Vittoz for help with sources and numerous burdens while he completed his own important study of labor and the state.

As before, to my wife, Joyce, I owe the greatest obligation for aid and encouragement in every way, and if this book has any merit it is to a great extent due to her criticisms and insights. For all its shortcomings and errors, I, of course, assume all responsibility.

GABRIEL KOLKO

MAIN CURRENTS IN
MODERN AMERICAN HISTORY

1

The Foundations of the Political Economy, 1876–1920

The essence of the American experience with the national government's regulation of the economy has been its limits and dilemmas. Partial and temporary successes in specific efforts notwithstanding, uncontrollable developments in the national and world economies as well as the integrated and continental structure of the economy have inevitably affected profoundly the fate of each major economic sector, frustrating the numerous political as well as private attempts over the past century to regulate, stabilize, and make prosperous this or that particular economic interest. Ultimately, only by understanding the origins, causes, and failures of the movement to manage the economy politically at the national level can one perceive the contemporary weakness and the very character of American capitalism. Crisis and change preclude the attainment of sufficient success in the attempts to regulate and make profitable capitalism, and this perception of historical dynamics carries the obligation to stress the constraints within the system as a whole. For in reality, no sooner has one problem within some important industry superficially appeared solved than other crises and new situations create additional dilemmas for the larger economic structure and, often, undercut the value of earlier concrete efforts at regulation or industrial cooperation. In general, the main tendency within American capitalism since the Civil War has been to require ever more comprehensive political, economic, and social solutions to the challenges it has confronted, even as the political and intellectual conditions both for articulating precisely and implementing these answers have become increasingly elusive and transcended the system's capacities.

The Myth of Economic Integration

Despite an amazingly durable conventional wisdom to the contrary, which Marxists as well as apologists for the system have shared, American capitalism over the half-century after the Civil War did not concentrate to the extent sufficient to impose mastery over the fate of finance and most industries without ultimately having to resort to some all-too-finite political solution. There was, of course, an immense growth in the size of individual firms, many of which by 1900 were truly big businesses, and Wall Street did in fact vastly multiply its financial activity; but large size is not tantamount to control, and without understanding the importance of this crucial distinction it is impossible to comprehend the economic motivations behind political efforts to regulate the economy.[1]

The primary contextual fact is that the half-century after 1870 saw, by far, the most rapid growth in manufacturing and mining industries that the United States has ever experienced, during which time new hubs of financial and economic power emerged without the existence of a dominating, centralized financial and capital control such as virtually all historians later erroneously attributed to Wall Street. Only by comprehending that decentralization and local and regional autonomy were far more characteristic of the economy before 1900 than the conventional image in the historical literature can one grasp the main trends. Whatever the criterion, whether gross capital formation, gross per capita national product, total capital in manufacturing, capital per unit of labor input, or the like, a unique pattern of unparalleled and largely uncontrolled growth was the defining fact of the first half-century of modern American history, during which time the financial sector was too crude either to stimulate coherently or to control this vast economic expansion. Even if the rising costs of efficient technology destroyed many small firms after the Civil War, the growth of larger corporate units did not dampen competition or, in innumerable fields, new entrants.

The absence of true financial centralization was due partially to the fact that American manufacturing produced internally 70 percent of its new financing from means such as profits and depreciation from 1900 to 1910, and 72 percent from 1915 to 1953, with much of the borrowed capital usually being obtained from local sources. Indeed, outside of Boston the investment bankers ignored Midwest and Western industry until the very end of the nineteenth century, and new firms west of the major North Atlantic coastal cities could not rely on stock flotations until well after they had by necessity developed their own mechanisms of capital accumulation. By that point they often could treat with New York or Boston bankers as equals. The latter preferred the lucrative railroad industry until its spate of bankruptcies in the 1890s tarnished its promise. As a consequence, manufacturers and miners borrowed locally, usually on a short-term basis, and maintained closely held corporations until the turn of the century.

Even so, when Eastern investment financiers did seek to invest in manufacturing and mining, which they were both more eager and able to do after 1898, they in turn still had to depend partially on tapping the European capital market until as late as 1914, when Europeans held $4.5 billion in American bonds and securities. It was because of J. P. Morgan's access to European outlets that the United States Treasury called upon him to help place its 1895 gold loans, but during the 1907 financial panic it was Morgan and his associates who pleaded with Washington to mobilize its resources to save the entire Eastern banking community from crisis. By the first decade of this century, the Treasury, inadequate as it was had assumed greater central banking functions than an allegedly collusive Wall Street, which remained sufficiently internally disunited as well as far too remote from the mushrooming new economic and financial centers to control its own economic welfare.

When Eastern finance did massively enter the industrial stock market after 1897, it was in response to the decline of railroad profitability as well as the desire of many of the early founders of new manufacturing firms to retire and diversify their economic holdings by selling the companies in which their fortunes originated. And a significant number of such sales were also attempts to solve problems of industry-wide competition or internal management that the predominantly family and partnership forms of corporate organization had created. If this merger movement, which reached frenetic proportions and then greatly diminished after seven short years ending about 1905, offered ample scope for New York finance to participate in the rewards of industrial capital expansion, it in no way diminished the trend toward banking decentralization—and the grave dangers it posed.

Since the geographic location of industrial expansion as well as population moved westward, and population growth was potentially one of the greatest stimuli to capital accumulation, centers of financial capital grew with it. The activities of the Chicago and St. Louis banking clearing houses grew four times during the two decades after the ending of the Civil War, while New York's remained constant. Because Wall Street would not and could not supply necessary funds to Midwestern manufacturers, some local industrialists created and dominated their own banks for those occasions when self-financing was insufficient, and access to cheaper capital was decisive to the successes of the Rockefeller and Carnegie empires. Moreover, the emergence of state banks free from the stricter national controls enacted during the Civil War resulted in the relatively uninhibited state-chartered banks possessing 58 percent of the total banking resources by 1913. In 1912, New York banks shared only 18 percent of the American banking resources, leaving such critical new industries as automobiles, Southwest oil, and the like for the most part independent of Eastern finance.

Limited by its conservatism and confronting the sheer magnitude of a capital explosion which it could not in any event have controlled sufficiently, the Eastern financial community still faced the dangerous problems that accompanied the vast rise of competition and banking decentralization. The capital market they had developed after 1897 was still heavily geared to paying off older entrepreneurs ready to sell out, but scarcely reversed the pattern toward internal financing, which indeed continued to dominate manufacturing in this century. Banking and finance needed a center of control which New York alone simply could not provide by purely economic means, and, as we shall soon see, it was for this reason that Wall Street turned to politics when its economic power and control no longer sufficed.

Despite the rhetoric and fear of "monopoly" which existed at the end of the nineteenth century, an anxiety which assumed a politically potent role even if it was a mythical description of most of the industrial structure, the image of the period held at the time and for decades thereafter led to a myopia regarding the economic dynamics of the critical period after the Civil War. Concretely, of course, there was vast growth and the emergence of firms that by any criterion could be labeled "big business," but a monopoly is a firm that not only is large but also sufficiently dominant in its industry to be able to control all prices and output. In this sense, "monopoly capitalism" in the half-century before World War One was both a fear for the many and an aspiration for a very few, but the vast majority of industries had not yet attained it, and the small number of exceptions—as in petroleum—did not last very long. Briefly, aspiring monopolists sought but could not attain conditions of stability and control by purely economic means.

The numerous reasons American capitalism precluded the widescale emergence of monopoly control before 1920 varied with each industry, but all were important. There was the astonishing growth of capital formation due to the readiness of local merchants and small capitalists to diversify; and the vast influx of mobile labor and its availability both as a work and consumer force in new regions was also critical. In addition, the geographic swing in the location of economic activity away from the Atlantic, so that something like a manufacturing-processing frontier existed after 1870, and the considerable creativity of new manufacturers in successfully employing new inventions, and thereby reducing their greater dependence on established capital markets, also diminished the chances of easily imposing monopoly power.[2]

Growth in the physical volume and capital in both manufacturing and mining made it doubly difficult for any one or a small number of firms to control the sheer immensity of the industrial explosion which took place during the last thirty years of the nineteenth century and at a somewhat slower rate until 1919. The emergence of a vast capital market to promote mergers among many firms, a phenomenon upon which historians and economists generalized into the future with projections which were wrong or misleading, began in 1898 and lost its steam in 1904, when investors failed to make anticipated fortunes and, indeed, even lost considerable sums. Moreover, the merger movement, which gave Wall Street its first real access to the industrial expansion, was largely confined to eight industries in which the number of competitors remained high or even grew—the most famous being iron and steel. For the branches of capitalism, the problem was how to attain economic stability rather than fend off the farmers' "anti-monopoly" attacks on which historians have lavished inordinate attention.

The relatively short life of the merger movement was inevitable because the combinations were much more often simply fine opportunities for promoters. Morgan was the greatest of them; and they all watered stocks to the extent that perhaps half the issues were purely speculative shares on which they often could not pay dividends. Promoters blended together weak and strong corporations with managers of very unequal talents, and created industrial units which had long since passed the point of the optimum size essential for efficient output. The limits of this process, which had little to do with organizational or economic efficiency but were merely promoters' responses to an artificial capital market, were translated in the inability of the new giants to prevent the entry of new firms and the loss of their original shares of the market. Indeed, what is more essential to understand is that the incipient condition of corporate consolidation which existed only briefly at the turn of the century produced an economy that firms within an industry, with precious few exceptions, could regulate less and less at the level of prices and output.

In the aggregate, during the decade after 1899, even as the merger movement reached its peak, the number of manufacturing firms in the United States increased 29 percent, while patents issued to individuals rose. Iron and steel was the industry most affected by the corporate merger effort, and United States Steel had 62 percent of the output when it was organized in 1901. Yet 446 individual firms still existed in 1909, and by 1920 United States Steel's share of output had declined to 40 percent as more efficient, significantly more profitable newer firms moved ahead of it. Standard Oil came the closest of any firm to creating a true monopoly, with 90 percent of the refinery output of the oil industry in 1899. Nevertheless, it failed to keep up with product shifts, as well as the movement of oil fields toward the West, and dropped to 80 percent in 1911, when the Supreme Court broke it up into individual but complementary units. By 1921, these firms accounted for but half the output, losing the markets, especially in gasoline products geared to the auto revolution, to newcomers. International Harvester, another Morgan promotion, passed from control of 85 percent of the harvester market in 1902 to 64 percent in 1918, while AT&T controlled the entire telephone industry in 1894 but only half by 1907. The top four copper producers controlled 76 percent of the output in 1890, and 39 percent in 1920.

By the time the war broke out, it was clear that numerous factors, important to varying degrees in different industries, were increasing economic instability in an industrial sector that was growing each year in its share of all American economic activity. Technological innovation remained high, and had upset the stability and control of such industries as chemicals and electrical goods. Changes in consumer tastes, as in tobacco, could occasionally arise to shatter existing firm domination. Industries with low investment levels for entry and efficient production—such as paper, textiles, glass, or meat—remained troubled with the instability endemic in high competition. And the larger question of the geographic shift of markets and resources availability remained a threat to established patterns in most industries. After 1910, as well, important firms that had built solid bases in one field began diversifying their product lines into quite unrelated fields, expanding competition in industries normally requiring large capital resources. American industrial capitalism, in brief, entered the twentieth century with conditions of instability potentially dangerous to short-term profits and market shares and to its future security.

Railroads, around which the organized capital market had existed until the Depression of 1893–1897 left roads controlling 28 percent of the mileage in bankruptcy, reveal much of the same pattern toward a continuation of competition and declining profitability dangerous to numerous railroads. Railroad mileage in the United States more than quadrupled between 1875 and 1915, and over that period the revenue per ton mile more than halved as cutthroat rate competition increasingly became the rule in an industry that in large regions had become unremunerative. While the number of lines increased until 1907, when 1564 operating railroads were in existence, only slightly over half this number were totally independent; but the quantity was still much too large for the profit of many large roads.

As with every other major economic sector—banking, industry, and mining—railroad growth had far exceeded the autonomous capacity of capitalists to restrict and control their own affairs so as better to guarantee their larger mutual interest to prosper and survive. Expansion and competition, and with them instability and economic crises, had become the essential hallmarks of the main branches of the American economic structure during the first half of modern American history.

National Economic Regulation

National regulation of various components of the economy after 1887, ranging from railroads to banking to industry, was an effort to find political means to resolve the economic problems which economic decentralization, competition, and a whole panoply of new challenges made endemic to American capitalism. It was not the exclusive method which various business leaders employed to attain stabilization and integration of their industry; for other nonpolitical means included trade associations and pools that sought voluntary price and output agreements and, of course, further efforts at mergers and economic concentration. Indeed, one can only view the American national reform experience from the 1880s until World War One as a frustrating cycle in which specific business constituencies moved alternatively between political and voluntary economic solutions to their problems, abandoning the one for the other as each in its turn failed to resolve their dilemmas or, what was as common, when general prosperity made past instabilities temporarily disappear. Beginning modestly with national railroad regulation in 1887, during the first fourteen years of this century the politics and politicians of economic regulation provided the dominant issues of the "Progressive Era," and not until the Great Depression was the issue of national reform to again occupy so much of the federal political structure's attention—after which point the political foundations of modern American capitalism were fixed. If national regulation grew elliptically, in a piecemeal and incremental fashion, collectively it laid the basis of the American political economy of the last half-century.

The fact that various businesses had strong incentives to use political modalities to attain economic goals eluded historians, who for decades thought that banking, railroads, or various industries were sufficiently concentrated and internally cohesive not to need the assistance of political agencies. But had the power they assumed to be in private hands been as extensive as they implied, then the emergence of "progressivism" as a means of seeking solutions to industrial problems would not have occurred. Yet it is expansion, competition, and decentralization that made national economic regulation appear increasingly attractive to this or that interest with a problem. For established firms in all sectors of the economy, the challenge was how to regularize their markets—price and output included—and for newcomers it was a matter of winning a slice of it. The former tried voluntary means first, and failed, while new entrepreneurs broke all accords that stood in the way of their growth—until success gave some of them also a vested interest in attempts at stabilization. While each major sector and industry had its own rules, reflecting their distinctive problems, political regulation was preeminently and most consistently a method of expressing rivalries among capitalists in which one type of firm—usually older and with larger vested interests—confronted and constrained another. We can never, in brief, overestimate the strength of specific industrial constituencies, and capitalism in general, to operate exclusively to find its rewards outside of a political framework. There were other elements, as well, in the national reform movement, but none so constant and important as this.

But intra-industry relations, whatever their form and however comprehensive national political regulation, could not solve the condition of economic demand and prosperity, which transcended all techniques of private or publicly sponsored cooperation. Indeed, it was the larger fluctuation of the business cycle that often upset and made inadequate existing forms of specific economic stabilization, for during downturns in the economy the constraints of earlier days melted before the new desire of once cooperative firms to restore their profits at another's expense. In fact, precisely because variations in the condition of the economy repeatedly made internal differences among firms inevitable and a voluntary unifying strategy and stabilization and control of their industry impossible, it often appeared to many businessmen that the political structure was the only place in which to find a unifying mechanism and establish a legally binding common denominator and rules for conduct.

Modes of capitalist rivalry are abundant, though not as numerous as the number of competitive industries. Generally, however, sectors of any industry often realize it is to their direct welfare to equalize those costs—labor or transport particularly—which allow some firms to employ lower prices to grab a larger share of existing markets. And established firms invariably favor efforts to reduce the ease with which new firms can enter their industry. This has also necessarily meant that some firms within an industry have ardently spoken against regulation, a fact to which historians later attached exclusive importance, and at the same time nonbusiness elements have also favored some mode of regulation or even policing of an economic sector. Anyone who sees this diversity as the essence of the era ignores the critical question of who benefits from a measure and defines its implementation, when in fact the motives of the losers, or those who created pressures others redirected for their own ends, should be of marginal interest. In brief, the issue is who succeeds rather than fails in attaining his main objectives in politics, and not so much the motives of reformers as the consequences of legislation. National or even state regulation is merely an instrument toward the goal of industrial regulation, and not an objective in itself, for when there are no useful, immediate economic consequences in political intervention, business has rarely advocated it. During the great expansion of economic activity and new firms between 1870 and 1914, with its destabilizing depressions and business downturns as well as long-term aggregate growth, political regulation of the national and state economies grew in frequency despite the long-run prosperity. After World War One, business attraction to national political intervention was more closely related to economic conditions, declining with prosperity. Indeed, for very diverse reasons, hardly any social element of American society was consistently opposed to some form of regulation.

The railroads were the first important economic sector to illustrate this cycle. The overexpanded industry had attempted to create voluntary pools and agreements to prevent rate-cutting and raiding of established territories, and new competition grew more quickly than significant efforts to concentrate ownership and control into fewer lines. Moreover, by the mid-1880s it was clear that large shippers would be able to create sufficient unevenness in state railroad regulations to increase costs and provide nuisances—though railroads one by one managed to control even the most reputedly "progressive" and "radical" of these state commissions. Removing such local inconsistencies in the national economy alone made federal regulation and uniformity more desirable not only to railroads but to the insurance and banking sectors facing comparable problems in their own industries. It was a critical sector of the railroads themselves that advocated and helped create the Interstate Commerce Commission in 1887, and directed it along paths the railroads charted thereafter. Other forces around some predominantly big shipping interests also competed with them and diluted in degree, but not kind, the nature of the regulatory effort, but by World War

One the railroads either controlled or overshadowed the influence of shippers, who in any case were but one more powerful rival economic group scarcely interested in some nebulous "public interest" that later writers have curiously attributed to the purposes of federal regulatory bodies.[3]

National regulation was not the only means railroads had for attaining stability and profits, and they never saw it in exclusive terms. Throughout the 1890s they continued, without success, to seek voluntary, nonbinding mechanisms, ranging from new price accords and pools to further consolidation of lines. What is most significant about the railroads' search for stability with profit was that they were never to find it by any means, whether private or public, and they were unable even to formulate a solution that held out the promise of genuine mastery over their economic environment, so that implementation of measures they favored is less significant ultimately than their futile search. They several times resorted again to new federal legislation, and the Pennsylvania Railroad's attorney even wrote the 1903 anti-rebating act, but the dominant fact worth stressing is that the most important single sector of the American industrial revolution ultimately became the victim of larger structural forces which eluded its control. In this sense it is unimportant that the ICC was not always composed exclusively of former railroad attorneys or their friends, of which there were to be many, or that shippers also influenced it on occasion.

In brief, the national reform experience produced during its first decades a situation in which business interests increasingly relegated economic crises to the political arena for solutions, but at the same time it was frequently impossible for the state to contrive efficacious answers that satisfied, thereby producing multiple frustrations in the management of American capitalism. For this reason it is extremely difficult to locate business advocates of political regulation who were literal-minded ideologists regardless of time and place, just as few businessmen matched the academics and preachers in their alleged dedication to Social Darwinian doctrines of economic and social competition as a desirable end in itself. Surely there were no businessmen who ever wished to have academics regulate them—for this they preferred their own lawyers and representatives. Businessmen advocated functionally rather than ideologically motivated political solutions, again, when other answers failed. With identical pragmatism they actively sought to implement private economic accords, mainly by means of trade-association codes, only if they were in highly competitive industries—such as textiles or bituminous coal—that were denied the stability of oligopoly or a few dominating firms able to regulate prices and output. Contemporary theorists were rare save in the university or world of letters, and there often by artificial hindsight. The one business organization, the National Civic Federation, to which a consistent interventionary ideology has been attributed virtually disappeared after 1916—precisely the time during which national regulation reached a peak. Hence there is a quite low level of conceptualization among business reformers, and what counts most are their functional actions and proposals. These proposals were invariably the concoctions of sick industries seeking help, and their definitions of desirable federal regulation rarely touched other industries content with their own lots. No one, in any case, ever advocated national regulation until they saw that their own interests were directly involved, and until then they often opposed regulation for others on principle. Consistency is a quality all too rare among specific businessmen favoring national political intervention. Political capitalism—the merger of the economic and political structures on behalf of the greater interests of capitalism—was incremental rather than comprehensive during its origins, and one misses the texture of the American experience in both implying excess rationality, efficacy, and coherence to it as well as denying its importance. Precisely because capitalism is not a rational system led by predictable men it resists a facile social analysis, and caveats and contingencies must be attached to any larger description. Yet the very ambiguity of a systematic description reflects both the economy's complexity as well as its vulnerability.

The experience in banking was, in principle, much the same as in railroads and embodied those essential elements that reappear often in the development of political capitalism before World War One. J. P. Morgan led Wall Street, but the Street had lost any capacity to exercise sufficient mastery over a national banking system. His importance was exaggerated all out of proportion because of his most exceptional and profitable servicing of the United States Treasury with a $65 million gold loan in 1895, but in 1907 Morgan and his associates were far more dependent on Washington's intervention in the financial crisis of that year and in the future—and knew it. By that time the Eastern banking community was fully aware of the dangerous decentralization of the banking structure as well as their need for integration via national legislation. "I would rather have regulation and control than free competition," Henry P. Davison, Morgan's partner, told Congress in 1912 in a truism that was widely appreciated at the time but overlooked by scholars over the next half-century.[4] And the legislation they obtained, as well as the personnel to administer the Federal Reserve System in Washington and New York, was in essence that which big bankers in New York first articulated and advocated. In effect, leaving the tortured details of the history of the origins of banking legislature to my other volume dealing with this theme, it can be argued that the preconditions for the emergence of Wall Street as the dominant force in banking and finance, with the power to command and be obeyed, depended on the far greater extension of political control over national banking. Indeed, only in banking was sufficiently appropriate and extensive action taken, and the environment adequately malleable, to make a real, even if temporary, difference. In the case of railroads the structural forces operating in the economy were to prove both unpredictable and overwhelming to the effort.

In certain economic sectors, such as insurance and utility regulation, advocates of regulation were stymied, but they further illustrated the fact that many businessmen increasingly saw politics as the arena in which to find solutions for wasteful competition, inconsistent state regulations, the easy entrance for new firms into their industry, and potential crisis. What was politically impossible for the moment because of divisions within the industry might prove relevant another year—and often did. Meanwhile, the numerous federal acts and agencies created during the "Progressive Era" left an important, if incomplete, basis for later reforms. In addition to the railroad regulatory system there was now a Federal Trade Commission and a Federal Reserve Board, food and drug legislation, a meat inspection that the biggest firms had much desired, and diverse other laws.

In the case of assorted industrial regulations, here too one finds the advocates of national legislation emerging in response to decentralization and competition in the various industrial sectors, from steel to meat; and their success in the form of the Federal Trade Commission is more equivocal because of the imprecision of the law and the ignorance of all in face of the sheer magnitude of the task of regulating a capitalism characterized all too much by its mythical virtue of competition. "Unfair competition" was made illegal under the 1914 law, curiously banning price cutting designed to reduce the number of competitors in a field, but more to the point was the desire of the FTC, in the words of its first chairman, Joseph H. Davies, in 1915, "that our industries shall be integrated and stabilized" to confront the national and world economy.[5] That the way to attain this goal remained a mystery to even its most ardent advocates was of less immediate significance than the definition of the goal itself. And what was most essential for later efforts in all fields was that, in a piecemeal and exploratory fashion, an extensive foundation of the modern American political economy had been laid and critical precedents established in a comprehensive fashion.

For the most part, before the war the advocates of this rationalization thought almost exclusively in terms of the concrete problems of their own industries, and the types of laws and commissions they propounded must always be assessed in terms of the economic context that made them desirable to one or another group. The Northern cotton-textile industry long advocated the passage of national child labor legislation not because of philanthropy or even some abstract pecuniary theory but purely and simply to strike a blow at their Southern rivals, who, enjoying a lower-cost labor supply, were beginning to dominate the market. Others began considering various forms of public unemployment insurance as an intriguing means of reducing labor turnover and thereby lowering labor costs. In addition to political actions to attain stability, profit, and rationality, business contemplated new innovations, for after 1911 trade associations begin emerging to standardize industry practices, with FTC encouragement following what eventually was to lay a critical basis of postwar regulatory efforts. The legal bases of this political capitalism were by no means fully completed over the thirty years after the creation of the ICC, and there had been many false starts and errors—not merely those political opponents dictated but, also, those limits of capitalist planning that ignorance and, above all, a changing structural environment in which men planned for the future on the basis of a quite different past imposed. And in a context in which goals always exceeded the means for attaining them, new improvisations and yet more change were foreordained.

The Political Dilemma

Economic rationality in a capitalist society can flounder because of the limits of technique and insight, divisions within an industry which neutralize the capacity of factions to unequivocally apply their solutions, and, above all, the alteration of external structural forces in the world and national context—whether war or depression—which make the essential foresight for planning rarely attainable. As for the political dimension, one cannot dismiss its importance merely by stating the truism that there is a consensus on the desirability of capitalism. In any specific case an analyst must take into account that interests clash well short of ultimate doctrine on such tangibles as conflicts by product, by size of firm, by agriculture versus industry and regions with differing specific needs, and any number of variables which always exist to make difficult the execution of a policy as well as, later, the comprehension of it.

Between 1896 and 1920 these differences were perhaps less significant than they were thereafter to become, but they remain important. The most astonishing political consensus was at the Presidential level, and only William Howard Taft tampered slightly with the orderly synthesis of big-business needs and national reform that characterized the unity of politics and economics some call "progressivism," but which more precisely should be termed "political capitalism."

Theodore Roosevelt was the linchpin of the period, and his belief in the inevitability of big business, and the need to distinguish between "good" and "bad" trusts, is now far better appreciated than the earlier naïve image of Roosevelt as "trustbuster." In fact no trusts were "busted" under his Presidency, and only Taft took several feeble steps in this direction, while Roosevelt's gentlemen's agreement to protect the "good" J. P. Morgan firms from anti-monopoly laws has been fully detailed elsewhere. Suffice it to say, such big businessmen paid handsomely to see Roosevelt reelected or remain in politics, and provided at least one million dollars to his chimerical 1912 effort to capture the GOP nomination and create the Progressive Party when Taft pushed his way into the Republican candidacy. Roosevelt's view of an integrated, paternal society, in which each class—especially workers—remained faithful to the prescribed rules governing their relations, meant that the banality and club manners of Harvard prevailed for eight years while various business sectors enlarged their views of desirable federal actions. With the exception of two railroad acts, meat inspection, and the Food and Drug Administration, as well as a hands-off policy toward Morgan-related firms, Roosevelt was to leave it to Wilson to implement much of what big-business elements advocated. Wilson, while nominally the symbol of the restoration of Southern Democracy to full equality in national politics, freely and accurately admitted at the time that, save for the tariff question, he could not distinguish between himself and the Roosevelt Republicans. In the intervening period after 1900 until the war, in which personal political ambitions melded with skepticism and opposition from agrarian conservatives who saw no need to assist industry and bankers, there are many details on which historians have focused, losing sight of the forest for the trees, but the fact is that by 1914 the most important business constituencies in the various key economic sectors had attained the essential legislation they sought from the federal government. There were undesired aspects to their triumphs, but these they were largely able to control, and above all they had virtually complete mastery over the implementation of the laws they advocated and the personnel of the commissions they created.

All this was logical given the fact that political power in the United States always responds to power and influence in the hands of businessmen, who often have more leverage over politics, given the consensual nature of the seriously considered social and economic priorities in America, than over their own business affairs—and are ready to use it. That nonbusiness groups shared a consensus which made capitalism the sanctioned economic order is not important; what is more critical is that economic reforms advanced class ends and were intended to satisfy class needs, and it was elite opinion and advocacy rather than the more numerous groups that shared it that moved social policy and political power. That the federal government between 1887 and 1916 associated the social weal with the welfare of the regulated sectors is reflected in the personnel and policies of the federal regulatory agencies of the period, and when key bureaucrats were not pliable, as in the case of Harvey Wiley of the Food and Drug Administration, they were unceremoniously muzzled.

But politics in the Progressive Era affected the execution of policies, and was but an augury of future dysfunctions as well as evidence of the ability of rich and well-born to have their way once they could agree among themselves. The personnel of the federal administration, ranging from Mark Hanna's man, William McKinley, in the White House, to the Cabinet members of his and subsequent administrations, revealed the continuity of power inside and outside government. Class, property, and power existed in tandem, always parallel and sympathetic on general values, sometimes independent in their actions, and often interacting. Politics became dysfunctional when serious interests were in conflict. At the very worst the dissidents within the ranks of respectability stood as educated, middle-class, generally younger spokesmen for the interests of the Western states not yet attached to this or that industrial development. They could delay and at times modify the reforms the specific interests of the industrial regions demanded, and occasionally they could stop them—as with insurance regulation. But to a lesser degree, all that the spokesmen associated with America west and south of St. Louis could do was fight a rear-guard action during the era of 1896–1916, and score more points later.

Meanwhile, the Presidents and their circles responded to the bankers and businessmen who sought their ears and actions, and any historian who works in the documents of the period finds innumerable recurrent contacts between important economic leaders and the main political figures both before and during the enactment of legislation they desire or oppose. It would be shocking if it were otherwise, just as it is predictable there was only one recorded case during this era of a black entering the White House for nonmenial purposes—and whether it was by the front door has been debated—and none, apparently, of real workers of whatever race to air their views. In effect, within the parameters of a class society, political life was administered according to its class character and political parties, and that fact, perhaps more than anything else, meant that business forces in need would have a reasonable chance to attain their goals, in part or wholly, by resort to political mechanisms. Incrementally, that process has provided modern American history with one of its main currents and defining experiences.

The Impact of War

The First World War did not bring to a definitive culmination the efforts of anti-competitive businessmen to rationalize their industries. It did create a skein of incipient organizational forms that were to be modified and revived later, deepened informal cooperation among firms so that something like oligopoly emerged in numerous industries, and produced a general prosperity and rising prices that solved all the earlier business problems which had stimulated the movement for regulation and national stabilization in the first instance. The wartime crisis produced new business-government integrative mechanisms, but the Wilson Administration disbanded them almost immediately after the end of the conflict, leaving precedents and experiences on which others would build.

The war organization's structure reflected the social context, and, in effect, existing power centers defined the new departures in a manner they deemed most useful. That the continuation of the dominant role of business men-of-power in new government posts will mean that the war organization will be managed in a manner favorable to the needs of business goes without saying. Despite the frustrations of the early war organization, which reflected both inexperience and the fact that the military and government bureaucracy could not match business for expertise in management of wartime mobilization, by July 1917 the Wilson Administration created the War Industries Board under the domination of men largely from finance and industry. Wary of elaborate bureaucratic codes and prone to informal yet binding accords, it was the first time businessmen had so comprehensively and profitably managed capitalism. Railroad executives ran the Railroad Administration, and an oil engineer and entrepreneur ran the Fuel Administration. Advocates of business-government cooperation were predominant, including those who had for some time urged national regulations which would have permitted industry-wide price and output agreements to attain stabilization. Briefly, the political and economic context of the Progressive Era delineated the personnel, policies, and forms the wartime structure pursued.

In essence, numerous critical economic sectors now could work out their own problems regarding price and output using government sanctions as a threat against violators, who in a period of lesser demand would have been much more common. Enthusiasm for the new wartime measures came from all directions—from business executives to the Chamber of Commerce, who saw in them the realization of the politically sanctioned national economic stabilization that so many business-association and industry leaders had advocated in diverse forms for over a decade. As it was, given rising prices and the vast market which Washington and its allies provided, there were relatively few critics of the wartime organizational machinery itself. Between entry into the war and August 1919, the public debt rose twenty times as expenditures skyrocketed to create unprecedented business prosperity, melting opposition to the vast expansion of business-government integration. Ironically, the good times diminished the memory of the events of less affluent years and split the industrial community's opinion on whether to perpetuate the new institutions in various forms. In effect, the war also proved that massive government outlays, loans, and subsidies were also means to assure business profits—an experience whose message was not to be lost—without creating new regulatory bodies.

The railroads alone were able to obtain new legislation in 1920 which allowed them legally to perpetuate the wartime rationalization of their entire industry in the form of pooling agreements and profit guarantees, but even this was never to prove adequate to assure them sufficient profits in the more straitened decades that accompanied the new competition of auto and truck transport. The biggest firms in the steel industry, who had been in the vanguard of the prewar movement to establish federal regulation of their industry on terms they defined, inclined to continue the new arrangements of price-fixing and output controls after the war, but found the Wilson Administration and smaller firms unsympathetic. The political environment and business divisions proved uncongenial to sustaining the wartime bodies. Trade-association advocates and executives in numerous other industries plagued by prewar price rivalries or overproduction also preferred—though not enough to fight hard for it—perpetuating the wartime measures which represented the culmination of the national regulation movement after 1900. But in the aftermath of their frustration and inability to mobilize sufficient business pressure and backing, all that they could do was to resolve to sustain or build trade associations which voluntarily accomplished the same goals—or privately to continue those new wartime ties and accords with specific firms, which, indeed, helped lay the basis of modern oligopoly.[6] The Federal Trade Commission agreed to review and approve a number of these congenial practices. Businessmen attained their ultimate goal—profitability and security—with the merger of peacetime reforms and war organization. On this basis they laid the foundations of postwar business reform, not in an ideological way—for not even the most ardent business advocates of the continuation of the wartime structures qualified for this designation —but as pragmatists who, when the older ways once again began to fail, were to remember how well the wartime departure had succeeded. The national government had built a vast administrative structure which businessmen had defined and guided from its inception, and they might yet do so once again.

The Dilemma of Political Capitalism

Any adequate vision of the foundations of the American political economy will necessarily be a very complex and contingent portrait, and hence the insufficiency of historical writing on the first critical half-century of modern American history. For indeed one finds an uncanny melange of business sophistication and clarity regarding some issues on one hand, inconsistency and ignorance on the other, and, perhaps above all, a larger social situation in which both the plans and reservations of business leaders existed in a context ultimately dooming any business or government approach to failure on its own assumptions.

But just as one cannot impute too much rationality and coherence to the emergence of the synthesis of economics and state power in America in the twentieth century, the far more common and traditional error is to assume that integration was aimless and without purpose whatsoever, save possibly to advance the "public welfare." Indeed, there is hardly any evidence capable of supporting the latter fashionable interpretation, which is a common enough mystification, since in the last analysis, despite the fact there is no specific agreement on the means, there is a universal consensus among all men on whatever level of power that capitalism as a mode of economic organization and social hierarchy must be preserved in America. And within that framework the options are necessarily limited and must perforce serve segments of the broad ruling class.

Because there were precious few business advocates of political capitalism preaching over time, and never a general theorist in the true sense of that term, reform became an incremental process intended to compensate for the failure of traditional means to cope with new problems. In effect, the whole of the American political economy consists only of its parts, which by 1920 were spotty indeed, and these were but efforts to apply concrete solutions to specific problems. And for this reason it was elliptical, often moving backward and forward in search of solutions to definite challenges—solutions often surprisingly indifferent to consistency or principle but merely deemed likely to work. Indeed, its advocates in one field were often stout defenders of laissez faire for others, as men favored political servicing of the components of the economy but not the whole. Because the interests of various business sectors are in tension on short-run issues, formulating a universally acceptable general strategy was impossible. But this curious myopia, in which men proved incapable of defining a comprehensive social analysis, should not obscure the collective outcome of the larger process. Yet at the same time—and here the dialectical tension arises to make history appear complex—the inability of advocates of political capitalism to articulate and convince different economic interests of the larger meaning of the system meant that others often resisted it and its implementation. This necessarily accentuated those frustrations intrinsic in attempting to regulate or plan capitalism. First, there were political constraints on action from politicians and business interests who saw they would lose from change; and after the unwillingness of the Wilson Administration to continue wartime control of many industries, there were comparable blockages during later decades. Second, the always changing domestic and international economic context meant that the difficulties that unpredictability always imposed coincided with the third dilemma of political capitalism, which is the recurrent failure of the leaders of innovation to know in advance both the necessarily precise means and the extent of the effort by which control and their ends could be attained. As it was, inability to plan for the unknown left a bitter taste among former proponents of regulation, who, if businessmen, were often quite ready to alternate back to voluntaristic techniques when the political failed. In any event, there was a remarkable correlation between business advocacy of political solutions to economic problems and their lower dividends, and its enthusiasm for innovation declined as profits grew.

Just as the deductive premises of capitalist economic theory occlude an appreciation of the role of politics in sustaining American business, to say nothing of the limits of social knowledge and strategy, so too, on the other hand, must one avoid imputing too much rationality and coherence to the system—all of which makes a descriptively accurate theory that much more difficult. Politics is not merely the tool of economic power, but during the short term it also divides economic interests and immobilizes this or that solution as conflict among capitalists finds expression in their competition for influence and control over political machinery, with national or regional constituencies eroding the solutions of those with a world focus, or some bloc or faction uses its political spokesmen to gain at the expense of others in one or another controversy—from tariffs to subsidies. The diffusion of power among conflicting political and economic centers makes a single-minded pursuit of a goal difficult, and it is often this struggle within a predictable matrix that creates the illusion of drift and conflict in American history when, given the minimal and shifting differences between factions, none exists in the ultimate sense of those terms. Still, the range of real options that policymakers can consider is prescribed by the defined interests and fundamental premises of the structure of power, and the political context to some critical degree determines the exact direction of the economic order. While this means that an acute observer may foresee possible policy choices, it does not mean that anyone, including those who make them, can predict the exact outcome their actions will have once they begin intersecting with unknown developments in the national and international political and economic scene that no one fully anticipates. It is this unpredictability that is perhaps the system's greatest weakness, and makes modern American history a sequence of events few could precisely predict during the first four decades of this century. Perfect social and economic integration, were it ever to exist, would preclude those elusive yet decisive forces which in fact have produced change and crisis.

In the decades preceding World War One the architects of a system of political capitalism elaborated piecemeal views on assorted subjects; and while no one man or group embodied them all, it can be said that main characteristics emerge for what is necessarily an artificial portrait. They were anti-competitive, and hence their attraction to federal sanctioning of price and production accords and insulation of the larger industry from cutthroat entrants. The trade-association movement was but the logical nonpolitical expression of this sentiment when political reticence and frustration with earlier efforts left the integrationists few options after 1920. They tended to oppose taxation as a tool of regulation, and gladly destroyed the wartime excess profits taxes which had been temporarily used to feed them more contracts. Equity in the social sense scarcely moved any of them, and their penchant for racism was a common social attitude of the period in any case. Order, hierarchy, and efficiency were more congenial notions, though not as ends in themselves but justifiable because they were profitable. Some saw social welfare reform outside the criterion of the cash nexus, but most were moved by what seemed pecuniarily rewarding. Northern textile-mill owners worried about the children their Southern competitors exploited, not the conditions of their own adult labor. Others saw company-organized unions as superior to autonomous organizations, and workmen's compensation and unemployment insurance systems as means not only of reducing labor costs via lower turnover but transferring the liabilities of employers to the state. Out of this melange of attitudes, impulses, and interests no consistent, overarching sophisticated philosophy could emerge, though indeed businessmen and their spokesmen never tired of banally defining their own interests and hegemony in universal rather than class terms. But it embodied the ingredients and contradictions in what was essentially a typically eclectic American philosophy for adjusting to a troublesome new reality that the merger of industrialism, growth, and space was distinctively creating in the United States.

The Agrarian Dilemma

A basic problem of industrialization is how one removes farmers from the land when their productive economic function has declined. All industrializing societies respond to underemployment in the agrarian sector and world agricultural gluts by deliberately or unconsciously stimulating the abandonment of the land. This transition has immense social, political, and human consequences, and frequently engenders more or less violence, but in the end all countries that hope to modernize must cross the Rubicon of too many farmers in a traditional social context. In the American case, the process of removing man from the land was unplanned but it was no less inexorable, and it was perhaps the major resistance, however inchoate its nature and ineffectual its protestations, to the entire epic of the creation of modern America. The events associated with this resistance, and its outcome, are a crucial aspect of the resolution of the problems that confronted American capitalism during its first half-century.

The difficulties facing agriculture in the United States, as in many other societies, were linked to the larger world economic structure over which Washington had little control. Hence the radical fluctuations in markets and prices produced immense variations in the fortunes of many farmers, so that the international context intersected with a distinctive set of domestic factors to produce a sustained agrarian crisis which was not politically resolved until the end of the nineteenth century, when agrarian discontent became less intensive and far more inchoate. What is perhaps most characteristic of agrarian protest movements everywhere is that they lack the sort of neat political and intellectual coherence that simplifies the tasks of later scholars, who often impose order on them where none actually existed; for farmers are not theoreticians and their impulses can combine atavistic respect for traditional values and institutions as well as a dedication to resisting the encroachments of capitalist economics. Indeed, a capacity to commit themselves to such a unity of seeming opposites may perhaps be the most enduring quality of peasants everywhere, and the source of their diversity as social actors in history.

The story of the crisis of late-nineteenth-century agriculture has been too well told elsewhere to require much discussion here, but suffice it to say that the fact that one-half of the American continent was empty after the Civil War was both a promise and threat to millions of Americans as well as immigrants ready to participate in the monumental expansion of farming that occurred over the next three decades. The rising value of land was overwhelmingly the main source of economic danger until 1910, and interest rates of up to 20 percent annually could be absorbed so long as prices for agricultural commodities rose and weather was stably good. Improved farmland more than doubled in the three decades after 1870, and between 1870 and 1890 the number of people engaged in agriculture was to increase by about one-half, and to grow at a somewhat lower rate until 1910, the peak year. The relatively greatest population growth was to occur in those regions that were to produce the most intense agrarian discontent and the collapse of the farm sector at one and the same time—the Great Plains, Texas-Oklahoma, and the Mountain states. The population of western Kansas alone increased 264 percent in 1885–1887, all good rain years in a normally semi-arid region. Town speculation and growth in such areas often equaled expansion on the farms, and even if farmers in the aggregate assumed only quite modest mortgages and debts, which was usually the case, their landholdings were too small to pay even these during poor harvest years. Overcapitalization and too great an investment in machinery crushed the big wheat bonanza farmers of the Red River Valley of the Dakotas most of all. If, as again in western Kansas, farm income dropped 59 percent in the one year of 1893, the human misery invariably affected the economic and political structure. The vast overexpansion of agriculture allowed plenty of suffering for all.

To consider the farmer as an aspiring entrepreneur ignores entirely the economic structure of peasants everywhere and the economic compulsions of excessively small acreage and output per farm which required the individual farmer to risk growth or face bankruptcy. All peasants, even those in pre- and postrevolutionary societies, are involved in risk-taking in the normal order of things, they aspire to succeed economically but rarely do, and the resemblance between this activity and any stage of capitalist enterprise is upon closer examination quite superficial. More important are the farmer's economic failures, which define his political responses and economic future. Some farmers, of course, succeed in becoming wealthy and conservative in this process, but the vast majority fail to develop secure and minimally comfortable existences, and their politics will sometimes reveal their misery. Agriculture, like the rest of an economy, has a class structure, and the distinction between large and small farmers is always a real one politically and socially. In such places as Kansas, of course, the local town elites and the eastern Kansas political hierarchy combined with a few large farmers to keep the new western populations out of political power as well as to monopolize state-controlled economic resources. Instability of population and institutions—clubs, churches, and such—meant that newcomers were less ready for political struggle against existing dominating elites, a fact that was to persist, save for a few exceptional and astonishing years during the brief Populist ascendency when both Kansas and Nebraska had Populist governments.

New settlers throughout the Middle West suffered most of all, and in general the rise of tenancy touched them deeply. Tenancy increased significantly in a state like Iowa from 24 percent in 1880 to 38 percent in 1910, and the process of land concentration in fewer hands begins evolving from this time onward both in the Middle West and the South.

Since the agrarian dilemma is one of the best-studied topics of American history, little can be added to a description of its causes. The world and national economic context of overexpansion and new foreign competition has been thoroughly analyzed, along with the importance of variable rainfall in triggering the crises always inherent in bloated economic booms. The political structure of the local Great Plains states has received more attention in recent years, and the ethnic and cultural complexity of the Midwestern states has been suggested as having major significance, though it is not yet clear that such cultural ties were strong enough always to transcend economic class and crises, as indeed they did not in the all-important election of 1896. The better-educated social composition of Populist leaders, and their ideas, has been usefully reexamined to reject blithe ideological fictions of the 1950s which dismissed Populism as an atavistic, neofascist, anti-Semitic phenomenon (it having been none of those things) and instead to show it to be the most truly libertarian social force relative to both the regions in which it temporarily emerged as a factor in the Midwest and South. If the intellectual ideas of the Populists were not highly structured, and local conditions colored their politics, the nature of the phenomenon was clear enough during the period the movement existed, which was very brief even by American standards. Indeed, its relatively radical, libertarian character even persisted in those quite isolated regions outside the South where Populists were to remain in opposition politics after the effective demise of the movement in 1896. In a sense, although historians have enriched our comprehension by focusing on such economic, cultural, and political history, they have avoided the central issues by failing to focus on the main question regarding agrarian discontent before 1920. And insofar as they assume the Populists created a transcendent agrarian ideology which affected later American politics and political attitudes, they have spawned misleading debates.

Specifically, the most striking aspect of the phenomenon of Populism, apart from the fact that economic disaster could sufficiently traumatize even a relatively stable social element to court a temporarily distinctively innovative and atypical response, is the manner by which a surplus agrarian population with incipient leftist doctrines was reabsorbed into a more integrated and cohesive social structure essential for the subsequent development of American capitalism in this century, and why Kansas and Nebraska and similar regions are today anything but the fount of political and social opposition. Mass politics in the Midwest disappeared without the slightest factual evidence, as Hofstadter implied, that poor farmers had been bought off with farm-parity prosperity. It is surely the case that the role of the federal government in the co-optive country agent and Farm Bureau movements played a minor role until the 1920s, in some regions by increasing the prosperity and efficiency of farmers and demanding, in return, their support for more conservative politics and leaders. The Populist rebellion far exceeded the effectiveness of such efforts to neutralize it, and later forms of discontent surfaced where the Bureau had been strongest. The problem of Populism's challenge to the emergence of a stable national capitalist society was not ended by co-option, prosperity for the dissidents, illusions or fickleness on the part of agrarian radicals, or any of the standard historical explanations. In the last analysis, it was resolved when the farm radicals, as in numerous other nations, left the regions in which they had created a politically cohesive force. Urbanization for some, new states and new farms for others—but all left involuntarily.[7]

In one sense, the Northern Populist regions more than any others had lacked a community and institutional life, and the capacity of the movement to create a surrogate sense of community and a social relationship was an artificial arrestment of the continuous disintegration of man in society which dominates America both with increasing time and mobility. The turnover of even Republican politicians in certain of these regions was as frequent as for Populists. Southern Populism, by contrast, had less of a problem with community instability, but in the end the underemployed poor black agrarian surplus and their white political peers largely experienced the same fate: they moved to Southern cities and, above all, to the North.

The South, of course, was scarcely a developing sector but instead retained all of the characteristics of colonial dependence and an agricultural export orientation. Its more than one million black Populist agrarians were heavily concentrated in those regions that produced the great post-1910 migration of two million blacks out of the South until 1940, in addition to the Southern cities, partially resolving the problem of agrarian black radicalism and the North's need for a new labor supply following the immigration restrictions of 1924, after which the misery of the rural South and seeming promise of urban life removed a vital portion of the former dissidents. And to a lesser extent, the migration to the North of an equal number of whites over the same period, including a significant proportion of poor whites who had backed Populism, performed the same political catharsis on the South's political monolith. However exceptional and paternalistic the pattern of black-white Populist unity that had emerged in the South from 1888 until 1896, nothing remotely comparable to it in scale and magnitude ever again reasserted itself in that region, with only rare and locally isolated cases of class rather than race unity ever managing to reemerge in the regional miasma.

Midwestern Populism's demise in the hands of demographic forces was yet faster than that in the South, and if one looks at the population of the counties where the Populists were strongest it becomes apparent that the radicals were neither converted nor prosperous—instead they moved. In effect, it was in the process of abandoning their region in desperation that they temporarily accepted a radicalized politics; yet the same mental and physical motion meant that they would not stay to consolidate their economic power by political means. In 1889 the first western Kansas counties began experiencing a population decline, and over the next two years some counties lost up to 77 percent of their population and whole towns were abandoned. In the decade 1890–1900 six southwest Kansas counties lost over 60 percent of their population, and in fifty Plains counties—mainly in Kansas and Nebraska—the population fell by nearly a third. This population movement is the overarching reality, more than any other factor, which explains the demise of Midwestern Populism.

This Midwestern movement, with its exodus numbering well into six figures in the critical decade of the 1890s, moved almost equally to the Far West—which gathered the loose spirits of the nation into the most rootless, artificial community of all—and to the more easterly towns, of which Chicago was the heart. To this extent, urban development provides the partial safety valve for the agrarian crisis, giving the industrialization movement a new supply of essential labor. Population movement, once again, solved America's structural dilemmas and gave it more time and space with which to grow, deferring its crisis to another day and social form. This process of agrarian population decline did not end even with rising agricultural prices after 1900, for in fact the drop in the population of counties extended to the eastern halves of Kansas and Nebraska over the next decade, became more intense in these regions from 1910 until 1920, and during this decade departures began also to affect the wheat belt of the Dakotas. Some counties in these states experienced growth, but with the high turnover which meant the persistence of the characteristic rootlessness of the region. Perhaps most disturbing of all to conventional wisdom is the fact that between 1898 and 1914 about one million American residents, the vast majority of whom had been previously in the states with large agrarian radical movements, moved to Canada, predominantly the rich wheat-growing provinces. Many had been Populists, and some outstanding former Populist political leaders were among their ranks, and this constituency and its inheritance became an important strand in the Canadian social democratic movement. Many, of course, were from the predominantly first-generation ethnics who composed the large majority of the population of the Dakotas and Minnesota, but the fact that one of the reasons agrarian radicalism disappears is due to departure from the United States entirely of a significant portion of its adherents is a reality too important for all but a few specialists to ignore.[8]

By 1900, therefore, the traditional problem of adjusting the farming population to the instabilities of their own sector and to the trauma of industrialization had been partially resolved insofar as the passing and eclectic radical Populist outburst was concerned. The transitional floating agrarian population had been reabsorbed in yet one more temporary context, and some were to be placed in the urban centers to assist the growth there with their minds and muscle. Later, the reduction of the nation's farm population, especially as aspects of war economies, was to continue the pattern of depopulation of agrarian regions prone to discontent and protest. Over the next half-century the problem of the social role of farmers in what was now irreversibly an industrial capitalist economy would prove immeasurably more tractable.

Social Organization and Social Control

The problems that a newly industrialized society confronts by their very nature and unfamiliarity look threatening, and to the established American ruling class their concerns about the possible disintegration of social life and emergence of class conflict seemed all the more urgent in light of the untested hordes of foreign workers entering America. A system that has problems does not need a theory to prompt action, but generalizations arose among writers, academics, and even a relatively small number of men of affairs. Such reflection was never systematic, though later students of the period artificially superimposed order upon it. Most were oriented toward problem-solving, so that they passed into relative obscurity when the difficulties appeared resolved or no longer threatening; social control adherents who were also men of affairs often engaged in functional action bearing slight relationship to their articulated mystifications. We can subsume the collective components of such notions under the rubric of social control and integration, and how to achieve it under American industrial capitalism. And, in essence, it might be said that integration dealt with the fundamental topic of how to solve or manage outside the economic sphere the problems of social decomposition, violence, and political instability that all capitalist economies invariably engender.

In the last analysis the social function of power is to serve itself, yet the seemingly vast threat of class conflict to a constituted order's capacity to do so still remained an enigma and a gnawing doubt. The problem of social integration which the two decades after 1890 saw debated reached a peak obsession during the First World War, when not only domestic cohesion but loyalty became a prime anxiety in a society, as Woodrow Wilson stated in December 1915, which had "citizens . . . born under other flags . . . who have poured the poison of disloyalty into the very arteries of our national life."[9] Social and political loyalty, in due course, merged to become common issues in the Red Scare, which carried to a logical conclusion the integrationist discussions of the preceding two decades, and for this reason most of the major "progressives" endorsed the deep abuses of civil liberties that occurred during the wartime period—the very years that saw optimum integration of the economy witnessed the extreme in superimposed social cohesion. Indeed, after 1920, when it became clear that the immigrants' and the working class's presumed threats to American capitalism were really much overexaggerated and quite manageable, the debate greatly subsided along with the sense of perceived danger. To some critical extent, Prohibition was the consequence of this mood and perpetuated its legacy.

Progressive theorists such as Herbert Croly and Richard T. Ely strongly defended economic inequality and capitalism, but with the critical proviso that property owners consider themselves stewards and act with social responsibility, a notion whose popularity won to it men like Theodore Roosevelt and such organizations as the National Association of Manufacturers. Classes could and ought to exist, but in harmony, for in their many discourses they stressed that durable, sustaining notion of the "public interest," which was served when business and workers forsook their claims within an intrinsic structure of inequality to respect the needs of an illusory larger constituency—the public. Truly independent trade unions could not, of course, operate in this context, and most leading progressives left few doubts that this was their view. The prevention of the emergence of an aggressive working class was a primary goal of the entire progressive theory.

This nebulous doctrine of social harmony rather than conflict within the framework of economic inequality found intellectual and organizational underpinnings in what historians have more recently called the cult of efficiency and the scientific management movement. It is easy to exaggerate the importance of these currents by assuming that articulate integrationist spokesmen truly reflected the broad mass of businessmen in American life—an assumption yet unproven and probably false. But the idea of regulating man's existence in the workplace and, ultimately, the home gained wider currency before 1920 than in any other period in American life, and the emergence of the prohibition of alcoholic drinks after 1919 was in this sense the logical culmination of such ideas. Institutional forms and modes for integrating the society's dispossessed and controlling violence—ranging from mediation to superior police departments—grew in importance as the seeming instability of the new industrial capitalism offered imagined challenges to existing authority and its consensus at the top layers of the social hierarchy.

The scientific management movement saw unionism as unnecessary protection of the working class, which experts in the cult of efficiency could best reward by determining the norms of work and wages. Not only unions but even some important academics rejected these class-oriented criteria at the time, and were it not for the fortuitous publicity that such men as Louis Brandeis gave the concept during the celebrated 1910 railroad rate cases before the ICC, scientific management would have fallen into obscurity yet more quickly. Despite the attention recent historians have lavished on it, the efficiency concept scarcely entered the factory per se, even though more technical criteria were employed in the preparation of lower-level executives, who, in the aggregate, were much more touched than workers, who in the vast majority of cases always remained locked into the imperatives of work standards which the economics and technologies of their industry imposed. Efficiency was a principle on which to administer political structures, as the progressive political scientist Charles McCarthy argued in 1912, and in this form, we shall see, it influenced the organization of local governments profoundly. But work itself was largely immune to "scientific" theories, for it did not take technicians to justify the always self-evidently profitable optimum as the norm.

On one hand the ideas of the period tended to emphasize a new solidarity, even one the state had the responsibility to impose over the occasional anti-social businessman and, of course, the much more common aggressive trade unionists. These criteria and the presumably nonpartisan and scientific theory of efficient social cohesion were to operate within the structure of inequality and hierarchy, a framework the objectives of which were the poor, foreign-born, blacks, and all others strange to the world of the white Anglo-Saxon Protestant college-educated elements largely in charge of American society at the turn of the century. This quixotic formula could only intensify and hasten the intolerance of the rest of the population that occurred: more racism in government bureaucracies, the repression of radicals during wartime, the forced acculturation of immigrants and the end of open immigration partially because of sheer bias, Prohibition, and, in the 1920s, the great popularity of the Ku Klux Klan. Eugenics soon quickly became associated with a pseudo-scientific racism and an anti-immigrant mood, and men from Roosevelt downward endorsed its most perverse ideological distortions. The most astonishing and persistent institutional expression of this larger mood was Prohibition, which originally had important cultural and middle-class roots but ultimately could alone never implement such values into national legislation until business elements concluded that sobriety among their workers was an essential, profit-creating goal. At a time when more and more business leaders believed in a more positive role for the federal government to eliminate the economic inefficiency of competition and the need for confronting the motley foreign-influenced mass which dominated the working class, national Prohibition gained those critical economic adherents that could bring it to fruition after generations of agitation. Enforced abstention was the logical concomitant of the compulsive Americanization movement and the ending of open immigration. Indeed, if lack of a national reflective frame of mind has deprived some Americans of coherent insight it has also prevented many others from tying together these strands of conventional wisdom into a specifically

American version of totalitarianism. Yet many of the elements of it were already there.

As it was, the integrative impulses in the economy and national politics after 1870 moved in an unsystematic, variable way that responded to need; and the contemporary reflections on the effort do not warrant as much attention as the institutional heritage transmitted to later decades and our own times. For ideas and writers come and go, despite their momentary successes and exaggerated importance, and the pattern of American life has scarcely been modified by any of them in a society no less immune to its numerous generalizers and celebrators than to its rare detractors. The concept of social control and integration gained currency because, in the aggregate, it was consistent with the end of optimizing profit for the dominant economic sectors. The precise formulas, whether political or otherwise, for attaining it were far less consequential than the objective of control itself, which gained in urgency in specific industries or the larger economy only and whenever hard times made it appear more relevant. Even without an ideology or a precise set of techniques, power has its own imperatives and a profoundly deep desire for self-preservation.

Because the economic and international environment in which American capitalism operates is always in flux, the exact means for reaching its objectives of profit and continuity have by necessity varied, so that the modalities appropriate to one period and set of conditions have usually differed from those of another. We must cope with change as well as continuity in the emergence of the modern American political economy, because it embodies both. To define the goals of security and profitability as part of the entire system over time is easy, yet to assume that the dominant techniques and institutions of one stage are necessarily those of another is impossible, for consistency in this regard is almost as nonexistent as tactical agreement among businessmen within a framework to which they are all united on ultimate principle only. After 1920 the direction and problems of American capitalism altered from the preceding decades, not once but often, as the insecurity and instabilities of the prewar period were partially obscured and yet new challenges emerged.

2

The Foundations of the United States as a World Power, 1880–1919

The oversimplifications dominating the study of the history of American foreign policy have produced a legacy of obfuscations and false debates to add to the natural complexity of the topic, creating the greatest single void in our comprehension of any central aspect of modern United States history. Such myopia unintentionally has reinforced the highly charged ideological definitions that the purveyors of conventional wisdom and the state have evoked to sanction the legitimacy of national conduct and, above all, the proposition that American foreign policy is largely unrelated to the nature and needs of a capitalist economy. Conversely, more critical historians, while attacking apologias for United States diplomacy that cite everything from philanthropy to missionary zeal to misunderstandings, have also slighted the obvious central reality that the problems of American capitalism and their solutions are not merely international but domestic as well, and that unless analysts interrelate the two in a more serious fashion all we can do is respond to bad ideological arguments with insufficient if not equally inadequate ones.

The difficulty of examining foreign policy is complicated as well by the reality that the writing of the history of United States foreign relations is usually based on concrete cases in which too much becomes important and relevant, thereby neglecting the structural framework in which American capitalism operates in a somewhat different quantitative fashion in every epoch. But specific studies are like so many fingers possessing unique prints, with most historians preferring to concentrate on the different gradations while ignoring the hand and body which inevitably circumscribe the possible individuality of each event. The confusion of partial details with total reality and an absence of a sense of purpose and integration leave anyone who wishes to generalize an unenviable task. The place to begin in earnest is with the structural context, both domestic and international, so that we may minimize ideological obfuscation and apologia on one hand and vague deductive abstractions on the other. Next we must consider the intentions, goals, and articulated definitions of actuality—whether false or valid—of men of power. Then the inevitable surprises and unintended developments, whether war, revolutions, or even the simple misperceptions and miscalculations on which most academics are wont to linger, and which so often arise to complicate reality and praxis—producing images opaque to the later historians—also require discussion. For the unpredictable in foreign relations is also predictable: not when and how it arises, but simply that it will. It is with a synthesis of these three interrelated if mercurial factors that anyone has yet to write an adequate history of modern American foreign policy.

The Structural Imperatives

The period 1871–1899 saw the most rapid expansion of capital and industry over any long period of American history, reaching a peak in the decades of the 1880s and 1890s, and leveling off during the first decade of this century. During this last third of the nineteenth century, the general trend of profitability in industry, railroads, and utilities was gradually and inexorably downward, especially during the depressions of 1873–1878, 1883–1885, and 1893–1897, though it is critical to note that the combined traded common share yields of all three of these main sectors averaged 4.2 percent even during the worst decade, 1889–1898. Indeed, this profitability was still sufficiently great to attract a large net inflow of foreign capital to the United States, reaching over 15 percent of total net capital formation in 1869–1876 and over 10 percent in 1882–1893, growing in dollar terms until it amounted to 4 percent of the total United States wealth in every form by 1914. Agriculture, of course, fared more poorly and played the largest single role in the export trade, yet not by any stretch of the imagination can it be said that American capitalism before 1914 had entered a general structural crisis which could only be resolved via exports or imperialism.

While it is perfectly true that foreign expansion and intervention could ameliorate specific difficulties of profitability, and for certain industries it may have done so sporadically, the *aggregate* problem of excess capital growth relative to profitability before 1914 was overwhelmingly resolved within the framework of the domestic economic sector. Of this fact one should make neither too much nor too little, for it merely sets a context whose relevance terminates after 1914.

This development cannot in any way, by itself, disprove the growing desire for exports which the "Open Door" school of critical historians has attempted with uneven success to document for the period before 1900; but unless one argues the thesis that desire for new export outlets becomes a kind of transcendent false consciousness, and that business interests failed to perceive where it was their main gains were to be made, then an explanation of how the fetishes of capitalists became something well nigh close to ingrained perpetual stupidity must also be offered. And if the argument holds only for specific industrial sectors, which is much more plausible simply because exports did generate profits and therefore built articulate vested interests, then the ability of a larger economy to profit without a vast export growth before 1914 is a commanding reality that must also be fully acknowledged. In any case, after 1899 the problem of unprofitable excess industrial capacity in the United States was partially brought under control with the expedients of mergers, a growing domestic population and market, the beginnings of government rationalization of banking, railroads, and industry, and the return of relative prosperity. Accumulation is based on internal as well as external possibilities, and perhaps the greatest weakness of the "Open Door" theorists is their lack of an overall model which treats the issue of capitalist profitability and crisis in this essential largest context. What they have explained well, of course, is how the concrete United States policies responded to the specific needs of this or that business interest, a scale of analysis still well below that necessary for a general theory of the role of imperialism in resolving United States capitalism's structural contradictions. In short, while their analysis may correctly assess American foreign policy in its particulars, it cannot explain capitalism as a whole. Nor can they so facilely assume that business attitudes relevant to one set of structural conditions are transferred *in toto* to later decades which are economically distinctive in their own ways.

It is most assuredly a fact that exports as a share of the gross national product of the United States rose from the 1880s through the 1890s, reaching 7.2 percent during the latter decade—a peak that only great war periods ever again permitted the Americans to surpass. It was in this context that ebullient businessmen and their journals praised the promise of exports, even though their intentions proved much more significant than their accomplishments. This growth was especially large, in percentage terms, in semi-manufactured and manufactured products, though agricultural commodities and raw materials remained the bulk of United States exports during the late nineteenth century. In dollar terms, the change was to appear yet more dramatic, and it is unquestionable that exports were one of a number of important factors which led to the restoration of prosperity after 1898, a fact which makes the incontrovertible details and quotations in the books of "Open Door" scholars necessary but far from sufficient history.

The data's complexity must not be allowed to slight one fundamental fact: The surge in the profitability of American railroads, industry, utilities, and even agriculture after 1900 and until 1913—which made listed common share earnings in the nonagricultural sector slightly greater than the 1890s—also saw a significant drop of almost one-tenth in exports as a proportion of the gross national product. In general, therefore, American capitalism's profitability, its options, and its structural dependency were not at this time self-evidently linked to the further internationalization of the economy, even though certain firms, such as International Harvester, were exceptions to this pattern. Compared to Great Britain, which in 1913 was exporting 22 percent of its national product, or the Netherlands with 50 percent, the United States was still relatively less integrated into world finance and commerce.[1] Contrasted to Europe, America was an example of late imperialism in the world capitalist order.

The dimensions which these figures contain also demand further attention, lest one misinterpret the data. Its balance of trade with Europe, to which fully three-quarters of its exports were directed by 1900 and two-thirds by 1910, was largely in surplus for the United States, while in 1900 less than one-tenth of its exports went to Latin America and less than one-twentieth to Asia. Apart from the fact that the nations in which the United States did indeed play an imperialist role at this time did not even remotely provide it with significant export markets, is the more complicated and vital function that Latin

America and Asia fulfilled in the larger well-being of the United States economy as well as in sustaining Europe's demand for American goods. United States imports after 1880 grew, above all, in crude foodstuffs and raw materials, and for the next two decades remained virtually constant in semi-manufactured and manufactured goods. Raw materials imports more than doubled in value between 1880 and 1900, and then doubled again over the next decade, so that by 1910 they accounted for one-third of all United States imports. By 1900 fully more than one-fifth of United States imports came from Latin America, and almost that amount arrived from Asia. Europe's capacity to continue importing American goods and resolve the settlement of payments was mainly due to its own surpluses with the Third World nations on which the United States was becoming increasingly dependent, and to whom American business related far more as importers than exporters seeking markets for surplus goods. It is this growing United States need to integrate Third World sources of supply, mainly to attain raw materials but secondly to sustain the flows of international trade, that is perhaps the most fundamental new development in its economic structure at the turn of this century.[2]

This dimension of the growing United States need for access to the Third World has scarcely been discussed in the works of historical critics and apologists alike. More important is the reality that this still small United States dependence was to carry with it vast consequences for the nations increasingly geared to American demand, leaving Washington with options to control Latin American states which were less a question of intentions or desire, at least for purposes of argument here, than of structural relations from which the United States could select any steps it chose. And even if these actions might not resolve the problems of American capitalism's profitability, they created the skein of dependency which over time was to bear fruit in United States oppression and intervention in the Third World. In effect, by 1913 fully 43 percent of the exports of Chile, Mexico, Peru, and Bolivia, and 48 percent of Brazil, Colombia, Cuba, and Ecuador, were directed to the United States—a pervasive reality which was only to grow with time. In the Philippines this integration with the United States economy was greater yet.

Structurally, therefore, the period from 1870 until World War One was infinitely more complex than existing historical narratives have portrayed, and it is within this context that diplomacy must be set in a fashion that explains the causes and extent of economic pressures to resolve. Without such a broad framework, reality becomes, at best, myopic. This said, the fact of incipient United States imperialism in the world after 1895 is undeniable, nor can one dismiss the export sector—much less the qualitatively more fundamental imports—just because critics of conventional wisdom have made too much of it. But expansion at *this* stage of United States capitalism could also be satisfied by internal demand no less than external, a lesson that became important during World War One and then was permanently institutionalized with the war economy after 1941. What critical historians must admit, as an aspect of coming to grips with a comprehensive, realistic economic theory, is that during 1900–1914 internal expansion satisfied most businessmen by far, even as an imperialist foreign policy placated some interests in need.

By focusing on intentions or aspirations rather than results, one can learn a great deal—but not enough—concerning the foundations of United States diplomacy; and the danger of purely aggregate structural analyses is that in practice foreign policy decisions may not always be taken with them clearly in mind, for they can often be nothing more than ultimate criteria to follow when their relevance or imperative importance becomes apparent. In fact, it may be sufficient in specific cases merely to do nothing which violates United States interests in this aggregate sense, but meanwhile to respond to shorter-range pressures and objectives. Such "small" actions, which were to have over time such immense implications for Cuba, the Philippines, and others, later were at times counterproductive. It was not always evident from the inception when the consequences of routine actions regarding one nation or one international problem might inflict permanent damage to United States interests elsewhere. What these needs may be, of course, will depend on whether there are conflicts within the ranks of American interests and men-of-power, how their disagreements are expressed via Congress and the institutions of social management—the press and universities, for example—and what else enters a picture to complicate decisions and actions.

Suffice it to say, the fact that exports were not required to resolve the problems of general capitalist profitability after 1899 and until 1914 did not mean they were not desired, for in fact the emergence of a "foreign policy constituency" among business interests after 1890 is a reality irrespective of conclusions historians have drawn from it. That there were other developments more important to the totality of American capitalism at the same time, and industry was far more concerned with protection of its home market than foreign expansion, does not alter this durable dimension. Men-of-power frequently have the capacity to deal simultaneously with the problems of international as well as domestic economies, but the weight they assign to each will invariably tend to reflect the importance the two dimensions have for each of them, and in the aggregate that shifts the main focus to the objective overall interests of the system at the given time.

The International Context of United States Expansion

The burgeoning American colonial role in the world came at the time when Europe's rivalries and mutual apprehensions left an unprecedented balance of fear and a vacuum which reduced the dangers to the United States and made its imperialism possible. Had the differences between the European states not been so intense, it is hard to imagine that the vast United States acquisitions and the creation of its own sphere of influence after 1897 would have gone relatively unchallenged for so long. As it was, the United States built a quite conscious commitment to the balance of power in Europe, which had offered it such freedom of action, and only after World War One shattered that fragile equilibrium among the other colonialist states did the nation's luxury of relatively conflict-free expansion in the interstices of global imperialist rivalries come to an end and the central role of America as the leader of the established capitalist world order become inevitable.

The cultural and ideological basis of United States expansionism after 1880 has been so well documented that it hardly requires more attention, save to note that the racist theories of "natural selection" and Anglo-Saxon or Teutonic supremacy so fashionable at the end of the last century left unresolved precisely which of the supreme should vanquish which less-developed region. From this viewpoint, the cultural arrogance of such writers as the Reverend Josiah Strong, John Fiske, and Herbert Baxter Adams was incidental rather than casual to American imperialism, for on the level of the "civilizing mission" the British were already well along in fulfilling that role. The United States, in short, would not have been any different had chauvinism and Social Darwinism been absent in the latter part of the nineteenth century. As Walter LaFeber has so ably shown, naval expansionism and the desire to spread abroad—and above all toward Latin America—were current by 1890 for essentially economic reasons involving the failures of the domestic economy as much as the existence of tangible foreign markets.

At first the main problem facing the growth of United States influence in northern Latin America was the presence of Britain; and, indeed, the issues emanating from Washington's relationship with the dominant imperialist power and, later, Japan, are the two central issues in the conduct of United States diplomacy between 1895 and 1917. By World War One's inception the vested interests the United States had built in its existing arrangements with, above all, Britain but also Japan during these two decades preordained its response to the nation's role in the war.

To state that the United States eventually became an ally to Britain perhaps exaggerates the relationship which was to emerge after much tension between the two over Nicaragua or Venezuela in the mid-1890s—with flamboyant talk of war. But after 1898, at the latest, Britain's growing concern for its rivals on the European continent made it determined, however reluctant its navy, to avoid any future serious problems with the United States and, at the very least, to get out of its way as much as possible as the new imperialism swept in 1898 across the Pacific and snatched the moribund Spanish empire in its "splendid little war" of 1898. That war, which primarily direct economic motives can explain in Cuba and more grandiose economic ambitions in the Philippines, was made all the more easy by Britain's benevolent attitude if not covert encouragement, thereby allowing the United States to satisfy its strategic as well as economic reasons for establishing a Pacific chain taking it all the way to Southeast Asia. Although earlier historians may have overstressed British policy as a deliberate courtship of the United States to build a new alliance against the greater menace of Germany, in fact Britain's careful respect for the new American power built up a serious, at least partially calculated, mutual interdependence. In turn, the avoidance of the drastic rearrangement of the world and colonialism which Britain's defeat in World War One would have engendered was vital to the United States. Sentimental preferences also existed, especially among such progressive imperialists as Theodore Roosevelt, Henry Cabot Lodge, Elihu Root, and others, who from a racist viewpoint admired British colonialism's role in the world, but mutual interest was the bedrock of the de facto Anglo-American entente that was to emerge.

Roosevelt, for his part, saw the studied cultivation of the balance of power in Europe as the best of all possible arrangements, since it both avoided war between the European states and prevented their upsetting a fragile equilibrium by their moving into the regions—above all Latin America—which the United States was increasingly to claim as its own sphere of influence. In this context, Roosevelt built a minor reputation as a peacemaker in his efforts to encourage arbitration of disputes among European nations. The results were surely propitious for the United States. No other imperialist power at this time claimed such open-ended privileges over so vast an area, and had another done so the result would have produced a European war.

In Asia the framework in which United States efforts proceeded was far more complicated and, ultimately, was to fail to preserve both peace and American power in an environment in which the balance-of-power diplomacy was eventually to become increasingly irrelevant before the tides of nationalism and revolution germinating throughout Asia. But the first American entry—and the most ignored—was the bloody acquisition of the Philippines and the long repression, eventually costing at least 200,000 Filipino lives, which was required when the Americans found that in order really to take the islands they had first to retrieve it by force and chicanery from a Filipino independence movement largely in control at the end of the war with Spain. Americans, with few exceptions, refused to reflect on the enormity of this crime, which it later repeated again in a yet more brutal form in Vietnam. But it was from this island base, held firmly in hand with terrible force, and then also co-option and cultural imperialism, that the United States was to embark on its Asian role, a role that eventually became the most demanding and troublesome in America's long history.

But the basis of United States foreign policy in Asia outside of the Philippines has become a favorite topic of research and debate among historians, who will never understand wholly the meaning of the issues which arise there save in a global context, including especially Latin America. For only in this manner can one comprehend such a doctrine as the "Open Door" as a more ephemeral basis for the conduct of United States foreign policy than most of its critics or defenders have acknowledged. While men-of-power in Washington thought little of the Far East by contrast to other regions of the earth, not to mention national affairs, taken together, however, the theoretical underpinnings of United States policies in both China and Latin America allow us to discern more clearly the marriage of convenience and principle which at that time and later guided the United States relation to the Third World and provided a tactical underpinning for its own brand of imperialism.

Inconsistency, or the response to the pressures of specific powerful constituencies less concerned with principle than the attainment of their concrete objectives, makes the articulation of a perfectly coherent, uniform doctrine difficult, if not impossible, to attain in foreign policy. Suffice it to say, in the Asian context the United States had to acknowledge the realities of the situation. In the Philippines, where it de facto created a colony regardless of its ultimate designs for that nation, the United States did not share any privileges with other powers. Moreover, it regarded its developing position there as a base for penetrating the China market, where the balance of forces, it always realized, did not permit great freedom of initiative. In China, because of the presence of England, Russia, Germany, and Japan, among others, the United States, by necessity, had to opt for inclusion on the basis of equality with the most favored nation within the framework of existing spheres of influence. Under these circumstances, Washington's advocacy of a vague sort of international morality was in that moment in historical time a precondition for its expansion in China. While historians have disagreed why it chose to underwrite this doctrine in the ambiguous first "Open Door" note of September 1899, the fact remains that it was impossible for the United States to relate to the division of China into dominated imperialist fiefdoms in any other manner, and in reality the Open Door doctrine scarcely concerned China but rather the relations between the expansionist foreign powers already there. It is true, of course, that the pressure of the American Asiatic Association—with its constituency of cotton-goods exporters sending perhaps one-half of their overseas merchandise to China and incipient railroad promoters involved with some of the highest-ranking Republicans—was critical in extracting the United States policy at this time and in this exact form. Later, when these articulate interests largely no longer existed, the policy remained essentially the same: not to sanction the disintegration of China and rising foreign domination to exclude the possibility, if not the reality, of United States investment and trade. From this viewpoint, the implicit political goal of the Open Door doctrine of equality of access within the existing spheres of influence proved more durable than the immediate economic constituencies seeking this or that tangible gain, and in due time it reflected a more abstract definition of the nature of United States policy toward China in which economics and politics were molded into a single concept.

The political integrity of China itself was never a question during the brief period these notes were formulated, and in fact the position of the American ambassador in China at that time was that the United States no longer needed to claim extraterritorial diplomatic status in those cities under foreign control, because "these ports have practically passed from the control of an uncivilized people to civilized," a position that Secretary of State John Hay was to share.[3] All the United States demanded was that the Germans, English, or whoever controlled the ports freely admit and charge no excessive tariffs to United States goods. By no means did the United States seek to retrieve China's lost political integrity for the moribund empire, which was disintegrating at a pace even the United States found a bit disturbing—though at no time did the United States ever desire a strong China able to treat with its potential invaders as an equal. In early 1900, while foreign troops, including 5000 from America, suppressed the nationalist Boxer Rebellion, the State Department, in a second Open Door note, responded to United States business fears of a final political partition of China that might exclude them altogether. Issuing the note a day before the Republican national convention, it called for no further alienation of China's territorial integrity—already well nigh lost. Such a position did not demand the restoration of lost sovereignty, and in fact the United States at the end of the year itself considered trying to get a naval base at Fukien. In reality, it was not ambiguous American reticence, which was scarcely noticed, that prevented a further dismemberment of China, but rather that the infinitely precarious European balance of power did not permit Russia or any other state to make a potentially dangerous move in China. Basically unsympathetic to the development of all forms of Chinese nationalism, the United States made the implementation of the notes contingent on China's "ability and willingness to make on its part an effective suspension of hostilities" toward Western nations.[4]

More to the point was the United States policy, which endured in various forms until the end of World War One, to try to create a balance of power in China which would permit relatively minor United States interests to operate in the fragile equilibrium. Until 1904, Washington saw Russia as the greater imperialist danger and cordially endorsed the 1902 British-Japanese entente designed to counterbalance the Czar. Roosevelt admired the Japanese surprise attack against Russia in February 1904 and hoped Japan would fight well without necessarily becoming the total victor and dominating Manchuria entirely, thereby unbalancing big-power relations. In mediating the war over the following summer, Roosevelt consistently favored the Japanese cause and emerged "far stronger pro-Japanese than ever."[5] His administration never feared Japanese intentions, and friendship with Japan became the keystone of his Far Eastern policy—with the Open Door notes being relegated, insofar as they implied support for China's political autonomy, to the dustbin. Indeed, it is common enough knowledge that secretly in 1904 and 1905, and publicly in 1908, the United States acknowledged "paramount" Japanese interests in the Yellow Sea area, notably Korea, in return for Japan's recognition of United States supremacy in the Philippines.

Objectively, of course, the China market was utterly inconsequential to all but two American industries—illuminating oil and cotton textiles—and it took 8 percent of the former and 28 percent of the latter's foreign trade in 1910. But the rising internal market within the United States by that time had greatly lowered the incentives to sustain the China market that had existed a decade earlier. Investments, on which far more has been written, largely lost all interest to the few United States capitalists who were ready to place quite small sums in Chinese railroads until 1908, and thereafter the case of United States investment in China is largely one of political leaders with little and declining success seeking to provoke business to enter China primarily for political rather than immediate economic objectives. While these political goals also implied future United States economic participation, this was at least temporarily abstract by virtue of the absence of potential American investors. More to the point was Roosevelt's anger over manifestations of Chinese nationalism in 1905–1906 which led to the boycott of American goods, even to the extent of his preparing to send 15,000 United States troops to show the flag as well as reverse the damage being inflicted on cotton weavers. In the end, the United States was to exhibit implacable hostility toward all forms of Chinese nationalism, opposing Sun Yat-sen during the Chinese revolution of 1911 as the next of a series of long steps to keep a China sufficiently weak to be open to eventual, if still amorphous, American activity.

In China the United States was ready or compelled to share the fruits of imperialism with others, but in Latin America it was a question of creating an exclusive sphere of influence in which the United States could at will write and revise the terms of its relationship to its southern neighbors. The first manifestation of this hemispheric system was outlined in the Platt Amendment of March 1901 permitting Cuba a purely rhetorical independence: the reservation of the right of reentry for United States troops, United States control over Cuba's foreign policy and all treaties, the freedom to maintain bases (one of which is still there), and the Cuban acceptance of all acts of the American military governor. With the Hay-Pauncefote Treaty of 1901 the United States retrieved from Britain total control over any future Isthmian canal, and it successfully opposed British and German presence in the period thereafter. In the Roosevelt Corollary of December 1904 the United States staked out its exclusive right to intervene, with force or otherwise, in the affairs of any of the nations of the hemisphere to prevent "a general loosening of the ties of civilized society," a prerogative it was to exercise countless times over subsequent decades not only for its own interests but to prevent the growth of European influence in the hemisphere. Numerous acts of domination and troop invasions of Central American states thereafter revealed no aspects of ambiguity between theory and practice for the United States. "Every great power has some 'doctrines' that it conceives to be as vital to it as the Monroe Doctrine is considered here," Huntington Wilson, Taft's Assistant Secretary of State, wrote in 1916. To intrude into other nations' spheres in a fashion that outweighed any commercial gain to be attained was poor diplomacy. "In return we should gradually crowd out from our own sphere of special interest foreign interests wherever they are predominant to an uncomfortable extent."[6]

This exclusionary policy was slowly but irresistibly realized, and became the foundation for hemispheric policy in what since has been accurately dubbed the "Closed Door," or a sphere of influence policy.[7] The United States assumed the unlimited responsibility for regulating the internal affairs of any Latin American nation in any manner it deemed of interest to itself. Despite all the verbiage of altruism, usually linked to better trade relations even in the most routine ceremonial speeches, the underlying policy was always explicitly the attainment of United States hegemony. The most candid example of this truth arose in June 1914, when Secretary of State Robert Lansing prepared a confidential statement on the nature of United States policy toward the southern nations: "In its advocacy of the Monroe Doctrine the United States considers its own interests. The integrity of other American nations is an incident, not an end. While this may seem based on selfishness alone, the author of the Doctrine had no higher or more generous motive in its declaration. . . . With the present industrial activity, the scramble for markets, and the incessant search for new opportunities to produce wealth, commercial expansion and success are closely interwoven with political domination over the territory which is being exploited. . . . Should a new doctrine be formulated declaring that the United States is opposed to the extension of European control over American territory and its institutions through financial as well as other means . . . ?" On November 24, 1915, Lansing sent the memo to President Wilson, who thought it impolitic to issue it at the time but responded, "The argument of this paper seems to be unanswerable. . . . Just now, I take it for granted, it is only for the guidance and clarification of our own thought, and for informal discussion with our Latin American friends from time to time, semi-confidentially and for the sake of frank understanding."[8]

Within the premises of this exchange, hardly anything new or unique was to occur in the conduct of United States foreign policy toward Latin America before or after 1915. If in foreign affairs one has at times to linger over the intent of a policy as opposed to its functional consequences, in United States Latin American policy this is scarcely necessary. The immediate outcome of these assumptions was a concerted United States effort to exploit the distractions the war created for Europe to systematically grasp all of Europe's Western Hemisphere markets. In this effort new governmental organisms were established to coordinate business activities, setting the stage for the next great step into the overseas market. American structural economic imperatives increasingly dictated no other course as the country embarked on its long, sustained effort to control the political and economic fates of the entire hemisphere as part of its own imperial domain. The war was the threshold for United States foreign economic policy, with need more and more replacing mere avarice, however different the weight of both these elements for each company. On these foundations, the history of Washington's defining role in that vast region was to proceed.

In effect, Europe's preoccupation with its own approaching storm allowed the newcomer to push forward in a vacuum that meant, not for the last time, that Europe's irrationality would give the United States an opportunity to grow disproportionately more quickly. This condition of relative freedom did not mean a total absence of challenges in preserving hegemony, as when Britain, pushed by its navy, sought to mix into the troubled Mexican civil war in 1913 to gain an assured oil supply; but what is most significant about such isolated forays is that until 1917 the United States always managed to gain its way—and after the war no nation in the world was ever again strong enough to reverse its political command over Latin America. After sufficiently chastising the British for interfering in the privileged United States sanctuary of Mexican politics, and offering to reciprocate to British acquiescence with concessions on canal tolls, Washington could count on Britain's backing for American strategy in Mexico and remaining docile wherever potential conflicts with the United States in Latin America might arise.

The Enigma of Ideology

Discussions of the role of ideas and ideology as the basis of American foreign relations will always necessarily be artificial; and divorced from the actual conduct of diplomacy, they will also prove grossly misleading. That leaders can or do relate each specific action to some intellectual frame of reference is to exaggerate the role that ideas are designed to play, yet standards and parameters of conduct exist and some are capable of being subsumed as principles. Indeed, the very lack of precision and the inability always to relate actions to final objectives and principles must be taken into account in order to comprehend the latent weaknesses and dilemmas of United States foreign policy. More pressing in the daily reality is the existence of constituencies and their concrete pressures to accomplish this or that goal, but even these have a minimally predictable coherence. Ideology, therefore, can be based on formal propositions and doctrines, or it can also be the merger of ideas and the functional practices which real interests impose on the conduct of foreign relations in a capitalist society. At various times and places it can be both, or either. More often, the practice searches for its own rationalization after the fact, and simply reflects the pervasive truth that the distribution of power in a capitalist society rarely had allowed Washington to conduct policies counterproductive to those tangible interests which could be measured not in terms of doctrinal purity but in dollars—or the promise of them. In this regard, the first principles of United States foreign policy can be considered as purely utilitarian: those which satisfy the interests of powerful constituencies are followed so long as they succeed, with doctrinal purity being less important than accomplishments. Historians, in brief, can make too much of the ideological basis of United States foreign policy, and are especially wont to do so when they separate ideas from practice. A speech, after all, is much more likely to be written to satisfy an occasion than to articulate a basis to guide future action.

Consistency regarding all details of the practice on which the broad principles of United States diplomacy rest is impossible, if only because the often vague ideological abstractions of the "Open Door," "liberal internationalism," or even "national interest," to cite only a few of the overall characterizations of the intellectual premises of United States conduct, cannot always be translated by decision makers into specific actions which satisfy all the priorities and needs of all the factions of American capitalism—who agree on the abstractions but have varying strategies to sell different commodities or attain privileges, often at the expense of each other. More practically, the men who administer policy usually are responsive to one approach to the achievement of United States hegemony or success which slights the needs of other constituencies.

Historians, in any case, have considered virtually *all* of the utterances of men of varying degrees of power involved in the shaping of United States diplomacy after 1880, from Presidents to business leaders. To precisely sort out the relative weight one attaches to McKinley's claim to have heard the "Almighty's" injunction to retain the Philippines to "Christianize" it, or to the cotton-textile industry's lobbying to open the China market, is a futile exercise, but it is surely a retreat from reality and an encouragement to wishful thinking to state that just because we cannot know everything we have no responsibility to attempt to strike some approximate syntheses.[9] For in the aggregate it is a fact that the final intended result of the whole course of United States foreign policy after the Civil War was to optimize the power and profit of American capitalism in the global economy, striving for the political and military preconditions essential to the attainment of that end. At times it is certain that the missionary impulse and doctrines of racial supremacy were operative, even for their own sake, and Roosevelt and Wilson's admiration for the cultural imperialism of Britain and Europe was a fact even when the profit of America was not an issue at stake. Few, if any, American leaders after the Civil War challenged the assumption that the expansion of Caucasian nations was synonymous with human progress. Roosevelt did indeed believe in "just" wars, and a certain admiration among him and his friends for combat and bloodshed as a healthy human activity existed at various times, even though in practice Roosevelt as President tried to avert conflicts among European powers and tried to preserve a balance of power there more congenial to American interests. A paradox, surely, but a quite common one that was to appear in the sort of convenient but genuinely sincere contradictions which so marked the thought of his numerous successors. Such an unconscious unity of seeming opposites is quite a common element in the development of such ideology as may have emerged, and is perhaps the best argument for stressing the practice and function of United States foreign policy rather than only the rhetoric used to justify it.

Woodrow Wilson embodied all of these paradoxes and strains of thought, and precisely because of his academic background he wrote and said more on which later historians have been able to focus. Insofar as Wilson was mainly preoccupied with national affairs until at least 1914, this inordinate attention to his every utterance is somewhat contrived, and in fact he did not worry about consistency as much as satisfying the needs of the moment. But even if domestic concerns took the majority of his time, Wilson shared an export consciousness which caused him often to note, as in his acceptance speech to the Democratic convention in 1912, that American industries "have expanded to such a point that they will burst their jackets if they cannot find a free outlet to the markets of the world."[10] And Wilson was indeed a Southerner who represented the full restoration of the South to equality of access to power, but his deep racism differed from that of his predecessors only in degree but not in kind. Racism in the most inclusive sense was respectable conventional wisdom throughout this period, not merely in the United States but among European liberals as well. More distinctive was Wilson's deep commitment to free trade doctrines so fashionable when he was a doctoral student, but also so universally shared by a South which, more than any other section of the United States, was integrated with its cotton and tobacco exports into the world economy. The foundations of Wilsonian internationalism were therefore congenial with both the theory and practice he and his region inherited, though in his conduct he also associated the fulfillment of these doctrines with the need of Northern manufacturing for new markets—as in reality it was. When viewing the relation of America to Europe and the Eastern Hemisphere, Wilson surely believed that freer trade and the integration of the world economy would produce the sort of natural harmony and prosperity the advocates of laissez faire had always predicted. America would benefit, but so would the entire world, in that sincere doctrine of the reconciliation of interests Republicans and Democrats so blithely shared at the time. Liberalized capitalist internationalism and integration, for Wilson, was an agency of civilization and peace. The advancement of United States trade and the interests of the world at one and the same time would be served—an article of faith American leaders have sincerely held in various forms until this day.

For the Philippines and Latin America, however, United States political leaders always evoked a consistent exception. By holding the Philippines, or giving aid to American investors in Haiti by sending in troops, or such, the United States made possible the future blessings of liberty and held out the hope of diminishing injustices. Later, by opposing Bolshevism and all manifestations of the Left, and by using food aid and the threat of starvation to force nations to American terms, philanthropy and national interest were both maximized. To state, as Wilson did in September 1916, that "Not only when this war is over, but now, America has her place in the . . . world of finance and commerce upon a scale that she never dreamed of before," was merely to proclaim what the constituents of American power also believed; but rather than being cynical, Wilson internalized this goal as genuinely best for the entire world.[11] That it was sincere made it no less acquisitive and dangerous, or perhaps more so. What is certain is that before the World War the United States had affected the synthesis of liberal ideology and classic national expansion which was to become the hallmark of United States globalism for the next sixty years. Moreover, after 1914 it created the organizations and honed the strategy that would allow it to move into Europe's traditional markets. Its internationalism and appeals to higher goals were integral to its expansion of its national economic and strategic interests, and its thin ideological and moral rhetoric was to become a standard handmaiden to justify its more brutal actions to serve itself in Haiti, the Philippines, Cuba or, later, Vietnam. For surprisingly large constituencies of other nations suffering from the void that the collapse of various national and reform social theories had produced after 1900, the political charms of this doctrine of liberalized capitalist internationalism were to provide the United States with a remarkably durable means of organizational mobilization useful to the attainment of its own concrete national interests—less with cynicism than because Americans too needed some faith by which to justify the bloodshed and expenses that their burgeoning imperialism required.

Hence the odd mixture of liberal international doctrine for the Eastern Hemisphere, a narrower, more classically imperialist practice and theoretical exceptionalism for the Western Hemisphere, and pragmatic attention, in the overwhelming majority of cases, to protecting and advancing specific United States interests wherever the need might arise without reference to such clarity and insight as larger ideologies are supposed to provide. Success was a better criterion for men of action than doctrinal purity. Ideas, in any case, are rarely so precise as to provide an exact guide for relating to each problem, and hence they can be bent accordingly to justify what the needs and interests of the moment require. Rarely do they lead to deductions as to which praxis the faith demands, for the essence of American liberal ideology was a broadness which allowed it to subsume the most diverse actions and become all things to all men. This universality made such abstractions useful not merely for American liberals but those of Europe as well. Hence its complexity and simplicity at one and the same time.

War Aims

It is pointless to try to attach weights to the factors historians have attributed as the causes of the American entry into World War One, but the question of war aims impinges on the ideological foundations of United States foreign policy as well as the larger, more complicated matrix of relationships on which the emergence of America as a world power was dependent. In the most general sense, the capacity of the United States to have expanded so quickly after 1896 without resistance was due to the fragile equilibrium in Europe and the British toleration, if not encouragement, of United States growth after that time. This meant, in essence, that should British power collapse in defeat it would require a complete revision of the United States relation to Europe on which its imperialism based its vast and unopposed successes in the Western Hemisphere and Asia. The other elements were important to a more or lesser degree, yet Germany's victory meant, in effect, that its triumph would likely require a testing and possible revision of the gains of two decades of American expansionism.

Hence the near inevitability of the growing United States support for England and the entente after 1915 and its eventual entry into the war. From the inception of the war, Wilson never feared the outcome of a decisive entente victory to United States interests, but only a successful Germany. For while the Wilsonian system could never be attained in a world largely dominated by an autarkic bloc, a German bloc was the most imminent, and Washington had to resist it whatever the nominal excuse. If Germany's actions with its submarines provided politically sufficient justification for doing so, that merely eased the making of necessary decisions regardless of circumstances. Moral factors and outrage as a cause of the American decision to go to war are not in contradiction with this premise if one probes more deeply into the institutional assumptions contained in the peculiar American brand of moralism. Even narrower explanations alleging that economic involvement via loans and trade was a cause of United States entry also require respect—though far less than was the wont in the 1930s, if all one means by economic involvement is several billions of dollars in loans or about three times that in trade. Even elimination of freedom of the seas and commerce, and hence subversion of the type of international economic integration and system integral to the fulfillment of Wilson's ideas, was not so much attacked by German submarine warfare during the war as was the prospect of its complete attainment afterwards, were the autarkic, nationalist doctrines of Germany to prevail. England, indeed, had more greatly violated freedom of commerce on the open seas in the initial stages of the war, but with far more acquiescence than a partial White House could later show Germany.

Sub warfare was a tactical threat to the objective of trade during war, but with or without the immediate problem of subs, Germany's victory would have made likely a strategic defeat of the economic and political basis of the type of world essential not merely to Wilson but to the future expansion of United States industry. And this growth, which had not so much occurred before the war as during it, was an option that many American business constituencies thought worth retaining. Before the war broke out it was an article of the faith among virtually all Americans with a real voice in politics and economics that open trade among nations was desirable, if not essential, and Democrats especially felt that freer trade and commerce was a key to both peace and prosperity for the United States. Republicans such as Roosevelt and Lodge, who had a lower opinion of laissez-faire doctrines, nevertheless even more passionately solidarized with the British cause for cultural and strategic reasons as well as economic—producing a larger consensus of growing support for the entente and, virtually, direct entry into the war.

Britain's victory would not have assured the future success of United States—defined liberal economic internationalism, though many powerful Englishmen were also dedicated to the American-adopted doctrine on which the empire had prospered, but Germany's victory seemed certain to eliminate the chances for its eventual attainment. The potential absence of British mastery of the Atlantic was also a strategic anxiety for American officers who saw the greatest menace in the rise of the German navy, but as an ardent navalist Wilson would have had little to fear with his intended largest fleet in the world regardless of the victory in Europe. In fact, it was mainly the potential purposes of any German navy that seemed to challenge American security rather than its mere size. It was not Britain's navy that guarded the United States Atlantic flank but its benign attitude toward the growth of the United States hegemony in the hemisphere, a toleration that Germany seemed unlikely to share.

Wilson, in any case, saw in the now ascendant United States economic power the possibility of dictating the nature of the peace to his future allies. "When the war is over," he wrote in July 1917, "we can force them to our way of thinking, because by that time they will . . . be financially in our hands."[12] What was essential was to guarantee a world in which all nations—by which he meant white European states—could participate equally on the basis of free intercourse. Controls, even to regulate commodity and raw material prices, were anathema to his ideal laissez-faire doctrine. His commitment to this set of goals deepened with the advent of the Bolshevik Revolution in November 1917, when his concern for the reform of cruder types of economically closed European colonialism, if not the destruction of German autarkic intentions, was largely pushed aside by the emergence of the previously unimaginable problem of revolution and a dynamic Left rising from the chaos of war. It was at this point that the desire to create a significantly reformed open world capitalist economic and political order was tactically blunted by the ever-growing obsession of preventing the further expansion and growth of Bolshevism and revolution. The compromises and alleged tragedies of Wilson's allegiance and principles at this point are exaggerated, if only because the fight against revolution was, from a purely American capitalist viewpoint, a necessary precondition to the reform of world capitalism in the Eastern Hemisphere.

With the articulation of the Fourteen Points in January 1918 as the most comprehensive single statement of American war aims, it was clear that the destruction of revolution would take temporary precedence over the reform of traditional capitalism in Europe and its exclusive imperialist blocs, but Washington's belief in the necessity of attaining both goals was never to wholly disappear. The economic reform and integration of its nominal allies is a current in modern American history which was to transcend the personality of Wilson as such. The advocacy of capitalist reform, in any case, was a useful political tool in intensifying defeatism among German liberals, and in principle the British Liberals also shared the articles of a free trade faith which they, after all, had originated for the Americans later to borrow. While the portion of the Fourteen Points dealing with Russia was the true immediate objective of the proclamation, intended to serve as a response to Lenin's more effective and simpler appeals, the idea of free navigation of the sea and the most extensive possible removal of economic barriers and trade inequality was already integral to the free trade synthesis Wilson had taken as his own. Open peace covenants themselves were innocent enough, and self-determination of nationalities under the heel of the Austro-Hungarian enemy was a gratuitous concession. Washington's studied ambiguity on the future of colonial regions was no accident: no American leader favored self-determination for Asians and races they felt inferior, and along with their white allies they later explicitly rejected a statement on racial equality in the covenant of the League of Nations charter. Not for a moment did it ever occur to the Americans to abandon immediately their own control over the former Spanish—and now United States—colonies.

This statement of principles and a more practical ideology were utilitarian for the occasion of fighting Bolshevism, but scarcely for the first or last time the United States proved ready freely to define abstractions to make them more congenial with the pressures of immediate demands. "The Fourteen Points themselves could not be applied without a vast disruption of the old state system of Europe," James T. Shotwell, American adviser at the Paris Peace Conference, later recollected, "and with the possibility of bringing economic and political chaos to much of Eastern and Central Europe."[13] Wilson did not dissent from such compromises to stem the greater risk of revolution, just as his own application of broad principles in practice had been incessantly flexible throughout his entire career, so that one overestimates the rigidity of this or that of his convictions, which was no less firmly held merely by being interpreted to suit the exigencies of some specific conditions or pressure. The role of ideas to men of affairs is not to create dysfunctions to the exercise of power, and no conflict between the two really exists. Practice in need of an ideology is not a dilemma, despite the frequently large gap between the two, because the implementation of policy has been so uniformly consistent and loyal to the real needs of power constituencies—even when not all, because of differing priorities and interests, have been satisfied at one and the same time. Though historical actors rarely spend time reflecting on their conformity with first principles, should the highly unlikely case occur that they develop a false consciousness dysfunctional to all important interests in society they will quickly be removed. What the decision not to try simultaneously to reform European capitalism and destroy revolution did show, however, is that when confronted with a choice the United States would decisively, firmly opt for counterrevolution. From the viewpoint of the larger interests of American capitalism, that decision appeared rational insofar as it preserved the framework so essential to the very existence of the system in any form. That principle, hammered out in the maelstrom of a war that was producing the negations of imperialism as a consequence of its own greed and self-destruction, became the firmest legacy of the Wilson period and one of the most durable premises of United States foreign policy for the remainder of the century.[14]

The United States and Revolution

The problem of the emergence of a world Left and revolution was one that transcended the intellectual equipment with which the United States entered the twentieth century and World War One. It was, in essence, unimaginable, and scarcely contemplated as the main outcome of the vast process of bloodletting called modern war. But any war will generate internal crises and upheavals appropriate to the latent fragility of a social order and the magnitude of the external forces, an unanticipated reality that neither the United States nor its allies could calculate, and one they found inordinately difficult to project into the future by virtue of their own confidence in the stability of traditional societies.

It was Lenin, not Wilson (much less his European peers), who by the fall of 1917 understood the trend of European history and could cope with it. The fact is that the European masses, in Germany and France especially, shared the disgust and apathy of the Russian people toward the whole bloody, insane war, and they wanted nothing so much as to see the torment cease. Lenin urgently wished peace in order to make revolution elsewhere and consolidate it in Russia, while Wilson and his advisers wished to destroy Bolshevism, or at the very least to fatally alter it as a precondition of modernizing and reintegrating Russia into a sustained anti-German struggle and, thereafter, a liberalized world capitalist order. The Fourteen Points were preeminently an effort in this direction, linking, as they did, vaguely defined reform of the European political and economic structures to a settlement "affecting" (but in reality in) a Russia with which the rest of the entente could cooperate. There was no chance, despite continued German aggression and disagreements within Bolshevik ranks, that Soviet Russia could accept the Fourteen Points, or even the more compromising modifications Colonel Edward House or William Bullitt proposed, and Wilson eventually shared Lansing's view that Bolshevism was a greater danger than German militarism and, indeed, probably a diabolical plot concocted and directed from Berlin in the first place.

A paranoid image of the nature of Bolshevism, which lingers in other forms until this very day, was intrinsic to the misplaced confidence that Wilson and Western leaders had in their own social systems, and it required too great a leap in their world views to perceive revolutionary socialism not as the cause of international chaos and capitalism's demise but as a reflection of them. Either way, however, it was not to their advantage to tolerate its existence, and from 1918 onward two grand themes shaped the world conflict which emerged at that time: classic rivalries and wars between states and, often simultaneously, international conflicts as civil wars and class alliances in which elite factions within nations preferred coalitions with the rulers of other states to the triumph of their own revolutionary countrymen and national independence.

Hence the entire byzantine American and Anglo-French involvement in Russia, which led the United States in the summer of 1918 to send almost 8000 troops to Siberia and Russia to join those of their allies, reflected these two main emerging currents in not only United States but Western European global strategy: to fight both Germany's atavistic nationalist imperialism and Russia's revolution, if possible at one and the same time. From the inception of Bolshevism, the leaders of the United States could not, in principle, tolerate its existence nor that of any other historic form of social revolution. Sending a small number of troops to support the fight against Bolshevism was neither a hasty judgment based on misunderstanding nor even an *opéra bouffe*—a banal theory which is even less serious than the naïve arguments that American forces were there to protect Russia against Germans or the Japanese—for they stayed much longer than the former were at war and left before the latter. While at the beginning Wilson had regarded such anti-Bolshevik intervention as synonymous with the anti-German struggle, he had no such excuse until April 1920, when the Americans finally left Siberia after it was clear nothing more could be done. The 1918 intervention, which Washington carefully discussed for half a year before approving, was the first small foretaste of a long series that have become intrinsic to the American response to a world in revolution and upheaval.

Nineteen-eighteen, as Arno J. Mayer has so superbly shown, marked the inception of the new diplomacy over the heads of state and directly to the people in hope of transforming the nature of state policies or even the social and class composition of the status quos of this or that nation. Such an effort was not merely a matter of issuing proclamations, such as the ambiguous American effort to liberalize Allied war aims both to sustain the anti-German struggle as well as reverse the pacifist and revolutionary appeals of Bolshevism and the

European revolutionary movement which had begun to spread in Germany, Hungary, Italy, and France, among others. It was also a question of sending troops and arms to assist counterrevolutionary social forces and classes; of appealing directly to the political counterparts of Western bourgeois liberalism in Germany and enemy countries to affect the political direction of those states; of using food, as was done with success under Herbert Hoover's direction in Hungary against the Left under Béla Kun and unsuccessfully in the Soviet Union, as a crude incentive in starving nations to extract far-reaching political concessions. In the crucible of Europe's revolution, Wilson and his circle first shaped the basic attitudes and techniques which were to later become integral to the conduct of United States foreign policy for the remainder of the century.

World War One, like its successor, was to prove far more significant not in the way in which it did or did not lead to a formal diplomatic settlement at Versailles or the creation of a League of Nations, which was predestined to fail regardless of United States participation, but because it created vast, uncontrollable social and economic forces; and, indeed, counterrevolutionary leaders could not begin to imagine their full extent. The war led to the emergence of a revolutionary Left, isolated territorially for the time but incipient many other places, as a historic force; it led to the metamorphosis of conservative bourgeois nationalism into fascism; to a panoply of new economic and social crises; to the vast upheaval and the direction of the world for the next half-century. War shattered many of the social and political equilibria throughout the globe to an extent few contemporaries appreciated when they began to try to reestablish some type of order.

The Dilemma of Japan

The new reality of instability in Asia and America's need to balance Japan's expansive power was ironic in light of the fact that Japan had received so much encouragement from the Theodore Roosevelt Administration to play its active role in Asia. William Howard Taft had less confidence in Japanese intentions, and from 1909 he slowly, hesitantly began divorcing United States policy from the legitimation his predecessors had given to Japan's sphere of influence. Taft wished to help United States business play a role in Manchuria and northern China precisely to prevent Japan's political domination should its economic growth remain exclusive and unchallenged, and for a time he was encouraged in this by Willard Straight of the J. P. Morgan Company, an ardent advocate of large United States economic penetration who had made the issue something of a personal crusade. But neither could make the risky venture sufficiently profitable to attract much investment interest, and the effort became essentially a politically prompted one in which Washington naïvely hoped that businessmen would risk the loss of money on behalf of the more remote United States strategic and political interest in becoming a power in China. But potential American investors did not agree, as their motivation dropped yet further and they sought for a way to disengage from the political pressures. This they accomplished when Wilson came to office and they posed what was known to be a politically unacceptable precondition for loans: a guarantee of the force of United States arms to collect from the Chinese should they default. When Wilson in March 1913 denounced the bankers for this position they were quite happy to drop the entire China question. And, paradoxically, the Wilson Administration shifted all too often on the danger of Japan's domination of China, thereby lessening its incentives to utilize funds to reinforce a political policy.

But in the ambiguous, often convoluted manner which characterized the rest of the Wilson Administration's policy on the matter, Washington also wished greater trade in China, and even loans to it, and to sustain the very nominal national autonomy that the blatantly repressive Peking-based Yuan regime proclaimed after it emerged from the 1911 Revolution. When Japan grabbed off Germany's posts in the Shantung Peninsula after the outbreak of war, plus a little more as well, Secretary of State William Jennings Bryan and President Wilson reluctantly tolerated Japan's "Twenty-one Demands" to China and threat of war of January 1915, which gave it a virtual economic monopoly of Shantung and Manchuria. Indeed, Washington even attempted to gain China's agreement to accept mediation of the outrageous assault on its sovereignty. Robert Lansing, who succeeded Bryan in June 1915, shared the explicit American acknowledgment that Japan had "special relations" with at least some of the districts it claimed, but mainly in the hope that the remainder of China could be kept open to United States interests—in effect, creating mutual spheres of influence. In fact, for the remainder of the Wilson Administration the State Department reverted to Taft's policy of encouraging investments in China to help create an economic barrier against Japan, or at the very least not allow it a monopoly by default. But lack of banker enthusiasm as well as Japanese efforts to stymie the United States caused most of the private undertakings to fail, and the administration eventually had to consider direct governmental loans to China to play the same role.

Lansing was quite aware that China and the future of the Far East had become a mainly Japanese-American question, and that conflict would be the outcome of their failure to reach an understanding. Mutual concessions and the demarcation of noncompeting regions seemed to him the most practical strategy. Despite Wilson's reticence and fear during early 1915 that Japan would seek to expand throughout all of China, the United States was surely not ready to take strong steps to stop it, and Lansing sympathized with the idea that any nation so close to an underpopulated region as rich as Shantung would naturally want to take it. The Secretary also hoped Japan would go no further. But the Russian-Japanese Treaty of July 1916 dividing North China into vaguely defined spheres of influence only renewed strong American anxieties, which remained relatively dormant as other matters intruded into the center of United States foreign policy. By the fall of 1917, after having again informally recognized Japanese claims in Shantung, Colonel House, Lansing, and others were ready to make a final attempt to concede to Japan a finite sphere of influence in China to prevent, "sooner or later," to quote House, "a reckoning."[15] The Lansing-Ishii Agreement reaffirmed that November the Open Door as well as Japan's "special interests" in "contiguous" areas of China. Japan was encouraged rather than satisfied, and Lansing grew increasingly hostile to Japan until, by 1919, he saw only danger ahead in United States–Japanese relations. Reluctantly, with the ambiguity and doubt that had marked United States policy for almost a decade, he endorsed the Japanese invasion of Siberia with over 70,000 troops against what he agreed was the far greater and immediate danger of Bolshevism. But he opposed Wilson and House's support for the Paris Peace Conference's decision to formally concede to Japan Germany's rights in Shantung when Japan, furious at the unwillingness of the West to insert a racial equality provision into the League covenant, threatened not to join the organization. By that time, however, it was clear that the existing situation pleased no one and a new, troubled era in Japanese-American relations would begin unless the United States were ready to withdraw from the direction of the affairs of Asia.

Nowhere was the new postwar change of forces more pronounced than in the Far East. For there other European nations had always provided a buffer between the United States and Japan as well as a modicum of balance, eliminating the need for the United States to stand as the sole direct restraint to a relentless Japanese expansion. Russia had been partially removed from the scene in 1905, and then wholly after 1917. Britain was too preoccupied with its affairs in Europe and elsewhere to remain of much consequence, and Germany was now wholly eliminated from the picture. By the end of the war it was unavoidable that the former cordial allies seek to negotiate a new arrangement in the Far East if possible, but whether or not they succeeded it was certain that a new, yet more unstable era in Asian politics had begun. Only the United States could—or had to—confront the issue, given its own ambitions in the Pacific as well as its strategic position.

War and the Distribution of World Power

The war wholly upset the pre-1914 relations between nations and removed the moderating preoccupations of common enemies that had smoothed the course of United States, British, and Japanese interaction for two decades. Former allies now had to seek a new equilibrium, and the entire world system of alliances and interests, in Asia as well as Europe, was at stake. United States dependence on Britain for the partial defense of its international status was no longer necessary. It was as if a convoluted game of chance had led to the table being thrown to the floor with fewer players reemerging—and two of them, Japan and the United States, being relatively far larger. Germany no longer appeared a factor, and the specter of revolution by January 1919 seemed to be something that capitalist nations now could contain and isolate—perhaps, thereby, even to forget. "Food relief is now the key to the whole [Eastern] European situation," Wilson concluded that month as they met at the Versailles Conference to dictate to Germany and set impossible conditions for Soviet Russia. "Bolshevism . . . cannot be stopped by force but it can be stopped by food," though the President soon endorsed ample force as well.[16] British economic adviser John Maynard Keynes later that year accurately described the conference's true historic significance as "the fearful convulsions of a dying civilization."[17]

Portraying Wilson as the sick, harried, tortured idealist at Versailles scarcely does justice to the President and his administration's carefully articulated plans for the peace. His faith in what a League of Nations could do with even poor peace terms was surely his greatest myopia, but beyond that he had supreme confidence in the economic capacity of the United States to define the nature of the future world order which it was to found, above all, on economic arrangements. "The American policy at Paris," the President's official biographer, Ray Stannard Baker, later naïvely but accurately wrote, "was to cooperate politically, and to go back to the old economic rivalries, with each nation playing a lone hand."[18] But the United States thought its hand, and the terms it could thereby impose, would allow a just, peaceful world order to emerge quite naturally and irresistibly for white European nations. To reduce the resistance of former friends and foes alike to this design was very much the plan and desire of Wilson and the United States. This meant that the struggle to reshape the world by peaceful rather than violent means would continue. That the conference could not immediately apply all of the erstwhile idealism of the Fourteen Points was secondary, because as one of his lesser advisers at Versailles has already been quoted as admitting, the consequence would have been "economic and political chaos."[19] The aspect of the postwar world to which the United States had given its main, most careful thought was the economic one, with itself playing the central role, and the League was only a later afterthought. Wilson passionately hoped for an American role in the League, and in this regard historians have quite accurately portrayed his personal efforts, but this was surely not in conflict with desiring even much more via unilateral action.

The passage of the Federal Reserve Act in 1914 had created the long-needed foundation of far greater United States involvement in world banking, a goal its authors explicitly acknowledged. Thereafter numerous federal and private organizations prepared to expand their role and the nation's profits abroad. The Webb-Pomerene Act in 1918, exempting price-fixing export associations from anti-trust laws, permitted American industry "to organize," as Wilson explained it, "for foreign trade just as the 'rings' of England and the cartels of Germany are organized."[20] By that time the eagerness of numerous United States bankers and industrialists to sustain the wartime-induced exports after the conflict, and to assume Britain's traditional dominant role in the world economy, was a consensus far more widely spread than had probably ever before been the case. The first place the United States had turned to attain this goal was Latin America, where quite important prewar preparations joined with abnormal wartime conditions to immediately create a vast success which by 1919 could only reinforce Washington's belief that its economic leverage in the postwar world would be its single most powerful asset in achieving the objectives of its foreign policy. By 1920 all of Latin America's dependence on imports from the United States had grown from 25 percent in 1913 to 50 percent. Almost one-fifth of all United States exports now were directed toward its southern neighbors, a share that was to remain relatively constant for four decades.

Given the time-consuming obsessions of the Versailles Conference with the problem of Bolshevism and Russia—"day and night" according to General Tasker Howard Bliss—as well as Asia and the future of the Ottoman Empire, to name but a few, it was a human impossibility to hammer out agreed-upon resolutions to numerous questions impinging on the economics and politics of Europe's future, and it is not quite certain that this truly surprised too many of the participants.[21] What was critical to the United States was the kind of world that would emerge from the new balance of forces in reality and, secondarily in my opinion, what the League might accomplish also in regulating the postwar era. The problems of Germany's postwar economic and political position, and war debts, were issues on which the United States rejected the proposals of its allies; but even before the conference ended, Wilson had authorized the serious consideration of existing United States plans for autonomous actions consistent with demanding full repayment of war debts, a policy which opened the prospect of a lack of European funds with which to sustain a high demand for United States exports. His intent was more significant than the results, and under no circumstances could he have undone the political and economic chaos which the Versailles decisions, piled on top of the economic impact of the war, were predestined to create over the next decade. Still, Wilson approved the development of a government-guaranteed export credit structure and bank to sustain the flow of American goods across the Atlantic. Originally the idea of the largest Wall Street banks and investment houses, who assigned to the Federal Reserve System control of the bank's stock, the gesture passed as the Edge Act at the end of the year. While private capital flows eventually made the act superfluous, the intent of the United States Government to adjust unilaterally to the difficulties before it was a better indication of how it expected to resolve the problems of peace.[22]

It was to this world in disarray, torn from its traditional patterns, with destruction throughout Europe and new configurations of power, that the United States sought to relate at the end of the First World War. Its strength in the world community now appeared preeminent, and to many of its leaders sufficient for the realization of the nation's foreign policies and objectives. The unfamiliar problem of social revolution had arisen to complicate the vision of the future, but by 1920 it appeared to be nothing more than a single diabolical event that could safely be isolated in Russia and, they hoped, forgotten. And America's decision makers and respectable academics speculated very little, if at all, on the social consequences of the war to the future of United States and world capitalism and bourgeois institutions—from parliamentarianism to colonialism. The economic consequences of the war and the peace seemed more manageable to the American businessman—in Chicago, New York, and Washington—who was an incurable constitutional optimist infinitely more out of reflex than insight.

But that it would nevertheless have to deal with the profoundly unsettled world was a foregone conclusion, for the objective role of the United States had changed dramatically in two short decades. It had ceased to be one of numerous powers in the Far East and was now quite alone in preserving the fragile equilibrium there that the weakness of China and the expansionism of Japan had created. In Latin America it had become the dominant imperialist power itself, a status which offered future promise as well as immediate gain—and one it had no thought of relinquishing. Even the objective economic imperatives impelling its expansionism had changed radically compared to the preceding decades and, indeed, in certain regards since the Civil War. During 1915–1920 over one-tenth of the gross national product went to exports—far higher than during the next war—and while Europe made war and death the United States made money and grew proportionately more powerful and prosperous from the follies of other states. The question of how to sustain the new field of endeavor was one of the highest national interest and priority, and the consciousness of the new institutional realities affected business and government alike in a fashion perhaps more profound and durable than ever before in American history.

Yet restoring new forms of stability and balances of power created a panoply of challenges: in Asia, in the overarching world economy, in Europe. Everywhere, in fact, the course of the world crisis of which the United States was now so much a part had yet to be resolved.

3

The American Working Class: Immigrant Foundations

Few leave their homelands willingly, and the notion that Europe's hungry and oppressed came to the United States because of its social or intellectual virtues may be good ideology but it is poor history. For it was less America's assets than Europe's failures that prompted 34 million men and women to immigrate in a little over one century. The vital relationship between the immigrant and his experiences in the United States, his continued aspirations toward his nation of birth, and modern American history remains far too obscure, notwithstanding the comparative excellence of recent writings in this field. For the complexity and richness of the topic also reveal much we have yet to learn about the nature and objectives of the American labor movement and the very character of the industrialization process contrasted to experiences in other capitalist nations. Only by examining the nature of workers and work itself during the formative period of American capitalism can one begin to explain why the American labor movement, unique to the world, failed to develop a commitment to one of the several historic socialist ideologies and the goal of sharing in the operational control of social power. In effect, in a society where the working class is an objective reality it fails to develop a consciousness, even from its structurally common experience, comparable to that of virtually every other industrial capitalist society. And only by seriously comprehending the immigrant experience, not only in their workplaces but in their homes and communities, can one appreciate *some* of the main sources of contemporary America's violence and social and individual disintegration.

The Industrial Reserve Army Escapes

Marx notwithstanding, no national ruling class ever passively allowed an industrial reserve army to emerge to destroy the existing order, and they attempted to rely on imperialism, migration, or whatever was required to sustain their hierarchal social orders. Nor will all workers wait for socialism to find bread. However reticent they may initially be, many will migrate before starving. The internationalization of the Western world's labor supply after 1800 is perhaps the most ignored phenomenon in socialist analyses, but this escape valve for the human consequences of economic crisis in one state by relying on the growth of others is among the central events of modern history.

Pushed by dire circumstances and sometimes haphazard and often deliberate national policies, Europeans reluctantly abandoned their communities and families in astonishing numbers after 1800, and for Britain and Germany the export of their superfluous human capital and culture as well as funds became integral to the very process of colonialism and imperialism. A slight majority of those pushed out of rural areas tried to go no farther than local cities or, if they possessed some skill, to stay in Western Europe, but many went to more distant nations, of which the United States was the single most important among many. Migration to the United States was an aspect of an international phenomenon which the emergence of European capitalism created. While data are often quite approximate, it appears that between 1821 and 1932, 34 million people entered the United States, while 16 million went to Argentina, Canada, and Brazil at about the same time. Asiatic Russia received 3.5 million voluntary peasants between 1897 and 1914 alone, and 12 million in the 140-year period beginning 1800. There were many "promised lands" to which to escape, and the British Isles and Germany—the first touched by the traumas of capitalism—provided the bulk of the reluctant emigrants until 1885. Immigrants from England and Germany equaled only 3.3 percent and 5.6 percent of their homelands' respective populations in 1890, but the Irish-born in America amounted to 40 percent of the population at home, and Norwegians 21 percent.[1] To some critical extent, Europe's potential social crises found temporary respites as those workers likely to form the most miserable portion of Marx's surplus labor army fled to other continents. At least insofar as the American case is concerned, the migration to its shores was a consequence of compulsive economic and social forces in Europe that produced unwilling migrants and a temporary American working class resolved to return home. The paradoxes in this reality are multiple.

The pressures forcing the European nationalities to migrate were as diverse as countries in the process of uneven development must be, and scholars agree on the essential factors. Famine, overpopulation, and sheer poverty for the Swedes and the Irish; the displacement of handicrafts and artisans by machinery, combined with agrarian depressions, in Germany and Eastern Europe; an inflexible land structure in Poland; industrial stagnation in England; the impoverishment of Jews in the Pale after 1885 and pogroms after 1905; the reduction of European restrictions on mass migration and even the European states' positive encouragement after 1840 to depart—all these and other factors, in multiple combinations, are well known. To these one must especially add the speed and relative inexpensiveness of ocean transport after 1870. By 1906 a southern Italian could go from Naples to New York in less than two weeks at a cost of about thirty dollars and, what has been slighted, return just as easily.

More fundamental about those immigrants who came to the United States from Southern and Eastern Europe is that, excepting the Jews, the vast majority came with the explicit intent of remaining temporarily, accumulating sufficient funds to reverse their marginal peasant existence at home or transform it entirely, and returning. On this point there is no dispute, and it means that in terms of subjective orientation a large section of the de facto American working class was a transitional one, just as it was to be in physical fact for an astonishingly large proportion of returnees.[2] In short, at a critical phase in its development the diversity and complex motivations of workers in America produced a specific consciousness unlike any known in Europe, with the emergence of a sizable working class that never regarded the place and difficulties of work as more than a transitional experience. For them, escape from such endurances was not to be found in social transformation in America but in their return to Europe at an elevated status. Both subjectively and often in reality, the 13.5 million immigrants in the United States in 1910 were part of a temporary working class slowly being integrated into what was always a permanent capitalism and social order to which many of them had neither the desire nor capacity to relate. Mainly reluctant migrants who would have preferred living a decent existence at home, those among them who remained produced an unwilling, even accidental working class stratified in a manner distinctive in the history of any industrializing society.

For immigrant workers a psychology of a "second-chance"—not in the United States but rather back home—was an enduring aspect of their relationship to the American class struggle. To a remarkable degree, from about 1880 until 1922, they indeed returned home, often after a stay of long duration. In the decade of the 1880s, emigration back home is estimated to have been equal to 30 percent of the total immigration, and in the following decade it reached 35 percent. By 1901–1907, before more precise data were collected, returnees were 39 percent of total immigration; and the same proportion returned during 1908–1914.Then, for the next period until 1922, making up for wartime travel difficulties the emigrants reached 53 percent of the gross migration. The vast majority of these were unskilled workers. The Jews and Irish had the highest rate of permanent immigrants. And in the period 1908–1923 the equivalent of almost two-thirds of the Rumanian and Hungarian immigration for that period, 56 percent of southern Italians, 52 percent of the Russians, 46 percent of the Greeks, 40 percent of the Poles, and 21 percent of the English returned home. Since both arrivals and departures were quite closely related to the business cycles in the United States, this return flow meant that a reverse safety valve existed at the point at which even greater surplus labor during American economic declines might have produced a yet larger and perhaps more miserable body of unemployed. The easiest mode of protest and salvation was to implement the standing intent to return home. Indeed, in the period 1899–1910, 12 percent of the immigrants to the United States arrived for at least a second time, making the work force a more transitional one yet.[3]

The intended temporary nature of the American sojourn was partially reflected in the lower percentage of females—34 percent—in the 1899–1924 migration. Jews, who had the highest ratio of permanent immigrants, also had a near parity of sexes. Yet the proportion of female returnees is about equal to that among males, indicating that here too the intent to return home was deep-rooted.

A majority of these returnees generally stayed in the United States ten or more years, and at least five in the case of the large majority. Comparative veterans, in brief, went back, and their example served to keep alive the hope among those remaining that they too might follow their course. America for such workers was always a tentative, transitional experience, and protracted exposure to it did not make it more enduring. At the same time, the object of work was to save, and while the data vary in degree, it is certain that the exceedingly penurious Southern and Eastern European immigrants hoarded amazingly large proportions of their earnings even as they served in the lowest-skilled occupations. Fifty to 80 percent of the earnings of immigrants in contract-labor camps in 1906 was "surplus" after deducting food and lodging, claimed one contemporary government report. "Italians come to America with the sole intention of accumulating money," *Il Proletario* complained in 1905. "Their dream, their only care is the bundle of money . . . which will give them, after 20 years of deprivation, the possibility of having a mediocre standard of living in their native country."[4] From 1900 through 1906 the value of international postal money orders sent to Italy, Austria-Hungary, and Russia reached $120 million for this one of many means of transmitting the fruit of one's sweat.

For most of the "new immigrants" of the post-1890 period from Southern and Eastern Europe, the United States was but a temporary stopping place, however long they were to remain in fact—and indeed two-thirds were eventually to stay permanently. Of male workers from these regions who were twenty-one or over when they arrived, and who remained at least ten years in the United States, just before the First World War only 38 percent were naturalized. Even one-third of English, French, and Dutch workers in this category failed to become fully naturalized, and well over a half of the Canadians. Indeed, the "old immigrants" from Western and Northern Europe who formed the bulk of pre-1890 migrants were significantly more reluctant to file papers essential to becoming an American citizen—and thus end the dream of return.[5]

As objective reality, the immigrant workers participated in the American industrialization experience as other forces elsewhere determined their fates. A remarkable number left and planned to leave. Subjectively, during his presence in the United States the immigrant worker found it overwhelmingly difficult to master the dilemma of his real existence and desired repatriation, the daily problems of adjusting to a new national culture and industrialism at one and the same time, and to relate with clarity to the nature of his workplace and community. The effect of these and many other conflicts, both in his mind and in his work and multiple communities, left a structural legacy which was to influence profoundly the development of the American labor movement and contemporary capitalist society. For it was on this foundation that a working class was built, making it something very different than the vanguard of social change it became in so many other industrialized nations.

The Nature of the Industrialization Process

However much scholars may disagree on precise causes of the unique phenomenon, there is no question that American capitalism developed within the context of a quite distinctive technology unlike that of Western Europe, and this in turn both created and built upon a no less diverse and unique working class. Capital- and technology-intensive to an unprecedented extent, American industry created a rhythm of life and an extraordinarily disciplined and numbing division of labor which made possible a higher standard of living even as it demanded more exhausting and alienating labor.

Whatever the causes, which Brinley Thomas and H. J. Habakkuk have most satisfactorily explained, the fact is indisputable that capital accumulation after the Civil War and until 1919 attained an amazing rate of growth, despite frequent depressions, reaching 14.7 percent annually in mining during the 1870s and 8.8 percent annually in manufacturing during the 1880s. Not until 1919 did the rate of growth in total reproducible wealth begin to drop off, but by then America was the world's leading economy. By 1919 the ratio of capital to manufacturing output reached a peak never equaled since, largely to employ an unprecedented variety of technological innovations. In mining, the ratio of capital invested to the value of product also rose to a high point in 1919 and then began dropping sharply with the stunning efficiency of technology. Between 1869 and 1914 horsepower per manufacturing wage earner increased by about two and one-half times. Up to 1919 capital investment was geared, unprecedentedly, to utilizing technological innovations to replace labor, and the man-hours worked as a ratio of manufacturing output fell by almost one-half between 1900 and 1929. Despite a relatively high wage standard which tended to grow in terms of real income, wages as a percentage of the value added by manufacturing fell from 48 percent in 1879—the peak year—to 36 percent in 1929. Until

1919, only the sheer growth of the output of American industry demanded an expanded labor supply. Yet at the same time the very availability of a large unskilled labor supply made a capital-intensive industry possible as well as mandatory; thereafter, technology and the efficiency of capital reached a point sufficient to eliminate the necessity of enlarging the industrial work force in the same burgeoning fashion.[6]

European investments, directly or even in the form of capital transferred by immigrants, assisted this explosion of output. Significant numbers of skilled British workers, escaping the crises of English capitalism, transferred critical knowledge, though not a sufficient number came to allow British modes of industrial organization to define those in the United States. By and large, therefore, skilled labor was too scarce and expensive, thus laying the basis of a capital- and technology-intensive capitalism unlike any to be found anywhere before World War Two. Necessity dictated such a course. Neither present-day historians nor contemporary observers dispute this, yet the issue here is how it defined the development of the American working class.

Unskilled immigrant labor after 1880 further accelerated the introduction of machinery that performed the work that was impossible for men increasingly of agrarian origins to master speedily, and their addition to the population also stimulated economic growth. Nearly one-third of the growth of the total labor force in the 1880s was due to the influx of foreign-born, and immigrants accounted for one-quarter of the increase during the first decade of this century. American industry eagerly adopted both European technology and such skilled labor as came or could be cajoled across the ocean, but it also produced its own inventions in almost every major industry. Mechanization was quite generally the rule, and it could incorporate a polyglot labor force with minimal talents into the operation of an industrialism that required skilled labor less and less. After a time it meant that the substitution of machinery for human skills led to two major developments in the life of workers in America: the dilution and diminution of skills on one hand, and the intensification of the speed and human and psychological demands of the quite unsophisticated, interchangeable work functions of modern factories and mines.

Skill diminution affected numerous industries by 1900: shoes, metalworking, iron and steel, and the like, and the collapse of the status and economic position of the machinist in the skill hierarchy of industry even temporarily led some to adherence to socialism. The magnification of the tempo of labor, culminating in the widespread introduction of the piece-rate system and assembly line after 1900, led to the driving momentum of the factory and rivalries among workers who were increasingly being called upon to perform at the level of output that the strongest defined. And in industries with very high innovation, in which changeovers in machines became the rule, new standards of production became the constant source of disputes between workers and bosses—and among workers themselves.[7]

Ironically, even as machinery led to a constant struggle against the dehumanization and increasing intensity of factory life, it meant also that American industry was better able to satisfy the economic demands of workers as labor as a factor in costs declined. Technology, too, resulted in an American capitalism which in many industries could with equanimity find substitutes for a floating, alien labor supply that had slight incentive to learn English before the illusive return home. And, as we shall see, after World War One it meant as well that machinery could help make European workers entirely superfluous in an economy whose capital growth rate and needs were beginning to decline dramatically.

The Immigrant in Basic Industry

From 1870 until 1930, as technology increasingly replaced skills and industry required masses of seasonally available workers, the foreign-born workers formed the heart of the American working class. In 1909, 58 percent of the workers in the twenty principal mining and manufacturing industries were foreign born; and, coming overwhelmingly from farm and unskilled rural origins, they composed 45 percent of all unskilled labor and 38 percent of the semiskilled in the United States. Between 1870 and 1920 the foreign-born percentage of the total white population ranged around 15–16 percent, with their children increasing from 16 to 24 percent of the population over that period. Typically, in iron and steel 58 percent of the workers in 1909 were foreign born and another 13 percent were children of foreign-born but Southern and Eastern Europeans occupied about four-fifths of the unskilled posts.

Their slight knowledge of English reflected the transitory goals of the immigrant masses as well as the nature of their communities.

Segregated by both desire and necessity, living in ethnic neighborhoods where the only strangers were other nationalities with an equally mediocre knowledge of the language, speaking mainly to fellow countrymen, immigrants mastered the new tongue slowly if at all. In 1910 only 45 percent of the male heads of households living in cities and coming from non-English-speaking nations could speak English. In the iron and steel communities it was but a scant 31 percent for males and 26 percent for females.[8]

Both from necessity and intent, the organization of work reflected the dominant ethnic character of workers. There is agreement on one critical point: that notwithstanding exceptions, the factory, during the formative period of the working class, was often subdivided into numerous ethnic bodies that lacked a linguistic, psychological, and operational basis of common action and development.

Within their workplace, relations between ethnic groups ranged from indifferent to often very aggravated and, at times, violent. The Poles in Chicopee, Massachusetts, disliked the new Portuguese, the Scotch detested "Hunkies," Welshmen fought Germans, ad infinitum —the local histories of life in mills and mines are full of such accounts.[9] Ethnic workers were objectively part of one class, but when brought together they became divided, suspicious entities, and a major virtue of immigrant labor to businessmen was its disunity and docility. Hence they structured the workplace to take advantage of this asset and avoid the costly demands that Yankee or English workers were more inclined to initiate.

Although some businessmen denied the reality was intended, and that ethnic segregation in the plant was confined to unskilled posts, the fact remains that three-fifths or more of the posts in many steel plants required only menial labor and that technology itself was reducing dependence on skills. Indisputably, ethnic segregation by tasks was the rule after 1880 and was to persist in various ways until well after World War One. Immigrant foremen and recruiters for specific types of jobs within the plants were common before the war, and new migrants invariably tended to move where friends, family, and fellow countrymen could be found—a natural instinct which made ethnic segregation easy. If "Slavs" became too dominant, Chicago meat packers decided, it was time to hire more Nordic ethnics. Mixing ethnics to make each more tractable was easy if twenty-six ethnic groups could be found in the northeast Pennsylvania mines, or at least half that many in Gary, Indiana. And well after mass migration to the United States ended in 1924, ethnic workers within many factories could be found segregated into branches of labor, with voluntary isolation during lunch hours and, above all, after work.[10]

A working class in name and fact only, such a melange of ethnics redirected discontent against each other or, later, against blacks—and was never to develop any united subjective consciousness. Exceptions notwithstanding, a temporary and disunited working class has its own distinctive style and critical goals, and in response to reality was not so much to produce a new consciousness among its components as a new escape within the fold of its local ethnic communities or, what was commonly hoped for, a return to its birthplaces. From 1880 until well into the Great Depression of 1929—the critical, formative period in unionism and the working class—such surrogates were the resolution of its troubles as the largest single portion of the industrial working class confronted the inordinately tortured tasks of adjusting to America and industrialism at the same time. For the managers of industry, only later did the liabilities of such a work force begin to emerge in the form of industrial inefficiency, accidents, and superfluous difficulties. Of this, more later.

Ethnics and Unionism

The ethnic worker's most common response to unemployment or dissatisfaction in the United States was far less socialism or trade unionism than a hastening of his planned return to his homeland. Emigration, not social transformation, provided him with the easiest and most commonly exploited solution to his personal troubles, and the remarkable correlation of emigration to downturns in the business cycle bears witness to the fact that Europe provided American capitalism with an escape valve of significance. Yet the interaction of the immigrant working class and American trade unionism explains their common weaknesses insofar as the emergence of a class-conscious radical proletariat is concerned, as well as its occasional small successes. For the majority of the ethnic workers stayed in the United States, albeit as transitional men both in terms of their aspirations and usually in terms of their objective economic status in a highly mechanized industrialism.

The European worker's familiarity with trade unionism in his homeland was generally insignificant, save for the British and, to a lesser extent, German workers. Heavily composed of unionists who often were encouraged by their unions to migrate in order to lessen the domestic labor oversupply, the English workers also frequently had bargaining leverage with their temporarily scarce skills. They were widely regarded as agitators, and where they formed ethnically homogeneous unions, as in the United Mine Workers, they were often drawn to the radical precepts of Populism and socialism. Indeed, a central theme in the history of the American working class and unionism is the extent to which it is synonymous with the ethnic character of workers and reflected the ethnic worker's problems and aspirations.

The mere fact of lack of familiarity with unions at home is not a sufficient explanation for the failure of unionism to influence the consciousness and political orientation of the workers during the formative years of American industrialization. Italian workers arriving in Argentina from the same backgrounds and with identical aspirations to those in America soon played a critical role in unionism only because the existing union leadership did not exclude them. Save for the Mine Workers and a few smaller unions toward the end of the century, American unions acted like status-conscious clubs in excluding the "new" immigrants. Added to this, the division of the workplace into ethnic sectors, the inability of the workers to communicate with one another, as well as their aspirations which minimized the present on behalf of the vision of a better future back home, all reduced the ethnic workers' propensity to join unions, so that the problem of ethnicity merged with the bigotry of trade-union leaders to produce paralysis in the development of a united and class-conscious working class. In the aggregate, workers with parents born in the United States tended by 1910 to have a union membership in major industries roughly half to twice as much as the proportion for foreign-born workers, which simply meant that until the ethnic structure of the modern workplace could be transcended, or the process of language and value acculturation proceeded far enough to allow the ethnic components of the work force to emerge from their cultural cocoons, American unionism would remain both organizationally and ideologically static during its most critical formative years. Indeed, that the process of acculturation was going to remain the decisive factor in the emergence of some type of minimal essential worker unity was shown in the fact that even in 1910 second-generation Americans tended in some industries to have an even larger rate of union affiliation than yet older generations of American workers.[11]

Formally or informally, an elementary cultural homogeneity was a precondition of common worker action, and a significant part of what passes for the history of American working-class militancy is in reality the record of the action of those fairly unrepresentative ethnic workers groups that acted in unison on mutual grievances. On the one hand this is expressed in the fact that exclusively ethnic trade unions emerged among Germans, Jews, Czechs, Italians, and others, often attempting the tactically hopeless task of organizing only a portion of a shop or plant in a fashion that transcended both the traditional craft and industrial union structure to make language the common denominator of organization. Yet it is significant that—save perhaps for the Molly Maguires among the Irish in the 1870s, and later the Jews, both of whose commitment to staying in America was greater than any other ethnic group's—these forms of unionism served a largely social and fraternal role. This type of organization was intrinsically hopeless because of the obvious ease by which workers of other ethnic origins could be found to replace recalcitrant or striking workers.

More important is the manner in which ethnic workers occasionally began to play a leading role in existing trade unions and gave them an informal ethnic character, either wholly dominating the union or, less often, finding the means by which to establish communication and rapport with other ethnic worker constituencies. At times this occurred as a consequence of deliberate decisions, as when the Yankee leadership of the United Mine Workers elected to create locals separated by tongue, a pattern that the packinghouse workers union followed less successfully. Or when the Amalgamated Clothing Workers Union established seven foreign-language papers to keep in touch with its constituencies. More often, spontaneous local strikes took place among ethnic workers, their success depending greatly on whether they had a sufficiently large portion of the work force, as well as the usual leverage. In the case of the famous 1912 Lawrence, Massachusetts, strike, it was an essentially spontaneous strike of Italian workers onto which a few Italian leaders of the Industrial Workers of the World pressed a distinctive strategy. Yet even in the Lawrence strike a facade of broader unity was sustained when all the ethnic groups working in the textile mills were given equal representation on the strike committee. Strikes by immigrants were rarer because their transitional mentality and aspirations made them more docile; yet, ironically, when they finally struck, the mere fact that they had come to America to save money for a return to redemption at home left them better able to endure long struggles. On the whole, however, a union succeeded best where it had cultural cohesion, and if it was also socialist or radical the presence of other ethnics tended to erode seriously this consensus. The socialist Brewery Workers, for example, composed of Germans, found strength in this common culture, but like the Marxist parties the Germans created in the United States in the latter third of the nineteenth century, their minor tactical successes led to later strategic failures. The well-known unions of radical ethnics had a precious small basis of common action because their constituencies were too particularist to build a transcending, broad-based radical and trade-union movement. They served the social and immediate needs of their own yet unsettled members, and rarely more.[12]

In the end, then, the creation of a common working class had to await not the domination of one or another ethnic group in this or that plant or town, much less an entire industry, but the minimal acculturation of the mass working class. Hence the loss of time and common experience and the failure to create durable radical movements among a working class which throughout the formative period of American capitalism was constantly in gestation and motion, unable to find a common platform because it lacked mutual goals, trust, and even a single language.

This process of creating a working class, which, even if it did not share a common set of cultural styles at least possessed a common tongue, took three to four decades, and its emergence in the form of the rise of unionism during the 1930s was a consequence of demographic patterns, the dissolution of Northern Yankee worker exclusiveness under the impact of the Great Depression, the growth of knowledge of English among workers, the weakening of the immigrants' resolve to return home, and a combination of forces that could not have been duplicated earlier. But it was still too amorphous to produce a mass united radical labor movement, and ethnic divisions remained deep, with racial bigotry added to them.

Ironically, the eventual acculturation of the Northern working class took place in a manner that brought with it the hope of new unity just as it planted the seeds of further divisions. The children of most foreign workers were never so touched by social and occupational mobility as to leave the working class, and from near parity with the foreign-born as a percentage of the white population in 1870, their children were almost twice their proportion in 1930—together composing 36 percent of the total white population. The second generation not only knew English, but it had earlier shown a greater propensity to join unions than the older established "natives," even though it retained its primary roots in the ethnic communities of the Northern cities. After 1914, when war and then law eliminated net migration to the United States, the North's imported labor supply came from the South, but in a form that gave it both a cohesion in communication sufficient to make possible industrial unions and disunity in new forms.

Nearly 4 million Southerners migrated out of their region from 1910 to 1940. They were evenly divided among blacks and whites, the latter largely coming from the mountainous districts, and provided Yankee industry with a fresh supply of new hands. Hill people, ethnics, and blacks held a few things in common: they were mostly from agrarian backgrounds, they shared many of the same tribulations of factory life, and they eventually hammered out a sort of common language. Thereafter, divisions set in. The white mountaineers, however, probably renewed significantly the American factory worker's dream of saving money on which to return to his open, green spaces. The Southern white farmer who moved to the factories within the region surely preserved the values of his nearby home, and often worked in mills or mines only long enough to save something to enable him to return to his farm somewhat better off than when he had left. Hence, both the foreign and regional migrant perpetuated the consciousness of a transitional working class even to our own time. Still, there was enough cohesion in this conjunction of elements to produce the CIO and an enlarged AFL, but precious little more. At its core, the industrial working class remained culturally stratified in terms of values, goals, and life chances.[13]

The Privileged Native Working Class

The very existence of ethnics as the major group in basic industry and mining created automatic pressures of upward mobility for those elements of ethnic migrants least prone to return home—the Western and Northern Europeans—and, above all, the old "Yankees" who had ceased to reflect the culture of their forebears. In short, the very presence of a psychologically and often physically temporary working class often made increasingly bourgeois and occupationally mobile the permanent workers to an extent otherwise impossible.

The qualifications for this upward mobility, in terms of occupational function, income, and status, were a knowledge of English and, if one stayed within industry or mining, the possession of skills. For the Yankees, the advent of the European migrant and economic growth meant a need for foremen, clerks, officials, and white-collar occupations of every sort. In New England cotton textiles, for example, almost all overseers were Yankees simply because workers of one ethnic group refused to obey sufficiently any "ethnic" of another nationality. Yankees were "considered superior" in executive posts in the iron and steel industry, and they were often recruited from the ranks of workers, while British migrants and, thereafter, Germans might also qualify, and roughly the same ranking was followed in skilled worker positions.[14] Until the 1930s, it may be fairly argued, the Northern Yankee working class could reasonably expect to find countless opportunities simply not available to Western and Northern European, much less "new," immigrants. That he moved out of the poorest working-class jobs is unquestionable, and one may debate only the extent to which he obtained success in entirely new class functions. Within the industrial system until the Great Depression, for reasons of experience, language, and status, the Yankee worker could not yet identify to any appreciable extent with the immigrant working class, thereby leaving a cleavage that was not easily surmounted. When technology eliminated his skills within the workplace, rather than falling into the mass of the working class the Yankee had available to him options closed to the immigrant working class.

Workers from the British Isles, the English particularly, formed a unique exception to the ethnic's confrontation with prejudice, for they not only carried with them a knowledge of the language but an unusual mastery of skills. Well over a majority came as skilled workers or professionals, and, comprehending the Yankee and his quality, these workers retained a distinct aloofness toward their new residence. Indeed, British workers gained the least, relative to wages back home, of any ethnic group; and while they quickly moved into high positions in mining and, to a lesser extent, industry, socially they preferred isolation. The "new migrants" forced them upward with the expansion of industry, and their children were socially and economically the most mobile of all foreigners. In effect, the almost automatic upward advancement of this element also produced a critical cleavage between the one group which most carried with it European traditions of unionism and social reform and the remainder of the foreign-born.[15]

Measurements of mobility may be gauged in terms of occupational roles over generations, social status and esteem, economic changes in one's position regardless of job, or even the relative compensation received by various professions. In the end, what is most essential is the structure and nature of a society at any given time whether or not it recruits democratically, for high occupational mobility is not inconsistent with great economic and social inequality. Moreover, given the sheer quantity of research on the topic, some sense of the question's intrinsic significance is essential to avoid both analytic and statistical inundation.

It is sufficient to suggest that for the immigrant workers coming from Sicily or Hungary the very act of crossing the ocean during periods of high employment produced an almost automatic upward economic transformation. Wages and living differences, even taking into account a quite stable pattern of real income in the United States, ranged from large to immense. In the aggregate, with variations for skill and location, at the beginning of the 1870s United States wages were two to four times greater than in Britain, France, and Germany, with the purchasing power of this income probably appreciably higher in America at this time—though less by the turn of the century. But an anthracite mining laborer in 1900 made anywhere from two to eight times more than a comparable worker in Poland, Russia, Austria-Hungary, or East Prussia fortunate enough to have a job. And since the large majority of foreign workers after 1890 were here, in their view, only temporarily, it made little difference that they were at least as far down the relative American pecking order as they had been back home. The immigrant was inclined to measure himself in terms of where he had been economically in the past in Europe and where he would be in the future in Europe, and the present-mindedness that might lead to action for the immediate was thereby minimized. The mere fact of coming to America created a reality of sharp economic mobility for the large majority of immigrants, and onto this ideologists plastered the notion of the equality of opportunity. Wages to the immigrant worker were often translated in his mind into the significantly greater purchasing power they would have "back home," and thereby greatly magnified in terms of satisfaction of his ultimate goal. The result was that a significant portion of the working class, the group that objectively had most to gain from resistance and social transformation, was the most docile.

In fact, the annual wage difference between Southern and Eastern European worker—mainly unskilled—and the occupationally better-off white native born of native father in 1909 was roughly two-thirds, and the gap closed only partially for the immigrants' children. The data are immense—far more than I can even mention in the broadest outline—but a few general conclusions arise. First, for the immigrants who came and tarried there appears to have been very low occupational mobility for Southern and Eastern European workers, and they remained among the poorest paid regardless of how long they stayed. Their children experienced appreciable upward occupational mobility, especially if they were of Western or Northern European origins, but save for the British and Jews they never caught up with the Yankees; and even in 1950 and thereafter the Southern and Eastern European Catholics formed a disproportionately large part of the lower-paid working class. What remains, in the end, are stratified American communities based on economic and cultural distinctions continuing within the framework of a class society that despite alterations in its composition endured throughout the century after 1876. The immigrants did not so much create or deepen the class structure of America as fall into it.[16]

The Splintered Society

The immigrant to the United States after 1880 largely moved into the burgeoning urban centers because that was where his labor was in demand. But within cities, by choice and necessity he isolated himself into his quite insulated nationality subculture, which effectively cut him off from the mainstream of the English-speaking environment and the other ethnic working-class components. The modern American city thereby emerges stratified by both class and ethnicity, the latter initially being roughly correlated to the working class but, at the same time, dividing it. National groupings, not class, are the dominant characteristic of the ethnic workers during the formative period 1880–1930, even though varying degrees of economic inequality existed among each nationality; and the complicated social and cultural legacies these divisions left to later generations is part of the history of our time.

Yet, depending on the ethnic group, the types of ethnic communities which arise exhibit varying degrees of both cohesion and disunity, and over the long-run both manifest themselves to dislocate deeply urban life as well as the class structure. Romanticizing the ethnic and his community in America is not more realistic than eulogizing his Pecksniffian Yankee detractors.

It was logical for the immigrants to concentrate in cities. For considerations of economy, the availability of jobs, and the existence of such family or friends as they possessed reinforced the impulse to become urban dwellers, above all in the northern Atlantic states; and in 1920, three-quarters of the foreign-born whites lived in cities. By 1900 the foreign-born composed 22 percent of the urban population, but 28 percent of all cities of 100,000 or over population. Twenty years later nearly 58 percent of the population of these largest cities was foreign born or of foreign parentage. In effect, the main centers of growth in America were ethnically subdivided. All this is familiar.

Indeed, the structure of the immigrant communities of all major ethnics is also no mystery, and there is hardly any disagreement that, although there were not necessarily wholly undiluted ethnic sections defining the map of each city, most cities were divided by roughly ethnic but essentially working-class neighborhoods, leaving divided workers who scarcely related to each other as a class at all. These ethnics, in turn, were often physically and organizationally subdivided according to villages or regions from which they hailed in the Old Country, and around these associations they built what has perhaps too casually been termed the "urban village." Sociologists and historians have been commenting on such patterns for a half-century. The existence of subgroups within the ethnic community—the *Landsmanshaften* among Jews, *contadini* among Italians, and so on —meant the separate festa, the initially exclusive club, the synagogues of nationally divided and mutually contemptuous Jews, a Catholic Church rent with seemingly perpetual disunity between the Irish and all the rest, and much, much else besides. Even the English workers kept themselves apart, and after 1910 black migrants from the West Indies were to maintain their own churches and clubs in Harlem. With workers internally divided even within the ethnic community, until the distinctions of region and dialect could be overcome, the goal of a united working class with common goals and values remained a chimera.[17]

Although the various ethnic groups shared certain experiences, above all the cultural shock and personal trauma of migration, they developed substantially different responses as organized communities, and the very term "community" is dubious because the institutional responses and defenses against the new environment among ethnics were uneven and, in the end, far less significant than the disintegration and loss of identity they all suffered. The twentieth-century city, after all, was too ephemeral and constantly changing to permit anything like the European village to emerge, and in fact the instability of both life and the people within it immediately eroded substantially those traditional bonds that were constantly on trial in Cleveland or Scranton. The second generation of virtually all ethnic constituencies substantially moved away from associational existences based on Old World subcommunities, to the extent that for the first time Italians began seeing themselves as Italians rather than as Abruzzians or Calabrians. But the Italians retained an integrative, traditional family structure as the basis of social life longer than most other ethnics, while Poles failed to institutionalize the larger ethnic community to the extent as did Croats, Greeks, or Jews. Suffice it to say, the lack of command of English, and the more or less dominating focus of the ethnic working class on its associational structure within the framework of cities which are quite generally divided by ethnic-class components, gives the United States a working class unlike any known in modern history.

More accurately, the ethnic working-class components change over the twentieth century in ways that have been appreciated, such as patterns of intermarriage among ethnics of the same religion, and they persist as well in terms of the residues of ethnic quarters found in larger cities. But to avoid erroneous stereotypes, one must see the immigrant in America since the Civil War both in terms of the cohesion of his community, which was sufficient for decades to divide the working class and the factory, and the transcendence of a larger American experience, which also eventually erodes the ethnic blocs rather unevenly and in vital ways to produce innumerable individualists whose outlooks were primarily lumpen and disoriented.

From 1880 until 1930, it is useful to focus on the ethnic working class in the context of its neighborhoods and cultural associations, but never to forget that migrants were, in terms of their aspirations and often in fact, temporary sojourners. The concept of the urban village that sociologists William I. Thomas and Herbert A. Miller proposed a half-century ago is functional. But to it the prescient thesis of William Thomas and Florian Znaniecki must be added, showing that forces quite disintegrating to its existence were attacking the ethnic community and character in the United States, producing unprecedented social breakdowns.[18] The ethnic community was scarcely united, save in the eyes of—or against—the outside world, and it was composed of people and constituencies with inherently autonomous goals—above all, to return to one's place of origin. Italians excepted, ethnics had a higher rate of organizational memberships in their own communities than Yankees, but these very bonds were a major cause of ethnic divisions in the workplace.

Moreover, the ethnic-working-class attitude toward neighborhood and home was less idealized than its present-day romanticizers would have us believe, if only because it took a significant portion of the immigrants decades to realize they were not, after all, going to return to their motherlands. It is true that immigrants both preferred and were forced into usually crowded ethnic quarters, but they persisted in them in a manner that differed in degree, but not in kind, from third- or later-generation Americans. Moreover, immigrant groups differed sharply among themselves in how long the neighborhood held them, with Italians and Greeks being far more loyal to their streets than Jews, Irish, Hungarians, and the always ubiquitous "Slovaks." Two-fifths of first- and second-generation Americans in the United States longer than a decade in 1909 had not spent ten years in their neighborhood, as opposed to 54 percent among "natives." From the outset the new immigrant was almost as mobile as longer-established groups.

Not unexpectedly, immigrants, once they sensed that return home was further off than they had initially expected, transferred their peasant attitudes toward house ownership to the American context, thereby laying the basis for later ugly confrontations with each other and, above all, with blacks. The migrant, after all, was often an insecure peasant with aspirations, which at first he articulated in terms of more secure or greater land tenure in Europe. If he was not to return there, he resolved to have his homestead in America; and from the inception, the "new" migrants were noted as far more aggressive home and property purchasers than the generally better-paid native Yankees. Home-ownership became something of an index of intent to return, and Rumanians, who were once among the most frequent returnees, increased their home-ownership rate from 3 percent in 1908 to 33 percent in 1928. Such attitudes, which were even more deeply implanted among second-generation Americans who had no illusions whatsoever about living in Europe, meant that the ethnic working class was far more locked into the debt system than natives. Home-ownership among the significantly lower paid foreign-born iron- and steelworkers in 1909 was 21 percent as opposed to 15 percent for the third- or later-generation "natives," but among their children it jumped to 27 percent. While patterns differ in other industries, where ownership rates were about equal, what is clear is that by the 1930s immigrants and their children transferred to America Old World habits that reduced their physical mobility somewhat, accentuating their cultural and physical isolation in poorer neighborhoods throughout America. And this tendency at the same time made their often lumpen bourgeois attachment to the value of their property and meeting payments a factor of no mean importance to their potential militancy and egalitarianism as members of the larger working class.[19]

Rivalry as a Way of Relating

If the violence that such ethnic divisions and segregation produced in factory and community is difficult to quantify, and thereby perhaps more imagined than real, nonetheless there was violence and disunity that no account of the modern American working class, city, or life dares slight. For the existence of rival city nationality gangs fighting each other, or forcibly excluding intruders from their neighborhood turf, was a vital, indisputable source of the present disintegration of American cities. To the immigrant still suffering from the confusion and trauma of having just arrived, ethnic gang taunting and violence loomed large. The tension such incidents between nationalities produced was also transferred to the workplace; and in mining regions, where the communities were relatively more transitional and the work more dangerous, inter-ethnic strife, bloody labor struggles, and the great excess of men to women all combined in varying degrees to produce much violence—the peak of which was perhaps reached in southern Illinois after World War One. Yet a half-century later Michael Novak quite fairly observed that each ethnic group remained intensely hostile toward all outsiders and, it must be noted, unionism's nominal organizational success did not significantly diminish that intense bias. Opinion polls were merely to reinforce what anyone could observe in the so-called white backlash and George Wallace's successes among Northern ethnics: good unionists, including many among those with the most radical social views, remained deeply suspicious of blacks, but also (and less well appreciated) of each other as well.[20]

The roots of this hostility can be traced not merely to the way ethnic gangs fought each other but also the manner in which their institutional efforts in the American environment clashed as soon as the "new" immigrants landed. For the Jews and Protestants who arrived and were kept out of established co-religious institutions there was no problem—they simply set up their own often minutely differentiated bureaucracies. For the deeply Catholic majority from Southern and Eastern Europe, however, finding scope for their deep and often particular religiosity was but one part of their struggle with the Irish. In the anthracite coal communities of Pennsylvania, where the Irish had first worked and then largely departed, well over one-half of the priests at the turn of the century were Irish, and their need to use English and their general inability to comprehend the Eastern European workers quickly led to strained relationships. The Italians had much the same experience in the major Atlantic cities, which meant that the Church in quite short order became far less powerful among the Italians than the Irish, even producing some Pentecostal schisms—although alienation was mainly expressed in the speedier growth of secularism. The Poles also were hostile to the Irish-dominated Church, finding it offered no community, and they organized a few of their own schismatic parishes. As for the Irish, despite a few eventual compromises with the ethnics, they preferred retaining control of their hierarchy, and even today most of the bishops and archbishops in the United States are Irish.

Immigrants, in short, found other ethnics adding frustrations to their life outside of the workplace. The Irish not only controlled the Church, which was potentially important to the Italian or Polish immigrant's social adjustment to the strange new world and secondarily an avenue of occupational mobility, but they virtually dominated politics in many major cities, and with it innumerable jobs, contracts, licenses, graft, and crime—in short, the wellsprings of boodle that since the founding of the American colonies have become traditional means for acquiring wealth and power. Politics, and the crime symbiotic on it, thereby became a source of disunity rather than cohesion among urban ethnics; and while the Depression of the 1930s was somewhat to modify this pattern, ethnic rivalry rather than a broader conception of interest and class still greatly, if not exclusively, defined the contours of American urban voting.

The decision to exploit the interstices of the system via crime reflected both the nature of the power configurations in the urban setting, which closed off more "respectable" channels of capital accumulation, as well as the corrosive impact of American life on the ethnic. In relation to the dominant Anglo-Saxon culture, America was a continuous assault on the integrity of the individual and his self-esteem. Combined with this was the breakdown of the ethnic's family as he underwent pain and anguish when his children rejected his values and prohibitions yet were themselves not accepted by the dominant culture. While I shall say more of this later, the net effect was to produce a much greater crime rate among the children of immigrants than existed among their parents—Poles, Italians, Jews, all—and far greater yet than in Europe. Crime then simply meant acquiring the material goals a society idealized by the only means left available to the dispossessed and scorned. Less invidious was to gain a political office or become a policeman, but for the ethnic it was in reality all a part of the same sordid game. Later those who could capitalize on their successes in these various enterprises were to encourage their children to take more respectable positions and attend "Ivy League" schools.

The Italians, Jews, and Irish were by no means alone in regarding crime as a means of social mobility, scarcely illegal because the police of Irish and all other nationalities both partially regulated it and, via fairly systematic fees, shared in its proceeds. But the Jews and Irish had other bases of power, and the vast majority of Italians either returned home or remained a part of the subproletariat. Italian leaders then used the organizational and economic foundations that crime provided to finally break the Anglo-Irish control of big-city politics, notably in Chicago in the 1920s and then less decisively in New York and the East.[21]

What is most critical here about this phenomenon is not the structure of American urban politics or capital accumulation, which I discuss in other chapters, but that ethnic divisions which have both a cultural and religious basis all too often have been transferred into a political arena which has prevented the emergence of a politics based on class and economic interest. Given the amorphous character of the two major parties and their consensus on economic fundamentals, in a sense this ethnic and cultural rivalry has been essential for parties that are required both by custom and necessity to contrive distinctions between themselves that really do not exist on even the narrowest definition of principle. Yet that transcendent awareness of the real economic interests which would be required to dissolve the ethnic nature of agrarian as well as urban politics that has manifested itself repeatedly over the past century, replacing it with a politics based on class, has been absent from modern American history. In the end, rather than fostering unity, politics in the United States further stimulated ethnic divisions—a schism that has been kept alive long after most ethnics mastered English, attained some significant degree of occupational and physical mobility, and retained precious little of the culture they knew either when younger or from their parents' recollections.

Most assuredly, some ethnics were far more economically mobile than others. But roughly half the Poles, Irish, and Italians were by the 1960s still solidly in the working class. Their disunity, as well as their common hostility toward blacks, tended to persist because of their reluctance to move, the residues of their ethnicity, their fears, and above all the continued prejudices which locked them into a too stratified order. Yet it was also the consequence of the historical origins of the organized ethnic community since at least the beginning of the twentieth century and, above all, the special role of the comprador class that early began to assist the exploitation of its own nationality by the larger capitalist system.

Despite the mobility that success in business, crime, politics, or such provided, the larger portion of Eastern and Southern European Catholics remained within the working class and marginal economic constituencies. Every ethnic community was in varying degrees internally stratified by class even if its richest members were not in the Social Register, and this process began immediately upon their arrival. The Italian *padrone* who gathered a large unskilled, mobile labor supply for Yankee companies epitomized the system, and regardless of what he did for workers—a topic on which there is still much controversy—he surely helped himself and those who used him. Every political boss who organized his ethnic bloc into a unified vote, the precondition of which was the maintenance of some level of ethnic identification and nostalgia, performed much the same service to a larger political instrument, which then rewarded him and his cronies with jobs and multifarious emoluments. Even in 1960 the ten largest American cities were composed of at least 30 percent first- and second-generation Americans, reaching 49 percent in the case of New York, and the effective ability to mobilize these constituencies one way or another was often of decisive importance in national, not to mention local and state, politics. To bind the ethnic working class to such institutions, minimizing as far as possible the politics of class, required a comprador leadership which became a vital part of those portions of the larger American political and economic directorate predominantly located in the Democratic Party. The occasional trade-union mobilization of ethnic voters does not significantly modify this conclusion, if only because union bureaucracies have either chosen not, or been unable, to alter the basic programs of either party.

Overlapping such a comprador class has always been a specialized ethnic bureaucracy, which began first with editors, religious and associational functionaries, and ethnically specialized businessmen, and which built rather uneven organizations within the various ethnic communities. Jews possess them in their most advanced form, and the Irish, Croats, Hungarians, and Greeks also have structures proportionate to their economic means. Recent federal grants that the racist ethnic backlash stimulated offer further scope to the more articulate ethnic leaders to represent their constituencies to the larger society as well as define for them a socially more "responsible" and integrative politics that averts race riots and denies votes to racist politicians. The very existence, and hence livelihood, of these quite well educated social technicians depends on the continuation of such ephemeral ethnic identity as was perpetuated over the past century and still remains today. From their inception, together with the political bosses and organizers of workers into gangs for mines and railroads, the function of these bureaucrats operationally has been to mobilize their clients' sense of ethnicity and diminish class as the basis of mass politics. Their success and the persistence of this larger framework of political life have meant the absence of a conscious working class which translates its awareness into a common program and action.[22]

"Americanizing" the Working Class

The incapacity, even minimally, to acculturate to America declined somewhat with the termination of open immigration after 1924, though in a subtler form it persists today, and in fact played at least a minor part in the movement to enact immigration restriction.

The structural force which permitted immigration restriction, and far outweighed all the other causes, was the termination of the American economy's need for a mass imported labor supply. The slowing down of the capital growth rate to 3.2 percent annually during the 1920s, or precisely half that of the period 1880–1909, in conjunction with the unprecedented efficiency of technology and capital investment in new plant, demanded that open immigration cease. From 1920 to 1929 the output of American manufacturing increased by one-half, but its employment remained stable. Such labor as industry might need it could now find in adequate supply from the normal United States birth rate as well as the poor whites and blacks of the South, supplemented by Mexicans as needed. Around these dominating structural facts, proponents of other justifications for immigration restriction could now, also for the first time, seem credible, but they surely were not the decisive cause of action.

In fact, the reasons for immigration restriction which most historians have commented on—trade-union appeals, nativism, desire for efficiency, fear of radicalism—had long existed without decisively affecting legislation, and they finally became utilitarian when the economics of capitalism dictated. Businessmen had run hot and cold on the question for decades, depending on the economic cycles or their fear of radicalism; and Protestant yahoos always joined skilled trade unionists in beating the drums for preventing European hordes from entering middle-class America.

Immigrant labor was relatively inefficient and had a high turnover that employers increasingly regarded as a costly nuisance, but its abundance made total labor costs far lower than they might otherwise have been and only intensified the transfer of skills to technology and machines rather than men. Indeed, the equivalent development of American capitalism after 1880 without access to such a pool of men was inconceivable. The division of the plant into ethnic-speaking components of mobile workers was an additional cost, however, as was the excessive number of smashed bodies in industrial accidents, and many businessmen unquestionably welcomed the opportunity to consolidate their existing labor force and dispense with their dependence on the flow across the Atlantic. And by 1919 they gave the political muscle to the familiar appeals of the AFL and racist Protestant preachers and professors whose conventional wisdom included the alleged superiority of Teutonic peoples. Yet behind them was the unquestionable fact, which social workers and academics alike articulated and businessmen experienced, that industrial costs could for the first time be lowered by controlling and integrating the labor force more carefully. That the existing melange of nationalities had prevented the emergence of a united working class never occurred to proponents of restrictionism.[23]

The overall accident rate in American coal mines in 1900–1906 was almost four times that of France and twice that of Prussia, with the gap increasing over time. And among Southern and Eastern European miners working in the United States, the death rate by accidents was almost twice that of natives and migrants from other European regions. In different industries the accident rate among immigrant workers was estimated to be roughly two to four times that of natives, and in 1908 alone, United States Bureau of Labor experts estimated, there were 30,000 to 35,000 fatal and about 2 million nonfatal industrial accidents. Ethnic workers often could not read safety instruction sheets, and the language factors that divided workers also made them prone to accidents and errors. The costly and widespread practice of hiring ethnic foremen or liaison personnel only very partially adjusted foreign workers to the increasingly dangerous high-speed technology they were being called upon to service. Maiming, blinding, and death were common enough destinies for immigrants who had gone to America searching for security.

The "Americanization" of the working class, the industrial safety and rationalization movement, and immigration restriction were soon to find common cause. The temporary emergence of an ethnically based Socialist and Communist movement during and after World War One and the ruling order's false perception of a political danger latent in the ethnics' culture, in conjunction with widespread postwar strikes, added force to restrictionism. But before World War One it was clear that a growing coalition of "Americanization" forces, of which business was now the most potent component, had decided that the existence of an oversupply of unskilled labor required action. In the Immigration Acts of 1921 and 1924 they won.[24]

Assimilation or Disintegration?

The process of adjusting to life in American industry, of establishing often stormy rapport with his children, of trying to decide whether to stay or return, of insulating himself against the derision of Yankees and fellow workers—all this and much more wracked the lives of millions of laborers in the United States at a time when the working classes of other nations were being politically mobilized. While the assimilation of immigrants and their children had been very uneven, proceeding most rapidly with Western and Northern European Protestants, the experience of being in America was painful to even the majority of privileged Englishmen. Few can leave their homelands easily.

In the aggregate, and especially after 1890, immigrants did not quickly absorb the dominant forms and assumptions of Yankee culture *nor* successfully preserve their traditional values, restraints, and communities; and their children found themselves in a cultural limbo that made them even more lumpen than their parents. Between the options of assimilation or disintegration, as Thomas and Znaniecki correctly noted a half-century ago, the immigrant was decidedly prone to the latter. And this was expressed in a retreat to individualist and egocentric norms to replace the constraints that the community or family had imposed in Europe—to crime, social breakdown, and atomism, which necessarily precluded the emergence of a unified and cooperative working class transcending ethnicity. Although the foreign-born share of prisoners sentenced for major offenses was no greater than their proportion of the white population 15 years and over in 1904, their share of those in prison for minor offenses—drunkenness, vagrancy, and disorderly conduct especially—was far higher; and foreign-born juvenile delinquency also greatly exceeded the rate among native whites. Immigrants, their children, and blacks, to very differing degrees, remained constantly anxious—about rejection, slights, and their far poorer economic chances in life. For the majority, experience amply justified their anxiety.

The male immigrant's dilemma was multiple. His contact with his children involved the constant struggle to impose family norms and constraints they simply refused to obey in most cases, and even the question of his wife's unprecedented if relative economic freedom could serve to draw his attention to his private—yet communally experienced—tensions. Yet despite his desire to retain an integrated family, and the fact his children mainly attained a marginal economic status and rewards by adapting to the norms of America, the average immigrant was a peripheral, ambiguous man. Many, including the English, had deep self-contempt for having persisted in gaining lucre in America, of losing even the minimum dignity they had back home; and all too many never finally were to resolve whether they would stay or return. But, ironically, a large portion of all who came to America were marginal, increasingly dispossessed men and women in their own homelands, and they were rarely carriers of the deeper cultures of their own nations. This, in turn, defined the character of their ethnicity in the United States.

Indeed, the mass culture which most immigrants brought was simply a knowledge—often very minimal—of their languages and the conventions of their native rural societies. Very few intellectuals or bearers of "high culture" migrated to America, and these, surely, were the most miserable and frustrated of men. Over time their main function was to supply the highly mobile children who would staff American faculties and the RAND Corporation, while they themselves manned ethnic newspapers and bureaucracies. These endured, and even at the beginning of this decade the ethnic press in America numbered more than forty dailies and 150 journals with a circulation of 4½ million, while more than 600 ethnic radio programs—overwhelmingly stressing music—retained 20 million or more listeners. Yet despite this persistence, it remained a fact that the descendants of the first generation quickly lost command of the language; and, above all, the immigrant's own familiarity with it was so superficial as to grant him precious little defense against his own acculturation to a kind of limbo ethnicity which left him with only slight knowledge of the most precious aspects of his own culture and only sufficient immersion in it psychologically to divide him from fellow workers who spoke other tongues. In the end, it produced a working class that was to a great measure both lumpen and insecure, accommodating but not assimilating in America, uncertain of its ultimate destination in the case of most, cut off from the larger society and even, to an increasingly remarkable and painful degree, his own ethnic community and family.[25]

Lumpen Society and Lumpen Class

The United States throughout its history was a nation of high physical mobility among all its peoples, who, motivated by economic need, ambition, or both, with increasing frequency moved what were by European standards vast distances. The price such individuals paid for their restlessness was great in social and psychological terms. Ethnics, in a parallel and overlapping manner, often shared experiences. There were aspirations and regret, nostalgia and overwork, the absence of family and constraints, and a much higher level of random violence than Europe ever knew. If natives and Wasps were spared the rejection and confusion which afflicted the ethnics because of language, customs, and prejudice, there is no doubt that a psychological and moral toll agonized them also, and this produced social as well as personal breakdowns—many now sanctioned and purveyed institutionally as amusements or military strategies—less well known in Europe. The United States, in brief, was a lumpen society of mobile individuals to an extent unparalleled in the history of industrialized nations; and this fact goes a long way in explaining the casual, impersonal violence Americans now experience at home and which their state proudly exports in infinitely greater quantity abroad.

Qualitatively, therefore, the ethnic's disintegration in the American urban context was not different than the rest of society's, but the extensive ethnic basis of the working class makes this phase of its problem important also. For the individualism of the economically ambitious immigrant, even within the framework of his ethnic community, helped produce a splintered working class of the twentieth century and a mass of quite aimless persons unable to relate as a community with a common interest and destiny.

Thomas and Znaniecki noted that after World War One the immigrant experience was producing a significantly higher rate of mental disorders and social breakdown, above all among their children, and since then a mass of data—good, bad, and indifferent—has been produced. Yet the very best has offered some persuasive conclusions, the most fundamental being that people who migrate—whether to another nation or just to another state—are significantly more prone to serious mental disorders than those who do not; and from this one can reasonably hypothesize that less grave psychological maladies are apt to affect many of those who elude data gatherers by avoiding hospitalization. Moreover, communities with high population growth rates are more likely to congregate or produce unstable types than those with lower rates of increase. And, lastly, the immigrant who came to the United States and returned home was, despite economic success, perhaps the most marginal, unhappy man of all, and this dimension forces one to at least ask whether many of the alienated immigrants from Europe were perhaps also destined to be marginal men wherever they might be.

For example, in 1939–1941 migrants to New York State who had arrived within five years were hospitalized for psychoses more than twice as frequently as nonmigrants. Migrants in the state longer than five years had a hospitalization rate only a quarter greater than native New Yorkers. Ignoring internal migration altogether, and comparing psychoses among foreign- and nonforeign-born whites in New York State in 1939–1941, foreign-born males were hospitalized only 11 percent, and females 21 percent, more than American-born. Almost two decades later, Massachusetts communities in the highest quartile of growth rates had twice the hospitalizations for depression as the lowest, and about three times the rate of suicides. Unanswered by all this, however, is the question of the psychological record of the children of foreign-born, who were at least as affected by conflicts of cultures and values. In 1903, second-generation white ethnics formed an only slightly larger share of those in hospitals for the insane than their proportion of the white population in the same age categories. Their parents, on the other hand, were more than half overrepresented among the insane and comprised over one-third of the patients in 1903. Yet what unquestionably emerges is that migration within and from without America produced a significantly more psychologically crippled nation than in most of Europe, with the main pressure on the ethnic coming relatively soon after her or his arrival.

This conclusion is best illustrated by Ornulv Odegaard's analysis of Norwegians remaining in their homeland, those who went to Minnesota, and those who returned from America. In 1889–1909, in Minnesota the Norwegian-born had a rate of admissions to mental hospitals almost one-half greater than the native-born. For 1909–1929 the differences decline somewhat but remain significant, the Norwegian-born still exceeding the rest of the population for hospitalizations by nearly one-third. Yet Norwegians who returned home from America had the highest rate of all, or twice that of non-migrants, which led Odegaard to note that in addition to the impact of the trauma of adjusting to America, "relatively many psychopathic or early psychotic individuals [could be found] among the emigrants, because the restlessness, dissatisfaction, etc., which is so common in such personalities is very likely to induce them to leave their country. . . ."[26] Indeed, the same quite modest conclusion also applies to native American whites who migrate internally. For all this too helps partially our understanding of today.

Odegaard's conclusions that migrants are a particularly unstable element are surely reinforced by the now substantial literature which exists on the one-third of the ethnics who repatriated home. While it is impossible to argue they were more unhappy than those who remained in America, the Greeks, Italians, Croats, and others who returned appear to have shared certain common characteristics. First, they were upwardly mobile economically, often challenging and being rejected in their claims for status by the local ruling elites. An astonishing number managed to lose their money again, either through poor management or war, and they engaged in the quite conspicuous consumption one expects from parvenus everywhere. *Americani* in Italy, and *Amerikansti* in Croatia, their clothes, speech, mixture of English and native words, and general independence made them both disliked and catered to within their usually rural communities. These misfits brought few innovations back with them but mainly articles of consumption; they quickly romanticized what life in America had been like, found it inordinately difficult to readjust to home, and congregated together even to the perverse extent of opening an American Legion post in Athens. In the case of a small minority, some went back to the United States. In Poland they introduced the street gang techniques they had acquired in America, making local reactionaries more unpleasant yet. In general, therefore, they appear to have been misfits—*kounesmenos,* or "shaken ones," they were aptly called in Greece—and perhaps the unhappiest lot of all.[27]

The ambiguity of the returnee (and the large majority of post-1890 immigrants were potential or actual returnees) probably exceeded the confusions and anxieties of those who finally elected to stay. As for the latter, their reluctance to take out naturalization papers revealed their residue of ambivalence, and their ethnicity after some decades became an expression of rootlessness long after their languages were largely unknown by their children and much of what they both shared in common culturally centered on food. In the end, the immigrants exhibited displaced commitments and values, lumpen individuals who had already become typical Americans and no better than all the rest.

For those who managed, for reasons of either sentiment or class, to stay within the complicated stratified entities called ethnic neighborhoods—which after the 1950s became the symbolic cultural and shopping centers of second and third generations, now barely literate in their parents' tongues, living in aseptic communities within driving distances of West and North Ends everywhere—the Wasps' urban-renewal bulldozers began delivering the final *coup de grace* to the vestiges of an internecine working-class structure which tragically had never developed a culture and politics appropriate to its own objective situation.

That ethnic willingness to transcend the suspicion of nationality toward nationality, save perhaps when it came to their common fear and hatred of blacks, at no time emerged during the twentieth century to help lay the basis of genuine unity from which class consciousness could overcome racial and ethnic identifications. Ethnic workers saw their grievances in an ethnic focus, which was essential to the very existence of political machines. Yet most ethnics were in reality primarily individuals and families, too preoccupied confronting their anxieties, conflicts of values, nostalgia, and private tears to politically or intellectually transcend the compulsive prejudices of their own nationality or religion. Such marginal socialist ethnic groups as arose, above all among Jews, Germans, or Finns, were scarcely efforts to escape their particularist culture but rather a transitional assertion of values temporarily useful in the diaspora and thereafter to become almost exclusively social and ethnic in function. It was not, surely, a creed they transmitted to their children.

Hence the temporary working class became the permanent working class with its own historically unique style and goals, lumpen people in a lumpen society, with that instability and frequently successful absurdity and triumph of demagoguery that often sways all the American people. It is in this context that the trade-union movement and the political expressions of the American masses evolved in the twentieth century, compounding the nation's problems while so far depriving it of the promise of real solutions.

4

The Political Economy of Capitalism in Crisis, 1920–1940

World War One was the turning point in the development of the American economy, marking the end of a long period of growth and relative insularity from the world economy. The decade of the 1920s, economically much more than politically or culturally, was a fundamentally new interlude between the no longer young industrial society, whose problems had largely been resolved through expansion, and an older and much larger nation in search of answers—increasingly political over time—to its structural economic dilemmas. The decade, in brief, witnessed an accumulation of unresolved difficulties and contradictions whose inevitable conclusion was the Great Depression.

No doubt the social-cultural experimentation and boorishness of the period alike have a certain fascination, as does the consideration of the odd if foreseeable human consequences which the effort to ban alchoholic drinks inevitably produced. The booboisie also has a certain amusing seductiveness along with literary alienation, but in the end the 1920s influenced the remainder of the twentieth century not because of this or that new habit or the outcome of a fairly predictable and usually secondary political development, but because the capitalist economy ended in a disaster whose effects indelibly shaped the lives of all Americans and the future of their history for the remainder of the century. That economic failure and its resolution, infinitely more than anything else one might choose to regard, was the main event of the period between the two world wars.

The Economic Context

In the simplest terms, virtually every important economic sector—workers, farmers, industrialists, and financiers—was in economic trouble during the decade, a fact which precious few of the more affluent of them acknowledged throughout the euphoria and superficial prosperity of the 1920s, not the least because false optimism was by then the central tenet of the national culture. The aggregate of these rather technical problems spelled collective disaster, even though the search for solutions to their specific manifestations began modestly immediately after the war and, of course, became the national preoccupation during the Depression decade.

For the capitalists, the major problem was to find profitable outlets for capital accumulated from wartime profits as well as during the course of the 1920s. As I noted elsewhere, the decadal growth of capital in manufacturing during the period 1919–1929 was by far the lowest since the Civil War, amounting to only 3.2 percent annually. Yet this capital, in contrast to earlier decades, was by far the most productive ever known—before or after—in terms of the quantities of products it could create. Output per man-hour in manufacturing increased over two-thirds in the decade after 1919, and almost as much by unit of capital input. In mining, as well, the increase was almost as great.

This astonishing efficiency of capital developed even as labor costs rose, in part because the decade and a half after 1914 saw the most unprecedented growth of workers' real income in United States history. Workers' wages after 1919 far outstripped increases in price of producers' goods and, taking advantage of the unusually low interest rates of the period, manufacturers wherever possible borrowed to substitute machinery for men, further intensifying the revolution in productivity. Between 1923 and 1929 the ratio of real average hourly earnings to output per man-hour dropped dramatically, but the ultimate meaning of this change was not wholly appreciated at the time. For the growth of per capita consumer outlays during the decade still made it at the same time the relatively most prosperous the United States had ever experienced, even if the reckoning was not far off.

The cost of production labor as a percentage of the value of manufactured products fell during the decade, but so too did the profitability of a more efficient industry. From a high of 43.2 percent of the value in 1921, the production-worker share fell to 35.6 percent by the decade's end, while the yield on the common shares of industrial corporations during 1919–1928 dropped one-seventh compared to the preceding decade. By any criterion, the profitability of American corporations was lower than in earlier decades, and in fact it was significantly less than any post-1945 period as well.[1]

But paradoxically, while the output of all manufacturing rose by over one half and by nearly that in mining, this increasing efficiency of capital in relation to output meant that the growth of American industry was no longer adequate to create sufficiently profitable investment outlets for all the available capital. The ratio of total capital to the value of manufactured products fell over one-fifth from 1919 to 1929, the first decline since the Civil War and the greatest drop over the past century. In fact, because internal funds provided the large majority of such proportionately lower amounts of new capital as industry or commerce required, the stock market and overseas investments became increasingly important to sustaining the profitability of the capital-saturated productive system. New financing within the United States, even so, less and less over the decade went into building new productive facilities, until by 1929 it was barely one-third of the total raised by security flotations. The remainder was essentially speculative. The foreign dimension I discuss in further detail in Chapter Six, but suffice it to say that during this period the export of private capital to presumably more profitable overseas outlets rose to the relatively highest point the United States was ever to experience. Mergers and the market for common stocks, the price of which rose about three times between 1921 and 1929, provided another temporary outlet for such excess capital. But all of these capital diversions merely reflected the fact that the interaction of a lower rate of domestic economic growth, technology, and expanding but insufficient consumption were producing the elements of a major crisis.

The paradoxes which an economy of relative prosperity and impending collapse produces are now obvious to all to observe, though contemporary analysts rarely drew the logical pessimistic conclusions from the abundance of evidence available at the time. The real income of labor grew, but in 1929 the total number of workers required to produce the decade's one-half greater output of manufacturing remained constant, while in mining (with output up two-fifths) it fell 14 percent. Only the expansion of the clerical, sales, and service occupational categories absorbed much of the work force that population growth and the last wave of immigrants enlarged. In the aggregate, the demand for industrial and mining labor fell, and fluctuating unemployment during the 1920–1929 decade averaged at least 4 percent of the labor force for seven of those years. But such data are misleading insofar as they ignore the fact, discussed at the time, of the widespread reality of part-time and underemployed workers.

But unemployment was only one of many major structural facts undermining the so-called prosperity decade's future. Income distribution, which has remained fairly constant since the first reasonably accurate data for 1910, during the 1920s left the richest fifth of the recipients with over one-half of the personal income. Despite the faster expansion of real income for workers after a long period of stability or modest growth, by 1929, a Brookings Institution study reported, 42 percent of the consumer units lived at or below a "subsistence-and-poverty" level that was poor indeed, while another 36 percent were at the "minimum-comfort" level. These consumers, who shared the other half of the personal income, left United States capitalism with the unresolved paradox of underconsumption relative to the excess industrial plant and the surplus capital available.

As always, nowhere were economic crisis and poverty more evident than in the agrarian sector. The farmers—also as always—were the victims of larger economic forces over which they had no control and which, despite the emergence of the politically much noticed Congressional "farm bloc" in 1921, were constantly to escape the constraints the agrarians' conservative as well as more radical spokesmen were to seek to impose on elusive economic realities.

Briefly, the prosperity which accompanied World War One enticed and then badly misled the farmers as their cash receipts roughly doubled between 1912–1913 and the end of the decade. During that same decade farm capital in new land and machinery expanded vastly, overwhelmingly coming, for the first and last time, from external loans rather than the farmers' own income and savings. Between 1912–1913 and 1921–1922 the farm debt, along with its interest charges, more than doubled. The American farmers were in persistent deep trouble as soon as the war ended. With the sharp decline of prices he received, the farmer was generally unable to meet his fixed expenses. Yet averages are misleading, since the typical farmer was a great deal worse off than the more conservative but politically better placed larger farmers congregated in the Farm Bureau but equally unable, despite much agitation, either to implement the Bureau program or reverse the plight of their sector either by private or public means. A million farmers simply left the land during the decade, but this was less than a tenth of those remaining, and the urban economy could not adequately absorb even this number. Economic crisis and poverty in the 1920s defined the existences of farmers more than any other major segment of the nation.[2]

In general, therefore, the 1920s produced a new epoch in the history of the immensely greater United States economy as well as a search for a new equilibrium in economic forces and development to replace the relatively stable, predictable prewar economy and the world in which it operated. The international economy weighed heavily on the American environment, even though domestic rather than world priorities tended to shape the decisions of those few men called upon to relate to both via the determination of interest rates and banking policy. But that fragile foreign structure offered one escape—and hence its importance—while the speculative mania at home presented another. The new maturity and increasingly unprofitable saturation of the United States productive sector, and the diminishing opportunity of growth capable of absorbing labor and sustaining sufficient purchasing power, were shadows that overhung the interlude of good times with its ephemeral cultural and social manifestations. Because of its greater complexity and size, the economy was also more vulnerable, a fact events would prove strikingly with an unprecedented severity that no respectable contemporary observer dared to imagine.

Perhaps no less important was the fact that despite the intensification of oligopolistic mechanisms in some industries with high capital requirements for entry, in which wartime collaborative arrangements persisted, or where mergers or acquisitions had lowered the number of firms active in an economic sector, competition in numerous industries left abundant collective dangers as well as a larger framework of instability in which economic and political leaders had to make decisions. Petroleum, textiles, coal, banking, chemicals, iron and steel, clothing, paper, trucking, and many others lacked order and discipline in the face of insufficient demand and, hence, overexpansion. To resolve their problems these constituencies were required to seek to develop adequate controls, means they ultimately were not to devise either in this decade nor the next.

Ordering the New Order

Herbert Hoover was the apotheosis of the 1920s, and in his aspirations, successes, and failures one finds remarkably crystallized the potential and the limits of capitalist "planning" after the First World War. Hoover, who has increasingly fascinated historians, was far less an original creator of ideas and organizations than an integrator of many discrete approaches to the problems of industrial capitalism which became current after the turn of the century. He was consummately able as administrator and synthesizer, but Hoover's ultimate demise was testimony to the utter inappropriateness of the economic irrelevancies that became conventional wisdom during the first third of this century.

If Hoover was the seeming genius of the period as Secretary of Commerce from 1921 to 1928, it is still vital to comprehend that he was a man who worked within the framework of ideas, organizations, and politics that preceded him and to which he himself conformed, and in no sense was he ever in fundamental conflict with the other leaders or premises of his time. As the ablest expositor of their ideas, he had immense attraction to both parties, which meant that Woodrow Wilson could both discover and make Hoover politically as well as provide him a more coherent foreign policy vision which the latter explicitly acknowledged for the remainder of his life. In 1920, factions of both parties even courted him to enter the Presidential race. Until 1929, he was both to succeed politically and fail in his effort to use administrative and organizational techniques to confront the effects of an economic crisis which was far deeper than he or his peers could acknowledge.

Hoover, in brief, was consummately the best example of existing social technology and disinterested politics in an age when Presidents were predictably inept and moderately corrupt, as was Warren Gamaliel Harding, or fatigued, dull men, as in the case of his successor Calvin Coolidge. Hoover was impeccable by contrast, but what is ultimately most striking and consequential is the extent to which the most powerful single Cabinet member of the period 1921–1928 and the Presidents shared certain premises which made Hoover's role not only possible but even necessary. For it was precisely because Hoover did what cigar-chewing, drinking, or sleeping men could not that he became a political power in his own right and built the constituency that made him, despite his apolitical past and presumably technocrat's present, the next Republican President.

Consensus, in brief, is more typical of the decade and made Hoover utilitarian to the men who designated him. Harding had been an Old Guard regular, but the 1920 Republican platform was sufficiently "progressive," and Harding himself suitably vague and humanitarian, to make the Republicans of the 1920s quite compatible with the bipartisan foundations of the national political economy called "progressivism." And while it is true that Hoover was the man who persuaded him so, it was Harding who in the spring of 1923 decided publicly to force United States Steel finally to relent and abandon the twelve-hour work day in its plants. Coolidge, for all his pervasive mediocrity, indolence, and endless string of quotable banalities, was still sincerely committed to the progressive tradition of Roosevelt Republicanism, willing to flirt with the older party insurgents if necessary, and he quite genuinely supported the regulatory legacy which his predecessors had bequeathed and his Cabinet members continued to sustain.

Hoover was not merely the inheritor of the political premises which his peers and superiors shared in common, but he operated within the framework of the sentiments of a sorely divided and undisciplined business community which gave him at least the minimum endorsement, without which most of his efforts would have produced total resistance. Hoover, of course, had earlier been a mining engineer but also simply another type of entrepreneur himself, and his substantial fortune testified to his success by standards Americans respected. Most important yet was the congruence between Hoover's own ideas and those of many key business groups and interests on the role of positive government in meeting their problems. Hoover reflected their impulses, but he also embellished in a rather original way the means for implementing them; and it was less the creativity of his means than the business-sanctioned-and-originated nature of his ends that counted. Hoover, after all, was not the first man to seek to employ state power to serve the needs of business constituencies, and it took no great act of bravery to assert a function on which political administrations before and after were to agree. What Hoover and various business elements eventually differed on were appropriate methods for attaining the common end of solving economic problems via political means, yet their diverse choices were due far less to principle or ideology than to the successive failure of modalities deemed appropriate at a given time to accomplish tasks which in differing periods were of varying magnitude. As historians have not tired of pointing out, the germs of the 1930s can be found in the economic ideas and organizational experiments of the 1920s and, of course, earlier yet. But this was due essentially to the fact that the structural problems, changing with the motions of the business cycles of capitalism, provided sufficient continuity to require this uniformity. The continuum of kind, if not degree, in twentieth-century United States political capitalism was hardly dependent on the role of a striking personality such as Hoover, but it was rather the logic of the interaction between the economic structure and the political mechanisms called upon to sustain its various constituencies in that incremental set of efforts which collectively produced the modern American political economy. If Hoover was later faulted for not comprehending the magnitude of the crisis which the United States and world capitalism confronted, the obvious defect was irrelevant. For had he dissented from the then almost universally held vision of the American economy as essentially immune to disaster, he scarcely would have qualified to serve loyally in a state apparatus which, if nothing else, had to preserve its confidence in its own viability.

Hoover's policies existed, therefore, as effect rather than cause, and as a reflection of the premises that Harding, Coolidge, their predecessors, and successors all would share. Still, the ability of the man demands detailed notice, for he was the best the constituted order could at the time muster to confront the complex and quite overwhelming structural crisis of American capitalism. Hoover's decisions were so multidimensional that they defy simple description, yet his basic theory for action was less complex.

The larger cycle of interplay between business constituencies and the state after the 1880s involved an alternation between primary dependence on voluntary efforts and then political regulation and compulsions to integrate economically specific industries. Behind political efforts could invariably be found one or another section of an industry that had come to realize that nothing short of legal sanctions would effectively bring recalcitrant companies into line, and periods of declining profits especially stimulated this sentiment.

Both the inability to devise legislation sufficient to control independent firms and the upturn of market demand and profits generally diminished the desire as well as need for new political controls, while the precedents of past commissions and legislation stood as a usually inadequate basis on which to confront ongoing problems. But when the economic crisis of a specific industry was sufficiently grave, then some of its constituents again were increasingly prepared to advocate appropriately sterner and more ambitious and compulsory political solutions. In the end, their efforts in the realms of both political *and* voluntary solutions failed to satisfy the needs of industries whose fates the impersonal general business cycle or the peculiar economics of their industries ultimately would control. Yet they were to attempt everything, and it is of this stuff, whether effective or not, that the history of the political economy is made. Hoover, preeminently of all men before or after him, was the astonishingly prodigious theoretician of the organization of voluntary regulation in an era that appeared prosperous enough not to require sterner measures. And, beyond his intellectual contribution, he was the implementor of many of his own proposals.

The rules of the game, whether one calls it the "associative state," as did Hoover, the "cult of efficiency," "business syndicalism," "voluntaristic capitalism," or whatever, were Hoover's forte. The elimination of industrial waste and duplication, scientific management, planning, empiricism, rationalization—all these techniques, familiar in varying degrees before and after Hoover, were approaches he cultivated. In essence, Hoover was convinced that every problem had a solution rather than presaging yet new dilemmas, and it was sufficient to use investigative, empirical techniques—usually via commissions of experts—to define answers. One never questioned first premises, according to such a view, but only sought to formulate and apply superior rules for a given game. This positivism, which ignored entirely the reality that differing concrete interests might articulate quite irreconcilable answers depending on their particular needs and perspectives, to say nothing of the fact that the problems to be solved were endemic in capitalism for as long as the system survived, was a popular myth then and thereafter. It was scarcely one Hoover originated, and it made technocrats play a role for the next half-century which their repeated failures scarcely diminished as less well trained leaders also failed. Indeed, such an increasingly popular belief in the efficacy of research and expertise was interesting as a reflection of a growing capitalist dilemma of attempting to substitute research and planning when their ignorance left them without reliable solutions, and it was the existence of both blindness and anxiety that is more important to comprehend than the pseudo-scientific jargon of expert mystifiers. The class premises of any inquiry were always assumed, and never challenged, but Hoover advanced the pseudo-positivist faith as never before.

Beginning with his study of waste in industry when elected president of the Federated American Engineering Societies in 1920, Hoover literally dazzled the decade with his empiricist answers to the problems of this or that economic sector. His unemployment conference of September 1921, which eventually brought to bear all that was known on business cycles at the time and advanced the belief they could be controlled, led to some unique proposals for tailoring the flow of public works contracts and nongovernmental construction to provide more stable employment in at least that field. Above all, he sought to expand vastly the role of the hundreds, and eventually thousands, of voluntary industry trade associations to reduce cooperatively and without compulsion waste and accidents by standardization of specifications, accounting and production techniques, safety procedures, market evaluations and voluntary output controls through the location and publication of statistics, and numerous similar functions. Such a strategy was hardly original and simply took an organizational form that railroads were long familiar with and which many industries before the war had also concluded might serve their common objectives. Indeed, the Federal Trade Commission itself had before the war begun such efforts to increase business cooperation and rationalize standards, which it intensified throughout the 1920s, and Hoover merely greatly advanced its pioneering work. The impetus to this purely voluntary cooperation, after Hoover's Commerce Department stimulated the creation of hundreds more trade associations where needed, was to be self-interest and mutual profit, creating within the framework of anti-trust restrictions an industrial self-regulation that was politically endorsed but unable to impose political sanctions.

In fact, during his eight active years as Commerce Secretary Hoover encouraged thousands of such voluntary groups of quite diverse types and interests to organize, on the premise that once having done so their common problems could be solved consensually and stronger government action would become superfluous. The government thereby created what Hoover later called a "regulated individualism," which was explicitly quite different than laissez faire.[3] This meant that vastly expanded Commerce activities took Hoover and his growing corps of specialists into labor and welfare regulation, foreign policy, the regulatory commissions, radio and aviation control, and numerous areas which made him the most powerful Cabinet member of the period—allegedly undersecretary of all other executive agencies. In practice Hoover's ambitious accumulation of bureaucratic responsibilities and programs led to government undertakings considerably greater than his theory proposed. If in fact his more grandiose schemes for government reorganization met defeats from other agencies—particularly the State and Treasury departments—also eager to protect their jurisdictions, his plans were always ingeniously advanced applications of engineering efficiencies instinctively respectful of the premises of existing economic forms. If nothing else, Hoover was supremely skilled in fields in which, unfortunately for him, far more than mere knowledge was required in order to find workable answers. The purpose of all this government economic regulation, Coolidge aptly noted in giving his key Secretary's philosophy, was to equalize the conditions of free competition, and Hoover's voluntarism seemed best suited for that purpose. But after all was said and done, the trade associations with their rationalized techniques, the new and expanded government agencies with their ingenious norms and mountains of clarifying documents, only managed to lift the once apolitical and quite recently obscure engineer into the White House. In the last analysis, Hoover had taken the pulse of organized business sentiment to catapult himself to the apex of political power just in time to see his constituency's and his personal theories prove utterly irrelevant to the collapse of the national and world economy that was soon to unfold.

The intimidating verbal density and endless statistics of Hoover's rationalization efforts and guided voluntarism can easily be misinterpreted as a type of profound business-government prescience leading, if not immediately then in due course, to an efficient corporate liberalism (to note but one definition of this cooperative process) which answered real problems with adequate solutions. It is always dangerous to impute to men-of-power, whether in business or politics, the contemporary conceptualizations of scholars, preachers, or intellectuals; for indeed businessmen in particular are by selection and training restricted to the specialized problems of their own industrial universe and, in the last analysis, the needs of their own firms. No less dangerous, both in this period and thereafter, is to impute to all businessmen total ignorance of the larger environment which will affect their interests. In any concrete example it is best to know exactly what the policies of specific elements were in cases where they were affected, and to remember that consistency for business can be a costly hobgoblin when it comes to means rather than the ultimately always unwavering end of stable profitability. Major decisions can be made by default, but also by the accretion of smaller judgments which at the time appear only as practical responses to exigencies.

The Limits of Trade Associations

Whatever the grand theory which Hoover melded from engineering theory and business needs, the practice of voluntarily regulating American capitalism through trade associations and cooperation among firms proved frustrating and ineffective to its advocates, and it set the stage for the conversion of many businessmen to sterner political methods of imposing economic discipline. Indeed, a strategy that could not work during a period of comparatively high demand was to disintegrate with quickly shrinking markets in the Depression. This development eventually brought with it a fairly predictable insistence by growing numbers of firms that the government do for them what they could not themselves accomplish.

Among the approximately 1000 true trade associations in existence by 1925, the practices and problems of each significantly depended on the degree of competition within an industry as well as the larger, more complicated question of the market demand for their goods. Nor did their ability after 1925 to indirectly fix prices legally alter these structural imperatives. Roughly speaking, and with important exceptions, where competition within industries was high or productive capacity exceeded the demands of the markets, the history of trade associations during the Hoover period was invariably a sequence of failure or ineffectuality. Even Hoover's successful fight to restrain the Department of Justice from applying anti-trust laws against the practices of many associations did not give them sufficient power to attain prosperity through voluntary self-regulation, which by 1931 was widely acknowledged as a rather utopian chimera.

Industrial variations were almost as common as the number of associations, but the general experience confirmed the hopelessness of controlling mature capitalism without political authority. Perhaps the first real trade association, formed in 1914 among finishers of cotton fabrics under the direction of Arthur Eddy, the influential chief theoretician of the association movement before 1921, logically arose in a branch of a cotton-textile industry plagued by excess competition, important regional wage differences, and overproduction. Similar problems had beset other industries long before, and less ambitious efforts at cooperation were numerous—and also an impetus to mergers among many firms—but the 1920s made cooperation appear more imperative as the economy, relatively speaking, slowed down and risked a surplus of capital in relation to the potential market. The cotton-textile industry, which by 1925 was losing money, desperately attempted to utilize its various trade associations and worked closely with the Commerce Department to stabilize prices and competition. Earlier, of course, the Northern branch of the industry had supported child labor legislation to close the wage differential between itself and Southern producers, and regional rivalry paralleled the struggle among firms to win greater shares of a limited market. Wartime cooperation with the government War Industries Board had allowed price fixing and higher profits, a relationship that was to appear much more enticing to the conservative industry leaders by the beginning of the Depression. But the consolidation of the various industry associations into a unified national structure in 1925 failed to attain voluntary stabilization and profit despite the fact the industry had extensively implemented the technical measures the Commerce Department propounded. By 1931 the leaders of the association, convinced that the reduction of night shifts would eliminate the overcapacity which the Depression was turning into an economic rout, were freely able to employ the moral approval of the Hoover Administration in their futile campaigns to recruit recalcitrant producers into their ranks. Indeed, the joint industry-government efforts enlisted even bankers to bring the nonconformist minority producers voluntarily under control, but to no avail. There was simply no way without full political sanctions to restrain numerous aggressive manufacturers who were determined to seek profit alone, and until 1933 that was not to be possible.

Even more elusive was the bituminous coal industry, whose low capital entry requirements led to production overcapacity by 1922, making roughly one-third of all mines economically superfluous and a danger to the rest. Spread throughout the country and in approximately 6000 firms, every associational effort was doomed to failure because producers controlling more than one-third of the industry's potential output were unwilling to join it. Voluntary price, capacity, and output restrictions, even when strongly backed by Hoover personally, failed. Technically precocious transport and distribution schemes fared no better. Only the United Mine Workers, which both the association members and independent coal operators tended to unite to oppose, advocated the use of public authority to introduce order in an industry which invariably sought first to solve its problems by wage cuts, thereby decimating the union. By the time the Depression brought yet new disasters, many industry leaders and larger firms acknowledged the failure of voluntary trade-association efforts and were increasingly prepared to discuss a wide variety of governmental controls to impose stability and cooperation on the unprofitable, competitive industry.

The garment industry, which like coal was so competitive that no common program among businessmen was possible, also shared the same economic problems, and like most other specific industrial associations tended to lose members during periods of declining prosperity. Incapacity to hold and discipline members on a voluntary basis was a problem common to a sufficient number of competitive industries, making the entire organizational concept frivolously irrelevant when real economic problems arose. Indeed, in such industries only unions provided the remaining nonpolitical hope for coordinating and restraining competitive conditions on a national scale, a fact that won the employers associations to the union cause in garments before the war and was eventually greatly to influence labor relations in coal and many other industries.

In petroleum, which had far fewer firms than cotton textiles or coal, it proved almost as difficult to obtain a consensus among producers divided by both regions and size, and overproduction and lower profits increasingly plagued an industry that was growing too quickly to stabilize easily. Throughout the 1920s, in the name of "conservation" sentiments, which the Teapot Dome oil-lease scandal facilitated, the larger firms unsuccessfully sought to impose output, price, and market restrictions with federal legal sanctions against recalcitrants in what was in the first instance to be voluntarily agreed-upon codes. Using the Federal Oil Conservation Board set up in the wake of the Teapot Dome affair, these big producers, of which Standard Oil of New Jersey was the most important, from 1926 onward futilely tried to reverse falling prices. Despite its initial hesitancy, the Justice Department by late 1927 was now ready to endorse the growing desire among the biggest oil producers and the American Petroleum Institute for production limits with federal sanctions, though the extent of the government's role remained a hypothetical source of division for some years to come. Despite the ability of the API to get quite widespread but insufficient state endorsements for its comprehensive 1928 code of ethics designed to scotch price competition, the big producers could never convince Hoover to favor the essential federal sanctions which alone, they increasingly became convinced, could discipline the new, smaller producers who continued to flood the markets and depress prices. Hoover until the end of his Presidency favored voluntary accords, but when these failed he retreated from the conclusions that practical businessmen rather than theoreticians were prone to draw in the disaster period after 1929. In this he was reinforced by politically formidable Southwesterners who feared that federal regulation would quickly become an instrument of the largest oil companies, though state controls appealed also to many of these smaller interests. Here, too, voluntary industrial regulation proved a failure, and politics the means by which differing economic constituencies combated one another.

If self-regulation and trade associations in the industrial sector proved dismal failures both to their proponents and by the standards of the questions they had to resolve, it was in the field of investment speculation that their limits became most apparent. There also, because of its interaction with the general problem of the rise of speculation during the 1920s, the absence of control assumed too great a danger and importance for traditionally dominant investment bankers as well as, eventually, the political leaders in Washington.

The Investment Bankers Association had first been created during the simpler year of 1912, partially as a professional group with status pretensions against the invasion of commercial banks and retail securities firms which began whittling off pieces of their buying and placement functions after 1900, but also as a lobby to attain uniformity among state laws affecting the industry. By 1919, although the IBA preferred a single federal law to the multiplicity of state regulations, and such leaders of the field as Paul M. Warburg urged federal controls against fraud, the association never supported existing legislation, and its anxieties partially melted with the 1920s boom. During the 1920s, however, two major problems gravely endangered the investment bankers, and their puny efforts could barely control them through voluntary codes and education. First was the critical new role of the Federal Reserve System and its eventual development of policies that were to increase the quantity of its own and other financial resources pouring into the New York Stock Exchange. In 1922 the Federal Reserve System began regulating the bank discount rate so as to control the flow of funds it judged essential for both the welfare of the domestic economy and the balance of international payments and, in general, its increasingly intricate financial relations with European central banks. Until 1927 there was no basic conflict between the national and international functions of the system, and the dominating personality of Benjamin Strong resolved such tensions as arose until late 1928 in favor of the Reserve Bank of New York's higher call money rates. Over the next year, trying both to dampen the wild speculation that inflated prices on the New York Stock Exchange fueled and yet not gravely endanger Britain's financial position, the Federal Reserve System was locked in a power struggle between the Board in Washington and the New York Bank, and then acted indecisively and belatedly to increase interest rates the following summer—too late to avert the panic that Strong the preceding year had predicted.

The second critical danger to the IBA was the fact that dealing in securities had become a business which far exceeded their membership, which in 1929 was perhaps one-tenth of all security dealers and less than one-quarter of the investment bankers. By 1930, in fact, commercial banks sold over 60 percent of the new security issues. Although the IBA opposed federal legislation after 1920 and confined itself to the improvement of state laws, the older, more established houses felt the impact of new competitors despite the growth of the market. Not only was the only existing trade association less and less able to regulate the conditions of the immense field, but it increasingly complained about the dubious and, as events were to prove, dangerous methods of peddling new issues. By the time of the crash, the trade association responsible for the voluntary regulation of perhaps one of the most important single financial institutions of the decade had worked itself into a position of frustrating impotence.[4]

Even before the 1929 crash the economic and organizational limits of the "associative state" had been reached, and voluntarism proved a chimera in dealing with price competition, market shares, and overproduction. The main lessons of the entire illusion and denouement were to shape profoundly the next period of reform and the development of the American political economy. The organizational mechanisms and regulatory devices of an epoch, their goals, ignorance, and assumptions, had once again proved inadequate for the economic tendencies and complexities which outstripped conventional wisdom and existing social technology. Neither the political mechanisms nor the existing personalities were a match for the problem of the first decade of what was heralded, not for the first or last time, as enduring prosperity. The objective compulsions for a renewal of the effort at federal regulation now existed. Firms and whole economic constituencies were in trouble—including other industries dependent on them. They would be ready to move, and the fact that their new proposals would not solve the problems for which they were intended was less immediately consequential than their necessity to act. The nonpolitical effort at economic integration had now exhausted itself, and although there was a growing consensus on the need for new and stronger solutions there was still a multitude of choices which differing concrete interests and perceptions—or misperceptions—imposed.

Every capitalist by necessity had to calculate in the last analysis on the basis of what ultimately best served the interests of his firm as he defined them, and many never fully understood their own system, its imperatives, contradictions, and how best to respond to them. For some this meant only disciplining other firms, not cooperating with industry norms and efforts to control their own conditions; and such men thought only that government power was merely to serve as reinforcement. To this predominant viewpoint, which merged the assumptions of the trade associations of the 1920s with the next great phase of national reform, it seemed inconceivable that the problem was not merely uncooperative inter-firm relations and overproduction but rather a far larger and more complicated economic crisis of capitalism which was the cause of excessive industrial capacity. Yet differing answers, even among relatively small sectors of an overall economy, meant that in order to find a measure of common agreement for industry-wide action more and more companies would call upon the state to impose a predetermined common policy and discipline on them. But while a growing number of industrialists wished to delegate responsibility to political authorities, they also sought to use their relative power to define the federal government's role in advance to serve their own needs. The question would increasingly move to the conflict among divided capitalist interests in specific fields to influence and control the political machinery, as firms differentiated by size, region, national, and international perspectives moved to influence the affairs of state.

Hoover and the Depression

It was the lack of a sufficient consensus among business leaders, as well as the need for the economic disaster further to affect individual business thinking, that reinforced Hoover's obduracy not to abandon the voluntarist faith which increasingly became an object of derision among those who once had shared it. In the last analysis, Hoover's confusion was shared by all those in business and Congress qualified in terms of power to give him direction, but as President he was called upon to assume responsibility for the collapse of the economy and culture of his times. It is moot to speculate what the President would have done had the traditional founts of legitimacy in big business and Wall Street acknowledged reality and taken a clear direction, but it was not until the end of his term that they even began to do so, and the failure of Hoover was in fact also the bankruptcy of the constituted order and its social perception and knowledge. Hoover supervised a disaster, but on assumptions and institutional foundations he inherited, and the cure for which was to elude his successors as well. Yet it was not only a universal absence of solutions that paralyzed Hoover and society's leaders, but also that traditional mindless compulsive American optimism regarding the future, a psychology which encouraged inaction in the present.

Meanwhile, Hoover's confusion was reinforced by his self-evidently correct but incomplete convictions that the war and world economy had produced the American Depression, and that without international reforms domestic palliatives merely treated effects rather than causes. "No one can maintain that such a calamity would have come to humanity had there been no war," he and his official biographers argued until the end, and the major domestic problems, particularly in finance, he saw as effects of the war and the subsequent disordered global economy as well.[5] This analysis was to an important degree accurate, but what Hoover ignored was that the United States itself had deeply contributed to the instability of the postwar international economy and helped produce that disaster in large part because of the weaknesses in its domestic economy, thereby prolonging a prosperity at home that might have ended yet sooner without access to the overseas economy. It is, in fact, futile to attempt to isolate the national and global causes of the Depression, for they were both, and either was capable of producing an American economic crisis because of the astonishing integration of the United States and world economies which the war brought and the limits and needs the domestic economy imposed. The October 1929 stock market crash came when it appeared inevitable that a world monetary disaster was at hand for an accumulation of decisive reasons, and all that specific cause did was to heighten already existing latent weaknesses and within two years destroy the international credit structure to which major capitalist economies were by then linked. The world economy which had resolved the numerous dilemmas and weaknesses of national capitalism for a decade now brought them to the fore, and for almost a decade the United States unsuccessfully tried to solve the problems of national capitalism largely isolated, both by circumstances and intent, from the international economy.

Hoover, in any case, directed power in a vacuum that business itself was unable and reluctant to fill. Essentially, the vast majority pursued the classic business role and responsibility of concerning themselves with the needs of their firms and industries, and to the extent they generalized on the future it was within this narrow context. The chaos that ensued in the wake of a gross national product that fell 27 percent between 1929 and 1932 was predictable. Some industries, such as oil, were in anarchy, and both in Texas and Oklahoma the states futilely tried to regulate an end to overproduction, even to the extent of imposing martial law.

It was not until September 1931 that the rare if sketchy business programs for general economic recovery began emerging, first of all in the famous plan that Gerard Swope, president of General Electric, released. Swope's ideas were not at all original or imaginative, but simply a logical extension of the trade-association theory which reinforced its powers with legal sanctions. The plan permitted trade associations under federal supervision, immune to anti-trust laws, to collectively decide upon production, prices, and investments, and made illegal "unfair" practices. Hoover, curiously enough, immediately recoiled: "It is the most gigantic proposal of monopoly ever made in history," and later called it the genesis of the National Recovery Administration.[6] In fact it was very much like specific industry plans Hoover had endorsed while Secretary of Commerce, and his rejection of the scheme was both inconsistent and politically unwise. Some weeks later the United States Chamber of Commerce circulated a somewhat modified version of the Swope plan, including a national economic council. In fact it was less compulsory than the Swope plan insofar as the legal force of trade-association agreements was concerned, and Hoover thought it would, as his official chroniclers phrased it, "drive the country toward the Fascism of which it was a pattern."[7] Not for the first or last time, a President showed his capacity for monumental inconsistencies, and his rejection only gained him an important new critic in the Chamber. The Chamber's membership, however, ratified the scheme, and the NAM also supported it. Despite the fact that important big businessmen publicly voiced skepticism as to what trade associations might accomplish in any form, the general trend of the program was as close to a business solution for the Depression as was to emerge. But Hoover's venomous response to a plan so parallel to his own ideas, and his obduracy in refusing to define meaningful alternatives, led to a significant political break between the administration and critical organized business circles. This rupture was, in essence, not different from the one his successor was eventually to confront. Later, during the 1932 Presidential campaign, Chamber president Henry Harriman warned Hoover that unless he endorsed the contours of the approach, many businessmen would support Roosevelt, who he claimed had agreed with it. For better or worse, the approach had sunk roots where it counted. But it was not so much a rejection of the assumptions of the premises of the 1920s as a further application of them, focusing on price competition and overproduction rather than internal demand and international crisis.

The President's immobility was in part due to his realization that the complex realities transcended the comprehension of himself and his elite peers, and such a view acknowledged not so much personal failure as the inadequacy of contemporary social knowledge. Incurably optimistic as to what might be accomplished once the facts were known, Hoover a month before the crash initiated a vast study of

American society that was not to be completed before January 1933, only unintentionally to reveal in a vast mass of data that it was not information but deeper structural problems and policy that were the ultimate problems confronting the reconstruction of capitalism. Empiricist and technological fetishism to most in 1933, in fact his Committee on Social Trends reflected the hubris of conventional wisdom—business as well as academic—on the value of social knowledge to the control of social institutions. Hoover, for his part, thought the social survey a prerequisite to defining rationally and unemotionally national priorities, which instead were decided by default. The project, which bogged down in time-consuming academic routines, was originally to have been completed in a year, and it finally came out as a quite pedestrian exercise on a plan to lay plans. Its only interest, ultimately, was its role as an excuse for procrastination as well as its deeper reflection of what was to prove then and thereafter to be the crisis of capitalist social knowledge.

In effect, just as contemporary American revolutionaries failed to replace capitalism, the capitalists were unable to discover the means consciously to save their own system, and the paucity of the Swope plan, the absence of others—good, bad, or indifferent—and the hollowness of the Hoover investigation all reflected this same incapacity. If the failure of the status quo did not guarantee the success of its challengers, at least not in the medium run, it did mean that continued crises were a part of the logic and limits of the system. Apart from the difficulty the domestic and global political and economic context always imposed was the dilemma of ignorance and the limits of unpredictability, as well as the frustrating conundrum of the point at which efforts were adequate to control destiny. The rule that problems exceeded the social order's capacity to deal with them rationally, and there was always a lag in perceiving and attaining political solutions to economic needs, was as important as the inability of the best brains to define them. But the significance of ignorance during crises was neither new to the Hoover Administration nor was he the last to confront it.

Despite his later blurred recollection of his own actions by comparison to the New Deal's, a myopia that further cultivated among others the image of Hoover as a stand-pat reactionary, Hoover was correct in arguing that "those who contended that during the period of my administration our economic system was one of *laissez faire* have little knowledge of the extent of government regulation," an admonition Hoover himself often forgot.[8] In point of fact, Hoover's response to the Depression defies easy categorization precisely because it floundered in many directions at one and the same time and its premises, both regarding the role of the world economy and the absence of an informed plan, precluded decisive action. On the one hand Hoover's first action was to urge industrial leaders voluntarily to attempt to sustain wages and employment, advice they heeded until it cost something tangible. Voluntarism was the keynote of his economic program even after it ceased accurately to describe it. For by 1931 his collective actions in vastly expanded public buildings and works produced the largest peacetime budget deficit (almost a half-billion dollars) ever known, and the following year it was yet six times greater—facts for which his Democratic challengers and Congressional critics were strongly to attack him.

By mid-1931, as the financial emergency threatened to produce a major banking crisis, particularly in the South and Midwest among banks too heavily involved in mortgages to farmers and homeowners, bankers increasingly favored the creation of a federal banking structure to lend funds to, and thereby protect, the private banks in trouble from a run by depositors anxious to save themselves. As is now well known, after some hesitancy during which he favored voluntary banker collaboration without government sponsorship, at the end of 1931 Hoover agreed to the creation of a Reconstruction Finance Corporation modeled after the wartime War Finance Corporation and run by men from—or close to—the banking community. A half-billion dollars in loans for banks and business was now available to buttress the economy somewhat. And $125 million to strengthen the Federal Farm Board and land banks was another measure to help the banks indirectly.

The Democratic Congress at this time, as Jordan A. Schwarz has ably proved, simply had no alternative to the Hoover program, and itself reflected the limits of capitalist social analysis and reform. Apart from Hoover's personal difficulties with his party's old guard, which never believed him to be a true Republican, or the dour, impersonal way in which the President failed to make or keep friends, was the far more significant fact of the general collapse of both analysis and alternatives in the political economy. Hoover had free space in which to bungle precisely because of the weaknesses, ineptness, and disunity among all those able to define and impose an alternative program. Hoover's ultimate failure was really the shortcoming of the age in which he ruled, just as his earlier successes had been a reflection of its illusions and drift.[9] All contributed to this dilemma: political parties and their leaders, businessmen, technicians, and academics. Wherever one looks during the period after 1929, there was an absence of clarity, division among constituencies, and confusion.

The New Administration, the New Deal

The men and party that inherited the responsibility of dealing with a depression that was to affect the United States more profoundly and longer than any other industrial nation were distinctly unprepared to transcend the limits of such conceptualizations and programs which were a part of the times. It is one thing to talk of the continuity of approaches between the Roosevelt Administration and that which preceded it, as historians are increasingly wont to do, but another to focus on their common limitations and confusions. Both, indeed, are essential not merely to understanding the origins of the New Deal but also its outcome.

The new President himself was easier to fathom, for as governor of New York State he had established a reputation for being an organization man, eclectic in terms of ideas, quite humanitarian in the sense of the noblesse oblige one would expect of Hudson Valley aristocrats, and superficial. He was no match for his cousin in terms of capacity to read, perceive, or write; and the endlessly complicated discussions of policies and administration, as opposed to politics, caused him to turn inward, listen, and nod as if comprehending. This quality, which was often misinterpreted as agreement rather than merely seeking to look intelligent, often meant that Roosevelt appeared responsive to the last person to talk to him, which frequently produced seemingly sudden changes of policy among warring advisers, who in due course had to hammer out a consensus, if they could, among themselves. Defining the national interest, therefore, was far less Roosevelt's role; it was instead articulated by those who controlled its implementation as well as concrete formulation. The President was less and less able to contribute to either area.

Ideologically, as Frances Perkins, his long-time associate, observed, "Roosevelt took the status quo in our economic system as much for granted as his family."[10] His knowledge of economics, his more acerbic intimate, Raymond Moley, noted, was "limited."[11] His education had been a gentleman's affair and quite casual, and for a short time during the 1920s he served the construction trade association as an executive. He was, both as governor of New York and Presidential candidate, in favor of reduced government spending and a balanced budget, and was aptly called a conservative reformer. His ambiguous criticisms of the Hoover Administration's economic program, and the paucity of his own alternatives, left him great flexibility to follow the advice he badly needed. He had avoided endorsing United States entry into the League of Nations in 1932, and thereby helped contribute greatly, perhaps decisively, to the coalition of Southerners and anti-League forces who won him the hotly contested Presidential nomination. For it was as a politician alone that Roosevelt exhibited great talent—the acquisition rather than the administration of power. And that could satisfy his personal ambitions much more than the economy's needs.

The Democratic Party presented a more complicated picture than the solitary President. It was polarized, to be sure, as always. On the one hand the traditional Southerners were seemingly as much agitated by the prohibition of alcohol and the Catholicism of the Al Smith machine as by a depression which as yet had not touched profoundly the elites who managed the Southern party. The Smith-Raskob coalition had a clear stand only on questions which most concerned the South, and Roosevelt ably maintained ties with both factions. Yet it was the Smith wing that largely wrote the platform, though by consensus the party agreed with its demand for a 25 percent reduction in federal expenditures and the elimination of deficit spending which cast Hoover into the role of economic heterodoxy. Such artificial distinctions, necessary above all shortly before Presidential campaigns, had temporarily upset the bipartisan harmony of the quite immobile, conservative Seventy-second Congress. Still, by their words and actions, the Democrats in 1932 appeared to be the anti-spending party, and beyond that they promised very little to end the Depression.

In one sense, 1932 witnessed some new developments in Congress which were soon to produce distinctive responses to the pressures which the now three-year-old Depression, with its 25 percent unemployment rate in 1933, inevitably had to create. The exaggerated importance of the 1928 election in consolidating the power of the Democrats over urban, immigrant-dominated politics notwithstanding, the fact remains that certain changes in national politics were to prove significant. Apathy during off-year elections remained the rule throughout this period, regardless of the extent of the economic crisis, with 30 to 40 percent participation in cities being the norm. In the 1930 election the Democrats, polling 2 million votes less than the Republicans, still gained a very slight majority of the House seats. With Congressional apportionment in 1932 the 5 million Democratic vote majority produced a vast Democratic dominance in both wings of Congress, and it filled the House in particular with a batch of new, inexperienced, and unsocialized members especially receptive to the desires of their urban labor constituencies. That fact presented the new Executive with both a challenge and opportunity that was to define its first programmatic response to the Depression and the temporarily unruly Congress at one and the same time.

Creating the National Recovery Administration

By the time the Roosevelt Administration assumed power the corporate community had largely failed to advance its own detailed programs for ending the Depression, leaving a dangerous vacuum. Specific industries, such as bituminous coal, had continued to explore various voluntary trade association accords, and the parallel Swope and Chamber of Commerce plans had acquired some additional business backing. But at the very beginning of 1933 the new administration leaders were rightly far more aware of business disunity and indecisiveness than the small measure of consensus. Despite this, both Swope and Henry Harriman—the latter particularly because of his frequent contact with Roosevelt and active lobbying at the beginning of 1933—had planted the seeds that were later to emerge in the NRA's main premises. In this they were joined by cotton-textile and National Association of Manufacturers executives, who energetically knocked on all Washington doors to promote their parallel ideas. They were all to succeed in part because of their power and influence but also because of the good luck of an utter paucity of conservative alternatives when more radical options arose. And because of the total absence of a Democratic and Presidential plan for the future, and scarcely any serious binding campaign pledges to help, it was essential for others to fill a void that the protracted Depression had created.

At the very inception of the new administration it became clear that the President's key advisers as well as top leaders from business and the universities, within the consensus of wishing to preserve capitalism, were divided, both in kind and degree, with varieties and mixtures between them almost as great as the number of interests involved. All they could readily agree upon were fairly abstract ends, with means, however, being the essence of social engineering. The greatest single division was between the remaining spokesmen of the Wilsonian "New Freedom," with its fuzzy notions regarding the restoration of competition and free entry into business, as opposed to the so-called Theodore Roosevelt New Nationalists, with their no less ambiguous notions of regulated big business. None, at least, had an incontrovertible scheme for ending the Depression, and all that their intellectual preferences qualified them to do was join the collective indecisiveness at a higher theoretical plane. And one can make too much of these distinctions, which usually were voiced when the freedom of others to experiment had proved a failure. Opportunism and flexibility were far more characteristic of New Deal thinking than dogma on any theoretical point, not merely among political leaders but among businessmen whose collective vast losses after 1931, which left corporations unprofitable for three years, had undermined fixed notions and self-confidence as no other event in this century.

Louis D. Brandeis and Felix Frankfurter were reputed to be the leaders of the Wilsonian position, with those who had experience with the 1917–1918 War Industries Board—Hugh Johnson in particular—being allegedly for some type of "planning."[12] Others favored the use of credit, or the elimination of government indebtedness, and fiscal techniques, and yet a few wished greater government spending and expansion into the economy. In March, as Roosevelt followed the advice of balanced-budget advocates and Congress cut federal salaries and veterans' aid by one-half billion dollars, Raymond Moley, Roosevelt's then most important adviser, asked James Warburg of the Kuhn, Loeb banking firm to try to meld the assorted and often vague proposals into a common program. By that time, the persistent lobbying of industry trade-association advocates seeking governmental sanction was beginning to have a deeper effect. But when Moley and Roosevelt regarded the divided results that came back, on April 4 they decided to defer national economic planning for industry indefinitely. Two days later they were forced to reverse their position when the Senate overwhelmingly passed the Black Bill and the

House Labor Committee favorably reported it.

The Black Bill, which had been under consideration since the preceding Congress, imposed a maximum thirty-hour work week on industry, which immediately denounced it. Roosevelt and his aides thought it both unconstitutional and likely to further paralyze business, and two responses were forced on them as, in effect, a Congress more eager to act lined up against what was to prove an administration-business alliance. First, he had Secretary of Labor Perkins prepare an alternative to the Black Bill, which ended only by increasing the momentum for the second, and ultimately successful, effort. Raymond Moley was directed to renew the project to come up with an industrial recovery plan predicated on business-government cooperation, and specifically told to review the matter with the Brookings Institution and the United States Chamber of Commerce. Moley immediately got in touch with Hugh Johnson, Bernard Baruch, and individuals who had served on and looked to the War Industries Board as a precedent. They took the Swope-Chamber plan, with federal licensing, as the economic framework which a new board would implement. Parallel to its deliberations, but then merged under Johnson's informal supervision early in May, was a group over which presided Senator Robert Wagner, Undersecretary of Commerce John Dickinson, and Brookings economist Harold Moulton, to which was added the decisive advice of trade-association lawyers, businessmen, bankers, academics, and several Congressmen. Their work was, perhaps unintentionally, facilitated when Perkins on April 25 submitted her alternative to the Black Bill just as the Senate seemed determined to urge the House also to pass it. Her bill, which allowed an increase of the thirty-hour week limit, also included a mechanism to establish minimum wages as well as restrict the output of plants engaged in unfair competition. It also permitted the imposition of trade-association agreements without fear of anti-trust restrictions. To many industry spokesmen, the new cure was worse than the old, and unions also joined the opposition for fear that minimum wages would then become maximum. But hearings on the Black-Perkins plans brought fairly sophisticated attempts by Harriman, Swope, and the president of Standard Oil of New Jersey to blend their own ideas with some of Perkins' mechanisms, and it was now evident that the trade-association concept—with its restrictions on output and price controls—was emerging as articulate business's main solution for its crisis. Undersecretary Dickinson, vehemently opposed to the Black and Perkins approaches, proposed the business synthesis to the Johnson group, using the concept of a ban on child, woman, or sweated labor, as well as minimum wages and maximum hours, to reinforce the very efforts of trade associations against competitive recalcitrants in their own midst. From this time until the President's May 17 release of the collective efforts of his advisers and their helpers, it was plain from press accounts that the trade-association advocates were going to prevail.

Johnson and Baruch had met with numerous key industrialists who came or were invited to Washington over the weeks before publication of the final draft, and they discussed all phases of it—including the famous section 7a presumably allowing labor to organize—in detail. Along the line they dropped key words and introduced ambiguity regarding unionism, and business satisfaction mounted. "Industry has accepted the plan with rather wide acclaim, almost enthusiasm, such as would have been nonexistent a few years back," *Iron Age* observed.[13] The NAM called a group of business leaders to Washington to meet with the drafting committee, and on May 13 endorsed the principle of the NRA. Cotton-textile trade-association leaders, who had labored hard behind the scenes, were delighted with the new proposal. Roosevelt, for his part, envisaged the new relationship with business as the fulfillment of his cousin's "New Nationalism." This sense of historical continuity Senator Wagner, sponsor of the NRA bill in the Senate, also shared. It was to him the realization of the 1912 Progressive Party demand for a "national planned economy" based on cooperation and efficiency in business.[14] How right they were in appreciating the unity of the reform tradition in the twentieth century.

The National Industrial Recovery Act finally permitted industries, after a consultation with the government that was to prove far more nominal than real, the right to draw up legally binding codes enforceable by the courts. It was not government control of industry, Roosevelt made clear in sending the message to Congress, but "a partnership . . . not partnership in profits . . . but rather a partnership in planning, and a partnership to see that the plans are carried out."[15] By any criterion, this was the most comprehensive aspect of the measure, yet at the same time it stopped Congress's near passage of the Black Bill for a thirty-hour week. Section 7a legalized collective bargaining and gave the President the right to fix minimum pay and maximum hours, but such regulations, by eliminating the wage variations that were a key cause of price competition, were mechanisms useful to enforcing trade-association or industrial codes as well. At least some key government experts immediately analyzed the wording as too ambiguous, and the impending administration of the NRA under Johnson too hostile, to help workers meaningfully. As labor soon discovered, it was only the willingness to strike that assured the organization of the unorganized. Unlike the industry code aspect of the bill, it left much yet to be clarified and resolved, particularly regarding the status of company unions. A public works program of $3.3 billion was an added fillip to melt some Congressional resistance, and a federal licensing clause presumably gave the government some new powers.

For business leaders who had favored the trade-association movement, or who had before the World War shared the concerns of Judge Gary and George Perkins regarding competition, the NRA was to become an old aspiration realized. During the first days after the administration released the draft, big business celebrated its success. The May 24 meeting of the American Iron and Steel Institute found an "overwhelming unanimity of sentiment" for the new order; "we gladly accept this offer of partnership," Charles M. Schwab of Bethlehem Steel declared.[16] The meaning of section 7a, Institute president Robert P. Lamont sagely observed, depended on the character of its administration. With many other industries, steel men appreciatively balanced the equivocal section 7a against what they considered the far greater dangers of the now defunct Black Bill—a point they were often to make and which the narrow passage of the final NRA bill in the Senate reinforced. *Coal Age* and *Textile World* shared the glad sentiments, as did the Chamber of Commerce and *Business Week*. Over the next weeks, as the more pro-labor House tightened the wording of section 7a, business spokesmen attacked the deviations from the original and they used the most exaggerated terms to denounce amendments. But in the end the Senate cut the edge of most revisions, and with the act's signature on June 16 the industry was pleased and confident that friendly administrators would interpret the substantial ambiguities of law; and the eulogies of labor leaders for the measure once again proved premature.

The Struggle for Industrial Control

The NIRA law said little about the substance of industry-wide codes other than that the industry itself might draw them up—and the President sanction or reject them—to promote such lofty but vague goals as fair competition as well as cooperation, greater production and purchasing power as well as employment, and the like. Industry codes were also to be drafted with the participation of consumers and labor, but they were never to be consulted. For practical purposes, the NRA was to create over 500 cockpits where the various factions of every type of industry might struggle for mastery of political authority as they had long since competed for shares of the marketplace. The controls of economic and political power, in effect, were now to become synonymous.

The NRA thereby became the main focus of the administration's initial response to the Depression, transferring to each industry the responsibility of bringing general prosperity via consolidation of its own. If other programs of public works and spending were carried on at the same time, until the end of 1934 industrial self-government remained the central New Deal pillar. In the aggregate, as Ellis W. Hawley has convincingly shown, the former trade-association regulations which could not be applied in the 1920s now became the NRA codes, but in the process firms within each industry continued their competitive struggle for domination of the market and each other. On the whole, the biggest firms within each industry were able to define the final codes that were to emerge—much to the unhappiness and disadvantage of smaller firms. It was as if, indeed, the events of the 1920s were being rerun with higher, more binding stakes. "Competition" and "individualism" became terms of opprobrium, on the assumption that conditions that had distressed larger firms rather than far more comprehensive, structural economic forces were responsible for the crisis. But General Johnson, surrounded by businessmen now serving as his assistants, gave ample scope for the association concept to finally prove its viability. With few, if any, restrictions, each industry was allowed to define its own price and production codes, which every industry was generally to do in accordance with the distribution of political power each faction of the industry possessed to impose its will. The NRA thereby became a tool of big business, with an only incidental relationship to recovery.

Several specific examples illustrate the structures the NRA encouraged.

The Cotton Textile Institute, the industry's trade association, viewed the NRA proposal as its major opportunity to impose stabilizing price and production codes with legal sanction, and both privately and publicly it celebrated the new era. In May, even before the passage of the act, at the behest of General Johnson it enthusiastically began drawing up its own code, thereby initiating a harmonious relation that gave the industry's larger firms full scope finally to test their associational theories. Johnson, for his part, in due course appointed a former cotton manufacturer to represent the government. Because the industry was already in favor of the forty-hour week to limit production, and Northern manufacturers favored minimum wages to increase the costs of their Southern competitors, the industry had fewer difficulties than all others in hammering out a common program of legal sanctions. It was the first code enacted.

Cotton textiles now had a legal basis for limiting industry expansion and cutthroat competition. The automobile industry, by contrast, was not competitive and had substituted working oligopoly for trade associations, which were most active precisely among those industries with a high number of firms or easy entry. Stated another way, from 1929 to 1932 auto prices dropped 21 percent while cotton textiles fell precisely twice that amount, and the auto industry was one of the last to cooperate with the NRA—if only because Henry Ford's obduracy created innumerable barriers to doing so. But although the new cotton-textile authority now had a free hand internally, its problems, much to its surprise, remained far greater than its means. For one thing, large industrial consumers of cotton products, such as tire manufacturers, attacked the premises of the new price-fixing and much preferred the old order of industry chaos from which they had profited. Critical was the fact that it was exceedingly difficult for the code authority to anticipate overproduction and time its restrictions accordingly, though it attempted to do so. More to the point, the objective of the entire effort was profit, and although industry income increased during 1933, the following year profits fell by three-quarters, and over half the firms in the industry reported no net profit. Disillusionment was inevitable, especially among Southern producers who had conceded many of their cost advantages in order to test cooperation. Many turned a jaundiced eye on all other New Deal innovations and concluded, especially after Johnson's forced departure in August 1934, that the collaboration was not worth the results. In 1935 profits again fell, and the CTI removed those leaders who had taken it into the NRA adventure. Hoping to head off chaos, New England producers in 1935 successfully sought to use their governors to organize a new federal effort to redeem the industry, and the White House cooperated in creating a special cotton committee. It, in turn, considered a wide range of proposals for government control of the industry, ranging from higher labor costs to machinery destruction, but only in the following year did legislation arise which dealt mainly with textile labor—and it was not considered at the time. In effect, what this rather typical competitive industry learned by mid-1935 was that the economic problems it confronted far exceeded any response based on organizational unity, whether politically enforced or voluntary. The industry that had invested the greatest hopes in trade associationism for the longest time was to finally find its illusions shattered.

But the Northern millowners only bided their time for a year before returning to their older strategy of equalizing labor costs with their Southern rivals by supporting "humanitarian" wages and labor legislation for all workers. Thus, in May 1937 an alliance of Northern conservatives and liberals, plus a few Southern dissidents, began what was to prove an over-one-year struggle for a national minimum wage and hours law which was widely regarded as primarily protection for the Northern cotton-textile industry. Its forty-cent-an-hour, forty-hour-a-week provisions and ban on child labor in interstate commerce affected the Southern textile producers most of all, and the movement to stop it in the House had the backing of four-fifths of the Southerners.

In the trucking industry, the great ease of entry and intensified competition after 1929 created among larger trucking firms a desire both for federal regulation that would end cutthroat rates as well as, in some cases, unionization that would equalize costs. Railroads, for their part, had throughout the 1920s favored federal regulation of trucking to reduce its increasingly costly competitive impact on their share of the market for transportation. Even before 1932 some large truckers began demanding Interstate Commerce Commission regulation of the industry, and at the end of that year the American Highway Freight Association was formed for the primary objective of passing a federal regulatory act comprehensive enough to eliminate the problems of one of the most competitive industries. The association enthusiastically endorsed the NRA and urged rate-fixing as part of the industry code, but opposition from more competitive truckers who had formed their own trade association in the hope of also shaping the code forced the NRA to demand that the two groups unite and create a common program. This they did by organizing the American Trucking Association, which agreed upon a modified rate-fixing system, which required truckers to charge at least the cost of the service. Backing rate-fixing, as well, was the Teamsters Union, which saw it as indispensable to ending the great wage inequalities in the cutthroat industry. Fair labor practices and unionism, bigger truckers appreciated, would drive up costs and undermine marginal operators. When the NRA code for trucking was finally approved, the ATA, with an important degree of industry backing, dominated the code authority.

Anti-union sentiment as well as business and personal reasons all led to resistance from other truckers, who then undertook to lobbying for the older formula of ICC regulation of all trucking as a way of circumventing the NRA. Early in 1934 such a bill was submitted in the Congress and its main attraction was inflexible tariffs. The struggle between these two viewpoints was not resolved quickly, because important shipping interests who preferred competition blocked more sweeping rate-fixing under the NRA authority. Given the complex nature of rate structures and the intensely competitive nature of the truckers, by 1935 large operators were increasingly disappointed with the laxity of the NRA system of regulation. During May 1935, days before the Supreme Court declared the NRA unconstitutional, the National Industrial Recovery Board ruled that cost could no longer be used as a basis of minimum prices or rates—thereby destroying a truckers' code that, in any case, was not being strictly applied. With the Court decision the ATA and its critics in the industry joined forces with the railroads to demand ICC regulation, which quickly became law the following August. Free entry into the industry was virtually ended, as rate regulation and safety and hours controls reduced the nuisances of competition. The NRA had failed, but regulation was deferred rather than ended.

The petroleum industry also sought to find in enforced cooperation the profits and stability that eluded its internecine nature, and during the NRA period the vast majority of the industry's leaders and the American Petroleum Institute supported the principle of national regulation, but since its details were left to them to define, their important divisions immediately came to the fore. Roosevelt, for his part, was close to J. A. Moffett, a Standard of New Jersey vice president, and the President inclined to reestablishing something akin to the wartime Fuel Administration. That organization's director, Mark Requa, provided a direct link to the 1920s' abortive American Petroleum Institute price and output accords. Requa, among other top oil industry representatives, helped define the essentially intra-industry dispute over desirable forms of regulation. While the potential NRA role was being ironed out in conference rooms, parallel efforts were under way in various oil-producing states, which began intensifying controls on output, and in Congress. In the House, Representative E. W. Marland of Oklahoma, himself a large oil producer, during April 1933 introduced a bill making interstate shipments of oil in excess of state-regulated limits illegal. This measure, which had Roosevelt's and Secretary of Interior Harold Ickes' backing, gained wide industry support. Over subsequent weeks, as overproduction in the industry reached crisis proportions, Southwestern governors and oilmen divided on the Marland bill, some wanting total federal control of output in Ickes' hands. But Roosevelt and Ickes circumvented the dispute by simply inserting the main Marland bill provisions into the final National Industrial Recovery Act. Oil in excess of state quotas could now be kept from the national market. All that was left was for the API to formulate a code for the NRA authority to review.

The API did its work during June in conjunction with the top leaders of big oil as well as independent producers, who deeply split on the question of minimum prices not by size of firm or even by enterprise but on the basis of personalities and their calculations as to what would best serve their companies' needs. But, at least initially, they approved output and price controls temporarily. When the API and major industry leaders arrived at the NRA hearings the following month, Walter C. Teagle, Standard of Jersey's president, was serving as the NRA adviser, and the top executives of the major oil firms immediately divided on government price-fixing and much else besides. Teagle opposed it, as did Johnson, but Standard's J. A. Moffett disagreed, and this division—which led to Moffett losing his job—led to total paralysis and adjournment. In the end, Ickes, who favored price-fixing, managed to obtain administration of the oil code and run it with contingent powers of price-fixing (which he was never forced to apply) satisfying to most of the industry. He had greater controls over production, and by the fall of 1933 had so reduced output that his support from the API and major firms now assured future cooperation. Regulation proved its merit for the industry, allowing it finally to place reins on a competitive structure that had become too volatile. Henceforth, the intimate cooperation of private and public officials for the welfare of the industry, whatever form it took, became a durable precedent. And when court decisions in 1934 weakened the NRA code, sectors of the industry endorsed a federal oil bill to control output, but it died in Congress. After the NRA was declared illegal the oil companies could return to the state regulatory bodies for assistance, which most now thought preferable if they could use federal law to reinforce their decisions, and in August 1935 Congress passed such an act. While for a time Ickes urged the major firms to attempt to force fixed prices, they made use of the existing system and their concentrated power to impose new stability on the industry. Thus began a process of industry-government integration that has lasted until this day.

While nearly 600 different industry codes provided ample diversity, the continuity between trade associationism of the 1920s and the NRA, and the use of political power by business constituencies to meet their goals of profitability during a crisis, in a number of industries meshed with the problem of unionism. The trucking and cotton-textile industries proved that the elimination of price competition was impossible without roughly comparable wage costs, and in labor-intensive industries this equalization was all the more imperative. If the industries were highly competitive, as in garments or coal, labor costs were a key—if not the only means—to price stabilization; but if they were controlled by a sufficiently small number of firms to allow oligopolistic collaboration independent of government enforcement, the question of labor became more a threat than a promise. In the latter case, the automobile industry was an excellent example.

Production-worker costs as a percentage of the value of automobiles during the 1930s were substantially higher than the national manufacturing average despite a near total absence of unionization at the inception of the New Deal. The handful of auto firms had no need for the NRA code to impose unifying price or output practices on the industry, its NRA code contained none of consequence, and the section 7a provisions simply reflected the industry desire to prevent the emergence of unionism. In the steel industry, which was even more labor intensive but somewhat less concentrated, the NRA code was left sufficiently vague regarding labor organizations to allow numerous companies to create company unions. The NRA labor board was powerless to challenge seriously the industry-dominated codes, which merely perpetuated the status quo and ignored union pressures. Ickes and Johnson, for their part, showed as much disdain for unions as did businessmen. Virtually all of the anxieties regarding the NRA, Johnson, and unions which the rare pro-labor New Dealers shared were realized.

In the garment industry, however, the union alone possessed the potential means for imposing price stability, for unequal labor costs were the key to "unfair competition." Trade associations, which had sought to work intimately with the unions, were alone unable to impose stability, and when the NRA received its first code submission from three New York employer groups in the women's garment industry they dealt almost exclusively with wages, hours, and working conditions—a focus that became the rule for almost a year. In the women's coat and suit industry code the wording was virtually the same as in earlier collective bargaining agreements. For both in women's and men's clothing industries the large majority of the employers were now ready to use the only organizational method of stabilization available—unionization. Under the circumstances, unlike any other mass industry save the comparable coal sector, the union membership in the two major garment unions—both of which considered themselves socialist-led—multiplied.

Still the industry remained thoroughly cutthroat, and geographical wage differentials accepted in some of the codes simply were a union effort to accommodate to the existence of runaway plants and sweatshops in return for the right to collect the dues of non–New York workers. In time, politically powerful clothing employers were able to get additional modifications imposed on the codes by arguing that the existing accords reflected the needs of the dominant portion of the industry and unions in New York. Thereupon began a litigatious and increasingly divisive struggle to use the code authorities—usually belatedly—to enforce what were essentially collective-bargaining rules, a process that the outlawing of the NRA terminated before total disintegration occurred. From that time on, the unions and certain branches of the ladies' garment industry sought to maintain substitutes for the NRA machinery, though in the men's industry the effort to reassert the control of effective unionism was attempted once again. In both sectors the effort to stabilize the industry by equalizing labor costs broke down, leaving the inexorable laws of competitive capitalism to levy their toll on workers and owners alike.

Bituminous coal, to cite another example proving continuity over the two decades, by 1931 was ready for outside control, and many mineowners regarded any externally imposed stability—whether government or union—as preferable to the chaos in an industry which saw its income fall by almost three-quarters from 1923 to 1932. In late 1931 *Coal Age* proposed an ambiguous scheme arguing that the heart of attaining the stabilization which voluntary efforts had for years failed to produce was the equalization of wage costs and working conditions, and although it denied that this necessarily meant unionization or government supervision, the sentiment reflected the fact that employers were searching for solutions. Those the United Mine Workers had proposed in the Davis-Kelly bill in January 1932, creating a government coal commission to supervise producer accords and encourage unionization, *Coal Age* rejected as a "legislative" bribe.[17] The coal industry, despite its economic collapse, remained both confused and divided. Still, less individualist interests, speaking through *Coal Age,* took the creation of the NRA as the opportunity to attempt to redeem the industry—even by putting a floor on wages.

Like all decentralized competitive industries, coal had numerous internal divisions which a common code could not easily resolve, and thereupon began a battle for its domination. A group of larger firms in the Eastern fields at first tried to preempt the rest of the industry, and it was quite prepared to bring the United Mine Workers into the stabilization effort. The UMW, for its part, embarked on a vast unionization drive, which in three months increased its membership from 100,000 to half a million, thereby establishing itself as a major factor in any coal industry accords. During this organization drive, strikes threatened to destroy code negotiations, of which John L. Lewis and the UMW had become an integral part; and Lewis, by forcing militant miners back to work, further consolidated the labor brokerage role the UMW was destined to play. But the factions prevailed, and the competitive structure of the industry continued with nothing remotely approximating the output and pricing power of other industry codes. The only uniformities automatically imposed—and here the *Coal Age* sentiment found expression—were minimum-wage and maximum-hour provisions, even though numerous regional wage variations were allowed. The status of the UMW was left ambiguous, though in fact its current strike demands were largely acknowledged obliquely. For the time being, the decentralized industry, too divided politically and in terms of interests to unite, was left to its own devices.

The UMW then turned to lobbying in Congress for a national coal commission empowered to fix minimum wages as well as prices and output restrictions, but it got nowhere until the NRA was outlawed. Then the coalition of the UMW and the major Eastern firms came back into de facto operation, using John L. Lewis' threat of a national coal strike to goad Congress into action. Dropping production restrictions to avoid the Supreme Court's certain wrath, in August 1935 the Guffey-Snyder Act embodied the core of the UMW and big operators' proposals dating back to before the NRA. Thereupon began the same struggle among coal producers over minimum prices and trade practices that had earlier divided them, until the Court outlawed the act in May 1936. Dropping the labor clauses, in early 1937 Congress passed the coal economics provisions as the Guffey-Vinson Act, but continuing disputes between coal operators, railroads, and big consumers of coal kept the law from being applied until late 1940. By that time the use of regulation as a mode of inter-firm rivalry had partially lost its value as impending war began bringing prosperity for all.

The NRA was soon attacked for serving as the instrument of big business against smaller firms, but this accusation was at best only partially just in those highly competitive economic sectors in which "big business" had no large share of the market. But almost immediately it became apparent that, on the whole, the judgment was valid. And assisting the small-business and labor critique were the political ineptness and hot temper of General Johnson and his increasingly unilateral and personalized direction of the entire NRA. It was not long before the NRA price and production controls were under mounting fire, and the administration's appointment of a review board under Clarence Darrow, despite its exotic, personal alternatives, only further reinforced small-business attacks on the NRA as an instrument of monopoly. More to the point was the fact that, political controversy apart, the NRA was not solving the problems of the Depression. Johnson was removed the following August, and, until the face-saving May 1935 Supreme Court decision outlawing it, the NRA remained on the scene as an increasingly uncomfortable and less utilitarian reminder of the failure of a major aspect of capitalist planning. The administration did not try to revive it.

Financial Reform

The New Deal economic program by 1935 had increasingly to depend on specific measures independent of the NRA as such, and the reform of the stock market and securities industry was perhaps the best example of these. While the Investment Bank Association had since the war endorsed the principle of federal regulation of investment securities without being able to agree upon some bill, by 1932, with over 2000 dealers out of business and many of the rest losing money, and with some of the very pillars of the industry on the brink of failure, the investment leadership strongly favored federal regulation to end the manipulation and marginal dealerships that had introduced many of the most competitive and dubious practices. And in banking, with 2300 bank suspensions in 1931, the largest banks desired new reforms of the national banking system to reintroduce stability.

In investment securities, many big banks that had entered the field during the 1920s were ready, even eager, to divorce the ultimately risky business from their normal banking functions, and both the Chase National—the largest in the country—and National City Bank shared this opinion. National City, indeed, actually did so before any new laws were passed. Winthrop W. Aldrich, head of Chase, particularly favored this change, and his public advocacy of such a reform in March 1933 pushed administration thinking in his direction. Such alterations impinged on both banking and investment-securities reforms, and it was in the latter field that the pressure for changes first bore fruit.

Drafting of the securities law began in early March, and, to the cordial approval of the financial press, Roosevelt at the end of March announced that new legislation would shortly follow. But the first draft was such "a hopeless and unintelligible confection," according to Moley, that he asked Felix Frankfurter to supervise an entirely new draft.[18] The IBA, too, thought it ineffective. At Moley's insistence, but to the increasing irritation of Frankfurter and his aides, W. Averell Harriman and a small circle of top Wall Street financiers and lawyers were consulted throughout the drafting process, but in the end, despite the Harvard professor's testiness toward yet more big-business interventions, a mutually acceptable law was drafted. Frankfurter later defined his role as a "moderating influence," and the official historian of the IBA called the law a "conservative response to a widespread demand for reform."[19] At the time, however, it was not sufficient to consult Wall Street and ignore the IBA, which, despite its advocacy of a model federal law, sharply reacted to the slight by criticizing numerous details of the bill that was to pass as the Federal Securities Act in May 1933. Its prohibitions against fraud and the concealment of information were the distinctly minimal changes that larger industry firms desired, and it was not long before aggressive operators located the law's loopholes.

More important to the investment industry was the Glass-Steagall Act of the following month, which required the complete separation of commercial and investment banking but was better known for its creation of federal deposit insurance. It was drawn up with the help of Aldrich, but the New York bankers nevertheless believed the law did not go far enough. Continued dubious practices and new episodes of wild speculation won yet more bankers and businessmen to the same view and convinced the administration as well that it could not rely the on the self-reform the New York Stock Exchange had promised.

The first draft of Congress's February 1934 bill to regulate the stock exchanges was surely not the measure Aldrich and his profession had hoped for, but it provided them a basis for extensive revisions and gave pro-reform New York investment bankers a handle for gaining needed changes. These they obtained, especially when they secured transfer of the enforcement of the new securities regulation from the FTC to a new commission. The final bill did not entirely please anyone, but it embodied provisions that New York investment bankers desired, and, apart from its full-disclosure and technical requirements, its broad purpose was to found a Securities and Exchange Commission with wide discretionary powers to regulate the industry. The law was enacted that June, and the appointment to its head of Joseph P. Kennedy, himself a former major speculator, confirmed to pro-reform large financiers that they would have their way.

Revision of the banking system rounded out the financial community's need for new institutional mechanisms for stabilization, and men such as Aldrich were convinced that the lack of a unified banking system had created the thousands of bank failures which had required Roosevelt, virtually as his first act as President, to declare a bank holiday in March 1933. Although most bankers had opposed comprehensive new reforms before 1933, they had generally favored changes leading to further centralization and uniformity in specific aspects of banking. By the spring of 1933 the American Bankers Association's policy committee had been jolted into favoring greater powers for the Federal Reserve System. They and other leading spokesmen supported the modest May 1933 banking bill that Senator Carter Glass—with Aldrich's help—had presented, save for its deposit insurance provision. But the new banking act left much undone, and many bankers knew it.

Aldrich was close to Senator Glass, author of the 1913 Federal Reserve Act as well as the 1933 law, and he had seen the President a number of times on an informal and increasingly friendly basis. Moreover, after September 1934 he became a prime mover in the ABA's committee on banking law reform. When the unorthodox Utah banker and Federal Reserve Board member, Marriner Eccles, had a vast revision of existing laws introduced into the House in February 1935, Aldrich and his peers seized the opportunity. Roosevelt himself, unable to comprehend the issues, stood aside while two groups of bankers-turned-reformers fought one another. Behind Eccles stood the House of Representatives and maverick bankers such as Amadeo Giannini of the California banking empire, Bank of America, who feared that anything New York attained would damage his interests. Glass and the Senate, along with some administration members like RFC head and Aldrich's friend, Jesse Jones, backed the Aldrich-ABA proposals. The ABA president reported that he and bankers across the country were also pleased with the final compromise, and as Aldrich's official biographer concludes, "The provisions of the 1935 act were quite close to what Aldrich and the ABA had advocated."[20] Glass thought he had completely emasculated Eccles' bill, but the latter thought he too had gained a victory—and all that is certain is that two rival banking factions had an acceptable new law.

In one sense, all the new measure did was to implement the centralizing intent of the original 1913 law by moving a large number of powers back to a smaller board of seven men in Washington. These did not exclude the New York Reserve Bank, which was sure to be one of the five districts the new board had to consult before reaching major decisions. But it also meant that hitherto ignored policies would have to be observed throughout the national banking structure, and a vital centralization was thereby implemented. Control over the appointment of regional chief officers, a much larger voice over rediscount rates and reserve requirements throughout the nation, and new means for imposing regulations on large state banks all reversed the dangerous deconcentration New York bankers so feared after 1929. Along with the passage of the Public Utility Holding Company Act the same month, giving the SEC the responsibility of enforcing it, Congress had rounded out the new stabilization of the banking and investment sectors via federal regulation that the Depression made imperative. Using political means, big banking could now impose its norms on a national banking structure that had proved elusive to its economic control. In the minds of numerous financial leaders, there was simply no way to restore the investor's confidence and prosperity under the old rules, which had brought disaster to many of them and might do worse in the future. They welcomed the new order they had helped fashion after such a close brush with fate.

The new order, of course, was the much more technically obscure one of administrative politics, and it further moved decisions from legislators to lawyers and the members of government boards who would thereafter listen to them. The history of banking and railroad regulation had proved salutary in creating a synthesis between a client agency and the industry it increasingly served, merging the technical personnel of each and assigning to the government the responsibilities for effective management of this or that industry. The ICC had begun this unification of political and economic power in 1887, and during the 1930s it had long since become assumed as a desirable relationship—one that the radio and aviation industries had also begun to pursue with their counterparts in Washington.

The new SEC embodied these decades-old premises of using government sanctions to back private power. "We . . . do not regard ourselves as coroners sitting on the corpse of financial enterprise," Joseph Kennedy immediately declared. "On the contrary, we think of ourselves as the means of bringing new life into the body of the security business."[21] The IBA, which for years had futilely tried to regulate itself and end the competition which had deprived the less aggressive of business but ultimately helped bring near-universal calamity, so welcomed the new standards that in 1938 it managed to get the industry's trade code, which the Supreme Court's NRA nullification had automatically wrecked, included under the SEC's jurisdiction. "In one month," an industry accountant observed in early 1935, "the SEC has set . . . standards . . . for the profession, which years of futile committee work within the professional societies have not been able to produce."[22] By 1939, as the exchange of personnel between the SEC and the industry deepened the ties of understanding and cooperation, the SEC was well along in wholly institutionalizing and stabilizing, within the framework of collectively agreed rules, the main securities institutions. Compared to earlier decades it was another era altogether.

In all this, the New York interests came out ahead of all the others, gaining stability along with mastery. Aldrich's official biographer judged correctly when he observed that "in his Washington activity . . . he was serving his bank as well as the banking community," for the results proved it.[23] From January 1934 until June 1939, twenty New York houses managed nearly four-fifths of all stock issues registered with the SEC, but they managed 100 percent of all those receiving a top-quality rating. By any criterion, the city's preeminence was now assured.

Despite stormy political words that were not to dissolve the financial reforms the New Deal created—words that were harshest from those businessmen who had gained the least or when elections and politics required them—the period 1933–1936 revealed which businessmen and interests were heeded during the programmatic vacuum which existed from the inception of the Roosevelt Administration. The business structure was composed of large numbers of interests with a great variety of necessarily quite conflicting needs and objectives, and to radically varying degrees their political power was unequal. The trade associations usually represented the larger sectors of any industry, and partially as a reflection of this fact specifically small business trade associations begin to appear after 1937. To the extent that differing groups had equal access to political power in Congress, or no overwhelming coalition of firms existed, as in bituminous coal, regulation of an industry became impossible as economic competition created a neutralizing political deadlock and prevented any decisive reforms. When such business disunity was absent, or no important group resisted lobbying efforts that the Chamber of Commerce or comparable organizations mounted, capitalists could define the essentials of the regulation they had conceptualized as desirable and politically expedient in such a way as to provide themselves with what they hoped would be political solutions for economic dilemmas. In the case of the NRA, the political structure showed itself to be socialized wholly by capitalism's priorities and personnel, and aggressive economic constituencies thereby imposed politically those economic constraints that otherwise would have been beyond their own capacity.

Politics becomes the means, once again, to engage more successfully in business. To Harriman, Swope, Aldrich, and men able to telephone and receive deferential, polite audiences, political responses to economic threats were conceivable in a way that would never enter the mind of a Kansas grain merchant. To the former, their political power exceeded their economic, and gave them a means by which better to solve their economic difficulties. Given the paucity of programmatic alternatives and the consensus of values and institutional mechanisms that bound together the ever-changing New Deal leaders and the directors of big industry and finance, it was logical that it was to the latter that Washington would turn. This consensual framework assumed only a predictable number of legislative alternatives, and it constrained the tactical social visions and political space within which the first New Deal could operate. Given, as well, the limits of capitalist social knowledge which the structural economic context and the compounded problems and policy failures of preceding decades had imposed, by 1936 the dilemma confronting both big business and a political leadership necessarily symbiotic on its vision and direction was that the economic programs the various influential capitalist constituencies had imposed on it were not solving the overall crisis of American capitalism that had existed since 1930 but had its roots in the maturation of the system after 1919.

The Effects of Crisis

The magnitude of the Depression defies description of the human suffering and consequences, just as it defied the New Deal's efforts to find means to terminate it. The Roosevelt Administration's intent, of course, was easier to discern, but the extent of the structural economic crisis in which American capitalism was locked has attracted far less attention. In the simplest terms, however, it can be argued that the government and the men it listened to had answers only to their immediate concerns of profitability and competition, and when these solutions failed, the fragile business-political alliance that defined the first New Deal's economic program fell apart, and business attacked Roosevelt just as it had his predecessor. Thereafter, a slower pace of action and increasing perplexity dominated what is called the second New Deal, which also failed. The government did not conceive of addressing itself to the structural origins of capitalist maturity that had helped bring on the Depression, and it scarcely tried to do more than palliate the human consequences of the collapse with relief and a multitude of alphabetized responses—AAA, WPA, CCC, and PWA. Two fundamental issues—underconsumption and the growing efficiency of industrial capital and its effects on employment—it hardly acknowledged and only incidentally touched with its programs.

Unemployment in 1933 amounted to 12.8 million persons, or almost one-quarter of the labor force. But in 1938, with the gross national product virtually equal to 1929, 10.4 million persons, equal to 19 percent of the labor force, remained unemployed, and almost 9 million more people were out of work than in 1929. Whatever the New Deal tried to do fell behind the inexorable crisis of a mature capitalism no longer able to expand sufficiently.

Despite the decline of capital input during the 1930s, industry's efficiency in terms of productivity continued to increase, both absolutely and in relation to output. Even if the productivity explosion of the 1920s was not remotely equaled, capital was still becoming more efficient in a condition of declining or stagnating output and low investment. In 1937 manufacturing output exceeded 1929 by 3.3 percent, but man-hours had fallen 11.6 percent, while in mining the change was greater yet. A manufacturing worker in 1938 could produce about 15 percent more goods per hour than in 1929. Changes in the occupational structure toward a greater white-collar population did not insulate the economy against this catastrophic trend, for urban clerical and sales workers on relief in 1934 were about 12 percent of the national urban recipients—only marginally less than their share of the occupational distribution. Seen from this perspective, there was a fundamental tension between the New Deal's necessary and predictable devotion to preserving capitalism and bringing the Depression to an end with the limited means available to it. In fact, by 1938 the structural problems of American capitalism had far exceeded the capacity of the political system to cope with them.

The NRA program itself was never concerned with the underconsumptionist dilemma of productive capacity exceeding consumer demand, or with fundamental revision of the income and tax structure. Yet it was only by vastly increased consumption, which the existing distribution of wealth grossly restricted, that industrial productivity could be reconciled with full employment. In June 1935, in response to the agitation and growing political appeal of Huey Long and a coterie of comparable demogogic proselytizers busy gathering a significant following, the Roosevelt Administration proposed a tax reform that even his later eulogists doubted he wanted passed in its original form, if at all. The President himself was distinctly reticent about the measure, in part because of upper-income protests, but in the end conservatives got the major revisions they demanded. Although the maximum possible income tax rate was sharply increased, so were the loopholes, so that the actual rate on the highest incomes collected in 1938 was lower than in 1932. Indeed, the Roosevelt Administration simply did not believe in relying on the income tax to finance the sharply augmented federal budget until the advent of World War Two, preferring to accept larger deficits. Federal receipts from income taxes as opposed to other sources fell radically during the New Deal compared to the Hoover period, and as late as 1939 only one-tenth of the national personal income was subject to income taxes at a time that the wealthiest fifth of the income earners received nearly one-half of the income. Not for a moment did the New Deal endanger the existing distribution of income and wealth, and hence it could not cope successfully with the collapse of American capitalism.

The enlarged system of welfare and social security institutions established during the 1930s also reflected a persistent conservatism prevalent in the Executive and Congress. The Social Security Act which Congress passed in the summer of 1935 was based on regressive tax principles and intended to be self-supporting and "actuarially sound," as the Social Security Administration later phrased it. It played no economic role at all during this decade, and even as late as 1967 only 26 percent of the income of the 65-and-over population came from Social Security. Its unemployment insurance measures were no less conservative, and its provisions reflected the ideas of a coalition of politicians, moderate social reformers, and businessmen like Harriman and the Chamber of Commerce who tailored the final draft. Long-time proponents of such a system thought the new measure worse than nothing at all, and wished to see it defeated out of justifiable fear it would prevent the eventual passage of an adequate bill later. The weaknesses of the system were immense, ranging from only partial coverage of the labor force to regressive funding and short duration, and its first real test, during the 1948–1949 contraction, showed that by making up only one-eighth of the loss of disposable income it was close to useless as an anti-depressionary device and cushion against suffering. Health insurance and the utterly inadequate state-based workmen's compensation system never even became issues during the decade.

The New Deal's response to the misery the Depression produced was always tentative and partially improvised because of its premature optimism regarding economic recovery. Beginning with the Civilian Conservation Corps for youth in March 1933, which was eventually to spend over $2.5 billion—and then an initial half-billion-dollar state and local relief-grant program that eventually and unexpectedly reached almost $3 billion and had as many as 5½ million individuals and families on its rolls at one time—the New Deal jumped from one agency and program to another as it found costs exceeding anticipations, and with few tangible results save new parks, airports, and the like. By 1935, with almost $2 billion spent, Roosevelt and his advisers thoroughly disliked the concept of relief and the budget deficits it engendered, but in that year they initiated the Works Progress Administration with the hope it could produce more useful and eventually less costly results. But any effort to reduce state or local programs merely created area relief crises, and such relief, with or without productive work, was reluctantly built into the system for as long as the Depression lasted. It was unintended and unplanned, but unavoidable.

The question of relief was greatly exacerbated by the astonishing and wholly unpredictable developments in the structure of American agriculture which the collapse of the urban sector produced. Throughout the 1920s, the number of farms but especially the farm population began significantly declining. Beginning with the Depression and until 1935, despite the calamitous drop which made 1932 farm income less than half that of 1929, migration back to the farms caused more than half a million new farms to be created during a crisis of agricultural overproduction. Thereafter farms fell off sharply. Affecting the Appalachians and the Corn Belt most strongly, this phenomenon touched the entire nation. The starkest poverty became more and more common.

In one sense, what is less surprising than the reemergence of agrarian discontent during this period is the fact that there was not vastly more of it than manifested itself in the much-investigated Farm Bureau, Farmers' Union, Farmers' Holiday movements, Southern Tenant Farmers' unions, and associated militant groups that blockaded roads, struck, marched, and caused occasional threats of a revolution that was never to occur. Given the magnitude of the farm crisis and misery, which in many regions was far worse than in the cities, it is more critical to understand that none of these groups managed to channel the great bulk of the farmers into their ranks, but that during this period and thereafter the virtually semi-official, conservative Farm Bureau, representing the better-off farmers and politically close to the Democratic Party, emerged as the strongest of the organized farm minorities. The rest, particularly the Farmers' Union, shared more in common with the Bureau than divided them, and the similarity in the higher economic standing and preference for political mobilization without deep ideological convictions of both these groups meant that the two main wings of the farmers' movement would not stray far. Both the Bureau and Union, in any case, by 1932 found it possible to agree on a common program, and that fragile unity was more important than that which separated them. As it was, during the 1930s they both landed in the Democratic Party with varying degrees of fervor.

In any event, both the new Secretary of Agriculture, Henry Wallace, and the New Deal's May 1933 Agricultural Adjustment Act pleased the Farm Bureau, which was duly consulted in the drafting of its parity payments scheme. The Farmers' Union, while more reticent, also indirectly backed the administration's efforts. The AAA reduced the quantity of basic crops by assigning acreage allotments, in exchange for which farmers were given government payments. Local committees of farmers assigned these critical allotments. Restricting cultivation and food production, despite national outcries, soon became less consequential than the successful efforts of larger farmers to monopolize subsidies for restrictions, farm mortgage help, and the numerous favors that piled up with each new federal program and appropriation. At the local administrative level, the Farm Bureau dominated the AAA until the Supreme Court nullified the law in January 1936, but controlled its replacements thereafter. On the whole, the wealthier farmers until this day receive the lion's share of the benefits of the New Deal's response to the agrarian crisis.

In terms of human consequences, the New Deal's farm program left the farm crisis largely intact. The fact that gross farm income increased during the first New Deal (at a rate not different from the 1932–1933 increase before the 1933 laws took effect) does not alter the fact that the income distribution among farmers left the very poor in misery. That deprivation, which became far better known after 1935, and which the New Deal's subsequent legislation could do little to mitigate, was ultimately only alleviated by the next war and the return of full employment—that is, in the resumed decline of the farm population.

In 1935 the Labor Department and WPA calculated a "basic maintenance" budget which they admitted "does not approach the content of what may be considered a satisfactory American standard of living," nor, to interpolate, the level of consumption that the structural dilemma of the economy demanded for full employment.[24] Minimally austere, it excluded a car, electric refrigerator, gas stove, savings, a varied diet, and much else besides. During 1935–1936, at least 49 percent of the nation's families and unrelated individuals lived below it, while 28 percent were at a much starker "emergency" level which, over time, threatened them with serious health hazards.

By any standard, American capitalism and its reform movements had failed on an economic level by 1936 both in the vast urban centers as well as throughout the countryside. No European economy save Germany's had been so profoundly affected by the Depression, or for so long. But while the United States economy had failed economically it was still not periled at the political level from the Left, which only grew weaker and was at no time strong. What assured stability was not the capacity of the economy to find solutions that permanently solved problems in a measurable way—for the unprecedented extent of poverty and the degradation of relief showed that was not to be the case—but the absence of a social and political threat from the working class. Accompanying its economic failure, American capitalism had a seemingly inexhaustible abundance of what may be called, for lack of a better phrase, "social time." Until the conditions that had produced that phenomenon—which had no equivalent in any industrialized nation save in a virtually identical society like Canada—disappeared, the effort to stabilize and revive the economy could afford the humanly vast cost of floundering from one failure at reform to another. What was to cushion the otherwise profound social and political consequences of the decade-long crisis of American capitalism was the distinctive nature of the American working class and the absence of a powerful Left. It was that critical void that alone explained the repeated political successes of Roosevelt with the poor, blacks, workers, and immigrants, as those who gained least economically from the New Deal gave it its political strength.

The Dilemma of Capitalist Reform

The experience of national economic regulation during the first Roosevelt Administration proved that while political intervention into the economy was a necessary condition of capitalism's viability it was by no means a sufficient one. But given the intrinsically ungovernable nature of the economy and its structural limits, the effort transcended the means available, and in effect the federal government did not so much plan during the Depression as improvise, with the advice of interested businessmen, a series of short-range responses which failed to cope with new yet quite predictable but insoluble problems. All theories of regulated capitalism—to say nothing of Weberian organizational concepts which assume that the movements toward integration and predictability are the direction of history—ignored the intrinsically mercurial and reciprocal, and inevitably unstable, framework in which American capitalism was now fixed: there were the dilemmas of the uncontrollable international context of any national economy, the profound limits of social knowledge and comprehension in defining solutions, the unavoidably fluctuating character of politics and personalities essential to regulation, the divisions within business ranks affecting both politics and policy, the inherent structural dilemmas of the economy at a given stage, and the endless possible configurations among all these factors. For it is one thing to desire rationalization, another to attain it. The rule that its problems eventually exceeded the American social order's capacity to deal with them sensibly was vindicated within a short time, as solutions always lagged far behind dilemmas. Capitalists and academics alike failed to discover the means by which to save the economy.

Business, for its part, had virtual freedom during 1933–1935 to apply those solutions that time and experience—plus a definition of the needs of influential men and firms with access to the political structure—had concocted. It focused on price competition as if that were the heart of capitalism's problem, when in fact it was hardly more than a small part of its difficulty. Business failed, leading to its growing frustration with the idea of national regulation and the New Deal, and a partial retreat from politics on the part of those who had been so instrumental in the 1933–1935 innovations. To some vital extent, both the men in Washington and in the economic centers partially were to reject each other, for both had failed during their period of intimate collaboration, and the discredited industrial reform plans had left business devoid of fresh solutions—to temporarily flounder alone.

Regulation surely helped specific interests in several fields, above all finance and banking, but it did not begin to answer the larger problems that the economic decline imposed. But since the ultimate function of the system was profitability rather than stabilization, this critical index naturally caused growing hostility to the New Deal from those large elements within business still suffering from the effects of the Depression. More precisely, this failure of capitalist profitability during the 1930s affected various constituencies in different ways, producing unequal political responses. In the aggregate, net income as a percentage of sales of all corporations, excluding finance, insurance, and real estate, at no time before 1941 came close to 1929 levels, and in 1938 it fell alarmingly to 1.7 percent. And again within the aggregate, manufacturing firms were to prove far more resilient in recovering than wholesale and retail trade corporations, though the former still were worse off than during the 1920s.

It was within this larger context that the important distinctions arose, even though every component of business—save minor exceptions—was less profitable than before. There was direct correlation between the size of a corporation and its profits, and during 1931–1939 all corporations with assets under $100,000 (in 1935 there were 286,000 of them), taken as a class, lost money. Those in the $100,000 to $500,000 assets class, of which there were 87,000 in 1935, barely held their own and were constantly on the edge of loss. During 1931–1933, of course, the combined corporate industrial structure lost money, though the powerful 600 or so with assets of $50 million and up about broke even. Pulling up the entire profitability of the system were the liquor and tobacco industries, followed well behind by the printing, foods, chemical and petroleum, and rubber industries. Service corporations, on the whole, suffered considerably more than any other major economic sector.[25] In brief, small business, which had opposed the NRA more than any other group and numerically comprised the vast majority of businessmen, gained least from the new order. By 1936 the New Deal could expect significant political opposition from this quarter. And as late as February 1938, with the President seeking to rebuild bridges with them, a group of 500 small businessmen he had invited to a Commerce Department conference on their mutual problems raucously excoriated the President and his New Deal in terms that more discreet and less discontented big businessmen generally avoided.

Searching for Solutions

Roosevelt and the large majority of his advisers had earnestly tried to work with big business, and in the fall of 1934, as his economic failures began to mount, he successfully renewed that cordial entente with public eulogies of private initiative and the profit motive. His later difficulties with big business, as opposed to the much more numerous small businessmen who had obtained the least from the New Deal, were surely not irrevocable and, in kind if not degree, no worse than Hoover had also experienced. The New Deal, after the failures of experience and the Supreme Court decisions that removed increasingly weak crutches, had to move somewhere, and for three years it became the victim of chronic indecision, which politics, its own fiscal conservatism, the dilemma of small business, and genuine confusion all imposed. Until the approach of war overshadowed all else and rescued the economy, the interaction between these elements defined the elliptical course of the second Roosevelt Administration.

Roosevelt and numerous key advisers had truly believed in the 1932 Democratic platform on reduced federal expenditures and budget-balancing, and the President was always surrounded by men whose firm objective was eventually to implement it. Hence his short-lived spring 1933 efforts in this direction, which necessity and premature optimism soon terminated. Hoover's $2.7 billion deficit in 1932 the New Deal exceeded by $900 million in 1934 but then about matched in 1935. In 1936, with a deficit of $4.4 billion, the administration finally chose to reverse its pump-priming course. Fiscal 1937, which ran to July of that year, produced a slash of $1.6 billion off the deficit, but fiscal 1938, which began in July 1937, saw another $1.6 billion chopped off the deficit and a budget fiscally more conservative than Hoover's last effort. Given large unemployment, which had begun to increase again in early 1937, the slashed WPA rolls and cancellation of numerous public works projects intersected with the already weakening industrial recovery to cause industrial production to drop one-third from mid-1937 to early 1938, driving unemployment back up to 19 percent of the labor force in 1938. In short, the economy was about where it had been in early 1931. Without relief funds, in many cities hungry men and women were forced back to scavengering in refuse heaps and garbage cans. Moreover, some administration leaders now expected massive permanent unemployment to persist indefinitely. It was during this period that the New Dealers began simultaneously floundering in several different directions for new economic solutions. It is perhaps exaggerated to assign philosophical bases to their differences, yet some such distinctions emerged, though what is more critical is that both failed to define real answers to the decade-old economic collapse.

The first school proposed to continue budget restraints and to return to some modified version of the NRA. Although men such as Aldrich had become increasingly critical of the New Deal during 1937, they never challenged the basic principle of regulation, and their channels to the administration always remained open. Roosevelt and Perkins had opposed the sit-down strikes and labor upsurge of 1936–1937, with the President pronouncing a "plague" on both "Little Steel" and the union in June 1937, and this alone was sufficient to reassure big business.[26] But over the very weeks that he was holding conferences with big businessmen to discuss a possible revival of the NRA principles, the President politely listened to the specious arguments of the second school of analytically superficial trustbusters who were convinced that the 1929 and 1937 economic depressions had been caused, after all, by monopolistic price restraints and collusion, and that if prices dropped as much as production, recovery rather than massive wage cuts and bankruptcies would be the outcome. This group, which included the advocates of higher federal spending, drew inspiration from Brandeis' presumably Wilsonian notions regarding the desirability of restoring competition and decentralization, but it had no social base and its strongest arguments consisted of pointing to the failures of other solutions.

Reasserting the fact that big business dominated the economy, it failed to note areas where size was not yet synonymous with control and those industries still too competitive to establish it save, possibly, via political mechanisms. Amidst an intensive effort by these competing schools to gain the President's endorsement for this or that legislation, Roosevelt's political sense made him comprehend the importance of resumed spending, which in fiscal 1939 caused the deficit to shoot back to $3.9 billion. And, at the same time, he publicly declared in January 1938 that a return to the concepts underlying the NRA was possible, three months later throwing a sop to the potential trustbusters by calling for greater competition and sponsoring the Temporary National Economic Committee's investigation of the economy—which effectively buried the issue in its arid hearings and reports for nearly three years. In effect, the policy of indecision continued save on the spending front, with the White House content to drift as the New Deal came to a disorganized close in 1939. In that year, 9½ million workers—17.2 percent of the labor force and almost 8 million more than in 1929—were unemployed.

By the spring of 1938 it was increasingly clear to big businessmen and politicians that the problem of the economic disaster that had befallen them would not easily disappear with trade associations backed by political sanctions, federal regulation, a massive government deficit-spending program, nor even trustbusting. By the successive defaults of all these answers, the vision of possible solutions returned to the Wilsonian integration of American and world trade in which Hoover had believed and which Hull had persisted in advocating throughout the Depression. The failure to revitalize world trade, Aldrich noted at the end of 1935, was a fundamental problem, and he strongly identified with the Hullian position thereafter. When all the others had immodestly failed, it was Hull who was to emerge as the Roosevelt Administration's last credible prophet of future prosperity, thereby providing continuity with the ideological precepts Wilson had first definitively articulated.

Businessmen, for their part, were far less confident in the solutions they had once advocated, solutions which had been tested and found repeatedly wanting. At the same time, Washington's answers had failed to restore economic activity fully, and so some big businessmen thought they could afford increasingly to criticize Roosevelt at least as strongly as they had Hoover—but only for a time, and only some of them. While they eliminated some problems in a small number of industries, they had not confronted the much more fundamental question of insufficient demand and the need for much larger markets—and that is what capitalism as a system needed most. To some extent, the disequilibrium in the international economy, which they could no longer ignore, seemed to preclude the restoration of full production, and here it was no longer a question of domestic economic consolidation or government regulations as much as the nature and effectiveness of United States foreign policy and the global environment in which it operated. By 1938 the normal rehabilitation of the world economy appeared far less likely than a new war, and while the Hullian interpretation and vision was to become much more widely held, and eventually become enshrined as official ideology as well as elite consensus, Hull's strategy could do nothing to solve immediate economic dilemmas.

During the spring of 1938, even as New Dealers and conservatives saw that the TNEC investigation would suffocate the bogey of anti-trust under mountains of talk and printer's ink, the White House and most of the President's key advisers were ready to smooth over frayed relations with big business. It was to prove quite easy, as feigned business discomfort with Washington melted away. In April, Assistant Secretary of War Louis Johnson told the Chamber of Commerce's organ, *Nation's Business,* that in the event of war there would be no conscription of capital or limits on fair profits. Both Henry Wallace and Commerce Secretary Daniel C. Roper advised Roosevelt to improve relations with big business, and over the rest of the year this view increasingly dominated administration strategy as more business leaders than in several years began wending their way to meetings in the capital. In February 1939 Harry Hopkins, now the President's most important adviser, took the occasion of his first major speech as Secretary of Commerce to reassure businessmen of the administration's realism and desire not to alienate them. The following August, as the federal 1940 budget remained about constant but the portion going to military expenditures inched upward, the administration created the War Resources Board, entirely composed of top businessmen and soon dubbed the "Morgan-Dupont" group. Its demise was due less to liberal-labor opposition than its inept sense of public relations, but assurances from top administration officials sustained the second and more durable administration integration of government and business beginning to unfold. Businessmen, in any case, throughout World War Two were to dominate war agencies much as they had during the first conflict.

The fiscal 1941 budget, which began July 1940, increased military expenditures by over three times, creating, without big-business opposition, the largest peacetime budget deficit in history, but one equal to a military budget which now comprised almost half of all federal expenditures. By that time the "dollar-a-year" businessmen, still on their company payrolls, were beginning to pour into Washington to direct the new agencies; cost-plus contracts were introduced along with a five-year amortization plan that in effect gave industry partially free plants; and in June 1940 the War Department attacked Congressional attempts to impose a 7 percent limit on war contract profits. That same month, Frankfurter, the patron of many of the New Deal's more verbally unorthodox administrators, agreed with the President that the appointment of Henry Stimson as Secretary of War would help create the "coalition" government the administration now thought desirable.[27] But 1940 unemployment stood at 8.1 million, or 14.6 percent of the labor force, and increasing military expenditures by about three and one-half times the next year brought the 1941 rate down to 9.9 percent. Save for 1921 and the preceding decade, it was still the highest peacetime unemployment the United States had known in the twentieth century. And in 1941 corporate profits after taxes for the first time since the crash exceeded those of 1929.

World War Two itself ended the protracted crisis of a mature American capitalism that had lasted, in increasingly grave forms, two decades. It made superfluous economic regulation by voluntary or political means as an enormous demand, vast governmental capital resources, and a seemingly guaranteed prosperity replaced the failures of purely economic and political controls of capitalism with what was to become the longest prosperity in American history. The galaxy of doctrines and concepts of planning and social and human mastery articulated during the first four decades of the century now became a rich lode of the forgotten past for historians to mine. The virtually total failure of the old order's assumptions about control, efficiency, rationality, planning, progress, and much else besides, and the irrelevance of the vast bulk of the institutions it had created to apply them, did not lead to capitalism's demise but to a continuing new integration of politics and economics that was to become a part of the permanent crisis of America and the world, assuming global rather than the hitherto largely national dimensions. What now underlay the system's success was not its social perception and capacity to apply it but its will to devote formerly unimagined resources to preserving its power, and in the process to risk all.

5

The American Working Class: Structure and Limits

The history of the American working class is not merely a chronicle of strikes, organizations, and personalities—the ingredients that have virtually monopolized the writing of labor history—but much more centrally is the story of the evolution of the relationship between workers and industry and the very nature of capitalism itself. No other class in American society has so little control over the forces that constrain and mold its existence, yet an assessment of this relationship of the working class to the general economy as well as to specific industries is still to an astonishing extent absent from what historians, regardless of their viewpoint, write. It is this larger, decisive institutional context that is the subject of this chapter.

Organizations are important, of course, but far more meaningful is to describe the objective economic status and dilemmas of workers who rarely share in the direction of their unions and whose lives are much more profoundly affected by wages, unemployment, and factors that unions, I shall argue, scarcely alter. Strikes are significant, of course, and they are the dramatic raw materials by which workers and their resistance to oppression are usually judged, but strikes are one thing and the attainment of economic security and genuine equity is quite another; and the frequency, and even the success, of strikes is not equivalent to the satisfaction of the essential structural needs and grievances of workers. There is always a danger in making analytic theories more complicated than reality and evidence warrant, but probably no field of modern American history has been so naïvely simplified as that dealing with labor unionism and workers.

By introducing the overriding nature of capitalism in estimating the position of workers in American society, there is at least some basis for perceiving the structure, power, and limits of workers and their organizations. And this necessarily also requires a more adequate, if complicated, notion of what the economics of capitalism, both generally and in concrete industries, is all about.

The boundaries on unionism are defined by the special nature of the industry in which a union seeks to operate as well as the larger economic framework—ranging from prosperity to depression—which determines the fates of specific industries. In the last analysis, it is this setting which has integrated all unions, whether led by self-proclaimed socialists or "bread-and-butter" conservatives, into the larger capitalist system and dictated to them their operational strategies for existence. Necessity rather than desire has been paramount, however interesting union aims. The economics of an industry may not perforce control the propensity of workers to strike, though in some trades it has, but it has surely defined what they attained for their sacrifices and, not infrequently, their heroism. Operational trade-union tactics and ideologies invariably flow from these economic constraints and do not create them. Whether one rejoices or wails over it, the fact remains that American unions have found it infinitely simpler to adjust to capitalism, or even to help manage it within their own industry, than to replace it. Given the conservative views of the larger bulk of union leaders, this should come as no surprise; but it is also at least as true of socialist unionists as of capitalists, and pragmatism and a passive acquiescence to a narrow orbit of concern are more likely to characterize unionists than any serious ideology. The industry and the larger economic context ultimately decide the course of a union's destiny, and whether that fact produces conscious collaboration or conflict is essentially a function of specific and general economics. Even where the union becomes another mechanism of industrial regulation—like the state, the trade association, or concert of dominant firms—it adapts to the economic necessities surrounding it. The result may appear to be many types of unions, performing quite different roles and experiencing more or far less strife; but to comprehend the essence of unionism today and its historic role, it is mandatory to perceive this process of its adjustment to capitalist constraints.

Essentially, therefore, what is vital to perceiving the history and condition of workers and their organizations is not only the character of the working class but also the concrete issues of how relatively capital or labor intensive an industry may be, the degree of competition among firms in an industry, and the capacity of workers and unions to affect the general distribution of America's wealth and power. Merely to probe these questions is to reintroduce the issue of capitalism as an economic and power system into the history of the working class, to consider again the structural and political dimensions of the existing social order, and to touch upon such overriding factors as technology, geography, violence, and power in their roles of influencing or reflecting capitalist America.

Economic Foundations and Constraints

Technical obscurantism and some very real disputes of economists notwithstanding, quite fundamental propositions arise from their work that historians and union apologists alike have almost wholly ignored. Stated in the crudest forms, to which important contingencies must be added, there is a large consensus among such specialists on certain basic propositions: First, the differences between unionized and nonunionized wages in a great number of industries are surprisingly minimal, and these are determined by the degree of competition within an industry as well as the extent to which labor composes the cost of production. The more highly mechanized or increasingly productive the industry, or the greater the degree of monopoly within it and the more inflexible the demand for its products (which is to say, its ability to pass increased labor costs along to the consumer), the less likely is business resistance to workers' demands. And a high-growth industry requiring workers is prone to pay higher wages regardless of the existence of unions. If an industry is very competitive, with marginal firms or slow growth, or if the general economy imposes restraints on greater wages, unions invariably modify their economic strategies. Even the frequency of strikes does not often alter this conformity to the constraints of an industry's specific economics. During economic downturns and recessions, therefore, unions become quite passive factors in the economic structure.

Although specialists in the field may differ in degree, there is a large consensus that workers' earnings in an industry depend on the extent of its concentration, with perhaps some modification for growth in demand for the industry's products, and that the wage effects of unionism are often quite minimal. The industries with the highest rates of wage increases between the two world wars were not the most highly unionized, and only during the period that union membership was declining—1920–1933—did money wages of organized workers appreciably exceed those of unorganized in the same industry. Thereafter, despite the large upsurge in union membership, the differential was rarely more than 15 percent and often close to zero. The total hourly compensation in unionized establishments increased only 15 percent more than unorganized during the period 1966–1972, to use a cruder but more recent figure which somewhat overstates the union gains.[1] Trends in the demand for labor are far more persuasive in explaining this difference and near equality in wage increases than unionization, and in fact unions have historically provided their memberships with a poor floor against the consequences of vagaries in the business cycle.

Nor can it be argued that the success of organization has sympathetically redounded to increase the wages of the nonunionized workers. Looking at the relative earnings rankings of workers in major industries before and after the advent of mass unionization in some of them, there has been almost no significant change for which unionization appears responsible. The workers in certain industries, such as apparel, have even declined in their relative wage ranking with the increase of unionization, and some have slightly risen, but the most striking feature during the first half of this century is the remarkable incapacity of unionism to alter the economic standing of its members within the larger industrial structure and, what is more important, to improve significantly the wages its members obtain over the unorganized in the same industry.[2]

The reasons for this failure to some extent compose the organizational history of the labor movement in the United States, and it is one that describes unions led by socialists as well as avowed capitalists. Socialists among shoe or garment workers conformed to the exigencies of the business cycle much as anti-socialists did in other industries. The economic limits that competition and depression imposed guaranteed the failure to unionize Southern textile workers between the two wars, and when success came later it scarcely modified the wage structure that this competitive industry imposed on organized and unorganized plants alike. Even if inter-union power struggles and political reasons prompted some unions at various times to press claims and demands, in the aggregate they have dealt with the economics of their industries on the terms businessmen defined.

Sensing this economic compulsion, at the beginning of the century Samuel Gompers and the American Federation of Labor openly admitted that industries in which a few large firms dominated were far easier to deal with than the competitive sectors. To attain surrogates for the stability that such monopoly or oligopoly provides was, as will later become clear, a main goal of unions in numerous industries from garments to trucking and maritime. Depending on the leverage that the general economic situation and demand provide, as well as the degree of mechanization in an industry and the size and special situations confronting individual firms, unions have defined their strategies largely conforming to the rules of the game as they inherited them. Specific power struggles, between or within unions, may create exceptions to the rule temporarily, but not indefinitely.

During the economic downturn of late 1957 and 1958, to cite one of many typical examples, the Textile Workers Union did not press for wage rises—still at their 1950 level—because, in the words of its president, "We must face the facts of life in our industry and adapt ourselves to these conditions."[3] As another labor leader put it, "If the company doesn't have it, we can't get it."[4] Woodworkers followed suit, and the United Auto Workers, true to their de facto policy of asking less from small companies than large, spared Chrysler from demands that might have undermined the then-wobbling company's future. Smaller firms in difficulties also have traditionally received union cooperation to sustain their very existence, and after 1950 in the technology-intensive telephone industry strikes were frequently accompanied by continued functioning of the struck firms.

In the end, while unionism was one of several vital factors that surely helped produce an inflationary economy after 1945, there is decisive evidence that it scarcely altered the basic position of its own members within the existing distribution of income, much less transformed that pattern of inequality. The share of the national income going to salaries and wages, as opposed to the "entrepreneurial" portion—a quite ambiguous category which still permits a vast income maldistribution—has fluctuated within a quite consistent range over the past half-century, with unionism only occasionally influencing it in relatively minimal ways. Indeed, the shares of wage earners have always had the dubious distinction of being larger during periods of mass unemployment, 1930–1933 and 1938 in particular, than during relative prosperity.[5]

Elements in Union Growth

Union growth and strikes also have more than their share of irony and failure, and success at these levels has never been translated into a capacity to transcend the limits of an industry, much less the larger capitalist economy.

During the period of peak growth of the labor force between 1870 and 1910 American trade-union membership was a quite inconsequential factor, which not until 1910 doubled its share of the nonagricultural work force to reach a paltry 8 percent. While immigrants accounted for a substantial minority of this labor-force growth, changes in longevity and high population participation in the labor force were more important, and throughout this critical period the growth of mass technology and the numbers of unskilled workers bypassed essentially craft-oriented unionized skilled workers. During its formative years, therefore, American capitalism developed essentially without the need to consider unions in their economic calculations, and only during World War One did the spread of unionism to a bare one-sixth of the nonagricultural work force somewhat modify this reality.

The paradoxes of the relationship of unions to workers that characterized it thereafter began primarily during the 1920s, when unionism's share of the nonagricultural work force was again halved and membership dropped by over one-third. What unions learned is that during periods of serious occupational and structural changes among workers or, later, declining employment, membership would fall unless heroic efforts were made. The objective of this effort to organize would be not so much economic betterment as the organization itself; and after 1941 the unions discovered that growth was in large measure a consequence of the expansion of the work force and the check-offs that automatically brought members with it. Economic gains, which in terms of real income growth were significantly greater in the 1920s compared to the decade after the 1944 wartime peak, had precious little to do with the success or failure of unionism, whose effectiveness was largely organizational and only marginally related to the control of economic benefits.

While union militants often made great sacrifices during strikes, their efforts generally did not produce durable economic benefits, which came, if at all, almost impersonally from broader economic and political forces to which unions rarely, at least until after World War Two, sought to relate. Strikes themselves, which continued at significant levels during the 1920s regardless of union weaknesses, did not alter the distribution of rewards any more before the Depression than after. Strikes frequently, as always, were concentrated in mining, textiles, and lumber industries, with little indication they gained more for their pains than what the industry structure could afford. Workers' propensity to strike in hopeless situations seemed as marked as in promising ones until the unions could inhibit wildcat and unauthorized efforts, though the short-term, purely economic rationality of both forms of strikes now appears dubious. After 1933, in any event, union membership grew with the increase in employment, and unions historically have been ineffectual and often only casually interested in maintaining full employment. As a percentage of the nonagricultural labor force, union membership eventually peaked at 33 percent in 1955 and began to drop to 26 percent by 1974. Unionism's initial success after 1935 was due not merely to the willingness of workers to act but also the interaction of a new militancy with the special vulnerability of such corporations as United States Steel after its financial losses of 1931–1934. Notwithstanding this success, which in the 1930s reached an organizational peak in what was to remain the poorly paid garment industry, industrial unions were to leave their members locked into a greater economic context beyond their control, save where, as in coal mining and longshore industries, they consciously exchanged greater productivity for significantly higher wages and much lower employment within the industry.

Labor Costs

It was the ease with which American industry would apply technology and the division of labor among unskilled workers without resistance that explains the capital-intensive nature of the American economy in what was surely a distinctive type of industrialism before World War Two. From 1870 until 1919 the annual growth of capital per unit of labor input reached an all-time peak in manufacturing, with output per man-hour in manufacturing doubling over that time, and it was for this reason that the production-worker payroll's share of the value of manufactures fell from 40.7 percent in 1899 to 35.6 percent in 1929. And, one must add, the historically unprecedented ability of American capitalism to substitute technology for labor explains partially the longer and higher unemployment of its workers compared to Europe's during the Great Depression.[6]

Despite contingencies to be discussed later in this chapter, higher wages for American workers were scarcely onerous to most of business simply because the cost of labor per unit of output was falling at an astonishing rate that was publicly acknowledged and celebrated as a national triumph. What was allegedly and, indeed, often in reality associated with it was higher consumption for the working class. The decline of labor per unit of output between the Civil War and Great Depression was so great that worker demands, whether union- or market-imposed, could easily be absorbed by those industries sharing in the technological and capital explosion. But in those generally more competitive industries without sufficient capital, or whose wages were a much higher share of the costs of production, the condition of the working class and unionism was generally very different. In these industries both labor leaders and businessmen related to each other in ways quite distinctive and usually more violent than in those industrial sectors with less onerous structural problems. Not only were labor relations unique in this more economically pressed component, but it was these firms that most frequently, though by no means exclusively, produced business advocates of political solutions to their structural economic and labor problems.

During the first half of the twentieth century, capital growth in relation to labor input was below the national average in textiles, furniture, food and beverages, leather products, and printing and publishing; and firms or sectors of these larger industries that also had a very high share of wages as a percentage of the value of their output usually had both labor strife and worker poverty. Textile and forest products wages hovered around 50 percent of the value of output from before World War One until World War Two, while those sectors had far more than their share of conflict and misery, and rank among the poorest paid in the first fifty-three years of this century. The chemical or petroleum and products made from coal industries, by contrast, had one of the highest rates of investment as well as a wage share by 1939 only one-fifth to one-quarter of value added. They were very highly concentrated firms that could freely transfer higher labor costs to consumers or absorb them in annual increases in the efficiency of labor, and there was a fairly inflexible demand for their output. Their workers, with and without unions, were among the best paid since 1899 and went on strike relatively infrequently.

It was within this larger structural framework that the history of the American working class evolved over the past century, and this context invariably compelled unions to adjust to the economic framework their industries imposed, while the latter in turn had to accommodate to the health of the general economy. These imperatives defined strategy and even, occasionally, such reflections on a desirable course for the union movement as were to emerge; and theory never controlled the larger conduct of any union—whether Left or Right. Because they could not alter these specific industrial conditions, a large number of union leaders thought less about the welfare of their workers, which was beyond their control on the truly fundamental issues, than the preservation of their organizations and their own specific positions within them. This bureaucratic political definition of conduct, about which I shall say more below, was possible in the context of unionism's role in helping functionally to try to sustain the prosperity of the industries in which many, if not all, of them willy-nilly became de facto junior managers. If on one level this is well known, as in the decision of the mine workers or longshoremen to accept wage increases in return for higher productivity and much lower employment, it not infrequently took unions into political arenas, including pleas for Pentagon contracts, central to their own interests as an integral part of an industry. And in several notable cases it led to unionism as a way for specific interests within an industry to regulate and control competitors.

Unionism and Industrial Stabilization

The equalization of wage costs among firms within the same industry often becomes the key to reducing internecine competition; and at various times in modern American history—generally after other solutions have failed—unionism has become a recourse for businessmen tired of some adversary undercutting them by paying lower wages. In industries where labor costs are a large portion of production expenses, eliminating this rawest exploitation can introduce stability. Moreover, in industries with a high number of firms and without effective trade associations or control by political authorities, union efforts at integrating an excessively competitive structure, and even creating barriers to continued entries of new firms into the industry, have on notable occasions appealed to capitalists unable to devise more effective solutions to their dilemmas. And while it is no longer the exceptional businessman who regards unions as rationalizers of worker conduct at the level of shop discipline, and many contracts now make this an explicit union obligation, the reliance on unions as a mode of inter-firm regulation is common enough to warrant being considered a major function of twentieth-century American unionism. Even if pragmatic adjustment rather than a positive affection for unions is more frequently the origin of such business attitudes, much the same may often be said about some business responses to government regulation. But while the big firms regulate many industries, such as automobiles, and the state oversees others, unions too, to varying degrees, play this role in several important economic sectors.

As early as the end of the nineteenth century, both in the pottery industry and in western Pennsylvania iron- and steel-finishing mills, there were important cases of industry assistance to unions, even weak ones, in the hope of eliminating low-wage competitors. The single most notable case in this century is the chaotic garment industry, which required little capital for entry and suffered a high rate of failures. Even before World War One important manufacturers concluded that the unionization of the industry offered the best, last hope against unscrupulous competitors. The garment unions from this time onward became the major enforcers in an industry in which labor costs were the key to competition, with employer associations at times even encouraging general strikes to impose discipline on recalcitrant firms. In the end the economics and decentralization of the industry were to undo all such efforts, even after the New Deal brought in political sanctions, but the experience (which continues today in this industry) offers a key illustration of the function and limits of unionism in highly competitive fields. Indeed, in 1931–1932 many Northern bituminous coal operators, with the support of key trade journals, concluded that only the spread of unionization could stabilize wages and working conditions, thereby equalizing costs of production and ending the industrial anarchy of price competition.[7]

Parallel, as well, was the decisive effort of the New England cotton-textile industry to pass a national child labor law, enacted in 1916, and thereby increase the labor costs of the burgeoning Southern producers who were then in the process of taking over a large part of the traditional Northern markets. Later, in the West Coast long-distance trucking and maritime industries, the unions in those fields gained the capacity to prevent easy entry of new competitors, save on terms which greatly restricted potential new entrepreneurs. And in 1937–1938 Northern textiles again used "reform" against their Southern competitors by successfully sponsoring national minimum-wage and maximum-hours legislation for all labor. The collective outcome of all these efforts was a substantial number of industries indebted to, and cooperative with, the unions who exchanged the benefits of higher wages for lower numbers employed.

In this context, unionism as a method of industrial regulation is no less vital in an assessment of the larger role of the organized labor movement over the past century. Equalizer of labor costs among firms and stabilizer of the work force within the plants, yet unable to transcend the larger imperatives that the economics of a specific industry as well as a larger capitalism imposed on it, the trade union as an institution throughout the better part of this century became one more institutional pillar—albeit a modest one—of the constituted order.

The Income of Workers

The quality of workers' lives transcends the statistical measurements that most social scientists are wont to use—and often compelled to cite for lack of more elusive and but frequently more essential insights. The introduction of a new machine, the transformation of a town from a reasonably sympathetic, personal community into an alienated one, moving from a friendly yet poor home to a hostile but richer city—such events have dimensions that transcend numbers. The consequences of this evolution can be seen at the end of the first century of America's experience as an industrial nation, when the cumulative impact of these seeming intangibles has created a reality of social and personal disintegration unknown in any other modern society, but one that a command of the statistics would never have allowed the futurologists of 1910 or even 1950 to predict. Yet the numbers remain, and few social scientists have the poet's capacity to ignore them.

The United States was throughout its modern century a nation in motion, uprooting itself again and again, with old Yankees to only a lesser degree sharing the same wanderlust of the newer immigrants. That demographic turmoil had social and psychological consequences, which remain beyond the purview of this chapter, and economic ones as well. And the intensification of capitalist industrialization brought with it alterations of the occupational structure, producing job mobility for Yankees and older settlers as well as a geographic mobility for new and old Americans alike. Collectively, all these developments shaped profoundly the lives of all workers.

The two most important changes in the distribution of the American population after 1870 until 1950 were the significant diminution in the South's share—from 24 percent to 19 percent—and the rise of the West's from 3 to 13 percent. Both the Northeast and North Central states declined in their shares about one-tenth over the same period, but still composed three-fifths of the nation. The surprising constancy of these aggregate figures eludes one more essential factor: Americans were frequent movers, to and fro, within the same region or to new ones, and they tended to go where living standards and economic opportunities were higher. By the end of the nineteenth century, wages in the South had declined to less than three-fifths of those in the Eastern United States, while per capita wealth was barely half. Although that gap closed significantly after 1929, the South remained the best place to find cheap labor, and three decades later the majority of the rural poor were Southerners. The existence of the South and lower-wage areas throughout the twentieth century affected greatly a trade-union movement that always was inhibited in its demands by the reality and, perhaps more importantly, the threat of runaway shops should they demand too much.

Yet in one larger sense the United States was a place for runaway people as well as plants, undergoing a demographic revolution among old settlers as well as immigrants. The migrant experience that so many shared so often, as well as an increasingly urbanized society—all this left an uprooted nation in which a class-conscious working class had, if possible, to develop. Combined with the immigrant foundations of the modern American working class, such a consciousness never emerged, giving capitalism a freedom and power which all of its many weaknesses and errors could not undermine. But ultimately the individual and collective disorganization of the working class, joined with the fragility of the entire population and social system, after one century of accumulated problems posed the real risk of social chaos without hope of social solutions.

Yet while American workers experienced physical mobility, their economic evolution presented a far more mixed picture. In large part this complexity is due to the fact that even radical analysts are not primed to regard the conditions of labor in one country in the often integral context of an international labor force of high mobility. Yet it is the very existence of mass migration to America that greatly altered the lives of European workers even as it affected in quite negative ways those who were already in the United States. If the history of the American working class is not precisely the use of native rural elements to contain the urban working class, it is most certainly one in which Europe's superfluous population performs to some great extent the same role. For while the real income of American workers rose in the aggregate before the First World War, during the periods of peak migration it increased much more slowly, if at all. Most important, from 1860 until 1913 the growth of average real wage rates in the United States was far lower than in Sweden, significantly less than Britain's, and slightly below that of France and Germany. While absolute wages of workers in the United States were higher because of an already greater base, this low rate of subsequent increase was critical in allowing the vast accumulation of capital for investment before 1919. In effect, the vast deluge of European manpower on America provided labor ready to work for less than natives might otherwise have been able to obtain without unions; and, above all, lower wages sustained the forward momentum of United States capital accumulation during its most critical period.

The real daily income of factory labor rose by about one-half from 1860 to 1890. During most of the next decade, with an unemployment rate of over one-tenth among the civilian labor force, monthly and annual earnings were quite stable despite a slight growth in the more abstract real hourly earnings, a measure that overlooks the impact of unemployment on labor's true income. Paul Douglas estimated that during the period of peak immigration, 1900–1914, real annual income of employed manufacturing workers remained relatively stable during the first decade and then dropped slightly, while several analysts argue that they fell more substantially. Still others, devising methodological techniques less justifiable than Douglas', claim there was a small rise in real income. Whatever the exact truth, America's growth was below known European rates, and all agree that 1900–1914 saw the lowest expansion of real income during the past century, and this was largely due to immigration.

From 1913 until 1939 the growth of real income in the United States ranked only slightly behind France and Sweden, in large part because the period after 1914 and until 1929—which coincided with war, the end of immigration, and an industrial boom—produced what was probably the greatest relative expansion of material gains America was ever to know. And this occurred while the American union movement became moribund and lost the organizational gains of decades. Not for the first or last time was it apparent that the status of trade unionism had precious little to do with the larger conditions —in terms of wages and employment—of workers.

During the 1930s, as the statistically illusory hourly real wage earnings continued to increase along with misery and the worst unemployment in American history, the central significance of full employment to the welfare of workers became clearer than ever before, and whatever favorable hourly wage contracts unions might obtain did not reverse this truism. With the end of unemployment which accompanied World War Two, the weekly real income of production workers in manufacturing increased 53 percent from 1939 through 1944, but only 17 percent over the next sixteen years. And after 1966 for all private nonfarm production workers it grew slowly to an increase of about one-tenth by the end of 1972, only to fall by an equal amount over the next three years. War, not unions, terminated the Depression's economic consequences, and with it came the deepening commitment of union leadership to the government spending—primarily military—that had become the best single post-1945 guarantor of relatively full employment and sustained wages.[8]

Unions could neither directly maintain employment nor prove their argument that by increasing wages they were averting the economic crises that underconsumption invariably brings. Nor could they prevent firms from passing wage costs in excess of productivity increases along to consumers, an inflationary process that invariably significantly deprived all workers of nominal contract gains. All of these structural factors determining the economic conditions of workers, and how they would live and consume, moved at a level of action that unions, individually and collectively, could affect only by increasingly reaching a consensus with business interests on government spending for the only large budget item they could both endorse, the military sector. But by May 1975, with 13 percent of the blue-collar workers unemployed, the capacity of the economy to reward the working class was being severely strained notwithstanding immense military spending.

The Occupational Structure and Transitional Working Class

The American working class evolved after the turn of the century in ways that unions could only partially anticipate, but in the end its increased complexity left what was unmistakably a quite traditional working class in the objective occupational sense, yet one without the subjective characteristics that socialists had anticipated. In part this was due to its immigrant character and the rising occupational mobility of many of the rest, but other factors must also be noted.

Perhaps the most radical transformation of the occupational functions of the working class came between 1890 and 1920, when clerical and sales labor increased from 6 percent of the work force to 13.8 percent, and later to 23.6 percent in 1973. This category absorbed many old natives who were being pushed upward by virtue of the new immigrant proletariat—and after 1940 women workers also swelled the clerical occupations. Semi-skilled workers, the ubiquitous operatives, were to edge up from 14.7 percent in 1910 to 20.4 percent in 1950, only to slip back to 16.9 percent by 1973; skilled workers went from 11.7 percent in 1910 to 13.4 percent by 1973. It was the unskilled nonfarm workers and service workers, who were 21.5 percent of the work force in 1910 and 18.3 percent in 1973, who suffered a real long-term decline. But despite this, a large classic working class was still as intact and significant as ever in the objective sense, and it was only the farm sector that truly diminished after 1890.

It was the composition and location of the work force that created new frustrations for the unions, since after World War Two a growing proportion of clerks and technical professionals—euphemistically called "white collar"—began moving into the durable goods industries until they composed nearly one-quarter of its so-called industrial work force by 1957, and left a group essentially impervious to unions in a critical position in many fields. Administrative personnel as a percentage of production workers in all manufacturing industries were to increase from 10 percent in 1899 to 22 percent after World War Two. To this extent, along with many others, unions were being bypassed as the larger occupational structure evolved, believing they should also organize this constituency. But they remained unclear as to how they would benefit clerks, much less protect them from the unemployment that unionized blue-collar workers had consistently suffered.

The problem of the working class was compounded not merely by immigrants but by the only partially overlapping phenomenon of women in the work force who were increasingly, despite a high turnover, an integral part of the working class and objectively among its most socio-economically oppressed. And women fell into two general categories insofar as their motives and possible future orientations were concerned.

Women sixteen years and older composed 40 percent of the civilian work force in 1975 but only about a quarter before World War Two, and nearly three-fifths of them were married. Indeed, between 1940 and 1955 the percentage of all married women (with husbands present) engaged in the work force almost doubled to 28 percent, and was proportionately about four times greater than in 1890. By 1976 it was 45 percent. Rather consistently, they were being paid one- to two-thirds of the salaries of men in the same occupational category; often they were working part-time. Over two-fifths worked as clerks and sales personnel, and another third as semi-skilled and service workers. Unemployment among them, therefore, was substantially greater than among adult men. Motivated by need of the most dire sort for a minority of them, including unemployed husbands or excessively large families, in the majority of cases working women pushed their families from the lower- into the middle-income brackets. Consumerism was as plausible a motive as any for this element, and wives with young children had the lowest participation rate of all. Many women workers were temporary, hoping to return to being full-time housewives after some often transitional burden or debt in their lives had been overcome. In effect, with over one-third of such wives married to skilled or semi-skilled workers, the seeming prosperity of these classes was significantly dependent on two breadwinners.

To working women not married, but divorced, abandoned, widowed, or single, there were distractions of children, housework, courting, or relating to the world in their institutionalized roles. The divorce rate per 1000 women increased more than two and one-half times from 1900 to 1950, and by 1976 women headed one-eighth of all households. For all such women in the working class and poorer income groups, their roles as workers were far less significant than the demands that their lives outside the workplace imposed on them, as the hardest work for most continued at home. In this situation, one-third of all workers joined their male counterparts in social passivity in American life, for structural as well as ideological reasons also unwilling and unable to challenge the existing order.[9]

With immigrants hoping to return to Europe and dreaming of a second chance at home, but meanwhile locked by language, prejudice, and preference into their own quite isolated communities; with wives expecting soon to cease working, or women being too busy to consider much more than the next task; with mountain people expecting to accumulate the bundle to return to open spaces, and older acculturated Americans being given white collars and men to oppress; with restless people moving West; with personalism and numerous socially approved modes of escaping reality both encouraged and utilized; with the pervasive illusions of mobility without the reality; with black people ruled out of everything and shunted aside; with all this and much, much more than prose can easily capture, it is no wonder that workers, the poor, and the oppressed counted for little in determining the fate of the first century of modern American history.

Still, seekers after attitudes could in various ways conclude that the majority of the working class in the period after World War Two still regarded itself as part of something called a "working class." But this self-identification often was a strange admixture of quite radical ideas on the desirability of nationalizing industry along with preserving racial segregation, many thinking that America remained a land where the average man could get ahead. While opinion takers could dispute with each other as to what anyone in their often diametrically opposed data believed, what was certain was that by its actions the American working class had failed to emerge as a directive force in the larger economic and political processes of American history, preferring to continue stratified by ethnicity, race, space, occupation, and all the differences separating people from each other. That much, at least, was undeniable fact. It remains now to turn from the internal reasons and more impersonal structural causes for its secondary historical role to consider those other external elements which sealed the working class to its course.

Violence and Social Control

The question of the role of the working class in modern American history is not simply its desires or nature leading it down a distinctive path differing from that of Western Europe's, but also the limits of social toleration that all forms of working-class or agrarian radicalism and militancy have confronted in American history. Fear of the masses has been a recurrent anxiety among America's rulers since the Civil War, and violence for social and individual goals has been a constant fact and quite unprecedented when compared to European nations during their nominally "democratic" phases. It has scarcely been confined to the interaction between social classes but increasingly pervades numerous aspects of human relations with a deepening intensity most urban Americans now take for granted. In the first two-thirds of this century there were well over a quarter of a million recorded homicides in the United States, with over 200 times more gun murders in the United States in 1963 than in England and Wales. By that time about a half of the homes of the nation were equipped with arms. "The United States," two quite conventional labor historians were compelled to admit in 1968, "has had the bloodiest and most violent labor history of any industrial nation in the world," to which they should have added that workers were far more often the victims than perpetrators of this bloody aspect of their nation's history.[10] That violence was so frequent and omnipresent that it created what was no less than a culture of intimidation in vast areas of the United States, an inhibiting fear that became far more of a deterrent than the assaults and murders themselves.

Polite society's fear of radicalism, communism, and a truly political working class antedated the creation of a significant Marxist party, and began during the 1870s, reaching a peak of close to universal hysteria during the summer of 1877, when a spontaneous national railroad strike, augmented by local strikes in specific industries, led to probably the greatest single labor crisis known in American history. Anyone who examines this strike closely will immediately perceive it was unorganized and wholly a response to the frustrations and wage cuts that accompanied the first serious industrial depression of 1873–1878. Yet to those in power, it was a clear harbinger of the arrival of the Marxist First International—which was wholly inconsequential before, during, and after the strike—and a justification of the need to mobilize force to protect property and the institutional structures built around it. "It is a pity," typically commented the New York *Tribune* with a callousness acceptable then and thereafter, "that the very first resistance to the law was not met by the shooting of every rioter within the range of a musket ball."[11] It was at this time that the federal and state governments, in response to the demands of "respectable" sentiment and with the aid of large corporate contributions, transformed the National Guard to maintain a system of repression adequate for future labor crises.

The significant moral of 1877 was one recurrent in American history thereafter: So long as political democracy and the social dynamics inherent in the tensions and crises capitalism produces did not impinge on the rights of property, a nominal freedom could be institutionalized and duly celebrated. Its allegedly minor contradictions, such as pervasive corruption at numerous levels of government or police repeatedly symbiotic with crime, could be dismissed as somehow peripheral to the essential order. So long as social stability and mass conservatism led to the voluntaristic endorsement of the existing monopoly over power and the institutions reinforcing it, freedom flourished and violence was less necessary—hence the illusion of consensus and democracy. It took only a depression, war, or effort on the part of workers or blacks to fulfill the rhetoric of nominal freedom to prove repeatedly how illusory and fragile it was in reality. Yet it was always the same during times of trial: vigilantes were almost always led by community elites, the police and troops invariably took the side of property owners against workers, those lynched or massacred were all blacks or poor whites, and the quantity and intensity of violence in modern American history—so fully if belatedly documented after the 1967–1968 riots—is without parallel in any industrial nation not under overt dictatorial rule.

From the slaughter of at least thirty black striking laborers in Thibodaux, Louisiana, to the Republic Steel massacre of ten men on May 31, 1937, that history is tragically and predictably repetitive, but always conveys the same point: that those in power will deal sternly with dissidence and occasional militance; and expressions of radicalism and militant workers would always, at whatever time, be subject to the constant threat of legal prosecution, harassment, and violence. All this has been integral rather than exceptional to the process of administrating power in America, and while it has varied in quantity and ferociousness according to the magnitude of the threat, it has been a decisive inhibitor to the emergence of an American radicalism when it has occasionally manifested itself. The few good books on the topic, which deal with the comprehensive destruction of the Industrial Workers of the World before and during World War One, or deportation of radical immigrants at the same time, do only partial justice to a phenomenon of repression of the anti-capitalist Left which is integral to the very structure of sustaining power in its largest sense. Although these movements can and should be assessed as minimal in potentially challenging the power of capitalism in America, their weakness in no way mitigates the reality that even when capitalism was wracked with depression or, as during 1929–1939, protracted paralysis, it repeatedly showed its capacity and willingness to retain social control via means of violence and repression. If it still was able to survive because of a consensus and dominant ideology which continued to bind the people to its politics and values—and its ability to satisfy the masses at that level was more crucial than its capacity to deprive them of jobs and economic sustenance—we are obligated also to appreciate the ultimate nature of society's cohesion. Violence was used in America more than in any other country that bothered preserving the facade of democracy, but what was clear from this, apart from the fact that the threat to constituted order evoked a response all out of proportion to the real danger, was the readiness to employ yet far more if it were required. That willingness to act, the prerequisite for maintaining power and a continuously repressive political order, is one of the crucial keys for understanding the basis of existing power in America since the Civil War, notwithstanding the fact that the half-century after World War One proved that workers had yet to pose a real threat to the social order.

The Business Response to Unionism

While business responses to unionism over the past century at first glance appear quite diverse, the overriding guide for its conduct —as contrasted to its words—has always been self-interest. But precisely because self-interest for one firm is not identical to that of another, and the economics of various industries can evoke very different conduct, American corporate behavior regarding unions and labor has a certain superficial complexity on which historians have lavished many books while usually missing its essence.

An easily discarded pragmatism characterized even the most pro-welfare businessmen who, ready to endorse the existence of a nominal union movement, gathered in the National Civic Federation from the late 1890s until World War One. Its rival, the National Association of Manufacturers, differed from the NCF only in the size and specific economic position of its members, who were drawn from generally less profitable small and medium businesses in the more competitive industries in which labor costs could not so readily be transferred to customers. Though somewhat of an oversimplification, the economics of this division still explains a very great deal. The NCF was indeed funded heavily by the J. P. Morgan firms, ranging from United States Steel to International Harvester, who at the same time were advocates of greater rationalization and stability in the economy both by corporate cooperation and integration and, in due course, by political intervention. Firms backing the NCF were large, tended to be capital-intensive, and were evolving toward effective oligopoly. And, outside of the NCF–NAM rivalry, which ceased with the decline of the NCF in the 1920s, there were always regionally based or specific industries which encouraged unions in the hope they would equalize labor costs and thereby reduce cutthroat competition—coal and garments were the most notable of these.

The overriding theme, therefore, of business responses to unionism was pragmatic self-interest, and anyone who looks for a genuine ideology of business-labor cooperation, much less a consistency in functional conduct, will be hard pressed. Judge Elbert Gary of United States Steel abstractly defended the right of workers to join unions even as he fought them, to the extent that as late as 1923 it was none other than President Coolidge who forced his corporation to abandon the twelve- for the eight-hour day it had bitterly resisted for decades.

Some corporations desired uniform state legislation pertaining to accident insurance and such matters as industrial diseases and pensions, but less because of their intrinsic merit than their desire, true in most fields, to overcome the costly inconsistencies between laws that states were enacting with or without corporate sanctions. When it came to de facto labor policy, the member firms of the NCF pursued their concrete interests, often with the sort of dissociation between words—and even perceptions—and actions which is the hallmark of business as a system. Because their specific economic positions varied, so too did their ideas and actions, but in the end most preferred resisting unions to a welfare capitalism if the choice had to be made—as indeed it did during the profitless years following 1929.

Until the Depression it was the large employer with more than 2000 workers who, with a frequency of about eight times that of firms with less than 500 workers, was likely to create an industrial relations department designed to regulate and, if possible, make more palatable business interaction with labor. Employee representation schemes were during the 1920s preeminently accepted by a small number of firms with over 5000 workers, but these too proved that it was the economics of the firm and industry that dictated action in most cases, with ideology of any sort being quite incidental. In the same way, just as the open shop movement of the pre–World War One era virtually disappeared with the high wartime demand for labor, the Depression swept aside all notions of cost-increasing concessions as the hard-pressed "benevolent" businesses of yesteryear cut wages and fought unions as their interests might require. Between the war and Depression, however, a declining union movement notwithstanding, the structural forces in the economy pushed labor's real income up to new heights.

In virtually every case, business responses to unionism—save where unions were vehicles of intra-industry rivalry—were hostile or paternalist insofar as the employer consigned to the worker whatever he thought was good for him *and* more efficient at one and the same time. Hence, by any real criterion, the vast majority of United States business was hostile to the most ideologically and politically conservative union movement of this century, preferring conflict to collaboration and integration. Co-option and liberalism were never necessary precisely because the alternative of a radical trade-union movement, much less revolution, was never present. Therefore the need to rely primarily on unionism—except in several unique industries—as the integrative mechanism for preserving class harmony was not essential either. Concessions which injustice pays to fear are proportionate to the extent of true anxiety, and the political development of the American working class made genuine collaboration superfluous in the twentieth century. Resistance to organized workers' demands when they were too costly therefore became the rule, save during periods of labor shortages and rising wages for all workers, and from this followed strikes and much violence, just as voluntary concessions came when the economics of the labor market dictated they must. When unmanageable problems arose, as they invariably do in an everlastingly cyclical economy, business preferred turning to the state for help against trade unionism. In the end, as we shall see, such pragmatism was also pursued by the vast bulk of those businessmen once nominally ready to accept unions as well as those opposed to them. For the goal of business was profit, not ideological consistency, and here too the state was increasingly to play a role that also defined the nature of the business stance toward unionism.

State Policy Toward Labor

One can at least make partially explicable the complexity and seeming unevenness of national policies toward labor since the Civil War by always asking the question "Who loses and who gains and what were their respective roles in prompting action?" For, given the nature of industrial economics, losses are never uniform or even general, and what is a greater cost to, say, a Southern textile firm is improved competitivity for a New England producer. While it oversimplifies history to view labor legislation as an aspect of intra-industry rivalry, neither can one continue to ignore that dimension. And just as one can easily misperceive the concept of efficiency and the rationalization of a labor supply, the fact remains that in a capital-intensive economy with a labor force as variegated, mobile, and costly as America's, serious analysts of that society should not gainsay the significant economic value stimulating the desire to rationalize the work force.

The federal government's role as strikebreaker is far better known, at least if the quantity of written history is an indication, than its uneven but parallel efforts over time to integrate labor into society by more subtle means. The former need not detain us long. From 1877 onward the use of federally controlled troops during strikes became commonplace, with seventy-one Presidential seizures of firms during strikes—largely during wartime—being accompanied by occasional but well-known federal anti-strike injunctions and criminal prosecutions of labor leaders. Twenty-nine injunctions to end and resolve strikes after the Taft-Hartley Act of 1947 sustain the legal basis of this coercive tradition down to our own day, setting aside the ambiguous 1914 Clayton Act clause that "the labor of a human being is not a commodity or article of commerce," as well as the much-celebrated Norris-LaGuardia Anti-injunction Act of 1932.

The yet more intensive parallel actions of the many states only greatly amplify a well-known picture. For if coercion is required, then it is no surprise that the government brings its legal monopoly over it to bear.

More interesting and far less well known have been the reform efforts since 1914 to stabilize and make more efficient the role of labor, if not unionism, in the social system. In large measure these efforts were the outcome of the increasingly polyglot nature of the work force since 1890, and the fact that after 1918 immigration was no longer needed—prompted, as well, by the coincidence that the most troublesome strike of the immediate postwar era, the Great Steel Strike of 1919, was largely manned by the traditionally docile immigrants who composed the bulk of the industry's members. Labor's "Americanization," via forced speeded acculturation in language skills as well as an astonishing period of prohibition of alcoholic beverages aimed mainly at the personal habits and efficiency of workers of foreign birth or parentage, was one dimension of the effort.

Another aspect, more subtle but continuous, was an emerging belief within the federal government that the stability, efficiency, and integration which the giant firms or trade associations of various industries sought to achieve could also be attained within the entire economy, with a concomitant social equilibrium and greater economic rationality. Beginning with the 1921 President's Conference on Unemployment, which Herbert Hoover initiated and promoted throughout the decade, and culminating in the passage of the Full Employment Act of 1946, the federal government sought by everything from promotion, scientific inquiry, increased compensatory capital expenditures from private or public sources, and other acts in "a technique of balance," to eliminate strikes, unemployment, and such as a part of the continuous process of desired economic expansion and full employment.[12] What was critical in this phenomenon was not the specific means used but the very belief itself, which over subsequent decades successive administrations could translate into every sort of proposal, from New Deal make-work measures to the durable Pentagon contracts to labor-surplus regions of our own day. Often, as we shall see especially in the cases of the New Deal, what was advocated as federal labor policy was really a means of intra-industry regulation utilizing governmental enforcement mechanisms. If war expenditures were to solve the problem of American capitalist crises and recessions at least three times after 1929—in 1941, 1950, and 1958—more to the point was that as the political authority was prepared to use force and repression to cope with an occasionally obstreperous working class, so too was it increasingly ready to find solutions to its own economic problems, or at least those of specific capitalist interests, which produced the frequent if aimless and unsuccessful strikes of workers. It was to employ the stick, but also the carrot—yet a carrot which, as I shall strive to show in subsequent chapters, eventually carried with it new obligations for Americans in wars abroad and anomie and dangers at home. Of this, our lives today, more will be said throughout this book. The stick, eventually, was reserved only for increasingly rare recalcitrants of the Left.

The Organized Left and Unionism

It is all too easy to attribute the failures of the Socialist and Communist parties in their relation to trade unions and the working class to their own shortcomings, which were enormous and surely major obstacles to their success. Their tiresome internal debates and almost continuous sterility of thought; their intellectual prima donnas, exotics, and floaters who divorced the assorted Left parties almost as quickly as they joined; the Left's deficiency of tactics, analysis, and discipline—all these were causes of organized socialism's weakness, but more importantly they were also reflections of an unhealthy structural situation which the Left parties inherited and could not overcome. The shortcomings of American socialism, I must contend, reflect the failure of American life and politics itself, and the weaknesses of both merely interacted. In the last analysis, however visible the inadequacies of socialist leaders, doctrines, and tactics, the essential problem was the very nature and interrelationship of the working class with America's social institutions. To an astonishing degree, socialists mirrored and catered to trade unionism's weaknesses largely because the development of the working class left them few options. This is not to diminish the crucial importance of their own insufficiencies, which were hardly exclusively the naïve faults of American as opposed to European socialism; but what is essential is to retain the larger social perspective and materialist context largely absent from the existing literature on the failure of American socialism. For whatever its shortcomings, the European Left always retained the loyalty of the working class.

The question of the immigrant's relation to socialism is ironic because the extensively immigrant character of the working class placed both a floor and a ceiling on the growth of the organized Left. The whole complexity of languages, aspirations, and instability among immigrant workers made it unprecedentedly difficult to organize the larger bulk of them for fulfillment in the United States, because so many of them were not going to remain there or were not able to literally comprehend the message. On the other hand, a certain number, above all among Germans and Jews, brought with them a socialist heritage and nostalgia from Europe which they retained, like beer and gefilte fish. The sentimental basis of their persistence with the very notion of socialism, like some holy relic, sustained them long after it ceased to have conceivable relationship to their actions and lives.

In any case, by the 1890s the one visible socialist party, the Socialist Labor Party, was not even one-tenth native born, and merely by partially mobilizing a few ethnics it was indeed able to form a visible constituency in what was still a relatively minor trade-union movement. But when a small number of Yankees and less sectarian ethnics who split from the SLP formed the Socialist Party in 1901, the outcome was not a qualitative increase in its capacity to communicate with the masses more effectively, partially because the new and dominant prewar Socialists mirrored the stratification of the working class and its particular weaknesses. While it is true that socialism from this time onward attracted various intellectuals and literati, the fact that it remained throughout this century a movement without one serious theoretician should not be overemphasized. For the function of socialist leaders and intellectuals was not to concoct revolution with ideas and organizations but to respond to the breakdown of a social system, which in this case did not occur in the manner anticipated, and to mobilize a persistently indifferent working class. Charismatic personalities, preachers, and lawyers can ultimately neither create nor undo a radicalized working class pushed by events to act. But it is a fact, the significance of which one must make neither too little nor too much, that the various factions sustained themselves not with new clarity specifically appropriate to American conditions but with the residue of British and European socialist doctrines.

American socialism after 1900 may be best perceived as a series of fairly autonomous constituencies in orbit with each other but ultimately reflecting the divisions and incoherence in the American working class and life itself. The native American group in it grew significantly and can explain the rise of the Socialist vote until 1918, but the party never sank deep roots in this constituency. Agrarian radicalism and Populism both assisted and hindered the Socialists. An important part of this element was among the million Americans who abandoned the Grain Belt for Canada's western provinces, where they indeed helped build a significant social democratic party. But others moved to the cities of the Far West, and of those who remained, above all in the South, an astonishing number were drawn to assorted demagogues. In the South the small Socialist Party excluded blacks from white locals until at least 1915, and the national party passed only one weak resolution on black rights during 1901–1912, even rejecting a farm program along Populist lines during the first five crucial years of its existence. Until the war, when the Yankees largely dropped out of its leadership, the party downgraded its work among immigrants and took essentially the AFL restrictionist position on immigration and a racist position toward Orientals. Its local electoral successes were largely due to its quite reformist local politics until 1917, when it briefly capitalized on anti-war sentiment and changed decisively the composition of the American Left. In fact, the Socialist Party was a kind of reformist faction somewhat to the left of the Gompers leadership of the AFL, an organization that represented but a small minority of the workers but was still oriented toward winning over better-paid unionists and the middle class. It was always equivocal toward endorsing industrial unionism as the exclusive basis of future growth, and remained wedded to the AFL despite its reservations. And even before attaining any real success, American Socialism was a party which bureaucrats, lawyers, and relatively well off devotees led. By that time it had consolidated a certain power in several unions, but its conduct within the labor movement was scarcely unorthodox or distinguishable from that of the Gompers faction of the AFL. What was common to them both was conformity to the economic parameters their specific industries imposed, with the Socialist-controlled garment unions being perhaps the most deeply integrated of any, whatever their nominal ideology, with the interests of the managers of their industries.

The First World War and the Wilson Administration's ferocious persecution produced the transformation of the American Left, turning it into a social organization of immigrants quite unable to relate to a vastly larger ethnic working-class structure too self-centered to notice the Communist or Socialist parties. Thirteen percent of the Socialists were enrolled in foreign language sections in 1912, but 53 percent in 1919, and most of the latter went with the Communists when they split. Thereafter, immigrants dominated the membership of both parties, which increasingly assumed a fraternal, leisure function for their members, a convivial assemblage of banquet-hall followers who funded the earnest, increasingly small membership still political in the true sense of that term. The Communists took greater pains to use English, making it the language of almost all their publications, but the majority of Socialist literature was in other languages. Only styles rather than constituencies differed. Neither party, during the most intensive, protracted crisis of American capitalism, was able to make any even modest but permanent gains. Both, in fact, had become just two of hundreds of improvisations immigrants devised to survive socially in a strange new land.

One could attribute this failure to the precocious sectarianism of the Socialists after 1933, or the opportunism of the Communists which led a large majority of their members into the Democratic Party—not just organizationally but, for many, ideologically after 1935—to remain there so that as late as 1972 as many as two-fifths of the party's members voted Democratic rather than Communist. For practical purposes, the Socialists disappeared in all but name, more deeply wedded than ever to the most conservative institutions of the union movement with a sectarian opportunism that only an exotic synthesis of American reality and European ideology could produce. The younger Communists, on the other hand, plunged heart and soul into the organization of the CIO as what John L. Lewis contemptuously referred to as his bird dogs, defending his pragmatism by asking, "Who gets the bird, the hunter or the dog?"[13] For their troubles the numerically unimportant Communists received many jobs and at one time dominated unions with anywhere from one-tenth to one-fifth of the CIO's membership, administering them precisely like any avowedly capitalist unionist might in conforming to the economic imperatives of their industries. In the end, Harry Bridges' International Longshoremen's Union worked as intimately with his industry as David Dubinsky's Ladies Garment Workers Union—with neither advancing socialism organizationally or morally. Throughout their history, American Left parties had always acted as the servants of the constituted labor movement, ultimately conforming to its implicit reformist premises.

The overriding, central fact was that during the worst and longest depression in the history of any industrial nation the American working class did not show any demonstrable change in its political and economic commitments. While some have attributed such remarkable conservatism to the Catholic Church, Lockean ideology, social or physical mobility, and much else, there is too much hindsight in all this, and ultimately no single explanation carries sufficient weight and some appear most dubious. After all, the Church was also as divided ethnically as the factory, and the doctrines of Irish priests meant little to Poles. And its power in Europe scarcely inhibited the Left there for very long. Nor was there much illusion or hope of mobility after 1929, even among those passing through America in fact or, increasingly, in their minds, though the persistence of their social and cultural distance from other workers remained a fact of immense significance.

More extraordinary yet throughout the Depression was the failure of all Left factions to develop an economic analysis of the limits of unionism under capitalism that would also have stimulated a reassessment of their own politics and inherent reformism. Instead, they supported unions on their own terms and reinforced those who were objectively, and often consciously as well, opposed to the elimination of capitalism. Their ultimate folly was to be both pedestrian and powerless. In this regard, American socialists differed profoundly from all their European counterparts, and never perceived their own dilemma and deficiency. All factions of the Left invested unionism with quite millennial qualities by which they deluded themselves as well as helped to deepen the narrow, essentially conservative, commitment of labor activists to a movement that promised much but delivered precious little—save to those on their payrolls.

Given the melange of factors—the stratified, divided nature of the working class, its tentative relation to America, its high mobility physically within and without the country, its cultural alienation and overlapping, confused identities, its racial irrationality, and much else besides—there was one profoundly different alternative to class politics and consciousness for the American working class, one for which there is no historical precedent: individual disintegration. Elsewhere economic crises produced social and political responses, and that is the history of defeated as well as successful socialist movements. In America, to an unparalleled extent, personal disintegration more than anything else was the reaction of the millions of individual victims of capitalism: crime, drugs, breakdowns, personal isolation, violence . . . In this sense, therefore, the failure of the Left was inevitable regardless of its numerous shortcomings, and the latter only further sealed an evolution for which one cannot identify any real options in the past. The collapse of the Left was ultimately but one more aspect and a reflection of the older, deeper, and intensifying generalized crisis of all American society in the twentieth century.

Trade Unions as Bureaucracies

From its inception, the American trade-union movement has been distinctive in possessing a leadership whose values and commitments were colored by those of the ruling class, and to an unprecedented degree they have shared the vision of occupational mobility of many of their constituents. This ambiguity of values among leaders and the led was, to a remarkable extent, translated into true mobility —even if within the framework of union bureaucracies. Directorship of trade unions, in brief, was but one of many means of power accumulation in American history, a kind of agency of individual mobility into a loosely defined managerial class. Once this is understood in historical perspective, the present degeneration of unionism—not simply its refusal to support some agency of socialist transformation but contrasted to the modest life style of union leaders in Western Europe—becomes explicable and predictable, and one may see as inevitable the phenomenon of George Meany and Nelson Rockefeller together at the same parties.

Any survey of early American labor history will illustrate this pattern. Being a union leader was to have a potential political constituency; and of two samples of 96 and 150 late-nineteenth-century labor leaders and reformers, anywhere from 37 to 46 percent were active in politics, mainly as candidates for office who in the majority of cases won or gained patronage—usually on major party tickets. Promotion of union members and leaders to management positions was quite common at this time in the iron and steel industry, and all but one of the Amalgamated Association of Iron, Steel, and Tin Workers presidents ended up in business or politics. Terence Powderly, the guiding light of the relatively more radical Knights of Labor during the 1880s, also operated a grocery business while union president, became mayor of Scranton, and ended his career with a political appointment from the McKinley Administration—which he had endorsed in 1896. Although the AFL was the most conservative union by world as well as American standards, the Knights under Powderly opposed strikes, and this in large part helped its demise when its organizational strategy of mobilizing along industrial rather than craft lines seemed so promising. No large institution of real or potential power in the United States ever experienced a weakness of leadership comparable to that of the union movement.

From its inception the parallel mentality of occupational mobility among the union movement's members reinforced the leadership's ambiguity and opportunism. And to some significant extent, at the beginning of the industrial century after 1870 the existing unions were benevolent and status associations, and hence the logic of their stratification along craft lines. "Respectability and standing in the community where we live," and acceptance from railroad executives, are recurrent themes in the words and literature of the Brotherhood of Locomotive Engineers, the top of the pecking order in the nation's single most important economic sector shortly after the Civil War.[14] The BLE opposed liquor consumption and even expelled a member for adultery, occasionally even adjourning its conventions to attend church. Good behavior, self-improvement, self-discipline, and cooperation with the railroads, it hoped, would in turn lead to higher pay for engineers. Strikes were forbidden unless authorized, under conditions difficult to attain, and those who disobeyed this restriction were expelled.

The Brotherhood of Locomotive Firemen, next in the rail labor status hierarchy, also conformed to this mentality in a remarkably consistent way. "The fireman of today is the engineer of tomorrow," as a speaker at its 1878 convention put it, and in 1876 its grand master declined to stand for reelection because he was soon to become an engineer, and quite naturally preferred that occupation. Despite the fact that many members were dismissed after the 1877 strikes, the Brotherhood—with its motto of "Benevolence, Sobriety, and Industry"—was to persist a while longer in its hope that, in member Eugene V. Debs's words, the railroads would not misinterpret its intentions and that "peace and harmony will prevail between us forevermore."[15]

Members and unions were to change, of course, by the 1890s, but the retention of the "success ideology" rather than job consciousness until that decade left an indelible mark upon the subsequent history of American unionism and the direction its leaders gave it. British unions had also shared this fraternal, status orientation, but their later evolution was far different. In part the craft basis of the AFL, which prevailed wholly in its theory if only partially in its practice, sustained the invidious social distinctions among laborers, especially after the chasms between them deepened with the "new immigration." Yet the continuation of unionism as an institutional mechanism by which individuals grew rich and powerful, playing increasingly important roles in machine politics, and helping regulate the conduct of laborers on behalf of a more stable, rationalized capitalism, did not alter with the greater readiness of unions to strike after 1890. If the specific economic structure and parameters of an industry to which the labor movement conformed were to constrain union strategy, they scarcely dampened the increasing extent to which American trade unions became sources of private power accumulation.

The Origins of Contemporary Unionism

Between unionism's values and institutions of the late nineteenth century and its reality today there exists a difference in degree but only rarely a difference in kind, and one key to comprehending that evolution is the growth of unionism as a mass-based structure with privileged elite domination, a paucity of real democracy and declining freedom of local control, and a kind of organizational sclerosis well suited for turning unions into political machines and mechanisms of industrial regulation.

If, as has been argued, the bureaucratization of unionism is a necessary function of the centralization of industry, a national market, and the increasing sophistication essential to dealing with them, the logic of this thesis would have to assume that bureaucracy is effective in economic if not democratic terms, and since 1870 there is not much to show that authoritarian *or* free unions qualitatively altered very much in this regard. What is certain about unions is only that they conform to their own power-oriented, elitist norms rather than those of idealistic socialists or their own public relations men, and that union constitutions as well as practice since the Depression have increasingly formally allowed restrictions on political dialogue and internal opposition. "A substantial minority [of unions]," the

American Civil Liberties Union reiterated in 1952, "engaged in abusive practices of a wide variety which deprived their members of basic democratic rights."[16]

The AFL, with several notable exceptions, had been plagued by bureaucratized, often corrupt, unions from its inception, and the emergence of the CIO only temporarily stemmed the pattern of centralized decision-making, substituting inordinately high officers' wages for the simple venality and often criminality of many AFL locals. Such criminality, as in the not uncommon case of vice-president Joseph Fay of the Operating Engineers or, later, president Tony Boyle of the Mine Workers, led only a few officials to prison sentences for offenses ranging from extortion to murder. Spontaneous workers' strikes in some industries, such as rubber, and highly centralized and expensive John L. Lewis–managed undertakings, such as in steel, produced another synthesis in the CIO. The anti-Communist hysteria after World War Two extensively destroyed whatever nominal democracy emerged from this unstable combination. Then officials never balked at the abuse of workers' rights, real or potential, in the name of purging the remaining few Communists who were not ready to make their individual peace with the system. No better justification than anti-Communism in this century allowed so many hierarchies to consolidate so much power for so long. But what was meted to CIO Communists was also applied later to rank-and-file protesters, such as the politically quite neutral "dues protest committee" in the United Steelworkers in 1956–1958, which the existing officers neatly crushed with a combination of intimidation and packed conventions. Later the Steelworkers' constitution allowed the central office to take over and directly administer dissident-led locals. Comparable measures over the post-1945 decades were scarcely less capricious or arbitrary than those of buccaneering entrepreneurs. By 1957, when David McDonald of the CIO Steelworkers was scarcely alone in rewarding himself with a $50,000 a year salary, the annual income of the union movement well exceeded $620 million in dues and the ratio of full-time union officials to members exceeded Britain's by over ten times. If by that time the recently reunited AFL-CIO could publicly wax righteous over corruption in its ranks and expel several of its unions, this newfound purity did not keep it from later quietly reestablishing cooperation with them. The fact remains that the unification of the two federations was now feasible because to some important degree the power and cynicism which united these leaders was deeper than their nominal concern for democracy and honesty.[17]

One cannot easily divide the relationship of workers to such a trade-union movement between cause and effect, for while the consciously manipulated elitist control and power accumulation perpetuated worker apathy and cynicism for some, worker indifference also helped make the bureaucratization of the labor movement possible. At various times, both phenomena are germane, for no one can deny that the ethnic working class's ambivalent relation to their lives as American workers left a vacuum others were happy to fill, and afterwards it was virtually too late to reform unions whose entrenched officials and hierarchies fully controlled. What is certain is that the labor unions increasingly lowered their capacity to influence members, who, to an increasing degree, were forced to join the unions and pay dues when hired.

While recent studies of membership participation vary in degree they all reinforce the fact that an extraordinary number of union members—perhaps as high as 99 percent or more in locals of over 4000 members—do not attend meetings. And in most of these locals there is no serious work for them to do on matters of fundamental policy, and hence their absence is based on a large measure of conscious or inadvertent good sense. Reflecting that growing alienation was the fact that the percentage of worker votes for union representation dropped from 82 percent in 1936–1941 to 58 percent by 1958 and 36 percent in 1975. More important to national union leaders, who after 1948 were rarely voted out of office, was that their capacity to bargain their members' election day votes for political favors was by the 1960s beginning to be very much in doubt. Given the cynical courtship of this or that potential candidate, including Republicans, or the banal platitudes of a Walter Reuther who wedded labor to the Democratic Party, workers became more and more alienated until, by no later than 1954, they had largely begun to oppose what was increasingly a major preoccupation of their leaders: influencing local or national politics.[18] By that time it had become apparent that union political strategies no longer addressed themselves to the needs of workers as a class, or even of the specific constituencies within it, but had become instruments of private egos, as in the case of a John L. Lewis or David McDonald, or state and local machines, as with a Sidney Hillman, or some other extraneous consideration. Since it was always quite dubious that unions per se ever controlled the bulk of their members' votes or attitudes, when workers to a significant extent began defecting from the Democratic Party—to which the unions had been a loyal, affluent appendage since 1935—for the Republicans or racist minority parties, no one should have been surprised. Neither the trade-union leadership nor the working masses had produced a spark of socialist consciousness, and neither had the capacity to overcome, much less redirect, a nation whose deepening problems and failures were increasingly defining workers' lives not just economically but universally—in their neighborhoods, the army, or schools.

The problem stemmed from the fact that unions had always operated as interest rather than class groups, within the framework of their own industries' economics and needs. And in politics they functioned on both the local and national levels as the passive rather than dominant member of the special factions and machines that made up the Democratic Party. That, in turn, left no common denominator with other workers as a class, for they had no identifiable, justifiable political party nor a larger conception of mutually beneficial solutions to common dilemmas. Divided by industry and privilege, ethnicity and race, union members were no more radical than non-members, and their proclivity by contrast to Europe for answers roughly identifiable with the Left was seriously in doubt. Indeed, for a large part of this century the ethnic divisions and differential chances in the working class were overriding, and when they finally began declining it became apparent that the labor movement's century-long refusal to cope with racism would leave the white working class seething with massive hatreds to replace earlier obsessions of ethnic hostilities.

The occasional if inspiring examples of class solidarity overcoming racial hatred notwithstanding—which as often as not died because national union leadership overrode the tentative, temporary unity of local initiatives even in the South—the fact remains that the failure of unions to confront the enormity of the historic significance of the chasm between white and black labor meant that the most natural and necessary alliance within the larger American masses could never be effected. That disunity was rooted in the very craft-union elitism which grew out of the immigration experience and the unequal skill and social organization of America's industrialization. Even after the creation of transcending industrial unions it was renewed and perpetuated until our day, when black workers left the

South after 1910 to be greeted by hostility and segregation in the neighborhoods and workplaces of other oppressed people. For union leaders all this implied little save impotence in regard to labor's possible direction of the larger society, which was never their aspiration in any event, and it surely did not diminish their personal fortunes. It meant, simply enough, that in addition to the alienation of their members, whose staying home actually facilitated the management of unions and labor relations, the union elites would remain passive throughout most of the crises of the twentieth century, save insofar as they chose to reinforce the initiatives of other power constituencies. De facto, it was only as mechanisms for regulating their respective factories and industries that unions by mid-century were to have any significant role in society.

Unions as Regulators

The interaction between unions and their respective industries has varied from product to product beyond the question of equalizing costs and affecting or even restricting competition, but unionism as a means of imposing discipline in the workplace is a problem about which less is known. And this obscurity is to some critical degree due to the repugnance with which conventional wisdom treats the very notion that unions accomplish the employer's work for him. If no industry has gone as far as the garment trades unions, which by World War One had extensive contractual responsibility for seeing that workers fulfilled specified labor norms, it is apparent that the value of unions in this regard has become increasingly real and perceived over the past half-century. Trouble in the shop was surely on the minds of employers who knew workers struck or deliberately produced less whether or not they had unions; and costly wildcat strikes and slowdowns, as one corporation president publicly congratulated union leaders in 1958, were onerous until unions came along: "We need the union to insure enforcement of the contract we have signed, to settle grievances, to counsel employees in giving a fair day's work for a fair day's pay, to help increase productivity."[19] The United Steelworkers, in seizing one of its large locals in 1958, stated it differently: "Enforcement of the labor contract with Kaiser Steel has deteriorated to a point where an abnormal number of work stoppages have cost and are costing the membership too great a loss in wages."[20] During the decade after 1946, and over worker resistance, the ostensibly more liberal United Automobile Workers raised work standards among a large number of small firms it feared would collapse. The overriding constraints of economics, both in the larger industry and its individual firms, inevitably led unions to conform to managerial imperatives and, in effect, help direct business at a level amenable to the latter's control.

The growth of multi-plant agreements after World War Two, to include two-fifths of all unionized workers, largely in competitive, regional firms and industries, meant more rationalized, efficient work standards for employers as well as equalized labor costs, less ennui for union leaders, and yet less autonomy for workers in their locals. The diversification of unions into every conceivable field other than the ones for which they were created, if only to sustain or augment their dues-paying numbers, has meant more consolidated negotiations with increasingly heterogeneous firms, a dubious process for which unions were technically ill-equipped but which meant bigger unions along with larger corporations. All of this tended at least partially to confirm the view, argued by some conservative academic specialists as well as a few radicals, that a major wellspring of union conduct was pure and simple power accumulation for its leaders and the organization rather than benefits to its members. The political and factional considerations necessary to retain or consolidate power therefore defined many contracts in assorted industries. If such a view minimized the economic constraints which defined union conduct in many cases, it surely had validity in others. Reinforcing it was the ultimate logic of this company-union managerial collaboration: many firms after World War Two saw clearly their need to influence the political control of various unions to suit their own goals, and this often required them to make timely concessions in return for continued collaboration. In 1953 General Motors helped Reuther's political position within the UAW by giving voluntary wage and pension concessions despite a contract with two years to run, and United States Steel gave the Steelworkers' still insecure new president, David McDonald, a generous first contract without the need to call a strike. McDonald, who the same year had been feted by Pittsburgh businessmen at an extravagant banquet and then had embarked on goodwill tours of United States Steel's plants with its president, was merely bringing to the surface a widespread phenomenon of firms reinforcing and cajoling union leaders with dinners, informal socializing, subsidies to assorted union functions, and small gifts. In the end, both the life styles and functions of union and plant managers had merged.

The rationalization of the trade unions meant superior control of labor in the capitalist work process, and that a measure of regulation—in some cases decisive—was attained within the framework of the specific components of the economy. So long as the general capitalist economy survived for its own larger reasons—often dependent as much on political and international factors as anything else—these rules of the game could operate within the context of a divided, increasingly alienated working class that could not be regarded as more than incidentally overlapping with the union movement.

In the end, the particularism and conservatism of the trade unions left the economic structure with its inequalities and dilemmas intact, thereby preserving for workers the origins of their own crises. In return it produced a privileged new class symbiotic on, but scarcely the equal of, the directors of business and politics—a group of men who attached themselves to the working class after the Civil War only to develop to maturity after 1939. Rather than modifying the structure, purpose, or control of American capitalism, trade unionism was quite willingly transformed by it, leaving America's destiny to others to shape.

6

The United States and the World Crisis, 1920–1945

The First World War rended asunder the economic, political, and psychological stability of the European old order and world capitalism. If that order had been fragile and divided, it had at least been relatively predictable and cohesive compared to the world that was to emerge. The war had been the reflection, not the cause, of the civil war within international capitalism, but the contemporaries of the event could not imagine that the process was only beginning rather than ending, much less that violent conflict between and within nations would become far more common than before. And those larger economic and political forces endemic in this protracted crisis caused and circumscribed the problems with which men of power in the United States and Europe ultimately had to cope. Given their confidence in their system and themselves, they could scarcely perceive the magnitude of the challenge confronting them.

Despite the instability intrinsic in the system, prewar world commerce had been economically centered in Great Britain, with sterling the standard of world trading and London the capital of world banking. The war seriously shook the value of the pound, greatly diminished the French franc, at least temporarily destroyed the German and Austro-Hungarian economies and their roles, and opened the door to the accession of the United States to its principal, though not wholly dominant, role in world finance to match the industrial preeminence it had attained before the war. The new United States control of world trade markets reflected this reality. Regardless of its own structural need for access to the world economy, the stability and power of the dollar, as well as the destruction of the traditional economic centers of Europe, so accelerated the relative American position in the world economy that the genuine integration of the United States into the global economic order was inevitable. This growing American ascendancy, however, was a trend in world economic power which other nations, and above all Britain, resisted, and it was the inevitable friction that accompanied this transfer of responsibilities and privileges which formed the central thread of United States foreign policy in the 1920s.

The vacuum which the decline of European power created had vital political and military consequences as well, especially in the Far East—where it was the United States alone that might aspire to check the emergent overt Japanese imperialism moving into the vacuum which the collapse of the prewar equilibrium made inevitable. These political and strategic questions were significant but less than central to the United States during the 1920s, but there was such a clear relationship between the economic and subsequent political evolution of the world that it is to the economic issues that one must first and primarily look to comprehend the origins and causes of the political and military controversies that became the center of the world scene during the 1930s.

The Structural Context

It is during the 1920s rather than earlier that the structural integration, even dependency, of the United States within the world economy occurs, but in forms quite different than the preceding developments to which historians have drawn attention. For the first time, the American economy after World War One confronted problems which only international solutions promised to resolve.

During the 1920s the American economy, particularly in manufacturing, expanded at a rate substantially lower than any preceding decade since the Civil War, truly posing the problem of significant but insufficient growth to sustain the levels of profit at home to which investors of every type had become accustomed. Capital in manufacturing during 1919–1929 grew annually by only 3.2 percent compared to prewar decadal averages which were usually twice or even more than that, though in fact this investment was the most productive ever known. Net capital formation as a percentage of net national product during that same decade was somewhat lower than at any time since 1869, with the decline being by far the greatest in business capital. Even so, the economy had no need for much of the capital invested during the 1920s, which went into increasingly less productive and high-risk investments until, in 1929, scarcely one-third of the new capital financing could be considered of a "productive" character. In effect, American capitalism had matured and was reaching a point of saturation internally.

If the United States had a long way yet to go before reaching a crisis of profitability, it nevertheless surely had a problem and trend that did not escape business attention. By any criterion one cares to select, profit during the 1920s was declining. Though the yield on the shares of utilities and railroads remained high, that of industry was the lowest for any decade since the Civil War save the equally lean 1901–1910 period, with dividends as a percentage of the capital of all corporations being the lowest since at least 1899. Excess productive capacity began appearing in critical high-growth industries toward the end of the decade, in part because of the new output restraints of oligopoly in some industries but mainly due to overexpansion. Industry as a whole during 1925–1929 produced at about four-fifths of its optimum capacity. Given the immense wartime accumulations of profit and capital, American investors for the first time on a large scale turned with enthusiasm to foreign outlets to supplement domestic speculative attractions.[1]

Nevertheless, United States industry was unable to resolve its dilemma of excess capacity by enlarged exports. The quantity of products exported during the 1920s fell sharply from the peak of 1915–1920 and, adjusted for price changes, was not again to equal the successes United States firms had attained throughout the war in Europe. As a percentage of the gross national product, exports of goods in 1921–1929 were almost one-half of the 1915–1920 record, and they even trailed behind the share of exports during the mediocre decade ending 1914. At the same time, the dependence of the American economy on imports of raw materials changed profoundly during this period as the nation developed a vast, permanent raw materials deficit. Between 1913 and 1929 the quantity of its imports of crude materials rose 146 percent, far higher than any other category of imports, but for items for which there was imperative need to sustain the American economy. This reversal in the nation's traditional role as a net exporter of raw materials and crude foodstuffs occurred primarily in the 1920s, though in fact the volume of imports had begun to rise sharply after the turn of the century. After 1925 the deficit of trade in raw materials rose dramatically until the end of the decade, and eventually would rise far more yet. It was particularly in metallic ores, of all imports, that the United States was to increase its dependency on the Third World. Of the 15 major world trading countries in 1927–1928, the United States accounted for 39 percent of their total imports of the nine principal raw materials and foodstuffs. This new structural dependence involved, above all, the United States' role in the Third World, for about half of all its imports during the decade came from Latin America, Asia (excluding Japan), and Africa. For the inevitable response to the need for raw materials imports is direct investment in foreign outlets capable of fulfilling those requirements at the lowest possible price. The political consequences of this elemental fact helped to define the diplomacy of the 1920s—and thereafter.[2]

All of the above factors intersected with the larger issue of war debts, the convoluted and partially frozen mechanisms for their repayment, and the monumental export of capital which was to prevent further overexpansion and declining profitability within the American economy. Debts due the United States Government because of the war amounted to nearly $12 billion in 1924. The economic and political implications of this sum absorbed an inordinate amount of Washington's attention, and its high tariff policy during the decade only exacerbated the issue's complexity. Compounding this corrosive matter were the reparations demands which loaded down Germany's—and thereby Europe's—search for economic stability. In any case, the United States temporarily resolved both problems through proportionately the most extensive export of private United States capital abroad before or after, in 1923–1928 amounting to one-eighth of its net capital formation and in 1928 equalling 1.6 percent of the gross national product. In 1900 the United States held three percent of the world's long-term investments, but almost one-third in 1929. Private investments and lending began in earnest in 1920 and reached a peak of $1.5 billion in 1928, for a net increase of United States private investment and assets abroad of over $10 billion between 1919 and 1930. Nearly half this sum went to Europe, but the raw materials producing Third World received about a third. The complicated process of placing these sums, the problems they were intended to resolve, and the new difficulties they produced set the context for United States foreign policy in the 1920s. And what was now at stake was not merely what some aggressive interests desired (but survived without) but the very health of the entire American economy and its power in the world. For the United States' new integration in the world economy created new structural imperatives, adding sources of profit as well as greater economic tensions along with potentially unlimited political obligations implicit in its global aspirations.

Political Perspectives and Contradictions

Economic affairs increasingly defined the political relations of the United States and Europe throughout the 1920s, until eventually the collapse of the world economy left matters too chaotic and grave for Western leaders to hope to resolve them with trade accords, entreatments, or loans. Violence, ultimately, was to become the inevitable outcome of unsuccessful economic integration. But before this apocalypse, which, the 1929 crash ushered in, there were also questions nominally independent of immediate money matters involving Europe as well. These included such problems as America's relations with the new League of Nations, the Soviet Union, a defeated Germany, and a tariff policy that brought political and economic dilemmas together.

The United States failure to enter the League has been overdramatized, especially in the wake of Wilson's personal struggle for it and subsequent mental breakdowns, and its significance misunderstood. Wilson saw the League as a political instrument, but independently of that forum he regarded America's economic power as a parallel mechanism for the attainment of a reformed, congenial world capitalism, and what could not be achieved one way he was confident could be accomplished the other. It was this economic instrument, embodied in the power of American capitalism to realize its goals, on which there was a large consensus among those for or against the League, including important business elements who had various objections to the proposed structure. The latter especially disliked the exclusive concessions on former German or Ottoman colonies given England and Japan at Versailles, where the League concept became tarnished with what they considered a colonialist's peace inimical to the Open Door in the Eastern Hemisphere; or they saw the League's control, in which the United States was only one among equals, as a diminution of their nation's real power. Few opponents to the League shared Senator William Borah's view of the organization as an imperialist alliance. But all this was ultimately superfluous to the political and economic outcome of United States and world diplomacy during the 1920s, for the United States was fully to utilize those means of power and leverage at its command, and had it entered the League it would scarcely have followed another foreign strategy. The impotent League was surely not going to become a substitute for the traditional means by which states relate, just as the United Nations never became a mechanism of serious diplomacy. American participation would not have altered that fact. As most historians now agree, the League decision was not a harbinger of an American retreat from the power and responsibility its now dominant status afforded it. Quite the contrary, the League was rejected at the very point the United States economy was obligated to increase its world role.

The question of the Soviet Union was scarcely one on which the United States and its former allies disagreed. The isolation of that nation, as if it were a bad dream that might thereby disappear, was their common response after their massive invasions there had failed to dislodge the Bolsheviks. Hatred of Bolshevism united the former allies and Central Powers in a transitory way, and it increased the fear of the Left everywhere in Europe, ultimately easing the acceptance of fascism in Italy, East Europe, and eventually, Germany. Still, given the sustained irrationality of the war, the loss of only Russia by the capitalist world was to prove a relatively small price for the system to pay, and after the next war the cost would vastly increase until, indeed, it was to become seemingly limitless. The League, with or without the United States, would not revise these realities, which were not based on defective organizational structures but on the very nature of world capitalism's inherited maladies.

Germany was another dilemma for Washington to confront. There was strong belief among many key Democrats and Republicans that the British were correct in arguing that overloading Germany with reparations had been a grave error at Versailles, but given the United States' unwillingness to write off the immense Allied war debts, these nations could only pay the Americans with the proceeds of German resources—a vicious circle that important American bankers soon saw as "leaky economics."[3] A few even favored a cancellation of all intergovernmental war debts and a cleaning of the slate. In the end, ironically, it was the flow of United States loans to Europe that largely sustained the repayment of war debts and reparations for as long as it lasted. And while this intricate maneuver was ultimately to produce catastrophe, temporarily it reinforced the already dominating power of American finance in the world.

If Germany was to prove one contradiction in both United States and British thinking, its tariff was to prove the greatest of all American inconsistencies. On the one hand the United States advocated an integrated world economy with reduced trade barriers, and it demanded the repayment of war debts. But on the other hand, by creating tariff walls too high for many nations to circumvent it made it much more difficult for the former allies to earn dollars, and even business internationalists favored temporary high tariffs to protect themselves against the commercial advantages which the depreciation of European currencies indeed gave industries there. While some important United States international bankers publicly denounced the consequences of the higher tariff Fordney-McCumber Act of 1922, which was followed by the yet higher Hawley-Smoot Act of 1930 even after it was apparent the apocalypse had finally arrived, most advocates of economic internationalism found no inconsistency between higher protection at home and the demand for greater access to cheaper resources and investments for the United States abroad. Among them, Herbert Hoover was to prove the most important. This dual standard was neither the first nor the last of the period, as the test of more and more American arguments became not consistency but convenience.

In the end, what is most essential in the decade of the 1920s is not so much the extent of United States foreign policy but the forms which it took and the weaknesses of the modalities and institutions it was to employ to advance its objective economic and political interests. Its ideologies produced contradictions and dysfunctions as well as profitable inconsistencies, and these created priorities—some it would later deem incorrect—which in turn were translated into regional strategies in Europe, the Third World, and Asia.

Europe and Mastery of the Third World

The growing United States need for imported raw materials profoundly influenced the interaction between it and Europe, and the issue became one of prime concern to major American business firms. Moreover, under Hoover's aggressive leadership as Secretary of Commerce and the most powerful single Cabinet member during

1921–1928, the United States sought control of raw materials both for strategic reasons and to obtain investment outlets. At the same time, it renewed its efforts to reduce the role of European exports to Latin America, both to win new markets and to consolidate further United States hegemony over that region. These questions impinged, above all, on relations with Britain.

Control of Middle East petroleum was to prove the most significant of all issues in the longer history of Anglo-American relations, though during the 1920s the dispute was relatively less acrimonious by virtue of the fact that Middle East oil output was still low and mainly a question of future promise. In 1919 the United States itself accounted for 70 percent of the world's oil output, and the Mexican fields it dominated (and which excluded Britain save on American suffrance) another 12 percent. Britain needed oil both for economic and strategic reasons, and with France sought to interpret the Versailles decisions giving them mandates over the former Ottoman possessions in a fashion that eventually would have eliminated effective United States mastery over the world's oil. Starting in October 1919, when the State Department protested Anglo-French efforts to divide Middle East and Eastern European fields among themselves, and throughout the following decade, oil became a gnawing, growing sore in Anglo-American relations. The United States repeatedly claimed, as when it disputed the legality of British concessions in Iraq in 1920, that it too shared a right to the fruits of triumph over the Ottoman Empire. "In view of the American contributions to the common victory over the Central Powers," it reminded its former allies at the Lausanne Conference convened in November 1922 to consider the political future of the former Turkish empire, "no discrimination can rightfully be made against us in a territory won by that victory."[4] The struggle remained stalemated because the region was still not a major producer, and Washington insisted on larger concessions on behalf of an "Open Door" in the region which scarcely concealed its intent to obtain a greater share in what was intrinsically an exclusive monopoly. But the major United States firms wanted access and eventually pressed for acceptance of a British compromise that would give the Americans 24 percent of the output of the Turkish and Iraqi fields in return for agreement to channel all efforts there through their common company—in effect, recognizing Britain's predominance in the area. In April 1927 the State Department relented to oil company pressures, and the next year there came into existence the famous "Red Line" agreement regulating the entire Middle East in a manner which reflected the British mastery until the new balance of forces in the region after the Second World War led to the elimination of the arrangement. Between the two eras, however, Middle Eastern concession disputes continued to exacerbate Anglo-American relations. Only the oversupply of oil during the world Depression minimized the need to resolve these obstinate disputes, and in fact three of the five United States firms in the Red Line group later quit it—at least for a time.

In Latin America, United States trade expansion, linked in part to the leverage which $1.6 billion in loans to the region during 1924–1929 gave it, resulted in a further diminution of European—preeminently British—economic power in the vast area. If this imposition of United States hegemony was not definitive immediately, one should regard it as a part of a longer-term trend whose ultimate realization came after World War Two. The struggle with vestiges of European power in the Western Hemisphere, which the United States both treated and considered as a closed, integrated part of its informal American empire, only highlighted the hypocrisy of Washington's consistent attempts to undermine parallel efforts of British and French imperialisms elsewhere.

Indeed, the Latin American situation, precisely because it so graphically revealed the dual standard in the peculiar American brand of international morality, only tended to intensify Europe's resistance to additional American incursions into their own colonial empires. The tools the United States employed to further its integration of the region were not simply loans, for which Britain remained a minor rival, but the location and bribing of local compradors ready to serve United States as opposed to European—much less national—interests. Although Hoover, as in Europe, wished to apply strictly commercial criteria for approving loans to Latin America, and disagreed with a number of the important flotations, the State Department's more political and buccaneering line prevailed, even though Hoover counseled against direct troop interventions—again over State Department objections. Commerce to Hoover, however, meant also the attack against raw-materials price-fixing, of which the most important purely Latin American effort was Brazil's attempt to stabilize and raise coffee prices throughout the decade. The Commerce Department was able to stop several direct loans to Brazil, despite the objections of United States bankers who correctly predicted the British would pick up the profits of the transactions, and Hoover partially mobilized United States coffee buyers to resist the Brazilians and develop alternative sources of supply. Loans, as often as possible, were tied to the purchase of United States goods or services, deepening the United States hold over all sectors of Latin America's economy. Not surprisingly, the United States share of total Latin American imports grew from 31 to 47 percent between 1913 and 1927, with the bulk of this trade dominating the northern half of the region. Britain still remained, at least for the time being, more powerful in Argentina and the southernmost areas. And, no less inevitable, the already dominant prewar United States access to the exports of Latin America was further extended, rising from 25 to 38 percent from 1913 to 1927. Europe could see in the Western Hemisphere a United States economic hegemony and political domination as complete and durable in its effects as traditional colonialism.

United States rivalry with Europe in the Third World above all involved the score or more of raw materials which Britain, France, and other European nations managed to subject to price and output agreements throughout the decade, creating continuous disputes that were to make a profound impression on Washington's foreign policy planners as well as key American industries increasingly dependent on raw-materials imports. These running controversies, which set a backdrop for the diplomacy of the era, attracted United States attention to that growing list of materials which it did not itself dominate. The principle of price-fixing for export purposes had been legalized in the Webb-Pomerene Act of 1918, even though only one-tenth of United States exports in 1928 were handled by cartels registered under the act. Yet it was a practice the United States sought to deny others. And insofar as it involved commodities found in the Third World, which was largely but by no means exclusively the case, it led to the American articulation of a type of hollow anti-colonialism which, as with the "Open Door" doctrine, required an equal sharing of the economic gains of Britain's or France's political penetration of other nations—a dubious advancement for colonies which scarcely impressed anyone as disinterested. Economically, in any case, the Europeans manipulated many, though by no means all, of the twenty commodity-control structures operating at one or another time at the end of the 1920s, a policy which increased their export and investment earnings originating from their colonies and offset the United States protectionism which reduced Europe's exports of manufactured goods. And this allowed Europe to amass the funds for the repayment of war debts owed the United States, in addition to importing more from it, as American political leaders always demanded. Washington rejected this European strategy of raw-materials cartels, and the matter was the source of much friction between former allies, producing one more utilitarian contradiction in United States foreign economic policy and another weakness in the world economy.

Washington, led by Hoover, had numerous tools by which to retaliate against British, French, Dutch, or German raw-materials pools: the threat to fix and raise the prices of such essential United States exports as wheat or cotton, the withholding of loans to some, the creation of buying pools among American importers, or the development of alternative sources of supply. By the end of the decade, however, the United States effort had only partially succeeded when the world Depression and oversupply made the question abstract, but the problem left a strong impression on United States thinking that was later to become important during World War Two.

The details of each commodity dispute involving Europe have been ably described elsewhere, but the contours of the struggle were fairly simple. With Germany and France, which desired United States loans, obvious levers existed to neutralize their potash cartels. In the case of rubber, Britain after 1920 tried to reduce its oversupply and declining prices, and both Hoover and the State Department agreed to United States rubber company demands that Washington make a test case of the issue. Despite the threat of retaliatory price-fixing, which did not succeed, eventually Hoover found the encouragement of substitute suppliers most efficacious, and it is at this time that Firestone Rubber turned Liberia into a virtual satellite and United States investments in the Dutch East Indies led to more direct control of the materials of those islands. Tin, which British and Dutch companies controlled, was less amenable to such pressures, and in the end the United States–European rivalry over control of the Third World's raw materials remained a point of contention to exacerbate foreign relations—one which League of Nations efforts to resolve came to nought. For the United States, other means would eventually have to be found to undermine the economic privileges of European colonialism which deprived the new colossus of the advantages and profits of domination. Given the growing dependence of the United States on imported raw materials, the matter was one of central importance in its foreign policy. The United States effort to break Europe's economic privileges would persist.

American and European Finance

The astonishingly complex problem of United States financial relations with Europe illustrated the main dilemmas confronting the capitalist world after the war. On one hand there was the conundrum of war debts and German reparations to solve, on the other the massive accumulation of United States funds in need of profitable foreign substitutes to wartime loans and domestic investments and essential to sustaining the market for United States exports. Moreover, in common with Europe's leaders the United States hoped to reimpose an international gold standard such as had unified the world economy before the war, little realizing that the new realities were far more recalcitrant, however hard they tried to find a precise formula that would allow world economic relations to return to the dependable, integrative old ways. The gold standard conception, which every nation defined to meet its own problems, eventually proved a greater source of division than unity—but its intellectual hold was so great that none of the world's major bankers could yet imagine abandoning it. Above all, there was also a strong desire among leading American and European officials to introduce both regularity and profitability with security into the world financial structure lest they lose control over it—with unforeseen consequences which eventually proved far more grave than any could dream. The unequal tension between the compulsions of national profit and the international effort to stabilize the world economy was, in the end, probably the most interesting and important development in United States foreign policy—with vast political as well as economic consequences—throughout the decade.

United States bankers were fully aware of their need to sustain the flow of loans to Europe. "But if the decrease in our export balance is to be gradual and not abrupt," Morgan partner and later top State Department official Dwight Morrow warned in October 1919, "it means that for some time to come there will be a substantial export to be settled . . . by foreign credits. . . . That is why we are all studying the problem of international credits."[5] At first major New York bankers hoped that the government-backed export credit guarantees that they designed the Edge Act to encourage would prove helpful, but the measure proved to be too little and too slow. The State Department itself was incapable of finding a solution, for on one hand it wished to see both the European economy recover and avoid a prostrate Germany hobbling that goal and again reopen the door to Bolshevism in Germany. But at the very same time that it insisted on the repayment of war debts owed the United States it also maintained high tariff walls which diminished Europe's capacity to repay the Americans, and also demanded the German delivery of reparations—a burden which by 1923 had helped make a trillion marks worth less than 24 cents and had totally paralyzed the German economy. Indeed, Washington persisted with the patently fallacious argument that there was no relation between, say, France's war debt and its ability to collect reparations, and that the United States was not in fact the final creditor ultimately responsible for the world's financial dilemma. Although Hoover and the Commerce Department enthusiastically promoted increased American exports, and thereby built an important political backing for the brilliant, aggressive Secretary, the fact is that his effort was, from a purely economic viewpoint, more notable for its inadequacy in finding a sufficient level of normal trade than its more publicized and studied successes. The main problems confronting the United States in maintaining its position and aiding recovery in the world economy were those of providing adequate credit and neutralizing the complicated legacy of war-imposed financial mechanisms and arrangements.

The United States bankers had to lend money or lose it, and the search for foreign borrowers became an essential function to them. And because of the inconsistencies of official United States policy, they took private actions which collectively produced that vast and increasingly large outflow of funds after 1920 and for the remainder of the decade which I have already noted. The State Department could resolve its ambiguity, it soon decided, by supporting the repayment of war debts, high tariffs, and German reparations at one and the same time, while mitigating the subsequent consequences of this punitive policy with private United States loans that also allowed Americans to make profits and restore the world economy. For this reason, among others, the State Department successfully opposed Hoover's desire to introduce stricter financial standards before making loans, lest the lenders eventually lose all.

It was this blend of inconsistent elements that led the State Department to transfer to a group of Anglo-American private bankers the entire question of restoring Germany's economy while it continued reparation payments. The Reparations Commission, which in late 1923 asked Chicago banker Charles G. Dawes to lead the undertaking, accepted the British idea—dubbed the "Dawes Plan"—which in its simplest form meant that private bankers would arrange for large international loans to Germans which would presumably simultaneously permit both reconstruction and reparations, thereby allowing the Allies to repay war debts to the United States while sustaining their imports from it. Secretary of State Charles Evans Hughes informally backed the solution, which for a time led to a stabilization and recovery of the German economy and, what was more important, a vast outlet in Germany as well as Europe for future United States loans.

For the American bankers who sold German bonds yielding a respectable 7 or 8 percent, the name of the game was not security but sales, for they took their profits immediately as a charge against the principal. From 1924 to 1930 over $1.2 billion went to Germany alone in what was a precarious though profitable business for United States investment houses netting at least $50 million in fees. That almost two-fifths of all United States foreign loans were in default by 1935 was not so much a confirmation of Hoover's warnings as an illustration of the compulsions and weaknesses which were increasingly becoming the very essence of the world financial system throughout the entire decade.

This fatal structural defect is surely the single most significant and instructive phenomenon to emerge from the increasingly fragile and crisis-ridden decade. Both in fact and desire the economies of the major capitalist nations were more and more integrated throughout the decade after the war, which made the growing weaknesses of each one the problem of them all—and that vulnerability was predominantly economic but also political in the broadest sense. For this reason, in an effort that was more and more characterized by futility, the United States, England, and France—in relation to other nations in lesser roles—attempted to develop coordinated financial policies among their central banks. Given the almost exclusive role the Federal Reserve System allocated its New York bank over international financial questions, until October 1928 this meant that Benjamin Strong, a former J. P. Morgan associate and now head of the Federal Reserve Bank of New York, led American policy. The major world bankers who dealt with each other, though often personally congenial, from the inception each acted on behalf of his national interests and needs. And because of the myriad conflicting economic and political interests and disagreements, this meant that the central banks were largely occupied with the increasingly futile effort to overcome differences among the major capitalist nations essentially moving from one crisis to another. The details of these inordinately complicated issues have been best described in the fascinating official Federal Reserve Bank history of the debacle, yet it involved such ever-changing problems as the role of gold in international reserves, interest rates in conflict with international as opposed to national economic objectives, German recovery, and the uncontrolled as well as directed flows of capital in the world.[6] At one point it was an American effort to get German banks to use dollars and gold as reserves and diminish British power in that nation, at another the excess flow of investable funds from the United States to Europe during 1927, when foreign interest rates were significantly greater there. It was the 1927 drop in United States interest, only partially designed to help the British attract capital and retain gold, that had the unanticipated effect of stimulating further speculation on the United States stock market after early 1928, which was one of several important immediate factors that triggered the 1929 crash.

By 1928, in any event, it became clear that each national economy was too fragile to allow cooperation to stabilize the others, and the difficulties that characterized the earlier period now were greatly aggravated. The world credit and financial structure, built on an accretion of short-range decisions which, from the American viewpoint, had nothing more in common than a desire to optimize national profit and power, had in fact become a kind of byzantine system far too vulnerable to any single weakness to survive much longer. It was sufficiently integrated so that problems in one nation could have serious consequences to another, but too decentralized and divided to even imagine finding common solutions. And the weakest nation in the chain was Germany, whose very revival and continued existence within the sphere of integrated, as opposed to rival, capitalism was dependent on access to foreign—mainly United States—credits. By mid-1928, despite the prevalent optimistic pabulum, some United States investment and banking leaders began developing a quite sophisticated model of the specific weaknesses of the world economy and their consequences not merely to the United States stock market, world economic power, or exports, but even to the future of capitalism in Europe. Seeing the crisis, both the Federal Reserve Bank of New York and other key investment interests took steps, all of which were to prove more or less futile, to correct what they misperceived to be the most urgent weaknesses, though the Federal Reserve System and its New York bank now split and neutralized each other's power. By October 1929, when American and world capitalism began breaking down with mounting intensity each passing month, all efforts to sustain cooperation only further confirmed that the entire system of voluntary integration had always been a chimera.

In fact, the effort at capitalist cooperation had also been a critical attempt to save Germany for a reasonably integrated and cooperative European and world capitalism, an undertaking also essential for the health of the American economy as it emerged after the World War. And, in the last analysis, bolstering European capitalism, especially in Germany and Central Europe, was indispensable to undoing the social and political effects of the Great War and protecting the world against revolution and the atavistic nationalist Right. The effort was not to succeed.

Also a failure was the assumption of capitalist rationality and the possibility of cooperation, even when mutual dangers were clearly perceived, when conflict was more profitable to national interests. Indeed, those real problems that official bankers could accurately identify transcended their capacity for rational, common action simply because their national interests dictated different solutions regardless of the clarity of their perceptions. The dilemma of managing a national capitalism both in its domestic and international frameworks repeatedly proved an untenable one of priorities and concrete tactics, especially with the increasingly contradictory, conflict-prone efforts of each nation to try to use others to solve domestic problems. Yet there was at the same time the disparity between capitalist social analysis, which might indeed be accurate on detailed aspects of a far greater context, and the richly textured social comprehension that the political, social, as well as economic aspects of the historic breakdown of world capitalism required. Even to admit the existence of that crisis was to accept a definition of reality which condemned to futility reform within the context of the old order. To a critical dysfunctional degree, the 1920s proved, a law of a capitalist society and its foreign policy was that it produced conflicts of national interests and that no mechanism or formula existed to undo the instability and crises inherent to capitalism from numerous political, economic, and social origins. The United States became the world's banker and used its funds both for temporary profit and to stave off further revolutionary changes for a decade, but ultimately its own limits and weaknesses were to merge, even heighten, with those of Europe to lead to a collapse that was bloodier, graver, and more protracted than the last. By 1930 the United States had largely failed in its effort to play Britain's prewar role in the stabilization and exploitation of the world economy, it had scarcely reintroduced equilibrium anywhere in the world which the military or political traumas of the war had touched, the Soviet Union had neither disintegrated nor disappeared, and the danger of revolution from the Left was now far exceeded by the reemergence of military capitalism dressed in exotic fascist ideologies. It was for the next decade to cope with the political and military consequences of the 1920s preoccupation with a world economy that began its unprecedented collapse even before the short decade of respite had ended. Ultimately, the 1920s would later appear merely as an exception in the longer epoch of violence, civil war, and crisis of world capitalism that was to sear the next decade and thereafter.

The Collapse of the World Economy

After 1929 the world economy for the United States was but a vast array of insoluble difficulties, and its former allure dissipated with each new shock. These growing frustrations are ultimately interesting because of the way they shaped United States planning for the future. In fact, like all the other capitalist economies, both out of choice and necessity the American economy turned inward as the fragile channels of world commerce capsized. While the 1929 crash did not immediately bring on a world monetary collapse, it made it inevitable by heightening the existing system's endemic weaknesses and undermining the international credit structure to which so many capitalist nations were tied.

The crash struck the United States and Germany hardest, and it affected the United States the longest, with 25 percent of its labor force unemployed in 1933 and 17 percent in 1939. In mid-1932 general world trade was only one-third of 1929, and by 1938 it was still far below precrash levels. As for the United States, its exports as a percentage of the gross national product were the lowest since the

Civil War, and in 1932 and 1933 its exports were valued at less than a third of 1929. In May 1931, after the collapse of the Credit-Anstalt, Austria's largest commercial bank, revealed the vulnerability of all Central Europe in the face of the maze of reparations claims and short-term loans that had accumulated, Hoover's one-year moratorium on all reparations and intergovernmental debts was too little, too late. That summer, as British finance stumbled from one crisis to another, the final encapsulation of national economies became inevitable as England on September 20 suspended the gold standard and payments and thereby began to consolidate a sterling bloc which removed one-third of the world's trade from normal intercourse. By the end of the year a system of rigid exchange controls, touching two-thirds of international trade, was in effect among half the nations, including the United States. The world, in effect, was now a melange of trade blocs and insular national economies, and their uneven economic recoveries—eventually the United States' included—were to come largely as a consequence of rearmament and preparation for war.

For the United States, however, this did not mean an end to empire in the Western Hemisphere, even though the objective value of the hemispheric system declined temporarily. Indeed, given the collapse of trade elsewhere, Latin America's relative importance and promise to the United States increased, if only because, unlike Europe, it and the Philippines were the two areas of which the United States could be sure and where its control was sufficient to shape reality in conformity to its needs. But the Roosevelt Administration's policy moved at a somewhat more subtle rhetorical level than that of its predecessors, even though Hoover is probably as much the author of the "Good Neighbor Policy" as those who later obtained credit for it. He had at the end of his administration withdrawn United States troops from Nicaragua and as well as partially from Haiti, and generally had opposed use of troops.

The Democratic Party decided to do no less than Hoover, and its 1932 platform condemned meddling in Latin American internal affairs. During summer 1933, however, when the venal and cooperative Machado regime in Cuba was overthrown, the State Department responded to its own instinct as well as United States business interests by opposing the nationalist government of Ramon Grau San Martin, with its labor and, allegedly, Communist backing. At the end of 1933, after unrelenting American political and economic pressures and ill-concealed threats of military intervention, Grau's fate was sealed. "Our own commercial and export interests in Cuba cannot be revived under this government," Ambassador Sumner Welles warned Washington, and in January of the next year the United States supported and immediately recognized a Batista-backed coup that managed Cuba on behalf of United States interests for the next quarter-century.[7] Shortly thereafter the fictitious autonomy of the new satellite was reinforced when the United States agreed to discard the Platt Amendment—save for a base at Guantanamo. Tariffs of both nations were altered to further integrate Cuba, and by the end of 1934 trade between the two states had increased well over 100 percent. "If the case of Cuba was to be the focus of Latin American scrutiny of our acts and intentions," Secretary of State Cordell Hull later recalled, "a happier one could scarcely have been chosen."[8]

Latin America, therefore, became a region in which the United States more intensively cultivated economic possibilities in lieu of options elsewhere, and Hull gave full vent to his trade and low-tariff theories, in effect to further integrate the hemisphere into a United States–led trade bloc. From this time onward the State Department busily mobilized Latin America to endorse United States trade policies at one hemispheric conference after another. And while its crude, overt intervention in Cuba belied the reality, the Roosevelt Administration tried to improve the rhetoric of its Latin American policy by repudiating the Roosevelt Corollary the President's cousin had announced three decades earlier by withdrawing the last troops from Haiti in 1934 even as it was consolidating its ideal example of the Cuban venal comprador regime. If in fact hemispheric commerce with the United States was not to recover during the 1930s merely by virtue of such political domination and despite the creation in 1934 of an Export-Import Bank that was largely used to lubricate hemispheric trade, what exchange there was became yet more reliably a part of the United States economic empire. Occasional exceptions, such as the Mexican oil nationalization of 1938 which United States firms crudely provoked when they ignored Mexican court orders, were possible because of the neutralizing role of United States silver investors in Mexico who counseled against rash action lest they too be seized, alternative markets for Mexican oil, and the erroneous American confidence that they could later retrieve the property at a more propitious time. Despite Washington's covert attack on the standing of the peso and boycott of equipment to its oil industry, Mexico's success was the exception rather than the rule—one that the United States would not again so lightly tolerate.

The United States Confronts Japan

World War One created a military and economic vacuum of power which Japan intended to fill, and to the United States and England it was both inconceivable and undesirable that a united nationalist China balance Japanese might. Not only would such a China eliminate the privileges of extraterritoriality that the United States and other nations had accumulated, but after 1920 it appeared for a time also possible that the Nationalist regime might even tolerate the spread of Communism. Yet the ideal solution of a compliant, weak China and restrained Japan was never to be found. The long, ambiguous United States search for a solution to these dilemmas was to take increasing time and effort in Washington until, ultimately, the next war that was only to confound both Japan and the United States in China.

The fact was that immediately after World War One both Japan and the United States were engaged in a naval arms race, and England wished to terminate its 1902 treaty with Japan because of the radically new power situation which made its former ally the leading menace to Britain's position in China and East Asia. To obtain Japan's explicit recognition of the terms of the Open Door as well as a naval moratorium which would both reduce the burden of arms costs and give the Anglo-American fleets preponderance in both oceans, the Anglo-Americans cajoled a reluctant Japan into participating in the 1921–1922 Washington Conference. By that time the United States loan and trade policy had failed to use economic power to neutralize Japan in China, if only because bankers refused to risk significant sums to back Washington's policy, and it was to prove a dismal failure over the next decade both in assuring United States access to China and inhibiting Japan via financial threats and inducements when it required loans for its own use. For the United States the stakes in China were interesting but not decisive, and Charles Evans Hughes made it clear to the United States delegates at the Washington Conference that the United States "would never go to war over any aggression on the part of Japan in China."[9] The ten-year naval agreement the conference endorsed gave the Anglo-Americans both individual and collective supremacy over Japan, but still allowed the latter some capital ship expansion and a de facto supremacy in the Western Pacific. The Nine Power Treaty on China reaffirmed the Open Door regarding trade and China's territorial integrity, but it mandated Japan and China to sign an alleged revision of the Versailles settlement on Shantung which in fact left Japan economic mastery of the area. China unsuccessfully attempted to get British and French troops and economic privileges withdrawn as well, and no one—the United States included—for a moment was willing to forgo the extraterritoriality which as much as any other factor denied China's sovereignty. In fact, the United States and the West wished a China weak enough to be dominated but strong enough to resist Japan, a hopelessly contradictory and utopian formula which proved the most unattainable of all propositions.

This ambiguity in United States tactics is perhaps the most distinctive aspect of its policy, for in the last analysis the United States never fought to make China strong or independent in Asia but primarily to keep Japan sufficiently weak and economically integrated with other industrial nations, and secondarily to preserve an option on participating in China's economic development if and when the seemingly perpetual frustrations to its attainment could be overcome. From the inception of this strategy, United States officials were divided on how to attain this goal, but for the most part it opposed the emergence of a strongly nationalist China that could resist the United States as well as Japan, and it always had important officials who regarded Japan as the natural leader of the region, one whose ambitions could best be controlled by being carefully directed and encouraged at one and the same time. Moreover, in due course the flirtation of Chiang Kai-shek with the USSR, and the later emergence of an active Communist movement in the north of China, made the Japanese role as an anti-Bolshevik force in the region appear compatible to American interests. It was precisely this calculation that had caused a reluctant Wilson Administration to support Japan's intervention in Siberia in 1918, yet to also then send American forces to watch the Japanese while assisting the struggle against the Bolsheviks.

By the late 1920s, in any event, the United States and England saw that Chiang was better able than his rival warlords to combine a moderate nationalism with anti-Communism (which he had bloodily confirmed in his 1927 mass liquidations) as well as resistance to Japan. While they refused his demands for complete abolition of extraterritoriality, the Americans and British made greater concessions to the Chiang regime and hoped to encourage a stronger, but not too powerful, China oriented toward the West—a gesture that caused Japan to regard Chiang as a puppet for whom their own option had to be found. In a very important sense, the United States refused to pursue a consistent policy toward China and Japan throughout the first half of this century, giving an illusion of endemic indecision to add to any description of its inordinately complex diplomatic relations in East Asia.

With the collapse of the world economy, Japanese militarists were able to prevail in taking their country to war in Manchuria in September 1931, hoping thereby to head off nationalist anti-Japanese forces emerging there, install their own puppet as a counter to the one they felt the Anglo-Americans had in Chiang, and to expand their already dominant power in the regional economy. Indeed, by that time Japan's investments and trade with China were, by far, preeminent, but in Manchuria only a very small fraction of total United States investments in China stood to lose by a Japanese takeover. By 1931, as well, United States trade with Japan was two to three times greater than with China—a fact that was to remain true for the rest of the decade—while its investments in Japan were almost three times as high as in China. The weight of these statistics had importance in creating within the United States a group of key investment leaders, of whom Thomas Lamont of the Morgan firm was the most important, who like most British officials sympathized with Japan's ambitions in Manchuria. And they in turn reinforced diplomats, such as Ambassador Joseph Grew in Tokyo or Nelson Johnson in Peiping, who urged understanding if not justification of Japan's seemingly natural ambitions in northern China, where it would serve as a strong barrier to Communism by ending local chaos. Accepting Japan's sphere of influence there, this group argued, would cause it to stop and accept the United States presence farther south and in the Philippines. In this view, the United States had to work for its own interests in the context of an aggressive Japan, a strategy perfectly consistent with Washington's main Asia policy since 1905.

This ambiguity was to find full scope in the much studied response to Japan's invasion dubbed the "Stimson Non-Recognition Doctrine." In fact Hoover and his Secretary of State were quite explicit that "these questions" involving China would never cause the United States to go to war with Japan, and Stimson himself wished the League of Nations to take the initiative in the crisis and allow the United States to follow it. At the same time, he was conscious that an unopposed Japanese success would cause "direct material damage to our trade" and "incalculable harm . . . to American prestige in China," and hence the United States backed the League's decision to study the situation while at the same time it urged conciliation on the victim and executioner alike.[10] The doctrine, which suggested that the United States would not accept the legality of changes in the Open Door policy or China's territorial independence, was both atypical of United States policy thereafter and nebulous enough not to offend. The League's Lytton Commission report the following October was critical of the Chinese by explaining the historical origins of Japan's expansion, yet condemned the Japanese and demanded their withdrawal without any mention of great-power action to compel it. The report was the sort of intricate balancing act the United States could endorse. Japan, of course, ignored it and withdrew from the League. Despite the unresolved matters of naval expansion in the background, relations with Japan the next two years improved despite disagreements on economic issues. But in April 1934, with Japan's own Monroe Doctrine of a "Co-prosperity Sphere in Greater East Asia," the United States felt but did not voice its displeasure at the virtual end of the Open Door which Japan's proclaimed assumption of responsibility for the peace of the area, and its opposition to any activity disturbing its imperialist relations with China, implied. The British, however, with their stake in China nine times greater than that of the United States, much to Hull's irritation were quite resigned to assigning northern China to Japan, and for the moment the United States could not circumscribe Japan. Nor was it able to do much when Japan at the end of the year announced it would not renew existing restrictions on naval expansion which were to terminate in 1936. The United States had, after all, begun large naval construction, admittedly allowed within existing treaties, purely to create employment at home, but that act mitigated its subsequent ability to complain about Japan's action.

After Japan's invasion of China in July 1937, Hull and others in the State Department were convinced of the inevitability of a serious confrontation with Japan, but excluded as solutions both diplomacy and collective actions with their logical European allies. Hull "doubted whether any joint action, unless it embraced a real show of force . . . would be of any avail. And I was certain that neither Great Britain . . . nor the United States . . . had any thought of employing force."[11] Joseph Grew advised no action, and the basic fact was that the United States wanted to keep out of the China conflict. Moreover, Chiang's criticism of the alleged United States abandonment of him irked Washington. It was also disturbed by the USSR's subsequent military aid to the dictator's Kuomintang regime even though it later opposed any Western loans to enable Chiang to buy arms elsewhere. The best the United States would do in 1937 was to urge both sides to stop the fighting and back League resolutions for a convocation of the signatories to the Nine Power Treaty—a meeting Japan refused to attend. Only the USSR in the West called for a strong stand in 1937, but as Hull recalled, "It might have led to reprisals by the Japanese and possibly to war. We were not prepared in arms or mind for war."[12]

The United States toleration of Japanese expansion which replaced its encouragement of it until 1917 had helped produce a grave crisis full of ironies. Washington did not intervene in China because its interests were only partially imperiled, but above all because it did not trust the existing regime and it quite correctly knew Chiang was too weak to help successfully. Later, when the United States was far stronger, it could not save him either. Imperialism was the logic of Japan's reactionary and nationalist ruling class as well as its objective position in the world economy after the Depression closed its traditional markets. Moreover, Chinese nationalism and Communism both threatened its hegemony, and it was ready to act. After July 1939, when the United States notified Japan it would not renew the 1911 Commercial Treaty, most American leaders assumed the die was cast, though the time of the clash was by no means certain and their increasing constriction of their raw materials exports to Japan only made their prediction self-fulfilling. The war in Europe only weeks later, and the isolated, weak colonial empires waiting to be taken in the Dutch East Indies or French Indochina, now increasingly became the standard of action for Washington's decisions. In the end, it was when Japan entered Indochina, a nation providing the United States with but one-half of one percent of its imports and consuming far less than that of its exports, that war no longer became a question of mere eventuality but of months or even weeks. Twice in the twentieth century was the United States ready to enter a major conflict in response to upheavals in the same small nation in which its objective direct interests were nonexistent, but which it believed impinged on its potential freedom to expand and to control the destiny of some major area of the world.

The European Disaster

After having helped sow chaos in Europe during 1914–1918, and having deferred it with money during the following decade, it was there that the United States was to turn its primary attention to the political and diplomatic failures of the old order. That priority was the logic of the United States' own industrial criteria of power, and that fetish was to prevail in its thinking about the world until this very day.

While it would be unjust to dismiss the role of neutrality legislation and embargoes—moral and actual—in the United States relationship to the European crisis and the spread of fascism, these gestures and moods were less the cause of United States policy than a reflection of a reality and a widely accepted definition of the world. In fact the world economy had become less important and isolation was a description as well as a desire as some members of Congress moved to pass the Neutrality Act of August 1935 and later laws. Both the term "neutrality" and the very existence of the Act impose an artificial criterion for evaluating the basis and conduct of United States diplomacy in the 1930s. Since the Act did not truly bind the President to an embargo against belligerents, save on arms and munitions until March 1936, and excluded oil and materials easily turned into weapons, businessmen, farm Senators, and moralists were all pleased. Later "moral embargoes" saw only increased oil and scrap exports to such offenders as Italy and Franco Spain, and simply did not work—save to the detriment of Loyalist Spain. Exporters, with various degrees of wrath, successfully objected to not being able to make a profit off of trade, and only arms and munitions producers, shipowners, and war loan financiers ultimately had reason to complain. Eventually the White House as well as original proponents of the "neutrality" legislation, such as Senator Gerald Nye, came to realize the Congressional efforts were both superfluous and dangerous. Nevertheless, the administration was glad to cite the prohibitions of law against Loyalist Spain when the pressure of United States Catholics made it expedient to do so. In fact, even more than in the Far East, the United States was searching for a relevant policy in Europe opposing Nazi Germany while also avoiding war. Roosevelt's oft-cited and clumsy October 5, 1937, "Quarantine" speech, which in reality merged four State Department position papers, led only to a denial of any intent to do anything capable of being translated into effective action.

The United States was confused as to what to do meaningfully to control fascism and tacitly, and later explicitly, fell behind British and French appeasement diplomacy. During the September 1938 Czech crisis and Munich, Hull took the position that the United States would not make appeals for peace or resort to force, while Roosevelt felt "It's safe to urge peace until the last moment." On September 26, Roosevelt wired Hitler and Edward Beneš "not to break off negotiations looking to a peaceful, fair, and constructive settlement," and after the destruction of Czechoslovakia was arranged the United States urged Beneš not to upset it.[13] Neither Hull nor Roosevelt felt that Munich gave the West more than a breathing space, but they were ready to take that much at Czech expense. To Hull, indeed, the solution to the European crisis was subsumed in his monomania, which I discuss below, but suffice it to say the initiative was left to a European diplomacy that blundered into a war in which friends and enemies were chosen only in the last moments of one of the most compromised chapters of the history of diplomacy, in which the Anglo-French were willing to save Polish reaction but not Czech democracy, in which the Western Europeans first tried to direct Hitler's attack against the Soviet Union and then either surrendered or refused to fight seriously when they failed, in which the USSR agreed to complicity with Germany rather than combat it, the Czechs surrendered rather than fight alone or with the USSR, and in which the West and Germany both wooed fascist Italy and tolerated Franco Spain.

The United States' initial endorsement of the diplomacy of appeasement and its common hostility with Britain toward an alliance with the USSR made it a passive partner in the game, and like its later allies, who did not enjoy the advantages of distance, it too sought to defer as long as possible the earnest fight against European fascism. The political assumptions in Europe and the United States that had made these policies arise did not disappear after 1939, and the alliance with the USSR was to become a brief exception in the longer stream of modern history, and to Western leaders a mistaken decision based on their erroneous assumption that the Left was less of a danger to their long-term interests than the unreconstructed, expansionist Right.

The Economic Foundations of American Foreign Policy

States often have ideologies which are not an index to their practice, and the disparity between the two can exist in constant contradiction. Ideology will not last long if it becomes dysfunctional to the preservation of power, but if it is merely irrelevant it can remain enshrined indefinitely. In any case, false consciousness is at least as old and common as the clear unity of perception, action, and principle, and it is important to know when it exists and powerful men believe that their actions should advance some goals and commitments. If in fact, as I think it can be argued, the practice of United States foreign policy since 1890 has never quite found its suitable comprehensive ideology which conforms to practice, and a benign tension between the two has existed since then, it was during 1933–1944 that Cordell Hull, whose tenure as Secretary of State was the longest in United States history, made a serious effort to formulate a suitable American theory of the world. One cannot, in any case, comprehend the motives as well as the theory of United States foreign policy after 1933 without taking Hull's accurate if incomplete official vision seriously.

United States foreign policy after 1890 was so deeply concerned with economics that it was no surprise that Hull should articulate what was a conservative economic interpretation of history and world conflict. In the crudest terms, to the Hullians the basic source of world conflict was trade and economic rivalry, and if nations could unhamper and free trade, then they would automatically attain peace. As a former leader of the low-tariff Southerners in the House, whose cotton and tobacco crops made it the most internationally minded of all sections, Hull also neatly reflected the interests of his most important constituents, but it would be wrong to reduce his commitments merely to those of the pork barrel. "But toward 1916," he later recalled, "I embraced the philosophy I carried throughout my twelve years as Secretary of State. . . . From then on, to me, unhampered trade dovetailed with peace; high tariffs, trade barriers, and unfair economic competition, with war. Though realizing that many other factors were involved, I reasoned that, if we could get a freer flow of trade—freer in the sense of fewer discriminations and obstructions—so that one country would not be deadly jealous of another and the living standards of all countries might rise . . . we might have a reasonable chance for lasting peace."[14] That neither the history of capitalist conflict nor logic made Hull's political conclusions or visions follow from his premises and the fact that the entire notion was no less ideology and false consciousness in his hands than in Woodrow Wilson's first American clear statement of the doctrine are besides the point. The United States was a trading nation that could benefit from the implementation of such doctrines, from which it could gain if others accepted them also. That it too was a high-tariff nation ready to dominate its entire hemisphere was irrelevant. Whether false or hypocritical, the Hullian doctrine was useful—and sincerely believed as well.

Hull did not at any time have exclusive mastery over United States foreign trade or political policy, and others often gained tactical ascendancy in advocating one or another approach, but they too failed and reinforced Hull's stature and influence. By virtue of twelve years in office he was to become the key architect in the formulation of the purposes of United States foreign policy and war aims. Because there was no division between foreign and domestic policy during the New Deal or any other time, the domestic priorities which the New Deal imposed precluded following Hull's counsel during his first years in office, and the economic and political realities in the other world trading nations made "Hullianism" irrelevant. Even the acceptance of his concrete proposals, such as the Trade Agreements Act of 1934, did not radically transform the commerce with the eighteen nations—mainly Latin American—who agreed to its reciprocal trade clauses. Hull was unable to decide United States policy at the London Economic Conference of June 1933, but Europe was scarcely any readier to accept his program, which in any case was irrelevant to the vast, complex matrix of unresolvable problems that world capitalism had accumulated since 1914. The United States during the first Roosevelt Administration largely opted for domestic economic solutions, but neither this nor Hull's program—which important banking and agricultural interests backed—could lift the United States out of the Depression. War was to do that, and it was far less a question of how this or that economic interest proposed to resolve the crisis of capitalism than how they actually did so. But the failure of the New Deal's domestic emphasis to end the Depression put the stress in future economic policy plans on that which had yet to be equally tested: the global economy. Foreign economic relations, of any decade after the Civil War, were less important to the American economy statistically but more significant in helping to define diplomatic objectives and war aims intended to avert another world depression.

Hull's economic interpretation of the causes of war was one that was shared both by businessmen and those Senators who thought neutrality acts could remove the specific economic causes which forced the United States into World War One. And since a concrete military or strong diplomatic response was one the United States was unwilling to employ against the rise of fascism until the end of the decade, Hull reacted to each challenge by referring to general economic principles and relations the United States wished others to both accept and implement. "It is the collapse of the world structure, the development of isolated economies," he argued in May 1935, "that has let loose the fear which now grips every nation, and which threatens the peace of the world."[15]

In fact, however, the change in the world economy most harmful to the United States was the consolidation of the British-dominated sterling bloc, and a good number of the largest firms of American big business reached their own cartel, output, marketing, and patent agreements with German industry to avoid economic conflicts. It was to the problem of Anglo-American relations that the State Department after 1936 turned most earnestly, attempting to win Britain's support not only for familiar trade principles but concrete changes in tariff and exchange policies. The former was not overly difficult, if only because the British still respected the theories on which their nineteenth-century hegemony was based, and the matter was inconclusively negotiated at the level of practice until 1938. For political reasons Britain was unwilling to break off such talks, preferring to cultivate American friendship and solidarity with its diplomatic strategy, but economically it could not afford to make major concessions—and was not to do so until after the next war. Hull, on the other hand, tried to persuade the British that economic causes were the origins of Germany's expansionism, and that diplomatic solutions went hand in hand with economic. "I kept hammering home the economic side of international relations as the major possibility for averting the catastrophe," Hull later recalled.[16] After much bickering the British agreed to minor and rather vague concessions in a November 1938 agreement they thought politically expedient to sign—though in fact the Anglo-American struggle over the theory and practice of world trade was only beginning. "I feel sure," Hull told the German ambassador during the Munich crisis, "that if the German Government decides to change its course and adopt our liberal commercial policy, it could move in our direction more rapidly than even German officials imagine. Capital and businessmen in other countries would immediately discover your Government's basic change of policy, and your manufacturers would soon get credit with which to pay for raw materials."[17]

This widely held economic interpretation of Nazism was not so much incorrect as immaterial and naïve for the exigencies of the moment and the nature of the needed cure of the malignancy that had grown on an ill German capitalism which, admittedly, had major resemblances with all the others. Publicly, not only for Hull but for the entire administration, the United States answer to the world crisis was economic accords and expansion. "I believed," Hull persisted in 1940 with his correct but now momentarily irrelevant thesis on raw materials and trade, "that the trade agreements program should be retained intact to serve as a cornerstone around which the nations could rebuild their commerce on liberal lines when the war ended."[18] By that time other officials did not disagree with Hull but knew that they would first have to find political and military solutions.

After 1937, the rest of America's leaders merely regarded Hullian doctrine as premature, yet it soon became the keystone of United States war aims and relations with Britain. Having defined its ideology, all that remained for the administration was to make practice conform to it—not only that of the rest of the world but of the United States as well—for its own high tariffs and hemispheric domination, to name but a few of many contradictions, were apparent for all the world to see. Without its own selflessness, the American brand of internationalism seemed to other nations to be one more subtle strategy for integration and hegemony. And, with Washington confident of its power, such a new world was sure to lead to a vast surge of United States exports and investments.

Hull's definitions always assumed trade relations would be between industrial capitalist states, with Third World nations being either docile, colonized, or otherwise integrated. The existence of the USSR, not to mention other socialist economies, was ignored, and revolutionary movements anywhere were unimaginable. That indeed there already existed an agrarian radical movement in Asia seemed not to enter into United States planning at all. In effect, what the United States was really contemplating was its relationship to Europe and Japan, and in fact the political development in the world immediately after 1920 made this preoccupation and desire and need to trade and invest comprehensible for the period. Yet the world had entered a new epoch after 1929, with new sets of political as well as economic challenges for the United States to resolve along with the traditional compulsions and desires. Not unpredictably, it confronted its new political problems with old or irrelevant responses and ideas, setting the stage for more frustrations and crises.

World War Two: The European Context

World War Two, like the first orgy of bloodletting that had preceded it, was profoundly significant to the following generation not in the manner in which it led to diplomatic settlements or even permanent new power relations, but in the way it unleashed forces in the world that no one—neither Americans nor Russians—anticipated.[19] For the war made permanent revolutions and the momentum from the Left the central irresistible theme in the history of our times, and while it temporarily resolved capitalism's difficulties it ultimately intensified them as it made the problems of world politics and economics yet more indivisible. However predictable aspects of it were, the war, in retrospect, ended in surprise conclusions, for many of the most important changes it engendered were neither deferred nor undone, as had been the case between 1919 and 1929, but immediately defined the mainstream of three more decades that were not so much the conclusion of the war in 1945 as a continuation of it in diverse forms.

World War Two was for the United States preeminently a European conflict, for America's priority of retaining the economically and politically most significant regions was a congenial one to Washington's criteria of power. On the other hand, not until June 1944 were the Anglo-American armies to open a true second front on the continent, and this fact was to profoundly color United States relations with the Soviet Union as well as the political outcome of the war in Central and Eastern Europe. America's leadership was keenly conscious of both these consequences, and therefore much more eager than the British to return quickly to Europe via France. As a surrogate, Roosevelt in May 1942 had promised Stalin a new front somewhere, and the quite minor and incidental invasion of North Africa in November of that year was the outcome, but subsequent promises to open a major second front were repeatedly postponed, so that the Russians had both reason to doubt the solidity of its new allies-by-necessity as well as the obligation to confront 70 to 75 percent of Germany's forces—save during early 1945—for most of the war. Russian military losses were therefore about twenty-five times greater than those of the United States, plus at least an equal number of civilians—amounting to 20 million deaths or more in all. And despite the loss of almost one-half of its population area, the USSR supplied itself with at least 85 percent of its own military supplies—and came exceedingly close to losing the war. The USSR's desperate need for greater help from its allies and its decision to subjugate ideological preferences to the imperatives of keeping the alliance intact and defeating Germany became the central motivation of its wartime policy as the Anglo-Americans focused on the periphery of North Africa and Italy until June 1944.

The obvious political implications of troop locations weighed heavily in the thinking of men such as Secretary of War Henry Stimson and others, and in August 1943 Britain and the United States authorized a mobile force to drop in Germany within hours should it surrender or capsize before the opening of the second front. Not until 1943, when it became apparent that the USSR had definitively stopped and reversed the thrust of the German advance, did diplomacy and politics become the main concern to the American decision makers. They tended to assume that the American ability to control the terms of the peace settlement would increase if these questions were postponed until the end of the conflict, when both its allies would be weaker and more solicitous of American opinion. In August 1943, as well, while the USSR was still fighting the Germans within its own prewar borders, Anglo-American forces invaded Italy and thereby raised the issue of whether, in lieu of a three-power political accord, possession would be nine-tenths of the law in dictating the nature of the European peace.

By that time the military and political problems of Europe had merged for both American and British leaders. The political impact of the war on Europe's masses was immeasurable but self-evidently very great, and threatening to the Anglo-Americans. Politically,

Europe's traditional Right had been allied with Hitler, and in many countries it was to an important degree in exile or dead. The Resistance in Italy, France, Yugoslavia, Greece, and elsewhere was predominantly Communist-led or ready to collaborate in a united front with them, and it was the Resistance alone that could merge patriotism with their social program. A constant preoccupation in Washington and London was what the Left and Resistance might do, and the relation of these forces to Russia. For while the USSR had publicly abolished the Comintern in May 1943 and often had publicly called upon all Communists to subordinate their programs to unity behind the effort to win the war, the issue of the Left for the United States was one of capabilities as well as intentions, and in fact American leaders always held Moscow accountable for all actions of the Resistance, as if it lacked any scintilla of true independence—despite massive proof to the contrary. That Russia would play the role of inhibitor of revolutionaries seeking to attain power seemed inconceivable, yet it was nevertheless true. But for the West's leaders the greater danger was the very existence of a powerful Left with the capacity and will to prevail, and that problem had to be confronted in 1943 independently of Russia's intentions.

As soon as the British and Americans entered Italy, Stalin asked that they jointly formulate a common policy for governing all defeated Axis states, but the United States insisted on excluding the Russians from determining the fate of Italy. The Anglo-Americans kept intact the structure of a discredited Right and systematically suppressed the Resistance, which eventually grew to about 150,000, despite its nearly exclusive uncompromised commitment to antifascism. As the British correctly argued, the Italian precedent was one the USSR too could follow.

In France, where the United States had backed the pro-German Vichy regime and Britain literally created a new conservative opposition behind Charles DeGaulle, the two allies remained at loggerheads over France's future orientation in the postwar world, with Anthony Eden and Winston Churchill openly committed to a France ready to collaborate with a British-led West European alliance after the war. Such a postwar bloc, which the British saw as essential to counterbalancing both Russian and United States power, posed a danger to American plans for an integrated world economic and political system, but the ineptness of the United States' chosen vehicles in France and the decision of many of Vichy's former disciples to move over to DeGaulle by 1944 left the contest in France between Gaullism and the Communist-led Resistance. And this struggle was decided definitively when the Anglo-American armies entered and installed an occupation of their own choice, to which the poorly armed and finally docile Communists—responding to their own instincts, the realities of power, and Soviet advice—acquiesced in return for minor government posts.

In Greece, however, the Left was autonomous and relatively more powerful than in any nation in which the Anglo-American armies were able to land. The EAM, which six Left and republican parties formed in September 1941, stood against the bankrupt forces of tradition in the military and monarchy as well as for the anti-Axis struggle, and its successful resistance was both a desire and an unavoidable necessity which ferocious German, Italian, and puppet repression imposed. By the late summer of 1944, when the Germans began to withdraw, the EAM was in reality a state controlling with popular support at least two-thirds of the national territory and able to take the remainder. When the British entered during October it was as an occupying army prepared to impose its puppet regime in Athens on the nation and retain Greece within the traditional British sphere of influence. A portion of the Communist leadership in the EAM, under Moscow's order, sought to compromise with British demands but, not for the first or last time, they could not impose discipline on the party, many of its military officers, or the EAM. The battles in Athens and the rest of the country during December 1944 and the following months cost thousands of Greek lives and were the bloodiest suppression of an indigenous, popular political movement by any of the Allies during the war. To all this the USSR remained silent, and indeed had written Greece off long before as an unavoidable appendage of the British sphere of influence. But by the end of 1944 possession had indeed become the ultimate definer of the political outcome of the war.

Italy and Greece proved that the Anglo-Americans, once they reached a consensus among themselves, had the will to impose their diktat wherever their troops were able to do so. It also illustrated the inability of the USSR and the disunited Greek Communist Party both to contain a revolutionary movement whose time had come, whose following was large, diverse, and sufficiently decentralized in hills and mountains to control its own action and space, and whose only option was to fight or to be repressed. Such a will to survive did not guarantee victory but it assured that Greece's struggle would not end with the imposed signing of a piece of paper in 1945. And these imperatives were to determine the future of Greece after the formal end of World War Two. The Communist parties of Western and Southern Europe proved to be as heterogeneous among themselves as Social Democrats had become from Communists after the first war; and, indeed, save for its Jacobin rhetoric, the French Communist Party's role subsequently became indistinguishable from that of the Socialists from whom they had split after World War One. There the party, almost certainly on Soviet advice, was an inhibitor of decisive working-class action, but elsewhere it proved divided and independent, and responsive both to the people and the possibilities reality opened to them. In Greece, Yugoslavia, and Albania in Europe were the other Communist parties, those the United States, and even eventually Russia, justly feared.

Eastern Europe: Diverse Patterns

The Soviet armies did not cross their own frontiers until January 1944, by which time the Italian precedent was firmly entrenched. But while the USSR often threw this example back at the United States in regard to the Axis nations of Rumania, Bulgaria, and Hungary, in Poland its political problems reflected the intense friction with the exile government that had taken refuge in London. These politicians had been anti-Soviet since the revolution, and Poland's war against the USSR until 1921 had cost the prewar Russian nation a vast territory of 70,000 square miles which was 60 percent ethnically non-Polish. The London Poles, moreover, shared the prewar Right's vision of Poland as a major power destined to lead Eastern Europe in the postwar era both against a resurgent Germany and in renewing a *cordon sanitaire* against Bolshevism. Not only did they refuse any boundary concessions to the USSR, which was firmly for the major revisions along ethnic lines that Britain's Lord Curzon had proposed in 1920, but the London Poles laid claims to major accessions of German territory. And since the 75,000-soldier remnant of the Polish army left the USSR early in 1942, eventually to fight on the Italian front, it meant that only a poorly armed but large and passionately anti-Soviet resistance force would be the representative of the prewar order when the Soviet army eventually arrived to liberate Poland from the Nazis.

The political strategy of the London Poles was to seek to mobilize Anglo-American diplomatic intervention on behalf of their original demands, from which they refused to waver until long after the entry of the first Soviet troops in January 1944. Indeed, the London Poles had earlier threatened to consider the Russians as invaders, and in 1944 refused to cooperate with them until their political position was accepted, and these episodes only more firmly consolidated the rupture between Russia and the exiles. Churchill, in the plainest terms, regarded the London Poles as nothing short of "absolutely crazy," as he put it in October 1944, and always urged them to concede the Curzon line to the USSR in return for compensation from German territory and the retention of political autonomy after the war—a solution the Poles would not even consider seriously until it was far too late.[20] The United States, on the other hand, conscious of the importance of Polish-American votes and in line with its policy of deferring all political questions until after the war, encouraged the London Poles' intransigence. Russia, having no Poles to talk to save a coalition of the Left in which Communists predominated, in July 1944 installed a new provisional government in Lublin and then the following month refused to alter its traditional successful offensive strategy of avoiding combat in cities when the London Poles' Home Army in Warsaw initiated a desperate uprising. While both the United States and British leaders tended to attribute this Russian decision not to assist the uprising, in which 166,000 Poles died and half of Warsaw was leveled, to their desire to see the London Poles fail in their strategy of taking the capital in their own name, the fact remains that the Soviet military did no more to aid a Communist-led uprising in Slovakia at the same time—and it too was wiped out.

While the United States was constantly to intercede on behalf of the London Polish cause, and the issue became decisive in Washington's evaluation of Russian policy in Eastern Europe, it refused to consider that Poland, to a greater extent than any nation of the region, had been structurally revolutionized and that the prewar order was obsolete and doomed to replacement whether or not the Red Army occupied it. Not only had one-fifth of the population been killed, but most of the prewar ruling officer class and bourgeoisie were dead or in exile. One-third of the population was non-Polish and indigestible, and the beginnings of Communist reforms of traditional agrarian problems had irreversibly altered the social system. Whatever else was going to happen, the United States could not succeed in putting the old Poland together again.

Soviet policy in Eastern Europe was far more pluralistic than the Polish pattern, where the London exiles largely defined Moscow's options. In Finland and Czechoslovakia it showed itself ready to attempt another course when it was possible. Edward Beneš, also head of an exile regime based in London, was aware that his demise at Munich was due to his unwillingness to utilize a military alliance with the USSR against Germany. During 1943 he unsuccessfully tried to convince the United States to back a pact with Russia in which Prague would refuse to enter into any alliance hostile to the USSR in return for the latter's non-interference in Czech internal affairs, as well as giving the London Czechs political control of the occupation authority. Since the Communists had been fairly strong during the prewar period but had gained a large following during the war, and were a part of the London regime, Beneš was confident his policy of avoidance of the prewar anti-Soviet *cordon sanitaire* would succeed. Washington, unlike the British, thought the Beneš pact with Russia ominous, and by May 1944 had written his government off as Soviet-controlled. Yet it was anything but that. Still, when the Czech resistance in May 1945 began its own uprising against the Germans and appealed to nearby United States forces for aid, the Americans refused for fear of strengthening the position of the Beneš government.

In Rumania, which had fought energetically on the Nazi front against Russia, the USSR set up an exact replica of the Anglo-American commission running Italy, and repeatedly threw the example back at the United States when it complained. Both in Bulgaria, where pro-Russian sentiment was strong for traditional reasons, and in Rumania the USSR openly favored friendly governments, but in Hungary they permitted hostile groups to take power and prevented local Communist forces from taking direct action to implement much-needed radical changes.

Yugoslavia was the prime example of Communist power in Eastern Europe, but it was so patently wholly autonomous of the USSR that the British during the last two years of the war, wisely but prematurely, sought to make their own alliances directly with the Tito-led mass peasant radical nationalist movement that had tied down thirty-three Axis divisions by the end of 1943. To the United States, which worked for the better part of the war with the reactionary collaborationist Serbian guerrillas under Draža Mihajlović, Tito was a Moscow agent, despite the fact that no visible Soviet aid went to him. But Tito's relations with the Russians, who recognized King Peter's exile regime in London, were already going from bad to worse. Tito's pan-Slavism and flirtation with the idea of an eventual South Balkan federation enchanted the British, who saw it as a barrier against Soviet influence, but it guaranteed an eventual rupture with Moscow. To such facts, of course, Washington was immune.

Until the end of the war, United States policy toward Eastern Europe refused to calculate the trauma which the war had imposed on the entire prewar social order. For such an altered region also would be lost to an integrated European capitalism ready to cooperate with the United States. Radical change it regarded as an extension of Soviet power, as if Eastern Europe's basic internal as well as international relations had somehow been fixed for all time. The demise of Germany's economy, which had so integrated Eastern Europe before the war, alone guaranteed that the war would upset existing patterns. While the United States refused to endorse an explicit restoration of the prewar Right, it assumed that somehow a politically uncompromised middle group would emerge in each of the melange of prewar nations to modify partially the tradition of irredentism, superstition, and exploitation to cooperate with the economic premises of United States policy enunciated in far greater detail than the political. The United States opposed outside interference in East European internal affairs, though in Italy, France, and elsewhere it had never followed such a practice. It preferred self-determination, save in Greece, Yugoslavia, or wherever it collided with United States interests. But the political forms Washington desired in Eastern Europe were less precise and were merely to complement its economic objectives. More explicit were the economic premises of a capitalism open to it with "general protection of American citizens and the protection and furtherance of legitimate American economic rights, existing or potential."[21] That type of permanently accessible underdeveloped capitalism was not merely wholly dependent on a political order Russia was not likely to permit but in conflict with the limits that the radicalization of the European masses was imposing. To strive for it was not merely to invite conflict but to aspire for the increasingly impossible.

The War in Asia

For the better part of World War Two the main United States commitment in the Pacific was its naval power, which permitted it to both fight an island war and extend its blockade of Japan. And while American leaders sought to keep Britain from any important military activity outside its own prewar empire to avoid consulting with its European ally on the political future of the rest of Asia, all were agreed on the need to avoid a major land war. The realities in China only reinforced this commitment.

By 1941 the unimaginably venal Kuomintang army had become a vast agency of the exploitation and radicalization of China, bringing both chaos and military ineffectuality wherever it went. This army rarely resisted the Japanese and often traded with them. The United States soon regarded the Chinese military theater as both dangerous and expensive, and the per capita cost of maintaining 28,000 American military personnel there was the highest of any theater of the entire war. China's inflation, which caused prices to rise 1800 times between 1937 and August 1945, was alone sufficient to make it too treacherous to enter in force. Chiang, for his part, preferred profit for himself and his clique, fighting only the growing Communist forces that spread throughout the north after the Japanese invasion of 1937, and he assumed that the United States would defeat Japan. American military leaders, in return, instead hoped that the Soviet army would enter the land war against Japan after the end of European hostilities, sparing United States losses in a conflict they expected to last as long as eighteen months after victory in Europe.

Chiang courted the United States, which traded financial and political support for his internal regime in return for Chiang's explicit pledge to follow the United States lead in international policy. And both the United States and the Soviet Union supported Chiang against the burgeoning Communist movement. Chiang assumed that Moscow could control the Communists for him, and in fact it unsuccessfully attempted to do so, and in due course he realized that Russian help in driving Japan out of China would also eventually be necessary. The USSR, in its strategy, preferred a weak and friendly China not able to challenge its claims to Czarist territorial acquisitions. But unfortunately for both Russia and the United States,

Chiang's regime was based on gangsterism and was doomed to eventual defeat, and by the end of the war Washington also regretfully had come to a similar conclusion.

If the United States could not base its future power in Asia on China, then its option was to depend on Japan. During the war this alternative became accepted with increasing clarity as Chiang inadvertently eliminated himself from the picture. The existing Japanese society was seen in Washington as more redeemable than that of Germany. Men such as Undersecretary of State Joseph Grew, whose influence rose throughout the war, felt that the existence of world-trade-oriented "liberals" within the Japanese ruling class gave the United States natural allies. Even the institution of the Emperor, suitably modified, became increasingly palatable. Moreover, unlike in Germany, where the United States had been obliged by 1943 to acknowledge the necessity to share occupation power with its nominal allies, in Japan it had no intention of doing so, because it fully expected to conquer the islands alone. Hence it could remake Japanese institutions to suit United States needs, reinforce the power of its local allies, and use Japan to prevent the chaos in Asia that looked increasingly likely after the beginning of 1945. If that strategy was not immediately unanimously accepted throughout key decision levels in Washington, after the Yalta Conference in February 1945 it began to dominate official planning.

Creating and Planning the Postwar World

The failure of the peace after World War One, and the objective need of the United States economy not to allow a renewal of prewar failures, led to a wartime planning for the peace far more intense than anything undertaken during the first conflagration. The United States was determined not to lose the peace again, nor could it afford to do so.

Indeed, insofar as the postwar principles around which the United States hoped to construct world institutions were concerned, Washington began at the inception of the war to try to gain the commitment of its allies, and above all Britain, to the letter and principles of its postwar system. For a reformed world economy, Britain was the single most crucial problem because of the preponderant role its sterling bloc played in the entire world trading system. The United States immediately linked its wartime aid to British support for American postwar plans and ideas, an integration which revealed the practice as well as the theory of the ideal world system it hoped to impose and lead.

The first important example of this American effort was the Atlantic Charter, which Churchill and Roosevelt issued in August 1941. By that time the British, for political reasons, were desperate to court the Americans but also unable to afford conceding everything they demanded, and these terms followed closely Hull's philosophy. While mentioning political matters quite superficially, the Charter called for free access on equal terms to the trade and raw materials of the world after the war, a point that Churchill strenuously insisted also incorporate respect for "existing obligations."[22] For the next four years the United States relentlessly moved from the general to the specific in mobilizing support for these goals, and spent an inordinate amount of time badgering the British, above all, to conform to all the subtleties of the Hullian doctrine of abolition of trade blocs, free trade, and open access to raw materials. After strenuous disputes which caused even the desperate British to delay signing it, London agreed to the only somewhat more specific objectives of world economic reform in Article VII of the Lend-Lease Agreement of February 1942, the precise meaning of which was to remain a source of controversy for the next five years.

For Washington the matter was not so much a question of principle as the prevention of another depression and the conditions that had brought the last one about. Concern over large postwar unemployment was widespread among economic planners from 1942 onward, and a Niagara of pessimistic studies and speeches on the dangers of insufficient postwar trade, access to raw materials, and investment opportunities gushed forth from official and private agencies and personalities. In effect, postwar planners hoped to avoid the mistakes made after 1918 on the implicit assumption that the two postwar epochs would not be politically dissimilar. From this viewpoint American strategists regarded the war and Depression as an exceptional development in history rather than one that would fundamentally revise the nature of the world and the problems and forces within it.

The Bretton Woods, New Hampshire, conference of July 1944 led to the creation of the International Monetary Fund and World Bank, which were intended to facilitate the quick restoration of "normal" world trade. Such a vision, quite as naturally, meant a firm

United States opposition to Axis reparations playing an important, if any, role in postwar reconstruction. Normal loans and investments, the United States felt confident, could accomplish that objective.

For the rest of the Allies, however, the issue was their own interests which their weaknesses imposed, as well as their clear awareness that what the United States was demanding of them was far greater than the Americans had ever accorded. Tariffs, agricultural export subsidies and import quotas, tied loans, a closed hemispheric political and economic system, and much else also made the United States an important offender of Hullian doctrine, which to others appeared increasingly like an ideological tool for extracting sacrifices of them.

This suspicion was especially widespread among the British, who were subjected throughout the war to a system of Lend-Lease manipulation intended to reduce London's foreign exchange reserves to an increasingly mythical point where it would be neither too weak nor too strong to collaborate with the United States trade program. The United States sought to manipulate the British reserves down to a level which would oblige London to borrow a large sum from the United States. Washington always intended to attach riders on trade terms and principles to such a loan, and eventually did so. More important, in the Middle East the United States constantly maneuvered in Iran to break into the British-controlled concessions, and throughout the region the two nations intrigued against one another in a manner that greatly exacerbated wartime relations. In Argentina, as well, the two nations disputed trade and political matters that went hand in hand. Everywhere the Americans sought to grasp the rewards of imperialist power that had once been exclusively England's domain. Hence British reluctance, and the need for a constant United States effort to impose its world order as quickly as possible, by whatever means available, lest the prewar crisis return.

Planning for the postwar United Nations structure was not so comprehensive and absorbed less of Washington's time, if only because United States leaders were themselves divided and both Britain and Russia saw the creation of a postwar surrogate of the League of Nations as no substitute for classic diplomacy—a view many key American leaders also held. Moreover, the problem of the UN was one independent of political settlements in specific nations, which the United States always wished deferred until the end of the war—a strategy that both its main allies resisted as being a ruse to impose

America's will on them when their blood was no longer needed and they were weaker. Britain, for its part, was more or less firmly committed to organizing a bloc, including its empire and Western Europe, with which to deal with the United States on more equal terms, a notion Washington firmly rejected and for which it hoped the United Nations would provide an antidote. Russia inclined strongly to the British view on the manner in which postwar diplomacy would operate. Roosevelt and Hull, however, advanced the UN concept strongly after 1943, but in a form that only intensified Anglo-Soviet suspicions of United States intentions.

Permanent membership in the Security Council and a veto were American ideas, and from the inception the Americans demanded membership for China because of the latter's explicit willingness to serve as what Churchill dubbed a "fagot-vote" for the United States in return for continued economic and political aid.[23] The original United States idea of the "Big Four" left Washington, in effect, with two votes in the Security Council, and the British then insisted on adding their own contemplated puppet of France. The original Council therefore had four anti-Soviet members, which only made Russia, with British backing, seek to strengthen the veto principle yet further. After the Dumbarton Oaks Conference of August 1944 the United States recruited all its Latin American satellites to declare war against the Axis and thereby qualify for membership at the San Francisco Conference called for the following April to draw up a UN Charter. The preceding February, moreover, the United States convened a hemispheric meeting in Mexico City to endorse its plans for the UN as well as a regional political pact which gave the United States a parallel option to the UN and, de facto, its own bloc within and outside the new world organization. Complete clarity regarding the American dual standard only deepened the Soviet and British expectation that the UN would not become a substitute for conventional diplomacy, and the American use of double criteria in its advocacy of alleged internationalist solutions only deepened the cynicism of other world leaders as well as such elder statesmen as Henry Stimson toward American policy. This exemption of regionalism and protectionism that the United States built into the new world order was never justified theoretically so that other nations could better comprehend America's conduct and ideals. But Washington nonetheless immediately reverted to a loftier definition of the UN Charter when the conduct of other states was to be discussed, confirming the reality that America's brand of internationalism was truly a plan for its own hegemony in the postwar world. The UN was born, therefore, without illusions as to what it might accomplish, and surely no American sacrifices, and doomed to failure before it began.

The Spectrum of Crises

United States wartime planning and practice went hand in hand, and it could not defer dealing with a whole spectrum of issues in nations in which the war was finally coming to a close by the beginning of 1945. This was true many places, but above all in Germany.

At first the United States had confronted the problem of the future of Germany by reflecting on the lessons of the past. Yet soon it became clear that both the presence of Soviet forces as well as the radicalization of the German masses required new approaches. But the question of the nature of Germany and the peace imposed on it impinged centrally on the future of Europe and Russia together. It was the most difficult issue for the United States to resolve, and it was not to do so during the war because its own leaders were also deeply divided and Roosevelt provided added confusion and no direction on this topic. In the end, the question of Washington's preparations for Germany proved a good example of the limits of United States "planning" in foreign policy and its inability to translate its extensive reflections on past events into a detailed scheme for the future—despite the broad consensus on ultimate goals which three or four disputatious agencies shared.

The issue of German reparations was linked to the role of United States credits in postwar reconstruction, and low or no reparations was about Washington's only consensus on the future of Germany other than the implied assumption it should not have any form of socialist society. Russia, on the other hand, until the last months of the war seemed certain to be in possession of the majority of German territory, an American premise which only Hitler's decision in January 1945 to fight to the death on the Eastern Front while permitting relatively easy combat in the West proved incorrect. But Russia as well as France wished German reparations with which to reconstruct. Treasury Secretary Henry Morgenthau, the advocate of dismantling German heavy industry, therefore also favored a large loan to Russia—a loan the United States was ready to extend only in return for Soviet political good behavior. Others, such as Stimson and Navy

Secretary James Forrestal, opposed a stern peace because they knew it would lead to a vacuum in Europe's economy as well as politics, opening the door to Communism. Hull simply wished a liberalized Germany integrated into the world economy, and the matter was not resolved into a common United States policy before the Yalta Conference of February 1945. There, with the Anglo-Americans having just been on the defensive and beholden to timely Soviet military pressure, with the USSR still likely to capture most of Germany and United States desire to get it later to fight Japan on the Chinese mainland, America's leaders were anxious to attain, at most, only general decisions on Germany and all other questions in the hope the crucial details could be more favorably interpreted afterwards, when the United States would be tactically as well as strategically stronger. This view was quite consistent with the general wartime policy of putting off all political settlements until the end of the conflict, and the late date the Yalta Conference was convened was in itself testimony to the astonishing United States ability to succeed in this effort as long as it did.

At Yalta, where the Big Three signed a general control-zone agreement giving Britain and the United States each about a third of Germany to occupy, including two-thirds of the prewar industrial and mining capacity, the main concession on Germany was an Anglo-American agreement to create a committee to discuss $20 billion reparations—a concession which later proved meaningless. The settlement on Poland proved as nebulous, and was also referred to a tripartite commission, leaving the Russians master of the situation. In China, to the Americans' delight, the USSR agreed to enter the war against Japan three months after the end of the European conflict, to support the political authority of the Kuomintang against the Communists, and in return to retrieve the Siberian port and railroad rights the Czar had lost in 1905. On the whole, despite acrimony on numerous questions, Stalin failed to press his advantage, and the ambiguous political decisions meant that the ultimate outcome would be determined in the fields by armies and, in Asia, peasants in arms.

In the months after Yalta and until the Potsdam Conference in the second half of July, acrimony between the wartime allies increased and the outcome of the war in Europe was to some great measure, if only temporarily, resolved by the location of armies. In Greece, despite the Communist effort to engage in parliamentary rituals, the repression that followed was to put 50,000 Leftists in prison and force others to return spontaneously to the hills to save themselves. In Yugoslavia, Tito and his Partisans were the masters and beholden to no one, though the United States was more certain than ever that he was Russia's agent. In Italy, much to the incredulity of the British, the 150,000-person Resistance gave up their arms, and the Anglo-American armies ruled the north as enemy territory until the end of 1945, when all remnants of danger from the Left had been eliminated. It was in Italy, too, that the United States and the British during the early spring provoked their worst crisis with the USSR by concealing surrender negotiations with the Nazis, efforts which Stalin misunderstood but which in reality were designed to prevent the Resistance from taking German arms. But in Italy, as in France, the Communists gladly on their own volition returned to being loyal to parliamentary forms, anxious to obtain petty government posts and resurrect the production of capitalist industry. For the United States held Russia accountable for the action of local Communists, unable to make the historically real distinctions between the Left and Russia that were later to become more patent yet. For this reason the Russians counseled moderation on Communist parties, but only in France and Italy did they find Communists who elected this course anyway.

From the Soviet viewpoint it was clear that the Americans and British would use force wherever possible to perpetuate societies to their interest, and already this was a demonstrable fact in Italy, France, Greece, Germany, Belgium, and elsewhere. United States bases in Europe after the war were already planned no later than June 1945, and the Russians were desperate to avoid a war with their former allies. At the same time, the USSR too imposed the ultimate parameters on developments in Eastern Europe essential to its security and interests, though it took longer to do so irrevocably, save in Poland, until well after the European war ended. And in Germany, where the masses had been radicalized and taken a large measure of power during 1945, Soviet policy was far more in conformity with local sentiments than were the fearful Anglo-American occupation policies. In the aggregate, therefore, military possession defined the political outcome in lieu of other mechanisms of reconciling the vast Anglo-American-Soviet differences. In Germany, the key to the European question, United States policy after April 1945 was to suspend rather than destroy German industrial power, prevent the socialist revival from holding and extending power whether by spontaneous worker councils or elections, leave the prewar social structure intact, "reeducate" the nation with American "values," and defer until later the main questions of Germany's future.

It was this larger political reality that defined the main outcome of the Potsdam Conference, which by July was doomed to the certain failure of inconclusiveness. By this time the United States was convinced that Germany was going to be partitioned into two ideological zones, and a renewed and denazified Western Germany as a part of a stable Europe and non-Communist world was now the main goal of United States tactics there. Hence the United States and Britain again rejected the principle of large reparations from their zones and referred the issue to another commission sure to deadlock. In the main, despite the ambiguous concession of the disputed Oder-Neisse region from Germany to Poland's temporary political administration, little was accomplished at Potsdam to patch up the wartime alliance-of-necessity whose exclusive rationale—war with Germany—ended. The tenuous allies exchanged charges and countercharges on internationally supervised elections with the Rumanian situation being countered with the Greek question, the Anglo-Americans refusing to discuss Spain, and the Russians resisting their demands on Poland. All that Potsdam proved was that the gap was quickly growing wider between the three nations, and would become far worse yet. In America's calculations, Russia bore the main responsibility for the social dislocations of the war, and was the major barrier to the attainment of its ideal world order.

The war in Europe ended in deepening discord, but in Asia the human and social consequences of the war were to prove far more profound. The United States navy had throughout the war planned on extending its postwar presence in the Pacific by acquiring the former Japanese-mandated islands and Okinawa as bases; and by consensus in Washington, Japan itself was to be an exclusive United States occupation zone, hence sparing the Americans the distressing difficulties that its wartime allies in Asia as well as Russia might pose. The British agreed to the transfer of Japan's mandated islands to the United States in return for silence on the future of its mandates. Though the United States' main emphasis remained on Europe, superficially it appeared as if it was in Asia that Washington had the greatest freedom to impose its hegemony, but in fact it had only growing problems there, eventually far greater even than those in Europe. In China the civil war was now raging more fiercely between the Kuomintang and the Communists, and Chiang's accords with the Soviet Union scarcely diminished the Chinese Communist determination to avoid destruction before Chiang's mounting offensives. On August 6 the United States dropped its first A-bomb on Japan, hardly expecting a quick surrender, while two days later the USSR entered the war and began the destruction of Japan's huge mainland forces against which the Americans could never employ A-bombs. A week later the war with Japan ended.

The last United States act during the Asian war provided the transition to the next stage of its much longer conflict there, and it was a rough if inadequate groping with the realities of the vast Asian drama and the magnitude of the war which was then tearing asunder the very structure of its old order and making revolution the dominant experience of its next decades.

In virtually every important Far Eastern nation, above all the former colonial states, there was a disintegration of power and a vacuum which the Left began to fill as the vast, hungry masses took to arms. In China the issue was who would occupy the immense Japanese-occupied territory. In the Philippines the Communist-led Huk guerrillas, the main anti-Japanese resistance, began replacing the collaborators who had once been United States compradors as well. In the Dutch East Indies a puppet independence government was in place, and in Korea, for which no occupation or partition agreement had been drawn up, a strong Left and independence movement existed everywhere. Above all, Vietnam was about to begin its August Revolution, which was to become the single most important test of United States power over the following generation. On August 14 the United States issued General Order Number One, attempting to define the political outcome of the war in Asia and reverse the immense danger to it of a vast sweeping revolution that could change the very future of all history. Asia had to emerge intact from the war or it could not be cautiously reformed and integrated into the contemplated United States Pacific destiny. The Japanese were ordered not to transfer either their arms or authority to forces that General Douglas MacArthur did not approve of, making them the de facto American agents. Korea was divided at the 38th parallel to stop the flow of a Soviet army capable of going far south of that middle line. The Philippines were left in the hands of the collaborators, and Indochina was divided between China and a French-British occupation, while in China the Japanese were ordered not to give either arms or territory to the Communists. All this had no relationship to reality, and it was a decision for a restoration of the old order that was to trouble profoundly the remainder of the century.

World War Two had been a vast, bloody attempt to resolve the crises of world power the First World War had created, and while it advanced the position of the United States relative to the European nations it also produced a host of new traumas which the United States could confront only as an aspect of its permanent struggle against the mainstream of history toward the Left which has irresistibly, if elliptically, characterized the history of our generation. International war had turned into civil war and anti-colonial struggle at one and the same time. Now internal social dynamics virtually everywhere in the world were to become a question for American concern and, very often, action. The Left might be co-opted in some countries, as since 1914, but it had now become a movement too large, diverse, and decentralized to master. Indeed, it was to become most dangerous and unpredictable precisely in those areas and nations not subject to Soviet constraints. The real events and trends to emerge from the war were ones the United States scarcely anticipated, and for which it had not planned, but its insatiable desire to direct the world's dominant course now imposed on it the main burden of counterrevolution. The modalities of loans and trade that had sufficed for a decade after the First World War to fend off the most serious potential political consequences of that bloodletting were now mostly irrelevant where they had once been efficacious, and the military prerequisites of economic integration became far more imperative. For whatever immediate economic problems the war solved only increased international capitalism's longer-range challenges. However vast the material resources of the United States, indescribably greater in 1945 relative to other nations than they would ever be, American ambitions were far greater yet, given the immensity of the world and the absence of Washington's means for controlling its infinite diversity. Internal civil conflict and revolutionary change had now become a major and ever larger item on the

United States global agenda, the precursor of endless crises over the next three decades. The Second World War ripped the world asunder, the international status quo would never again be restored, and the traditional American solutions for the rest of mankind's problems as well as its own were to prove increasingly futile.

7

The Accumulation of Power

Power includes the ability to manipulate the levers that affect profoundly the material lives of many people, and in United States history it has rested in sufficiently diverse places at any given time to reinforce the inclination of the vast majority of writers on American life to avoid confronting what is not only one of the most complex but also sensitive and vital of topics. Yet not to attempt to understand the directorship of power in modern American history is to be ignorant of both politics and economics, their interrelationships, character, and possibilities. Apologists for the status quo find that the simple denial of the class nature and function of society and decision-making within it is adequate, and the descriptively elusive character of the social system and its management is the best reinforcement of their thesis. Radical simplifiers have contented themselves with quite primitive models which tend to lean heavily on explanations which are at best historically limited, often quite irrelevant, and almost never linked together into a broader analysis. And defenders and critics alike of the constituted order of power erroneously attribute to the existing system a strength and coherence which invariably underestimates the weaknesses and limits intrinsic in it.

Power is expressed by a vast, interwoven, and quite complex series of political and economic institutions the direction of which rests in the hands of persons whose selection over time becomes a central question given the undeniable reality that the economy and political structure do in fact historically define the larger contours of the application of American power institutionally at home and abroad. How such people accumulate various forms of political and economic power, and the ways in which elites are created in the United States, can alter over time, though one can also define a fairly limited number of quite predictable mechanisms whose relative importance may change in degree if not in kind. The economic and political universe and the criteria within which elites operate are durable, despite the fact that no single, much less simple, model suffices to explain the variations possible within this ultimate limit. Selection methods may more or less fluctuate, but the systems they are designed to serve do not. At the economic foundations the business leadership works within the premises of capitalism; at the political levels there has been a larger consensus and historical continuity in domestic and foreign policy that both transcends and defies the recruitment process. Yet as the conditions and needs of American society have altered, the role of traditional means of recruitment and the accumulation of power for this or that constituency or group have not so much been replaced as supplemented.

In effect, the issue in this chapter is "who succeeds" and "who runs America" at a given time—and less the nature of the institutional order, though clearly the two issues intersect—and how such men acquire that power of direction. And certain historical examples of the accumulation of power—in the early stages of industrial capitalism, the choice of top political administrators during our own epoch, decision-making in foreign policy, and the role of the military—help provide building blocks essential for the construction of a more accurate and viable historical model which accepts the premise that in different epochs changing combinations of factors may operate within a constant structure with different historical specificity. Though these examples surely do not exhaust the dimensions of the problem, they at least illustrate how we must create a more realistic assessment of the historical accumulation of power in modern United States history.

Established Elites and Economic Development

Theories of economic development in the United States still tend to explain success in the accumulation of fortunes and economic power in impersonal terms, a technique sufficiently accurate to obscure a historical reality that was far more subtle. Exceptional success due to purely impersonal economic and technological factors, or the triumphs of initially modestly placed new dynamic and innovative entrepreneurs and firms bent on reaping the joys of creation in psychological as well as material terms, cannot be wholly dismissed as explanations of United States economic history during certain periods merely because all too many have exaggerated these phenomena into ideological apologetics. When used simply to argue that the emergence of American capitalism was based on pure mobility that competition alone defined, creating a sort of equality of economic opportunity, such theories mystify without explaining history. But their degree of irrelevance or utility is independent of the eulogies of capitalism deduced from them, and one must consider their usefulness during periods with specific types of economic development.

The Horatio Alger vision of United States economic development surely has deserved the contempt a growing number of historians gave to it after World War Two, but merely to rip apart an absurd notion without constructing an alternative model leaves a vacuum which the critics of high social mobility in the accumulation of economic power did not end. That void tentatively was filled after 1955 when Richard Hofstadter skirted the entire controversy to argue that a new economic group led post–Civil War economic development and challenged the status pretensions of an economically declining, essentially middle-class "status elite" that increasingly turned to reform to challenge the raw, amoral arrivistes. Hence the alleged origins of "progressivism," a notion Hofstadter immediately saw embraced as historical conventional wisdom despite his curiously inconsistent acceptance of the studies that proved that there was scarcely a scintilla of validity in the Alger assumption of a new class of capitalists. Critics of the Alger myth demonstrated statistically that during the period 1870–1910 the most important businessmen of the period were the sons of wealthy or middle-income parents, highly educated by contemporary standards, overwhelmingly native-born Protestants, and likely to have begun their careers with important economic assets available to them. About one-tenth were really atypical: Jews and Catholics, foreign-born, sons of poor farmers, and the like.

Yet such iconoclasm, while in fact on the right track for the period 1870–1900, was also circumstantial insofar as it slighted the immense gradients possible within income and occupational categories. Economic mobility does in fact occur when the well-educated

Protestant son of a prosperous grain merchant ends life a hundred times richer than his father, and their change in relative status and power is sufficiently important to measure in terms more precise than those the critics of Algerism employed. Projected into the future, of course, the vision of the United States economy as a monopoly of the old elite slights important changes that occur later. Less oblique, and therefore more useful, for the critical decades after the Civil War is a more exact model of how and by whom economic power in the United States was accumulated, and the relationship of that founding period to later developments.

In the barest outline, existing evidence shows that economic development in the United States after 1865, and for at least the next four decades, was significantly controlled by existing long-established social and economic elites, and not merely in the hands of sons of "businessmen"—even though transitory factors of new settlements created increasingly important exceptions farther west. But given New York, Boston, and Philadelphia's critical role as the center of United States corporate headquarters which dominated their regional economies—and thereby the main national developments until 1900—the evolution of urban centers is critical. In essence, who succeeded in these cities largely depended on their status—family and social connections—and access to existing economic power. The crucial groups in economic development after 1870 had both a high degree of status and economic privilege before the Civil War, and existing models of economic history do no justice to a reality in which not all men entered the initial period of United States industrialization as equals, but in which those men with a "head start" in the accumulation process tended to share heavily in the control of the future as well as the past distribution of economic power. This well-placed constituency laid the foundations for their political influence and, to some variable but always critical extent, defined the basic ground rules for the distribution of power in America until this day. Even if time has seen modifications of its original forms as the structure of economic activity and rewards has altered, it is still a central foundation of American power.

Despite the existence of the culturally alienated and disenchanted among the sons of such older social and economic elites—critics whose complaints have attracted intellectual historians who have implied that the old families produced not much else—the fact remains that the mores and values of the established families in the three main economic centers made business the natural, even compulsive vocation of many of them. Indeed, some of the most oft-cited grumblers about the conflict between culture and capital, such as Charles Francis Adams, Jr., and Henry Lee Higginson, were themselves major capitalists and no less obsessive than most of their relatives and peers about making fortunes. In fact, by the end of the Civil War the social and economic elites of Boston and Philadelphia had been sorted out and, in a manner of speaking, rationalized. Families whose fortunes were not well invested or renewed before the war, or whose marital alliances were not cunning, were pushed aside and eventually forgotten by their more aggressive but no less well born peers. Prewar squanderers who could not manage to keep up with the new pace largely passed into obscurity, especially if they lived in a much more ascetic Boston region, where the elite generally held all forms of excess consumption and display in contempt. The rule was that old status and fortunes now moved further up the economic ladder, though by no means all of that class shared in the ascent.

A crucial foundation of business activity was the extended family or kinship system, which immensely facilitated the eager young elite Bostonians entering businesses "with all their force," to quote one sour contemporary, and provided the decisive universe for recruitment of key personnel and leaders.[1] Founded on fortunes initially amassed largely in commerce and mercantile activities, real estate, and finance, the established families had the capital essential to master the economic revolution that after the Civil War took place in manufacturing, railroads, and mining. Massachusetts and Pennsylvania had the highest average capital investment per manufacturing firm in the country in 1870 and more than enough for regional needs—a fact that drove the capital of these cities westward. "The family and social connections of the firm," observed Henry Lee Higginson, the head of the critical Lee, Higginson investment banking house and arbiter of Boston finance for decades, "assured to it the best possible clientele; there was sufficient capital. . . . The firm owed in some measure to family alliances its well-advised connections with the best financial enterprises of the day."[2] Key firms, such as Higginson's and Kidder, Peabody & Co., in Boston, tended to provide the crucial coordination for vast undertakings involving numerous areas of activity, removing the dangers of costly or even fatal errors that exclusively narrow family undertakings were more likely to make.

To manage new activities the heads of enterprises everywhere preferred recruiting on the basis of blood ties, a fact that greatly colored individual behavior, goals, and responsibilities in a manner that formal conventional economic theory has not attempted to describe. In Boston, recruitment on the basis of blood, or, lacking sufficient quantities, club and school affiliations, was the rule. Higginson himself, after losing money on assorted ventures of his own, later confessed, "I was taken in at the beginning of 1868 as a matter of charity to keep me out of the poorhouse."[3] Subsequently he employed and also complained about relatives in similar straits. John Murray Forbes, merchant prince turned railroad tycoon, retrieved his indigent cousin, Charles E. Perkins, from Cincinnati, and eventually Perkins became president of one of his lines. Forbes always hired relatives first, and the children of other Boston elite families afterward. Charles Francis Adams, Jr., when president of the Union Pacific Railroad, made it a point to hire "my kids"—Harvard men—if possible.[4] Investment banking in New York relied on blood ties first as the basis of recruitment, and the German-Jewish banking firms in New York were manned at the upper levels by what was a series of interlocked extended families. Superimposed on kinship were marriage bonds, which not only saved some family fortunes but provided others with new managers with whom affiliations of blood and kinship meant that much more than mere profit motivated individual behavior. Key families, in effect, formed the basis of primary economic networks managing and owning economic activities as collectivities whose exact shares altered with new marital liaisons, tax avoidance structures, occupational choices to continue in the business or outside it, and similar variables. As a kinship group the family could much better afford to lose some children to other occupations, diversions, or death, and it gave sound management to the kin group's general interests, which, with the addition of tamper-proof trusts, assured its future control of large and growing economic resources.

With this "head start" and astonishingly extensive efforts to keep key positions within the clan or club, the elites of the key Eastern cities established the continuity between the pre- and post-1865 fortunes to an extent that cannot be crudely measured simply by just noting that business leaders of 1900 social origins were not confirmation of the rags-to-riches myth. To a critical degree, however, the mastery of this class over the first phase of modern capitalist accumulation was a founding stage whose hegemony was *partially* challenged by developments which even the entrepreneural audacity and expansive character of established urban elites could not wholly control, especially after the turn of the century.

Existing economic elites could retain their relative national economic power so long as the regional economies upon which their original fortunes were based persisted in importance and if they could master new economic potentials elsewhere. In manufacturing, this was difficult to accomplish, though Massachusetts ranked as the third most important state of the union in value of its manufacturing output from 1869 until 1909, when it fell to fourth place. But the fact that economic growth moved manufacturing's economic heart from the Pittsburgh region to mid-Ohio between 1870 and 1920, and much farther west yet in the metal mining, coal, lumbering, and oil and gas industries, overwhelmed the ingenious capacities and capital of the primary economic centers. Moreover, the development of internal financing among manufacturing and mining firms after 1900, to the extent of over two-thirds of their requirements during the first decade and thereafter, reduced the need of potential new entrepreneurs in the more westerly regions to rely on more conservative outside capital sources. The economic prerequisites of absolute continuity in economic control in the hands of a traditional economic elite are a concentrated control over necessary capital, a fairly low rate of economic growth and sufficiently slow product and service innovation, and a geographical area small enough for the elites to administer. Virtually none of these conditions existed after 1910, and this inexorably meant that important new entrants into the economic elite would emerge everywhere in the United States.

Still, the established centers of economic power did astonishingly well in keeping up with many of the most speculative new developments, retaining a large, if not majority, share of the growth outside of their own regions. The Boston Stock Exchange was the first major national market for industrial shares in the 1880s, and Boston interests dominated the Michigan copper industry, controlled the strategically critical General Electric and American Telephone and Telegraph firms, participated actively with New York in the 1890s merger boom, and later even assumed the first large responsibility for the reorganization of General Motors. The Kansas City Stock Yards had a no less august president than Charles Francis Adams, Jr., who was also at one time president of the Union Pacific. It was in railroads, indeed, that Boston carved out perhaps the most significant position nationally and made itself a key center of railroad financing, thereby also moving into timber and iron mining. Other key seaboard cities could report comparable successes.

The older American elite thereby retained economic power throughout the nineteenth century, though less exclusively as the twentieth century progressed, and with it automatically came renewed status, though it was something it surely never lost. The importance of being in the *Social Register*—which began in 1880 along with comparable clubs and schools around the same period to protect and confirm the pretensions of the elite and absorb some of its surplus capital—has been greatly exaggerated. Suffice it to say, all in the *Register* do not have significant economic power, and those with important fortunes not in the *Register* because they are Jews, Catholics, divorced, or for ephemeral reasons are much too numerous to ignore at any time, but particularly as the twentieth century advances. The *Register* and exclusive clubs, schools, and churches are the effect, not the cause, of wealth, and the socially and educationally integrated relationship of this elite is merely a perfectly predictable if increasingly unreliable mechanism for controlling marriage—which is to say, economic—choices crucial both to a family's objective welfare and preferences. The key Philadelphians in 1940 number under four dozen and are the main architects of the economy the city controls, and the thousands of others in the *Register* are of small importance by comparison. The majority of millionaires both in Philadelphia and Boston at the turn of the century were in their *Registers*, yet what is most significant is the one-third to two-fifths of the millionaires who in 1902 were excluded. Personal reasons explain many of these omissions, but despite the importance of the older high-status "Establishment"-type elites in the foundation of industrial capitalism, it was evident even by 1900 that interests that did not conform to this stereotype were already important (about one-tenth of the key business leaders) and, with the economic development of the nation in ways the old elite did not or could not control, likely to increase with time.

The first group to emerge was the German-Jewish banking families in New York, who were composed of a set of older families who intermarried and had their own tightly knit social world excluding most Jews and all Christians. They, in turn, where ostracized from the Establishment social world and, of course, the *Register.* Speyer & Co., J. and W. Seligman, and Kuhn, Loeb were but some of the main names in this orbit around 1900, and later it was to grow beyond even the bounds of German Jews to encompass numerous other Jewish interests in finance, merchandising, and such branches of mining as the Guggenheim empire. Jacob H. Schiff in 1900 was surely one of the ten most important financiers, yet not in the *Register*—a fact which in no way diminished his very substantial importance.[5]

Eventually new *Registers* had to be created to accommodate local snobbism busily segregating itself into clubs in Cleveland, Detroit, or Chicago. The *Register* also initially excluded Catholics, though in fact they too began emerging after World War One as an economic force, eventually to create enterprises of the magnitude of the Bank of America or General Tire; and like the Protestants and Jews they also managed to impose restrictions within their own set of social organizations that excluded their poorer religious compatriots. In the end, to project ahead, Jews today compose at least a third of the Harvard undergraduate enrollment and with Catholics make Protestants a minority of that elite body from which Adams once selected his "kids." What was the case in the mid-twentieth as at the end of the nineteenth century was that whatever their religion or family position in the *Registers*, students at elite universities such as Harvard were drawn from the same economic and occupational origins, and their increasingly Jewish faculties shared the same respect for the status quo and its wisdom as their Brahmin predecessors had shown. Within the framework of a class society, equality of privilege left constituted orders and interests entirely intact and equally celebrated and defended.

The elites of the post–Civil War period of economic growth persist until this day, having retained their absolute mastery over their original industrial and financial empires by the same cooperative kinship structure which gave them the collective "head start" on which so many of their fortunes were based. But the class structure of United States capitalism broadened automatically to include a parallel system of economic accumulation as new products and regional interests emerged outside the framework of the Boston-New York-Philadelphia-Pittsburgh axis, and once this began occurring "status" as defined by rich Protestants in the East with family fortunes had less and less utility for comprehending class. Most recent sociological definitions of social mobility, including occupational origins, have diminishing utility after 1900. Too many Jews, Catholics, children of immigrants and workers, and non-Ivy-League-educated persons begin playing too many vital economic roles to allow static and simple models of class and power in America to be employed. What emerges after the first four decades of modern capitalism is a significantly higher economic mobility into the elite, but in a manner which in no way alters the economic and social structure of capitalism or the distribution of income and wealth. Whatever the form of economic accumulation or the propensity toward broadening the directorship of capitalism, the system defines social and human relationships in precisely the same fashion regardless of the family, religious, or racial origins of the most important owners and managers of the economy. Intrinsically significant in capitalism is not the manner in which it is constructed by one or another group of individuals, but the economic and human outcome of the effort itself. Yet insofar as the exercise and purpose of political power reflect the nature of the distribution of economic power, the alterations in the accumulation and distribution of economic resources become a key to comprehending the changing nature of political leadership in this century.

Still there is a significant historical value in perceiving the social and family organizations and continuity that made for success in the accumulation process, and the manner in which they persist even to this day. Indeed, even major corporations built wholly by individual rather than collective kinship and peer-group efforts, after the First World War as well as before, for tax as well as other reasons frequently passed to family control—Ford is the best-known example—and in any case family domination during the 1960s explained the operational control of 45 percent of the 300 largest American corporations, while another 15 percent were under possible family control. The forms that had succeeded after the Civil War retained efficacy a century later, and many of the men who created the corporate structures then still had heirs continuing a century later with strategic blocks of stock and directorships. Joined by new corporations and now new families along the way, both persistence and change had marked a century which was completely constant only in the purpose and profits of economic activity.

Leadership and Social Mobility

In the most fundamental sense, the very debate over social origins and social mobility throughout American history has been a false one and itself an inadvertent victim of ideological mystifications. Focusing on the social origins and recruitment of personnel in business and top federal government bureaucracy to some analysts has implied that their origins alone will define the distinctive nature of their actions and ideas—and nothing could be further from the truth. To others, high mobility has been equated with classlessness and even equality, while the opposing effort to prove "Establishment" preponderence invariably introduced an obverse form of simplism.

For all the essential contingencies, the most reliable single generalization about the mobility into top bureaucratic national leadership in American history is that the extent to which this colorful phenomenon occurs is essentially unimportant, and that the quite constant function of leadership is far more significant than the means by which it is recruited, and were this process wholly altered the social order would remain precisely the same. This said, in the aggregate one can note leadership recruitment in American society after World War One as following two largely parallel and intersecting patterns which perpetuate the authority of the older elites while absorbing numerous key men from outside them. For just as the traditional accumulation of economic power in the hands of established elites led to the later emergence and equality of new, important capitalists of different religions and ethnic origins and status, so too does the distribution of offices become more diversified during the course of the last half-century. There are inevitable exceptions and reservations, but in general the model of a tightly knit, integrated Establishment partly diminishes in its analytic value and requires with time a more elaborate definition of the accumulation and distribution of offices. It demands greater attention to the real distribution of economic power in America historically as well as the imperatives which war, social needs, and technical and scientific challenges impose on the problems confronting the entire social system. Yet unless one clearly perceives the consensual, interlocking, and common purpose which binds leadership together—regardless of its origins—excessive attention to the mechanics of accumulating power will dangerously obscure its function and outcome.

The function of the top federal bureaucracy is to serve constituted power, not itself, though usually the abstract nature or divisions of that power give it a flexibility in articulating policy that is tantamount to serving a faction of the power structure. Indeed, the concept of an independent bureaucracy free to ignore the reference points of constituted interests affected by their decisions, or not wholly socialized by training or inclination into a more comprehensive social and ideological consensus, is as close to a perfect error in the analysis of American society as one can devise. Rulership at the very highest level, in any case, does not begin or end with career bureaucratic elites, but it is a web of interlocked men and institutions which links political and economic institutions at many and diverse levels—ranging from a lawyer's ability to place an urgent telephone call to an old associate to the post outside government the official may someday wish to return to—and it may operate in different fashions at different times, however predictable its ultimate purposes and ends may be. At the level of these differences, leadership may consist of elites that are rivals or that overlap on short- and medium-range issues; but on comprehensive issues they unite as a part of a class with a commonalty that transcends such routine, predictable differences. Economic and political diffusion virtually guarantees the emergence of tactical elites, who become rivals and partners at one and the same time in the process of rulership, just as the absence of social challenges at home allows this diversity to persist—yet if endangered as a class the factions of the larger ruling class cohere as a class. This, however, occurs only rarely at home, but often arises in various forms in foreign policy and United States globalism. Effectively, therefore, the American experience has seen almost continuous rivalry among elite factions, including the effort to define who governs at the critical level in Washington. Between the ultimate functions and daily decisions there may be immense discretion, and this freedom often determines the manner by which particular men are chosen for posts that allow them to bring political decisions to bear on economic, international, and social questions confronting the larger society as well as specific constituencies within it.

However, political decision makers often are transitional, and this makes them less durable than the main economic institutions from which most of these national bureaucrats came and to which they will return. Particular bureaucrats depend on elections and appointments, instabilities which do not affect those key economic forces confined to some hundreds of corporations and banks. The economic sector, therefore, is the fount of the larger part of the political bureaucracy, and vastly more important than elite schools or clubs in determining who qualifies to administer the higher levels of the political structure.

Schools should not be wholly gainsaid, because they too are important preliminary institutions in the socialization process and measurably influence who succeeds and fails in business, but they are not decisive in recruiting key political bureaucrats. From 1933 to 1965, 40 percent of the 1032 key federal executive appointees in domestic as well as military and foreign-policy posts attended eighteen universities, and the three most important—Harvard, Yale, and Princeton—accounted for almost half of these. Catholics were only 19 percent of this total number, though their share increased over time to reach 26 percent under Kennedy and one-third under the first two years of the Johnson Administration. Jews were 4 percent overall, but reached 7 percent under Kennedy and surely increased yet more under Nixon. What is clear is that non-elite-school bureaucrats, Catholics, and Jews when in power acted in a manner quite indistinguishable from those conforming to the "Establishment" model, proving that the power of the office imposes absolutely clear reference points on any appointee, and whatever his origins, no one who is not wholly predictable and conforms to the parameters of consensus on the function of power is able to obtain a vital post. So deprived of individuality are these bureaucrats, and so impersonal and devoid of sensibilities the office and the power structure that produces executives, that public resignations for reasons of principle become virtually unheard of as bureaucratic mechanisms wholly displace even the most elementary scruples.

This quality increases as international demands and warfare require technologists and specialists in office, for crises of every sort intensify hiring by non-Establishment standards and enlarge the federal bureaucracy at one and the same time. For worse than a lack of status is incompetence, which neither old nor new elites can afford very long. After declining between the Roosevelt and the Truman Administrations, the percentage of top officials with Ph.D.s rose unprecedentedly, reaching 19 percent under the Johnson Administration—particularly among Assistant Secretaries of Executive agencies and specialized functions in agriculture and the military branches. These Ph.D.s, despite a markedly greater propensity for dysfunctional ideological mystifications than characterized virtually any other group to enter government, were often merely the anointed technicians of traditional power centers—the most notable example being the Rockefeller family sponsorship of Henry Kissinger's own initial key assignments after he had loyally worked for them for well over a decade.

By and large, business and law provided half of the key federal appointees in the period 1933–1965, with big corporations and big law firms preponderant among this group. Other private occupations closely allied to business, excluding education, added another 8 percent. But businessmen congregated where the money was being spent or managed—the Treasury, Commerce, and Defense departments. Their lawyers went to Justice, Treasury, and Defense. As synthesizers capable of defining the needs of many clients rather than single interests, big lawyers played the most vital role of all in advancing a broader definition of class interests as national policy. Well known by virtue of their private successes in representing business to the state, they could freely represent the state to business—thereby neutralizing those rare efforts to draw a conflict of fundamental objectives between the two. The constant interchange of such men between business and government, some holding many posts over time and circulating back and forth, made the social values and objectives of the national bureaucracy and key sectors more intimate and responsive than would have otherwise been possible. Often this process decided exactly which competing elite interest would find its goals satisfied. Hence there were indeed differences, particularly when bureaucrats sided with one branch of business and managed to alienate others, but that the consensus by far outweighed the distinctions was a pervasive and defining fact of the structure of American power.[6]

Indeed, the big-business and law community had in fact become the fount of the top federal bureaucracy in the twentieth century, greatly simplifying but also helping to articulate the tasks of a state committed in principle, and needful of assistance in its practice, to the larger interests of business as a system. From this viewpoint, the nature of the top bureaucracy was essentially an outcome rather than cause of policy. The interaction of personnel at the highest level thereby became both logical and convenient, and a permanent aspect of modern American history.

Recruitment to the top occurred on the basis of many criteria, with "Establishment" norms increasingly, though surely not wholly, giving way to others as well. A class structure and predatory rule can quite comfortably exist within the framework of high social mobility and "democratic" norms for rulership, perhaps all the better so, as it integrates the elites and experts of the potential opposition and more fully incorporates talent into a vested interest in the existing society. Former socialists and civil rights leaders, Jews, or blacks, all act the same, and self-made Texas buccaneers and Groton-Harvard grads all become indistinguishable. Society is not democratized by this process, but only broadens the standard by which some men are chosen to run profoundly destructive institutions whose direction and purpose are predetermined. In this task, the less talented members of the older elites are simply bypassed and rarely, if ever, qualified for responsibility over the last forty years solely because of personal connections.

Personal contacts are important, however, as one component of a much broader selection process: the existence of family and personal dynasties that offer ample scope to their more talented members. The Foster-Dulles dynasty produced John W. Foster, Secretary of State in 1892, and Robert Lansing, Wilson's Secretary of State; and their grandsons and nephews, John Foster and Allen Dulles served as Secretary of State and director of the CIA long after. The Henry Stimson dynasty included successors in Dean Acheson, the Bundys, and John J. McCloy to carry on the tradition Stimson's law partner—and also Secretary of State—Elihu Root had helped shape. The Rockefeller dynasty was economic in origin but soon moved into numerous key political roles, and with the sponsorship of Kissinger's career eventually magnified its own power. The Kennedy clan is yet another, based largely on the mysticism of names that also helped make a second Roosevelt President. Such dynasties, which intersect government, top corporate law, finance, clubs, marital alliances, schools, and much else, have a certain deceptive fascination and are instructive in showing the integration of political, economic, and social power at various points. Indeed, at any given time one or more exist as quite important selection mechanisms for the administration of power. Yet viewed alone, or even as primary recruitment systems essential to the organization of America at the top, they become seriously misleading, for there is no evidence that family or power dynasties are a necessary prerequisite to the continuity in policy and practice of American capitalism in its larger context. W. Averell Harriman, born into one of these dynasties, was no more important in post-1945 history than Joseph Dodge, son of a poster painter, high school grad, and one-time car salesman who became a successful Detroit banker. Both fulfilled their numerous key responsibilities in precisely the same way, for exactly the same ends. Alone or together, Dodges and Harrimans were sufficient to give continuity and leadership to America's established order. Neither could transcend the imperatives of conduct the larger principles of that order imposed upon them, nor undo its personal or institutional limits.

Decision Makers and Foreign Policy

From the inception of modern United States foreign policy, the role of businessmen, their lawyers, and their spokesmen in the formulation of means and goals has been integral to the definition of American diplomacy. And while it would be too much to say that historians agree on this reality—and most still fancy the purposes of policy a broader, amorphously defined public interest—the details of this interaction have been so extensively documented that there is not really a serious debate left. Ranging from studies of McKinley and his policies, to the United States in Cuba, Mark Hanna and Willard Straight, or to the role of cotton-textile exporters in the formulation of the Open Door notes, the reality has time and again been incontestably proved. "To get as near as possible to the source of power," as William Endicott, Jr., commented to Attorney General Richard Olney in April 1893, has always been the ambition and accomplishment of those with interests to protect and advance.[7] "I, as counsel for the National City Bank, have a long-standing acquaintance with many members of the State Department," another put it three decades later.[8]

Diplomats, even after the Foreign Service Act of 1924, came from elite families and were educated in elite schools; and whether their fellow students and friends went to Washington, law, business, or the university was merely a matter of taste and inclination. The channels of contact—family, marriage, clubs—always existed, even though I would argue that such personal ties were incidental rather than causal to the nature of decisions made. For whether foreign policy personnel were well-born or not, their visions and consensus transcended such intimate links. It is, of course, germane that Franklin Roosevelt, himself a patrician, recruited 44 percent of his key personnel from business or law, and that one of his two key diplomats responsible for overthrowing the radical Grau government in Cuba in 1934 was closely associated with major United States sugar investors, but it is difficult to imagine American Molasses being dissatisfied with any of the other personnel that might have been chosen to implement a policy exactly like dozens that preceded and followed in comparable situations. The larger foreign policy consensus which existed meant it was natural for some firm or interests with a need —as the rubber companies and British price manipulations after 1920, or the J. P. Morgan & Co.–initiated federal export loan guarantees in 1919, or Owen Young of General Electric's successful promotion of a Bank for International Settlements after 1929, and numerous other possible examples—to stimulate a government action or obtain its endorsement of their own. In cases such as the Federal Reserve Bank of New York, the Wall Street banks administratively organized it and the Bank was in charge of official United States overseas monetary policy, thereby leaving matters more directly in business hands, especially when its own agents staffed the key posts. Both the selection process of decision makers and the purposes of policy were circular and mutually reinforcing: it made sense to have a knowledgeable former oil-company executive or lawyer directing a program of overseas petroleum diplomacy if one automatically assumed that acquisition of new fields and profits for United States firms was the purpose of policy.

Suffice it to say, over one-half of the key posts within the State Department from 1944 to 1960 were occupied by men who had first been with major law firms, in banking and finance, or with big-business firms. It was that understanding and contact with big business which defined the conduct of diplomats and provided the standard to which they were obliged, at risk of losing their posts, to conform. And such premises reflected, in turn, the broader consensus within all institutions—business, press, education, politics—that the prosperity and security of capitalism as a system was integral to the larger national interest and welfare. That assumption, so uncontested at meaningful levels, excluded a vast range of foreign policy decisions which were never taken, regardless of whether or not specific interests lobbied against them, or who and how foreign policy personnel were chosen. The United States Government always opposed the loss of American property, and hence national revolutionary movements; it never voluntarily relinquished markets to another country at the expense of United States exporters; it automatically opposed foreign bases as close to United States soil as American bases were to foreign territory; and it always objected to foreign actions which precluded future United States involvement in local economic development. The larger assumptions and parameters of decisions, therefore, are fixed by an overriding consensus and the collective nature of political power and capitalism in the United States; and although the tactical means selected to reach ends can be quite variable, even the limits of that variability are predictable in advance, regardless of who specifically makes the choice.

But stating this much only diminishes the importance of such matters as elite recruitment which so many scholars have thought to be causal rather than incidental to the larger process of United States foreign policy. It *is* germane when it comes to the differences admissible within this consensus, and these are critical to understanding why some steps are taken at a given time, why others are blocked or modified, and which priorities are applied from the numerous options available but still, ultimately, *all* subsumed by the consensus on protecting United States capitalism and power in the world. For the broad consensus on capitalism is alone too abstract to comprehend causes of short- and often even middle-range decisions, though if we ignore it as the contextual framework we also discard concern for the larger nature of reality. There is not one interest among many capitalists, save on abstract theory which is meaningless should the profit go to others, but only the individual need to accumulate. What helps New York bankers may hurt Chicago, and Chicago or some region may neutralize the former, or, more frequently, the biggest bankers of all cities may dispute with small banks. High tariffs endanger one group, and may cause it to resist different interests. More often, what happens in regard to one area or commodity may affect only one constituency, which may push its cause without resistance by others; and, depending on who they are and the conjuncture of circumstances, they may affect United States foreign policy whether or not their gain has any objective importance to other business elements or the larger system.

From this viewpoint it is unimportant to argue, for example, that opening a small market in China was not essential to the economic health of the United States economy at the turn of the century, but merely to show that the State Department listened to relatively small interests who were unopposed because of the indifference of others and able to influence its actions. Conversely, it is vital to note that the overseas success of this faction alone did not save United States capitalism from non-profitability, and that the State Department and larger political community's attention were overwhelmingly elsewhere than in the China market. Advocacy in a void, however, works only for those who speak for power and can mobilize it, but often the priorities or even the simple lack of time within the State Department may cause proponents of this or that action to fail. Bureaucratic rivalries within government are more fashionable to study than economic conflicts outside it, but these too cannot be gainsaid if one also respects the limits of variability that consensus and overall purposes impose. Personalities clash for often absurd reasons, but at some critical point, the nature of which more clearly reveals the motives and needs of a system, their differences are finite. Political agencies struggle for funds and prerogatives at each other's expense, and repeatedly these types of tensions prove fruitful to comprehend. Often, as with Hull, Acheson, or Dulles, a Secretary of State or high official will try to define some larger aggregate interest than that of, say, a dollar-a-year man who feeds contracts back to his employer, but even these generalizers invariably fail to satisfy the diversity of power constituencies all must reckon with in foreign economic affairs.

Within the framework of a broader collective vision and purpose, foreign policy becomes an aggregate of specific policies and concrete priorities which respond to immediate pressures and needs, but to focus on them alone is to ignore the most significant aspect of United States history: its unity and purpose. Collectively these decisions may unwittingly undermine the rational attainment of broader goals, but never in the history of United States foreign policy have men been able to fully and sufficiently gauge the implications of means to final goals and to rationally move toward their attainment without complicating decisions which often require others to be made in the attempt to neutralize miscalculations. Crises are the outcome of such failures and unforeseen errors which responses to specific pressures as well as the application of a general strategy produce, and crisis is the rule rather than the exception in United States foreign affairs—a testimony to the profound limits of social knowledge in capitalism and its inability to be the final master of its own destiny.

The Military and Power

Military power is the instrument American political leaders utilize to advance their increasingly ambitious objectives abroad, and the growth of the Military Establishment to its present vast size was the logical, necessary effect of expansionism after 1945 rather than its cause. The concept of a "military-industrial complex" which assumed that the military was co-equal with the state and business, if not, to use C. Wright Mills's phrase, in "ascendancy," was utilitarian social criticism but a poor basis for durable social analysis. But violence is the means to implement the quite purposeful political and economic objectives that self-styled "liberals" and "democrats" define, and the increasingly technological and organizationally complex nature of warfare since 1914 has, if anything, constrained and eventually reduced the importance of the military in the decision-making structure.

The notion of an independent military dynamic and ethic occludes the real interests and purposes of American foreign policy and implies that greater constraint of the military would somehow transform the objectives of American foreign policy. But in fact the military has ultimately been the neutral instrumentality of that policy's resort to arms after other means of persuasion fail. The "militarization" of civilian tactics was thereby self-imposed and only the logic of the failure of nonviolent techniques. A distinctive military ideology, indeed, has never existed in modern American history, and the few ideological glorifications of the alleged military ethic by men as diverse as Theodore Roosevelt, Brooks Adams, or Samuel P. Huntington were all civilian-inspired and without influence on the real world's actions. Invariably conservative in inclination, if only by virtue of the traditional recruitment of the officer class from middle- and upper-class origins, with an unusually strong weighting of Southerners, the military has still failed to articulate anything remotely resembling a distinctive social doctrine that would set it apart from the mainstream of rulership.

More important, the officer corps could not develop a sufficiently exclusive skill and expertise which would allow it to pursue its course independently of civilians and their civilian institutions, whose importance in the management and direction of military power was to increase immeasurably with each war and consistently after 1945. And since 1945, with the emergence of a permanent war economy, the involvement of interested business constituencies rose as the Pentagon budget became the single most important economic regulator and source of lucrative government contracts. It was not even consequential that military men increasingly intermingled with business and political leaders, often joining them, or that they shared a common social origin and outlook—one that was civilian in its genesis. More critical was the issue of whose interests the military serves.

In fact, the military learned during World War One, after almost paralyzing the war effort, that the logistic and managerial problems of the vast new undertaking far exceeded their talents and resources, and businessmen largely ran the war mobilization after initial wartime chaos left no other recourse. Interwar planning followed that precedent, and corporation executives and business school professors dominated the program of the Army Industrial College after its founding in 1924. That pattern of increasing dependence on business executive leadership in the war agencies was accentuated during World War Two, and in fact experience then confirmed finally that although generals might know how to fight a war they could not logistically prepare or sustain one. This fact alone insured civilian domination of the military.[9]

This process of growing dependence on civilians working in or for the Defense Department, as it was dubbed after 1947, greatly intensified with the technological revolution in warfare immediately after World War Two. Given the enormous complexity of atomic and nuclear weapons, electronics, and propulsion and rocket systems, the services formally acknowledged, in Eisenhower's words in 1946, that "there appears little reason for duplicating within the Army an outside organization which by its experience is better qualified then we are to carry out some of our tasks."[10] These tasks proved eventually to be far more than incidental, but were in effect the keystone of United States military doctrine, a doctrine for which the military services lacked the essential expertise. Thereupon began a vast research and development program that was to marry industry, universities, and the economy of the nation together, bringing more and more civilians into key Defense posts. The air force in 1948 created the RAND Corporation to advise it, and from 1953 to 1958 it assigned direction of its missile program to the Ramo-Woolridge Corporation, while it left the coordination of its specific weapons systems to the prime contractors. In 1955 the multi-university Institute for Defense Analysis was created to undo a near-collapse in the Pentagon's in-house weapons evaluation group, and by the end of the decade almost half of the three services' supervisory procurement personnel were civilians with business experience. The military alone simply could not cope with modern warfare. The technological fetishism underlying military doctrine effectively displaced officers from planning for the short flash of devastation that war had allegedly become, until 1962. What generals could not master, the fast-talking and -thinking business executives or Ph.D.s allegedly could.

The weakness of the Military Establishment was significantly intensified by the rivalry for a larger share of the Pentagon budget between the three main services—air force, army, and navy—and the special branches overlapping each. This division involved often giant corporations allied with one or another service and producing different types of weaponry, politicians from areas that particular contracts favored, and the conflicting ambitions of key officers themselves. Eventually it touched the fundamental question of the basic strategic premises of United States military policy, and since some wars "cost" less than others—strategic nuclear war being cheapest of all to prepare for, if not live through—the magnitude of the national budget also became a central issue arising out of inter-service conflict.

This inter-service rivalry began sharply as soon as the effort to impose a unified Defense Department over the War, Army and Navy departments started at the end of World War Two. It persisted in the struggle for autonomy and power after 1947, and was translated into its first great public fight over the issue of the long-range B-36 bomber versus the super aircraft carrier versus universal military training—a conflict that was ended to the air force's satisfaction because of the political influence of its contractors, the assumption of an atomic blitz against Russia, and the administration's desire to confine military expenses to a predictable, relatively lower sum. Tendentious arguments and smooth organized public relations against other military rivals thereafter became common as other weapons systems and budget conflicts emerged. When the rivalry could occasionally be suppressed and the generals and admirals spoke with one voice (which only rarely occurred on major issues), their opinion carried great, but not decisive, weight in the councils of state. But after mid-1947, in part because its internal disunity filled some key leaders in Washington with skepticism toward the reliability and objectivity of the Defense Department, the newly created National Security Council significantly downgraded the nation's dependence on officers for military advice. The three service secretaries, all of whom were civilians, voted at NSC meetings, but so did many other branches of government. Not until the Korean war did the Joint

Chiefs of Staff, who had merely attended NSC meetings, obtain the right to share in vital staff functions. In fact, after 1949 even the service secretaries confronted long periods during which the real decision makers sought their advice only on technical matters, or the military implications of foreign policy decisions already made. The creation of the CIA after 1947, with its quasi-military as well as political functions, offered policy makers more covert means for applying low levels of force and violence than the more visible Pentagon branches. With the service officers divided much of the time and thereby neutralized, and unable to manage many of the vital tasks of modern warfare, the civilians could shape the Military Establishment to their own purposes with no decisive opposition.

The main instrument for keeping the increasingly economically important Defense Department under firm control was the choice of civilian executives to head its services and the entire Department itself. Every reorganization of the Defense Department after 1947 further consolidated the decisive role of civilians within the Defense Establishment. In 1949 the three services were deprived of independent executive status, and the creation of an autonomous office to control all missile developments within the three services left the Secretary with domination over the most essential element of future military technology. The 1953 Reorganization Act increased civilian assistant secretaries from three to nine, assigning them many new responsibilities in which the military voice had once been more important—including representing unified Defense policy on international affairs within the National Security Council. Five years later the civilian secretaries were further strengthened, and the Secretary himself retrieved the last responsibilities for all important weapons systems developments.

At least three-quarters of these secretaries came from big business and giant corporate law. Lifetime government employees at these highest ranks were only a tiny fraction. The integration of the business and military sectors largely bypassed professional officers, who were not qualified or able *as officers* to administer all of the critical functions of the new Establishment. Those who did acquire some technical or contracting expertise soon found they could make far more money representing industry to the Pentagon, and in ever-increasing numbers high officers began retiring to enter business, so that in 1968 over 2000 former officers with at least colonel rank were working for the hundred largest military contractors.

It was under the leadership of the former president of Ford Motor Company, Robert McNamara, that the civilian ascendancy over the military officers became the most extensive—and the Pentagon the most destructive. McNamara candidly stated "that the techniques used to administer these affairs of a large organization are very similar whether that organization be a business enterprise or a Government institution, or an educational institution."[11] His model was Ford, and he made technical competence the highest virtue, and further downgraded the generals and admirals. It was when civilian mastery over the officers was total, a relationship that was purely a coincidence rather than a cause, that the Defense Department became engaged in one of the greatest efforts of human barbarism in all of modern history—one which all the ingenuity of cost efficiency, "package programming," utterly self-confident businessmen, and liberal professors could also not prevent from becoming the worst defeat America was to suffer in over a century.

Civilian mastery of the military made the latter an instrument of a policy that others defined, preeminently big businessmen, their lawyers, and politicians, and insofar as the Pentagon was a factor in the American power structure it was as an adjunct of the traditional institutions of power. The concept of the "military-industrial complex," of the triumvirate of politicians-business-military, and similar notions simply ignored the manner in which the generals had been neatly absorbed into a larger, more durable historic framework. The military budget, which was qualitatively a new factor in the economy, businessmen managed as they did the civilian expenditures. And when the key decisions to embark on organized destruction took place, civilian counsel prevailed—with no less inhumane results.

The collapse of McNamara's empire and the failure of his "crackpot realism" did not end civilian supremacy over the military, and businessmen who managed the Pentagon and then returned to their older affairs remained the rule. The Vietnam war proved, more than any other event in American history, that the ideological premises of those in favor of civilian supremacy over the professional officers had always been wholly warlike in means and ends. It revealed how fully the Military Establishment had become the instrument of warfare liberalism during the Fair Deal–Great Society period of American history—as well as how futile this technically precocious ideology is in asserting the mastery of the United States over determined and ably led revolutionary mass movements.

The forms of the accumulation of power have altered historically within American capitalism even as the general social and economic functions of that system have not. Different economic, political, and social modalities for attaining success have emerged, not so much to replace each other as to become parallel means by which individuals have played duplicate and interacting roles. These constituencies have interrelated comfortably in the world of affairs. The traditional modes coexist with new ones for personal advancement as the criteria for recruitment have become far more flexible even as the purpose of rulership has remained unchanged. Within the worlds of business and politics this pattern of recruitment and success has varied significantly over time. The existing pre–Civil War economic and social elites parlayed their accumulated assets into a significant mastery over the early growth of modern American capitalism, only to be increasingly joined over time by newer entrepreneurs of diverse social and ethno-religious origins: men who succeeded largely because of their relevant capacities rather than whom they knew from school and club days. In time, they too formed exclusive new elites, with their children also succeeding on the basis of a "head start" that was decisive for all those willing and minimally able enough to exploit it. Beneath a common structural role, numerous configurations in American power developed, based on differences in regions, types of economic functions, social origins, and much else. Both the political and economic organizations readily absorbed such distinctions without perceptibly altering.

When new institutional structures emerged, of which the gargantuan post-1941 Military Establishment was the most notable, for a spectrum of reasons existing economic and political leaders immediately dominated it and absorbed the professional officers into an integrated power system as secondary influences. Success for an officer came not from within the military, based on uniquely martial criteria, but by wholly conforming to the political-economic system's ground rules to capitalize on his fame or, far more likely, experience in the armed forces to enter politics or business as a man essentially indistinguishable from all the rest. The military thereby became a tertiary institution for power accumulation for rare generals, like Eisenhower, and some thousands of businessmen who had once been officers, but in itself nothing remotely resembling an autonomous power coequal with business and politics.

Because the accumulation of power and the formation of the various components of power occur in different ways, even at the same time, despite a certain number of parallel mechanisms for personal and group aggrandizement, the economic universe within which they all operate remains constant. Studying the changing layers which compose the structure of capitalist power and how these layers interrelate therefore becomes a major task of social analysis, but one which can become exceedingly misleading if one assumes only that the historical process is merely one of a clash of factions—regional, intellectual, or based on interests—rather than a finite social universe in which different constellations are always in motion even as the whole moves with the ultimate unity which is its essence. The accumulation of power in the hands of various constituencies can affect aspects or even the timing of the social order insofar as its ever more integrated economic and political aspects are concerned, but not its general function or direction. It may even greatly affect its capacity to resolve problems at a given moment in history, yet to assume that the problems would not exist were the structure of power somewhat differently organized is a favorite error of liberal optimists who personalize social defects in sections of the order—the CIA, Texans, and the Pentagon being some of the more favored—rather than capitalism as a total system of economic power which by its very nature and needs must be surrounded with diverse political elements. The components of the system alter with historical changes in the accumulation of power, yet capitalism remains the very bedrock of modern American history—the overriding structure which predetermines the purposes for which the United States today exists.

8

Politics and the Foundations of Power

To assert the existence of a society which rules with the consent of the people can be a specious ideological rationale, a statement of reality—or both. In the United States, the notion of "consensus" as the basis of political legitimacy has become conventional wisdom among academic theorists and Fourth of July orators alike, but the validity of the doctrine touches the nature of the political order, the basis of the mandate on which it reigns, and the very character and purpose of politics. Indeed, it is patently incomplete to discuss politics in modern American history without first determining the foundations of power and the role of the masses in shaping political life.

Analyses of these fundamental questions invariably leave one in a bewildering descriptive and theoretical limbo from which the status quo is inevitably praised as grounded on democratic sanction. Traditionally, consensus theory focuses on ideological precepts and the way a nation purportedly holds them, with the existence of shared values and goals being crucial to some essential unanimity which most people allegedly hold. Even critics of capitalism, such as Thorstein Veblen, believed in the overwhelming predominance of class values that all Americans shared within the framework of a class society that in fact benefited relatively few. Later theorists, convinced of the entrepreneurial, class-based Lockian ideology's absolute permeation into the alleged mass values, argued a quite similar position. A system that rules with the consent of the oppressed, who strive only to be counted in at the top also, thereby reconciles the notion of consensus with the structural reality of classes.

The fact remains that men-of-power as well as their critics have always found it extremely difficult to articulate the goals, ideology, and structure of American politics and power, an ignorance which conservatives such as Daniel Boorstin now celebrate as a virtue in which anti-ideology itself becomes a pragmatic doctrine rather than, to add another possible interpretation of the phenomenon, mindless conservatism and a reflection of the system's incapacity to control its own future. Yet this theoretical and analytical void surely exists, regardless of the reasons for it. Even theorists of political pluralism who distrust the masses, but instead discuss how such vast institutions as business, states, and unions interact, argue that some sort of neutral consensus unifies their efforts to find an equilibrium among themselves—but they cannot describe it. The concept of legitimacy in politics and power is sufficiently complex and frustrating to encourage this myopia indefinitely. Yet if it is ever to be clarified and demystified, whoever studies and comprehends clearly will have to confront some central questions involving the ultimate nature of power in America.

Apart from how it might appear in theory, the locus of decision-making in society in practice is a central issue, and no less important is the description of all forms of power—political, ideological, or economic—in objective terms. How decisions and actions in the world of power are arrived at, and whether they would alter were the mass attitudes and consensus different or more stratified and complex, is primordial. Stated another way, the question is whether power is administered because of some indefinable consensus which somehow guides it, or whether it has a more short-range, functional focus of concrete needs and interests in which references to basic principles are rather irrelevant. Correlation, in short, may not be causation in the world of affairs. Indeed, the question of power is not whether consensus and class or all group interests coincide in the structure of power, but what happens when they do differ. Is consensus relevant to the direction of power, or does it merely happen to usefully coincide with it? And, ultimately, is the concept of consensus and legitimacy something that can be reasonably measured, say, by elections or opinion polls, or is the notion too elusive to be usefully employed as an explanation of the sources of political conduct? And, if it cannot be measured, then well might we ask if the very proposition of legitimacy is but a means for justifying a social order grounded on the needs of power—political and economic both—and its capacity and will to prevail rather than some ultimate euphemistic "public interest."

These questions simply do not admit pat answers or more rhetoric, if only because it is a fact in modern American history that internal resistance to the constituted order is, at best, minimal, and the kinds of historic socialist parties which have succeeded virtually everywhere else have not taken durable hold in the United States. Even during its moments of worst failure, such as the 1930s Depression, capitalism has had plenty of space and time to make a succession of errors which in many other countries had a profound social impact. That the constituted system has ample "social space" is a fact that successive economic breakdowns have revealed, and for those on the Left to deny this pervasive reality is merely to engage in more sterile fantasies about the imminence of a mass-based articulate radical movement that is now nearly a century overdue by the standards of other industrialized nations. At this relatively late point in the history of the United States as a modern nation, one cannot develop an analysis of consensus or mass opinion on the basis of the implications of one or another definition of reality to the efficacy of what one desires. If nothing else, a candid confrontation with realities now is less frustrating than the cultivation of illusions which are unrequited later.

The primary question is not to prove the degree to which consensus exists on an issue, but to show whose opinions can and will be translated into action regardless of the existence or not of consensus; in short, who has power, who rules, and how? And this requires a weighting of the consequences of specific opinions to social practice rather than a mere counting of hands. In this view, it is less important that mass approval of the larger contours of the social order exists for whatever reason, or even fluctuates considerably with wars, depressions, and the material basis by which the order affects people's lives and welfare, than that the degree of social sanction is as irrelevant as it is difficult to gauge. Mass consent in a society based on a relatively small elite's predominance is not significant, and the operative causal agents in society are the goals and power of those able to impose their wills rather than masses who allegedly sanction in some indefinable way those objectives. It is the weight of specific opinions and class interests, as opposed to the powerless' endorsement of society's direction, that is most vital. No less important, in estimating the "social time and space" United States capitalism has during periods of failure which generate alienation and even opposition below, are the foundations of mass opinion. In effect, the bases of both power and powerlessness are critical.

It cannot be denied that since the Civil War there has existed an astonishingly pervasive belief among many—though to say "all" would be unwarranted conjecture—that the banal, vague ideological model of American political power and purpose described in elementary school "civics" courses retains a fundamental influence. On the role of Congress as an agency to affect state power the large majority of Old and New Leftists and prowar yahoos agreed throughout the period after World War Two. False consciousness among instant and pop radicals naïvely speaking truth to presumably sensitive or misguided power, or a middle class morbidly afraid of "creeping socialism" in Washington, is a basic cultural phenomenon that analysts have yet to confront with even partial adequacy; and leaders too often share, in quite important ways, false perceptions which can lead to costly errors both in terms of money and overall priorities—"credibility" during the Indochina war is the best example of this. Yet ultimately it is less important that the elite have false consciousness than that others share theirs as well. For those who do not count for much in the weighting of opinions, their misperceptions of the limits of their freedom and the modes of serious social change lead only to utopian futility and, for a very few self-proclaimed liberals and reformers, ceremonial opposition. Here "freedom" becomes merely the right willingly to consent to a type of action which reinforces the illusion of individual potency while in reality it does not touch a mechanism of power and decision-making which thereby gains additional tolerance and social time to continue according to quite different functional, if not celebrated and articulated, rules. The illusion of "freedom" helps make possible its suppression via a politics which, as a historic fact, never transcends predetermined orbits and assumptions. Indeed, simply because of American leaders' almost endemic inability since the Civil War to articulate comprehensive ideology which brings practice and theory together, save quite partially for rare conservatives such as Theodore Roosevelt's Secretary of State and War, Elihu Root, illusions among significant numbers of the masses may be no less shared in high places where men are trained to act without reflection as to purposes and ultimate questions.

The Limits of Conflict

Problems confronting men-of-power make their relation to consensus theory quite different, involving as it does profound conflicts of interest over matters that are far short of the nature of the existing order and the premises on which it is based. Not infrequently the collapse of perception among businessmen is translated into fear of socialism or the creation of paranoid organizations, of which the John Birch Society is the best recent example. Yet the businessman with a loss of intellectual equilibrium differs from comparable eccentricities at poorer economic levels only in that the former has the money by which to make his eccentricities seen and heard. Save for quite rare personalities, such as Charles Francis Adams, Jr., at the beginning of this century, or H. L. Hunt later, such examples of business myopia usually include mainly small businessmen, and they serve as further proof of the power of even such cases of unrealism to make their odd views known by simple virtue of their access to sufficient money. More to the point is that a genuine theorist—as opposed to a clever polemicist—of explicit American conservatism has never emerged, and the phenomenon is still far more a question of intelligence rather than interest or ideology.

Even when socially sanctioned potential dysfunctions arise, and 2000 or more politicians and generals meet to pray together or in small groups, while governors in forty states and mayors of over 1000 cities ask divine guidance as to what to do, or even the Pentagon maintains a room for prayers, the system protects itself against the marginal risk of such rituals leading to disturbances to traditional methods.[1] False consciousness among the masses is more utilitarian and leads to misperceptions no one stands behind them to correct. Consensus theory includes a place, as the United States currency states, for a trust in God.

Conflict among men, groups, and nominal ideas about the way to confront reality in the consensual process divides spoils and defines priorities in often quite different ways save one: the very function of capitalism as a desirable system within which to struggle for mastery. Within this abstract framework, which binds those who can affect policy only on matters one step beyond all their plausible options, a very real, definitive, and irrevocable consensus exists and may be freely perceived. At this level, an identifiable economic ruling class exists which subsumes all diverse elite factions. Power is revered, and for the businessman it means articulating the social good in terms which, at the very worst, will not cost him his privilege, and which more often will enlarge it. Within the more immediate world of practical affairs disputes become short and medium run in their significance, and can even produce mutual neutralization and ineffectuality among the numerous competing elites at times, but never intentionally touch the very existence of the constituted order and the class structure. Obtaining a contract or road appropriation will lead power constituencies to disagree and often concoct disingenuous reasons to justify such short-range disputes. When it comes to medium-range decisions they may differ on important national priorities, preferring far greater attention, say, to Latin American problems than Indochinese, or greater development of the domestic oil industry than imports from abroad. In this domain, business lawyers are eminently satisfactory in transcending parochial interests and priorities to try to articulate broader ones most men-of-power are likely to support, or at least clustering together the interests of various constituencies and arranging a sufficiently broad policy accommodation to fend off weaker challenging elites. Hence their large importance at the top of Washington's officialdom as referees in a ring with many contenders. What all will agree upon is the purpose of the effort and the desirability of capitalism, but this is also an accord too broad to avert continuous struggle within the consensus save during time of war. How long a coalition of interests can reign depends on its satisfying its components and retaining their loyalty. But disagreement, which often impinges on the manner in which political power will determine the divisions of economic spoils, has been intrinsic to the American economy since its inception.

At this high level, consensus also includes a healthy respect for retaining power and the ability to affect decisions, a fact which led to a phenomenon unknown in Europe—the man who almost never publicly resigns from a post for reasons of principle. For an attribute of consensus is that one reveres power, a mentality that encourages individual toleration of official policies long after personal disagreements warrant greater independence in adequately protecting other interests. Disagreements over how it is applied are transcended quite easily in this fashion: the name of the game is the game. Differences are generally so small that top officials often learn how to put up with them and never, in any case, vocally cut their bridges definitively in a manner that is unseemly and likely to prevent future personal opportunities from emerging. Hence while men are occasionally fired, as with Gifford Pinchot in 1910 or General Douglas MacArthur in 1951, only rarely does a senior official call in the press to excoriate the government. During all the years of the barbaric Vietnam war not one top official so left office over the intrinsic criminality of the event. Pervasive conformity and consensus are at the highest levels a part of the same game, and reveal the voluntaristic authoritarianism which leads to the application of repression against rare dissenters outside the institutions of power. And at the level of power constituencies, this passion to be in contact with authority leads some of them to finance quietly also that party they really prefer to lose.

Consensus may exist in two forms, one of which carries with it quite different implications and connotations than purveyors of standard theory will admit. It may be articulate, expressing itself in quite measurable ways, or it can exist as indifference and apathy which merely functionally reinforce elite control. If conscious accord becomes its criterion, then there is considerably more evidence that consensus is a quite irrelevant description of the relation between men in power and those they rule. To state that American capitalism exists because of the power, interests, and agreement of a minority and the non-opposition of the larger remainder is another, less ideologically rationalizing concept—for which more proof exists. In effect, according to this definition, the system exists because of its capacity to rule and, more certainly and importantly, the lack of a real opposition. Hence the consequent social time and space that also exist. Apathy, in turn, can be the result of political cynicism and some more or less coherent alternative in which important segments of the masses believe, a proposition for which there is very little proof, or withdrawal from political and social concerns for personal reasons. In terms of the institutional and individual explanations for it, a serious comprehension of the extent and sources of apathy is the main gap in all thinking on United States politics and society, and a vital key in its past and future.

Personal explanations for social withdrawal are many, and self-evidently important though not necessarily comprehensive and sufficient. Immigrants in transit in mind and fact and caught up in segregated communities by choice, people busy courting, and such are a few of the main causes of apathy. What is sure is that in politics the demise of Populism and the election of 1896, as Walter Dean Burnham has so persuasively shown, marked a threshold in modern United States politics and began a vast constriction which both choice and institutional limits—such as the poll tax or grandfather and literacy clauses which wiped the poor blacks and whites out of Southern politics—imposed. The year 1896 was the high point of the mass-based party and electorate, and not until 1916 was the number of votes in a Presidential election to exceed it. Thereafter, off-year Congressional elections in the major non-South urban areas involved a low degree of participation which meant that during 1922–1930 the majority of eligible voters, often to the extent of two-thirds to three-quarters, stayed home. By contrast to the period 1876–1896, when 78 percent of those eligible voted in Presidential elections and 63 percent during off-year Congressional races, the twentieth century saw the withdrawal or removal of the masses from United States politics to an unprecedented extent. Presidential election turnouts were 51 percent of the eligible 1920–1928 voters, 59 percent of the eligible 1932–1944 voters, and 60 percent of eligible 1948–1960 voters. By 1964–1972 it was 59 percent. Off-year participation grew from 35 percent in 1922–1930 to 44 percent in 1950–1970, but slid back to 36 percent in 1974. Despite the long-term increase, 1876–1896 was never again rivaled for participation, and national elections still failed to attract nearly half the electorate over the past generation.

Populism's demise offers an impersonal explanation for political withdrawal, and implies that the nature of the parties and the men leading them was a central cause of apathy. Demographic changes and increasing and more frequent physical mobility cannot be ignored, especially in explaining the disappearance of Midwestern Populism or the astonishingly low rate of voter participation in rapidly growing cities like Detroit, Cleveland, and Pittsburgh during the 1920s.

It is the burden of proof for defenders and critics alike of the notion of political legitimacy to confront and candidly assess the relative importance of all these factors, which must indeed all play some key role in a general theory of United States power and politics. But there is no evidence today that public opinion per se ever determined a key foreign or domestic policy decision in the exact form in which it was taken, and the form itself generally profoundly affected the content of legislative and diplomatic action—and it was at this level that the weight of opinion carried most significance. Indeed, circumventing such opinion—apathetic and articulate alike—became an increasingly verifiable preoccupation of United States foreign policy after 1946; and many of the major stages of the Vietnam war—from the Tonkin Bay "incident," to the secret air war over Cambodia, and the very character of the United States intervention itself—were geared to either consciously deluding or keeping ignorant the public. Bypassing the opinion of the masses that is alleged to determine ultimately grand political policy is today infinitely more institutionalized, via deceptive public relations and covert agencies, to name but a few means, than anything designed to define and reflect it. The implementation of foreign policy by ritualized deceit is the starkest challenge to the conventional wisdom of consensus theory yet to emerge, but one that has not yet led to any great revisions of what thereby increasingly becomes an ideological apologia. The gap between all the dimensions of American reality by the 1970s—its violence, racism, repression at home and abroad, its increasing personal and social disintegration and cultural mendacity, and so much else—and its still purveyed liberalistic doctrines was perhaps the most astonishing dissociation between reality and theory ever produced in a nominally literate society.

Modes of Integration

If consensus has historically included conscious approval, apathy, and co-option, when it has broken down in some visible manner it has also led to a resort to the law, a great deal of outright socially directed and legally sanctioned repression and violence, and the emergence of temporarily fashionable racist theories. The vogue that eugenics enjoyed during the Progressive Era, being taught as "science" in universities and receiving widespread endorsement from Theodore Roosevelt downward, is just one of many temporary but repetitive aberrations in United States social thought when challenges from below were perceived: in this case largely from Southern and Eastern European immigrants. Each crisis has tended to lead to similar authoritarian expressions, usually less elaborately structured and often as quickly forgotten as uttered. The Great Strike of 1877 was one such period of outright totalitarian effusions, and the practice of violence as often as not had its verbal rationalizations. Repression and violence, in all cases, make explicit what has historically always been implicit in "consensus"—those who do not agree by their own accord or indifference must submit in other ways. During the rare moments that non-consensus finds expression in some usually unpredictable fashion by virtue of its lack of institutionally sanctioned means, reference to law and order is exploited to destroy the effort to make formal freedoms an instrument of real freedom in the social process. "Freedom" thereby becomes a posture the powerful tolerate among the powerless, and those in power make certain they will remain ineffectual. The large body of law for suppression always in readiness is a pervasive fact that the celebrants of American freedom refuse to confront. For authority and power exist because of special interests in society and their ability to impose restraints rather than on any general social sanction, thereby making an enforced consensus from above the ultimate arbiter of the direction society takes. The very concept of the existence of true freedom in America among the larger population thereby becomes a means for undermining its fulfillment and binding together with ideology what otherwise requires courts, police, and armies. But it is at the moment that a substantial number of individuals seek to translate formal into real freedom with those minimal resources at their command that the true basis of social cohesion is revealed. "Consensus," at this point, becomes an ideological phrase which wholly obscures the real basis of authority in United States society since the Civil War—law and the threat of repression. Terms such as "cohesion," "order," and "integration" are far more descriptively accurate in revealing how the system of American power operates in historical reality. Succinctly, the state of repression depends on the extent of real opposition to constituted power. And in the United States very little opposition, and the glad willingness to submit to authority voluntarily rather than involuntarily, has evoked repression disproportionately greater than the real challenge. "Liberalism" is not a descriptive phrase for the experience with civil liberties and rights in America, but an ideological mystification to hinder it.

At the inception of the United States as an industrial society there were the courts, which, to quote Otto Kirchheimer's more general observation, "eliminate a political foe of the regime according to some prearranged rules."[2] A battery of laws and legal precedents immediately began with the first railroad strikes, abetted by the fact that so many judges and government lawyers of the period were themselves close to railroad interests. Each major railroad strike after 1877 tightened a web of law around the capacity of the working class to act, and fear of the masses among lawyers and judges by the 1890s was the rule. The courts thereby became the effective defense against the presumed dangers of mass government.

To the extent that critical strikes were not common, and other forms of dissident political behavior rarer yet, there was no conflict in the status of freedom and law together. It was only when some socially critical and potentially dynamic groups ceased to endorse the prevailing consensus that the state had to employ or consider authoritarian measures. Eugenics, scientific management, Prohibition, commission government, and much else grew out of this essentially totalitarian and paternal articulation of the limits of freedom in mass society. The existence of institutionalized racism for so many generations was not merely consistent with this elite sentiment, shared by Presidents on downward, it was its logical conclusion, and it links the full "progressive" elitist ideology with the repressive practice quite consistently. "Freedom" thereby flourished in public pronouncements and slogans as well as practice only for those who could afford it, who were white, contented with their lot, and not eager for equity. In fact this may have included the vast majority of Americans at most times, yet the critical difference between their false consciousness of being free and their objective status should not be confused to reinforce ideology. Functionally, whether voluntarily or otherwise, they could only submit.

In this sense, the notion of "illegitimate" authority so fashionable among dissenters in the 1960s was always an unrealistic view of the nature and control of American power and law since the Civil War. It is true that the use of state authority illegally against peers is unacceptable, and in one critical sense the Watergate crisis of 1973–1974 was but the logical result of the illegal use of authority against the strong. Against the weak, in trials, with laws whose value depends only on access to money, false accusations and arrests, or legal harassment, legitimate repression has always been exercised inexorably and routinely many thousands of times in any decade. During wartime, when national security is allegedly at stake, it has been applied with special ferociousness. The system of power, in short, always has ample sanctions and resources to give it teeth, and the allegation that repression is an illegal aberration is itself a way of sharing and perpetuating a false illusion which becomes a measurable obstacle to both rational social analysis and action.

War, above all, tests the limits of "consensus" and "freedom" and shows that repression and authority are the ultimate guarantors of social cohesion. While the progressive theory of the neutral state led to a hubris that naturally encouraged imposing class interests on those few not willing to accept it in reality, jingoism was no less important in provoking the outbreak of repression which accompanied World War One.[3] The dissenter against the war had only the freedom to become a victim in the social process, as a battery of sedition and espionage laws joined existing criminal-anarchy legislation to prove that law was the natural underpinning of repression. Advocacy, to say nothing of action, in all its forms simply became illegal, and the thousands of arrests and deportations from 1917 until 1920 only led to the extension of repressive state legislation in the immediate postwar period. Thirty-five states passed anti-"Red" legislation in the few years ending in 1920, and the creation of what was to become the Federal Bureau of Investigation was a no less enduring legacy in the anti-radical cause.[4] Free speech as a war casualty proved only that its use in the form of dissent was not tolerable, and the whole sordid history of the next decade, from Babbittry to the rise of the Klan to the Sacco and Vanzetti case, was hardly atypical of the treatment received by the Industrial Workers of the World in the prewar decade, and by strikers of all types earlier yet. Repression of dissent is intrinsic to modern American history.

The relative decline of federal repression of radicals after 1929 was as much due to changes in the two main Left parties themselves, which endorsed the New Deal or virtually disappeared, as to any other factor. No less critical was the nation's preoccupation with the Depression itself, and the Left's support for World War Two eliminated the need to do more than arrest a handful of Rightist cranks and a few Trotskyists. After World War Two the Smith Act, which had originally been designed for wartime dissenters, was generously employed against the remnants of the Communist Party.

The anti-war movement and New Left again posed a challenge to authority, which responded with intensive infiltration of numerous new groups and eventually the employment of both the CIA and Internal Revenue, along with the FBI, to gather data on at least 10,000 key black and anti-war leaders in addition to a less select concern for the lives of a yet far larger number. Opening their mail, tapping phones, provoking groups, and surveillance became acceptable state practice. In the case of the Black Panthers it involved the liquidation of some of their key leaders by the Chicago police. Beginning with the Spock case in 1967 and running through numerous famous trials, the Justice Department initiated a process of legal harassment that eventually proved nearly all of the accused innocent but distracted them and millions of dollars away from their "freedom" to dissent. For many hundreds of solitary, unknown individuals who objected to war with burned draft cards and other ceremonial gestures, fate was less kind, and prisons long and hard to endure. One century of American history, if nothing else, proved that behind clichés the state exercised authority, and when freedom moved from rhetoric to social action, however slight its real threat to constituted power, repression followed almost as a rule.

Enforcing the New Order

The American social order needed stable politics and institutions to ensure the unchallenged hegemony of the broad economic principles of capitalism on which it was based. By necessity, almost incrementally and without any comprehensive design, this meant ever greater control over the population, its modes of thinking and action, its aspirations and potential dangers. Social integration and cohesion were not the spontaneous result of a universally shared set of values, much less some mystical bureaucratic, organizational impulses to impose order on society in some neutral fashion, but an evolving class response to potential or real social challenges. The history of social "scientific" fads in the United States is really one of anticipating or responding to dangers inimical to the elitist consensus from above.

The cultural environment in which the late-nineteenth-century American elite responded to the apparent risks confronting the social order was unabashedly racist and nativist, with the university system as the most disingenuous fount of common prejudices. The Teutonic mysticism of the late-nineteenth-century political scientists and historians was merely a rhetoric-laden justification for the anti-Catholic, anti-Semitic, racist, anti–Southern and Eastern European immigrant views of the greatest names in American letters: John W. Burgess, Frederick Jackson Turner, Henry and Brooks Adams, Charles Norton, E.L. Godkin, and so many others. The masses—unwashed, unlettered, hardly speaking English—"a surplus of undesirable citizens who never think at all and who feel wrongly," as Henry Lee Higginson typically phrased it, were a potential menace to American society under the hegemony of the traditional ruling classes.[5] As voters, their danger was that much greater; as a floating labor supply they were imperfect, inefficient, and threatening; in terms of the nature of the demands of an orderly society based on stable politics and political assumptions, the people were at best a challenge, at worst a menace.

Hence the spate of concepts of social control and social order: Prohibition, scientific management, eugenics, and forced acculturation. The socialization process was speeded wherever possible for immigrants, until finally the declining demand for labor ended free entry altogether in 1924; the birth of modern public relations, geared to shape mass values and opinions and Congressional votes at one and the same time, begins at this time amid the consciousness, as AT&T vice-president E. K. Hall put it in 1909, that "the public mind . . . is in my judgment the only serious danger confronting the company."[6] That "public mind" was never permitted to evolve undisturbed along "consensual" or other lines, if by that term we mean something more elevated and philosophical than manipulated accord. From the turn of the century until this day, it was the object of a cultural and ideological industry that was as unrelenting as it was diverse: ranging from the school to the press to mass culture in its multitudinous dimensions.

In the aggregate, it must be concluded, men at the top and their conservative professors worried far too much about the social crisis, and thought excess the better part of wisdom. The rare expressers of opposition from the amorphous Left they had only to jail, deport, and wreck on relatively few occasions, and surely not continuously. But if the dangers to them were not so ominous or pervasive, the consequences of their own integrative efforts were no less comprehensive in shaping the American mind. If in fact the masses were more likely than not to avoid politics altogether and not vote, and if unionism became a mode of social and industrial control rather than a vehicle of transformation, the scars that preventive social regulation left behind were indelible and major; and the astonishingly neglected task of comprehending them is one essential key to the way modern America evolved—and why—toward consensual approval by default as well as conscious endorsement of the institutions of capitalism that developed after the Civil War and were far less challenged in the United States than in any other capitalist society.

The "new immigration," perhaps most of all between 1890 and

1924, crystallized the threat to the elite from below. Though I discuss this larger issue in greater detail in Chapter Three, it should be noted that the problem of "acculturating" this vast mass to the values of the predominant elite consensus was simplified greatly by the fact that the poor folk who came to America rarely brought a deep command of their own culture on which to survive, but only a simple knowledge of their native tongues and customs—neither of which bound their children very long to an alternative cultural or life style. Rejected by the majority rulers and value setters for one or usually more generations, such ethnics became insecure, marginal, and even lumpen as acculturation and socialization in an impersonal, mobile nation often broke their identities before it replaced one fragile peasant culture with an even more ephemeral melange of clichés, public relations, and a kaleidoscopic intellectual and cultural Tin Pan Alley always brutally in noisy motion toward nowhere.

The acculturation process met varying degrees of resistance from its objects, but in the aggregate the larger proportion of immigrants shed their external cultural attributes relatively quickly. This threat from the "masses" never materialized in a form the elites once feared. Blacks, of course, were different, since no amount of acculturation in the North ended the ghettos, job discrimination, and the vast wall of racism which kept *any* black, however white or even accomplished he might try to be, out of the mainstream save as the rare ceremonial professor or official to be pushed up front defensively. In the end, the larger socialization process produced the ends desired, but with human and social consequences the advocates of integration unquestionably never anticipated. Mass apathy gave the system plenty of social space in which to make errors, and the failure of the period 1930–1941 to see the emergence of a real Left opposition among even the unemployed indicated how well the elite-defined consensus had become a fortification against threats from below.

What was not anticipated was that the banality and emptiness of the new integrated culture, spread over a vast continent with a population always perturbating and moving, would destroy the original values and intellectual and socio-cultural moorings of its objects, and in the void of consensus-by-apathy leave a lack of community and norms by which people could relate to each other and their common problems in socially rational ways. For it was precisely this social rationality, this threat of blacks in the North working together and with whites, of whites transcending their ethnicity to relate to each other and blacks with common problems—that was the danger which had so disturbed elite leaders and professors during the decades after the Civil War. Having fulfilled their desire to break the possibility of opposition, they also destroyed, as well, social cohesion and community. Integration in its numerous diverse forms had triumphed, but only for the elite in its relations with those below. Underneath, however, the danger of radicalism had been eliminated only to be increasingly replaced toward the end of the first century of modern America by disintegration—a disintegration expressed in violence, rootlessness, an absence of community, and the collapse of unprecedented numbers of individuals in socially tolerated but no less debilitating forms. If the extent of this triumph of personalism could not be said to truly constitute a challenge to the established order, and in fact was only its further reinforcement, it was surely in a form not anticipated by the bureaucratic theorists of class consensus and stability earlier in this century.

Violence

The fact that America after a century of modern industrial capitalism had become like a perfect trap for developing and then containing within it all the problems and dilemmas—individual and social—that can plague relations between persons or within institutions was not surprising. Violence in America antedated industrialism and urban life, and it was initially a product of an expansive rural-commercial economy that in the context of vast distance and a hastily improvised and often changing social structure saw barbarism, violence, and their toleration ritualized into a way of life. Slavery consisted of institutionalized inhumanity and an attack on the very fiber of the black's personal identity and integrity, yet the ultimate restraint on its violence was the value of the black as property. Against the Indians, who owned and occupied much coveted land, wholesale slaughter was widely sanctioned as a virtue. That terribly bloody, sordid history, involving countless tens of thousands of lives that neither victims nor executioners can ever enumerate, made violence endemic to the process of continental expansion. Violence reached a crescendo against the Indian after the Civil War and found a yet bloodier manifestation during the protracted conquest of the Philippines from 1898 until well into the next decade, when anywhere from 200,000 to 600,000 Filipinos were killed in an orgy of racist slaughter that evoked much congratulation and approval from the eminent journals and men of the era who were also much concerned about progress and stability at home.[7] From their inception, the great acts of violence and attempted genocide America launched against outsiders seemed socially tolerated, even celebrated. Long before Vietnam, that perverse acceptance of horror helped make possible the dominating experiences of our own epoch.

It was internally, between people and within the community, that violence in America became integral to the nature of existence. In the West it was common, partially as a substitute for police-sanctioned controls which simply did not exist, and local elites generally led vigilante actions. "The United States has had the bloodiest and most violent labor history of any industrial nation in the world," two conservative labor historians recently concluded in their report to a United States Government Commission on the Causes and Prevention of Violence.[8] The South, more violent than any other region both in reputation and fact, eventually saw its lead over the rest of the nation closed as a by-product of its own economic development as well as increasing violence elsewhere. For the rural South was less bloody than the urban South, and it was initially urbanization throughout the United States that was to increase the rate of homicide and violent crimes. But urbanization was not an antiquated and temporary event, like the frontier and its permissiveness, but integral to modern American life. While statistics are variable in accuracy, and ignore much about trends in anti-social behavior that is not measurable, it appears that big-city crime for personal gain reached a peak in the United States after the Civil War, declined substantially after about 1908, and began rising after World War Two to a point now approaching the all-time high. Crimes against property nearly tripled in the two decades after 1948, with the fastest growth after 1960. Homicide rates grew appreciably with the urbanization of America, reaching a peak during Prohibition, declining sharply thereafter, and again began to mount significantly after the mid-1950s. Early violence might be said to have been the result of the partially transitional process of urbanization and ethnic group hostilities, but that of our own times the consequence of the increasing dissolution of the social system in more permanent ways. In reality, however, that larger tradition of hostility continued in various forms until our epoch. If one takes into account large-scale racial conflict, then the aggregate amount of internal violence in America since 1960 is the highest in history, and just as no other industrial nation has seen the failure of a common working class to develop politically, so none has had an experience with violence remotely comparable to the United States. For violence without radical political purpose automatically leads to chaos and disintegration. With over one-third of the nation's white families owning firearms in 1968, and a somewhat smaller percentage among blacks, widespread interracial violence would not be too surprising if quantities of guns alone were a simple cause. But the fact remains that cities from their inception were not communities, and a class that was divided within itself in too many critical ways to enumerate here were part and parcel an aspect of United States development and the social space and unprecedented security that American capitalism as an unchallenged system enjoyed. In such a form, a sort of consensus and elite hegemony had been maintained, not by shared values but by common disintegration and estrangement among increasingly large sectors of the nation.[9]

Violence thereby became a kind of irony overhanging the larger drama of American history. A nation that had slaughtered so many Indians, enslaved so many blacks, butchered so many Filipinos, and believed in domestic integration and order imposed on diverse, potentially unruly sectors of the working class also emerged as the most violent nation in the industrial world, both at home and abroad. Even as its politicians decried crime, they themselves were purchasing and dropping 15 million tons of munitions in Indochina, only to confirm the fact that whether calculated in dark urban alleys or the highest offices in Washington, Americans accepted more than any other people the practice and contemplation of violence. It had, indeed, almost become the national calling around which a true consensus might be said to have emerged. For those not acting in slime or governmental sessions, there was always the television to watch and the family gun to hold. "It is unbelievable that a secretary should have to write this kind of a letter," the executive secretary of the Organization of American Historians wrote his membership in February 1973 in warning them about the muggings in the Chicago hotel in which they would hold their next collective discussions of the nation's past, ". . . but living in the kind of society that we live in right now, these problems are becoming increasingly more demanding."[10] That history had not only ironies but also poetic justice. Social cannibalism and disintegration were now becoming as American as the Fourth of July.

The Politics of Democratic Elitism

It remains a disturbing fact that the deepest insights into American politics and the political process have come from foreigners, from Alexis de Tocqueville to Lord Bryce to M.I. Ostrogorski and Harold Laski, who have not been bemused with the patriotic conventional wisdom of academics and who have regarded reality with candor rather than theory. For the study of politics still is deeply bound in ideological shibboleths, with a need to justify existing institutions as equitable rather than a concern for the rougher world of action. But even if this ideologically prompted view of politics is transcended, the fact remains that American political history is inordinately complex and persistently defies simple categorizations.

The tendency to focus on the short- and medium-range aspects of politics necessarily emphasizes this obscurity, for the realities of the post–Civil War period break down by the end of the century, only later to be again changed by some dramatic "critical elections," as political scientists have too facilely called them, which presumably reflect some deeper underlying structural current in American life. To call the theory of the American political party underdeveloped is perhaps too generous. And those two parties are all the more difficult to comprehend because their genesis, so intimately linked to the struggle over slavery and the preindustrial capitalist society now more than a century past, has left them as kinds of artifacts and intellectual anomalies whose real justifications are far more implied than explicit. What is essential about the political party is how it performs a critical role in the larger social order and distribution of power in society, its relation to the people, and the manner in which the two major parties find a common consensus as well as differ. The fact that parties are stratified by regions, numerous types of visible interests, ephemeral cliques, personal ambitions, and so much more makes them difficult to comprehend, save if one stands back and asks the more basic question: How do parties relate to the masses and the broader institutions of capitalism that have defined modern American life since its inception? No less central is the issue of how consensus, in all its dimensions of elite definitions and mass apathy, molds the constituted parties.

There is a cautiously worded agreement among a growing number of political scientists that American political parties are neither mass based organizationally nor disciplined elite parties. They have no formal credos or membership requirements, yet their agreements and distinctions are quite well known and predictable: the Democratic Party's Southern wing has its traditional differences, both within and in relation to the Northern wing, and the latter is stratified historically in ways that are predictable, though they change over time within a certain finite ideological framework.

To say that American parties are elite parties with mass bases makes them not wholly exceptional. Conventional social theory is familiar with the universal proposition of a Robert Michels or Gaetano Mosca that the inevitable trend in all political parties is toward oligarchical domination, or, as with Max Weber, toward rationalization and predictable impersonal bureaucratic succession and control. In American history, however, despite the useful germs of truth in these concepts, none grasps the flavor and essence of an experience in which charlatanism, infantilism, cynicism, apathy, and gangsterism have all merged in ever-changing ways with the regulatory functions of the political mechanism and its responsibility to perform essential and predictable tasks. The existence of corruption and patronage in erratic forms, but as a constant if varying element to be counted on in politics, the absence of a predictable succession, and the changing relationship of parties to economic power over time make iron laws of American politics impossible if all one attempts to do is describe the past and future content of elections and factions. It becomes almost a law that one cannot predict the "future of American politics" but only delineate its social function in relationship to the larger problem of the control of power in American society. Politics in this manner becomes many things: a means for the accumulation of economic power as well as an arena in which to try to attain its orderly administration; a vehicle by which the already rich and their children can find distraction and the fulfillment the world of business no longer holds as allure; a slot where lawyers find life more interesting and remunerative than back home; a place where those who have influence of some sort can get things—of every nature—accomplished; an institution where the vain, the charlatans, and even the naïve can seek their goals; a sinecure to which cynics too can retire.

Even when nominal "mass oriented" forces, such as oligarchically led unions, have become important political influences, it is still a fact that the major American parties have remained elite parties which occasionally have had factions that engage in selective mass mobilization to attain their ends, but which in essence have never tried to institutionalize mass participation and control of party mechanisms. Quite the contrary, the fear of the masses is an articulate basis of many "reform" efforts of the late nineteenth and early twentieth centuries, and what alters thereafter is only the manner in which various machines—ranging from traditional boss-dominated cliques to "Chicago-style" gangs and unions—provide control over people. In this regard, what is made systematic is the form of non-participation and calculated exclusion of specific constituencies or the terms on which others can join the race. Mass mobilization as an end in itself is never the aim of politics, which is to win offices by harvesting such votes as are sufficient to that end. Still less is the articulation of political principles or ideologies the cement of the party or the people whose votes it seeks to gain.

Given the astonishing degree to which the electorate ignored politics after 1896, elite management of politics intensified both out of desire and necessity; and the occasional rise in voting to make upsurges politically important, as when urban immigrants and their children began voting to a greater degree after 1928, in no way altered the means or purposes for which parties ran their affairs. The significant aspect of the rise of the ethnics in urban politics was not the facile machine manipulation of them but the fact that their ethnic differences and hostilities kept them from forming a party based on class rather than distinctive cultures, and it was this aberration that left the machine bosses and other oligarchies a vast uncontested void in which they maintained their free reign. If politics is full of surprises at the short- and intermediate-range levels, and if the dominant caucuses of one period can be the losers of another, the fact remains that all of the sectors of both the Republican and Democratic parties are inalterably wedded to the desirability of capitalism as a general economic framework, if not the specific interests within it which are to be most favored. As Woodrow Wilson put it in 1912 in a moment of splendid candor, "When I sit down and compare my views with those of a Progressive Republican I can't see what the difference is, except that he has a sort of pious feeling about the doctrine of protection, which I have never felt."[11] If these differences provide most of the distinctions which we have come to associate with political issues, this larger framework within which they occur is quite constant and primary. Despite the curious insistence of some commentators that American parties, unlike European, are nonideological, in fact what is true is that they simply share a common and quite cohesive vision of the nature of the desirable society, and however much they may disagree on the details, that vision has been unwavering for a century. If these premises are never articulated into formal doctrines required for membership, but merely expressed as traditional commitment, American political culture has been kept mindlessly lower thereby than in any comparable Western European nation, a condition not exclusive to American politics only but which has given its people less intellectual defense against demagogues and rogues than perhaps any other country with equivalent literacy. In effect, such utilitarian mindlessness has made the United States a politically underdeveloped nation more easily and willingly manipulated by elites than any.

The great reform periods, beginning from the "Progressive Era" onward, in no way touched the nature of the parties' decision-making. The President's control of patronage remained the key to the nominating process, and when Theodore Roosevelt in 1912 objected to Taft's control of the party's convention in precisely the same manner as he had himself employed earlier, he still modeled his new Progressive Party along the lines of the traditional parties, with the few major contributors and himself quite firmly in charge. At no time during the Progressive Era or thereafter did the concept of democratic politics based on democratic organizations emerge as an issue, for in reality the de facto totalitarianism of elite machines—fashionably labeled as pluralism in our own day—was so much the accepted rule as to appear unquestionable. The issue of how a nominally democratic state could operate without democratic politics was a tasteless point that simply was never to arise. The problem of American politics, from the end of the Civil War until Watergate and our own day, was not the misuse of political power but the intrinsic assumptions and structure of party politics which left even the most ephemeral activity only to those occasions when it was necessary for a few professionals to ask the party elites for assistance or, every two or four years, to mobilize mass constituencies for the one critical day in which their voice could be heard and then ignored again. The logic of such a structure was insularity for men of political power in operational fact, save from peers and others with time and leverage to extract some attention and, even, response. The ultimate consequence of this process, and an unusual distortion of a system of elite politics in which the powerful albeit small party constituencies were normally paid attention and often assuaged, was Nixon's rupture with even men and institutions that traditionally counted for a very great deal in the political and power structure—a process that was eventually to lose him his post.

That the operational American political organization is the elite-dominated party does not necessarily mean that those elites are closed to new entrants ready and able to conform to certain fundamental tenets irrespective if they disagree on the division of spoils or even, as in the case of the Mugwumps after the Civil War, are opposed to the very institution of spoils itself. There is some evidence, of which too much is made to justify conservative conclusions, that such hidebound bastions of conservatism as the Senate were in fact surprisingly open to new entrants and that social mobility of a sort—within the framework of a tight elite politics—did exist. True, Senators, as always, were in the majority lawyers during the last third of the nineteenth century, with businessmen making up most of the remainder. They disagreed on many immediate issues, if only because businessmen and their lawyers rarely find unanimity on any short-range measures, but even the apologists for the system admit that whatever the intent and outcome of this fact, Senators commonly took money from outsiders and made business with each other. And it is unquestionably accurate that the larger visions of such men were scarcely modified by petty, self-serving transactions, and even had they been beyond all reproach it seems likely that most would in any case have been committed to the general policies, if not detailed measures, which they supported. The halls of legislatures have never been removed from the world of personal fortune-building from the very inception of capitalism everywhere, and for many politics has largely served as a means for amassing personal wealth. But unquestionable is the fact that this is an effect, not the cause, of a larger consensus among the elite that is the fount of policy. Crooked or honest, men of political power historically think in similar ways. Indeed, to make the Senate or House into a monolith on concrete questions of national policy at any given time merely because of common social or economic origins is a gross error, because comprehending the way Congress became a vehicle for specific, conflicting particular and regional economic and social constituencies is indispensable for appreciating its repeated role in introducing obstacles and dysfunctions to the coherent, systematic, untroubled direction of capitalism as a total system. As the kaleidoscopic mirror of an economy of competitors in a society in which ultimate power rests outside the parties as such, Congress becomes a key focus of rivalry as politics and economics intersect with increasing regularity in modern United States history, and the arena for rival group struggles within the abstract higher consensus.

However structured, and whether honest, corrupt, or the more usual varying mixture of both, the parties and their leaders relate to power constituencies throughout society, and how they do so will determine their political fates and public image. There is no period in modern United States history when one or both parties has not finely attuned itself to the needs of the existing loci of economic power or, ultimately, failed to be rewarded for its solicitude. For parties cost money, and in that mundane fact the central phenomena of American political history often can only be understood.

During the period that the federal political structure had no civil service requirements and patronage, and officeholders could be taxed to sustain their parties—and jobs—the dependence of the two major parties on business was nominally reduced. If in fact both parties were pro-business, this was only further proof that buying politicians was not essential to explaining the conduct of federal politics. Ironically, the fear of the mass party catering to the people's whims, and the patronage which prompted an elitist group of wealthy and patrician civil service advocates to successfully lobby for the reforms which began with the Pendleton Act of 1883, only led to the further triumph of businessmen over federal and state political machines. If the reform was scarcely drastic—and even by 1910 one-third of all federal employees were exempted from its coverage—it accentuated the need to get money from capitalists that earlier officeholders had otherwise been obliged to contribute. Yet this triumph of the civil service reformer was not sufficiently decisive or quick to explain wholly the rise of business tycoons such as Mark Hanna to the main leadership of the Republican Party for a decade and a half. Both parties, of course, needed more money after 1884, but that alone scarcely illuminates the nature of political policy but merely the growing importance of businessmen in party councils, especially around election time. Hanna's official biographer, Herbert Croly, was unquestionably accurate when he proposed that both Hanna and William McKinley, his protégé, sincerely and disinterestedly thought "the most important object of political policy was the encouragement of business."[12] That premise, held long before comparable business domination of the two parties, was to persist later, even when the elites in the two parties changed. The central question in the history of the political parties was not the misuse of power but the very assumptions and structure of politics as a vocation.

Most striking proof of this constancy of ultimate purpose was the impact of those elites in the Democratic Party who nominally could mobilize the ethnics and the workers, thereby promising victory in local and national elections. After the stunning but certainly not irreversible increase in the 1928 Democratic urban vote, it is a fact that the reemergence of the Democratic Party as one that could win a majority of the votes in a national election—as opposed to Wilson's 45 percent plurality in 1912—was coincidental with the ability of leaders such as Alfred E. Smith and Franklin Roosevelt to bring a sufficient number—but hardly a large majority—of hitherto indifferent or disqualified immigrants and their children as well as blacks to the polls to vote Democratic; and with the disappearance of the party's charismatic leadership after 1944, the CIO and, later, AFL-CIO performed an equally critical mobilizing function with generally decreasing efficiency. More important, this Democratic focus on mass mobilization in no way changed the machine, faction, and competing elite organizational structure of the party. What did alter was the relative leverage opposing elites had in imposing their candidates on the regional and national party.

But for men such as Smith, the party's program was important only insofar as it touched Prohibition and quite minor questions of reform, and in no sense did the fact that ethnics and blacks were now the key to the new Democratic majority define the fundamentals of the party's 1928 or later platforms. The take-it-or-leave-it options the elitist machines offered these constituencies meant simply that they could vote in a manner that momentarily relieved their deep frustrations but nothing more, with the reality outside the voting booth remaining quite constant. The unions compromised far more with the Democrats' traditional leadership and programs than the party felt willing or obliged to reciprocate, if only because the leaders of the AFL and CIO were not prone to demand much and generally satisfied themselves with their domination of traditionally weaker local machines. Despite the lack of conclusive evidence that the workers who voted paid any special attention to the advice of their union heads (and with the rise of the George Wallace movement it became clear many workers openly ignored them), what was certain was that the AFL-CIO had become a main pillar of national and local party funding—a fact that surely was insufficient to write the party's platform or, more critically, determine its elected representatives' actions. Within the framework of the pluralistic political theory that so many academics celebrated, this process of interaction among the leadership of mass constituencies left the consensus as to the purpose and direction of politics quite intact. A party made of congeries of smaller machines scarcely left any place for mass politics but only occasional mass mobilization.

The Politics of Money

Since the Civil War, the viability and leadership of successful political parties at the local, state, and national levels have depended on their access to money with which to campaign. This overriding fact has changed somewhat in form but not in principle, and to divorce political history and theory from the question of the cost of politics, as is the wont of most academic specialists seeking to impose schematic systems and clinical, impersonal order on political phenomena, is to ignore its essence. The absence of ideology or a serious political culture, save in the far vaguer consensus which is more assumed than articulated, makes money and jobs—or the promise of them—the adhesive that binds the party's workers to the organization. In one way or another, without a deep political culture the American political man becomes by necessity a professional.

In this context, the decision-making structure of either major party is intrinsically hierarchical and totalitarian: those who control access to jobs—the boss or the elected chief—have the voices that count most. This oligarchy is not imposed so much as it is understood by players in the political arena to be part of the given rules of the game. What is exceptional rather than the norm of United States politics is the absence of favoritism and chicanery, kickbacks, patronage, and payoffs. Rogues hold sway far more often than not, and they differ only in terms of the extent to which their appetites are bridled and their manners suave. From Grant, whose secretary shared handsomely and without retribution when the Whisky Ring cheated the Treasury of millions, to Nixon, the process of systematic, ritualized corruption has in some manner or another touched the offices of many of the Presidents and most of their higher administrations. At the lower ranks, it has been more the rule than the exception. Corruption, whether in the service of individuals or interests, is endemic to the very purposes and means of American politics over the past century. The root of the problem—personal greed apart—is money and the cost of successful politics.

This system of organized, routinized corruption was built into local, state, and national politics at the very inception of the modern period of American history, though its roots stretch far back into a colonial past in which politically well placed men who had access via charters, land grants, and government aid and contracts built some of the earliest fortunes. Beginning with the Crédit Mobilier scandal in 1873, which implicated fifteen Congressmen and James G. Blaine, who became the Republican Presidential nominee in 1884 and missed victory by 30,000 votes, and ending with the personal fortunes that Lyndon B. Johnson and Richard Nixon accumulated while in government, the history of money and politics has scarcely altered. Save for theorists who wholly divorce themselves from operational realities, scarcely any student of the last third of the nineteenth century has denied the deep role that patronage and peculation had in coloring the American political experience. Even the critics of the system, the Mugwumps, and later civil service reformers, included some disgruntled office seekers among their more prominent leaders. Most were what one would properly call conservatives on social issues. The federal government, in any event, was even in the 1870s the nation's largest single employer, and the introduction of civil service by no means diminished its ample supply of benefactions for the faithful. It was assumed that the reward of loyal political work was a job or jobs for the activist or his friends, all of whom would sustain the party or caucus out of their salaries or other means of obtaining revenues. Locally, of course, reform of hiring and patronage procedures was slower yet in coming, and never completed.

Even defenders of the existing system admit the corruption which prevailed in customs houses and the Senate, though in the latter case they with good cause argue that the main legislation of the period was not settled by the admittedly significant amounts of money that moved into Senatorial hands. To some critical extent it is true that at a grand policy level the opinions of key leaders were the products of the larger values of the dominant class of the age. Yet the decisions that Senators made on land grants, mail service contracts, or rights-of-way did not involve ideological consensus, and here patronage and corruption were frequently decisive.[13] And the way ward heelers mobilized their neighborhoods, bar owners advised and treated their customers, policemen enforced the law, and numerous functionaries performed their tasks of mobilizing the vote all revolved eventually around the amounts of money and jobs dispensed for their services. Corruption was so universal by the end of the century, as Robert D. Marcus points out in the best of the recent accounts of the period, that it probably simply canceled itself out, save that one must add that it still left those with funds master over both parties. Vote-buying, in any case, was common enough, and could cost a great deal, though it generally never went so far as in Adams County, Ohio, where it was learned that 85 percent of those who cast votes in the 1910 election had sold their choice at least once in their lifetime, though on that particular occasion only 26 percent were convicted of vote-selling. In 1905 New York City was alleged to have had over 170,000 purchased votes, though rural areas were credited with greater venality than urban.[14]

The enforced as well as voluntary decline of political participation after 1896 and civil service reform failed to reduce the potential costs of running a successful political machine, and after 1888 there emerged the business-dominated party to accompany the increasingly insufficient self-financing machine based on kickbacks, selective contracts in return for campaign donations, and such. At the level of national campaigns, 1888 was until then the most expensive in history, and its funding for the triumphant Republicans was largely Mark Hanna's accomplishment—with the aid of his business friends. Many of the most famous state political bosses of the period—Tom Platt of New York, Simon Cameron of Pennsylvania, Zachariah Chandler of Michigan—were themselves merely wealthy businessmen in politics, but with Hanna the predominance of business became more comprehensive. Hanna's ability to have his former attorney, William McKinley, nominated and elected President in 1896 was an event that caused politics to transcend the struggle between rival cliques, whose main differences were the division of spoils, and to impose a more coherent and controllable standard for the Presidency—service to business. Herbert Croly appreciated the significance of Hanna's ascendancy over the Republican Party: "In one way or another every kind of business was obtaining state aid, and was dependent upon state policy for its prosperity. At the very moment when both business and politics were being modified by specialization and organization, business itself was being fastened irretrievably to politics."[15]

This new rationalization of politics was only partial, since professionals remained a potent force, however increasingly symbiotic they were to become on big business, but it increasingly transferred to the political arena the rivalries between specific business constituencies. At most it merely furthered the process of eliminating the masses from political participation, as circumscribed as it always had been intrinsically within the framework of elite-dominated machines and hierarchies. The mass-based activist party existed only a few years in the form of Populism, and in this regard the Populists were perhaps more innovative and radical organizationally than ideologically. Capitalist money made the rules of national politics somewhat less arbitrary and sordid insofar as personal illegality and milking public treasuries were concerned, but it imposed business domination on the two major parties in a manner that was irrevocable, durable, and to a degree more utilitarian to the needs of a capitalist society.

The first great expression of this new form of business domination was the relation between Theodore Roosevelt's progressivism, and later the 1912 Progressive Party itself, and the interests clustered around the House of Morgan as opposed to Standard Oil of New Jersey. Roosevelt's sympathy for Morgan firms, his model of alleged "good trusts," was genuine; but when tempted to prosecute a Morgan firm, he was reminded, as Henry Knox Smith, head of the Bureau of Corporations, put it in September 1907, that "it is a very practical question whether it is well to throw away now the great influence of the so-called Morgan interests . . . and to place them generally in opposition."[16] Standard had also contributed heavily to the GOP, though by emphasizing the Congressional election of men such as Senator Boies Penrose of Pennsylvania, on whose favors it could reliably call. It sought futilely to relate to Roosevelt's specific designation of it as an "evil trust" in 1907 and 1908 by offering to help secure the President the GOP nomination in 1908. Roosevelt assiduously guarded his connections with Morgan leaders, who donated hundreds of thousands of dollars to his 1912 efforts to capture the Republican nomination, and then at least a quarter of a million dollars to his new party campaign—whose platform was preeminently the work of Morgan executive George Perkins.

For practical purposes, access to increasingly vast sums of money was not a sufficient condition of political victory in a Presidential campaign, yet it surely became a necessary one. In 1868 the Republican National Committee raised approximately $200,000 in large part by imposing levies on office and contract holders. By 1892 it expended $1,700,000, only to lose the election, and twice that amount in the following campaign. After 1912, when nominal reporting requirements were enacted, figures on total party outlays became somewhat more reliable, though still far from accurate. But by 1928 the Democrats spent well over $5 million, while the Republicans exceeded $6 million. Carefully calculated assessments on jobs helped produce some of these sums, especially in local elections, where spending could legally remain largely confidential. As C. K. Yearley has shown in his brilliant, systematic analysis of Northern party finance from 1860 to 1920, every hope, every post, each candidate, had a price to pay into the party coffers, depending on the town, state, and time. Police applicants in New York handed over as much as $500 cash at the end of the last century, promotions went for as high as $10,000, and throughout America brothels, liquor dealers, saloonkeepers, sidewalk peddlers, bootblacks, and myriad others all paid into pockets money that in turn moved up the hierarchy of authority. Reform campaigns came and went, and more puritanical days were forgotten, but the kickback and payoff and systematic corruption endemic to local and state politics remained pervasive in the United States throughout these formative generations. What is at question is not the existence of de facto legalized corruption as intrinsic to politics at this level, but only its extent. It was rarely, if ever, expunged from the routine administration of such cities as Boston (by 1910 perhaps the most corrupt city of all), New York, Chicago, Philadelphia, Buffalo, Denver, and innumerable other Northern cities. It surely made the police in many of these urban regions, as the New York State Commission of Investigation once more and tiresomely showed in 1973, the largest, most systematic organized source of crime and theft of public funds in many of the cities that were dangerous to live in, as Denver, Philadelphia, Chicago, and Albany, to mention only a few of the more recently scandalized centers, were also once again to learn. In fact the police had always served both as tax gatherers for their own class and those who appointed them as well as regulators of the accumulation of wealth based on vice. Successful syndicate-scale crime, thereby, became symbiotic on efficient police, who eliminated the petty potential rivals to established entrepreneurs.[17]

But at the preconvention nomination level and national campaigns, local political taxation was of declining significance, leading to the growing importance of business donors and, in due time, the very rich candidate for office. By 1928 both parties were dependent on contributors of over $1000 for a large majority of their national committee funds, with bankers and brokers composing the largest single identifiable occupational group in the critical $5000-and-up donor category. By 1968, with reported national campaign expenses at almost five times the 1928 level, but with estimates of real costs at $100 million, and Congressional races adding another $50 million and local and state campaigns the equal of both, the parties had become far too costly to survive on the cruder if systematized techniques of the first half of the modern century—even though aspiring ambassadors provided continuity with it. Even erstwhile anti-organization reformers, like the unsuccessful Eugene McCarthy in 1968, required vast sums—about $11 million in his case—to supplement efforts of their often comparatively sizable cadres of free campaign workers. The Democratic Party, contrasted to earlier years, had at the national level come to depend largely on the contributions of elite Jews, a smaller group of elite Catholics, and the trade unions, who accounted for the large bulk of its funds, while the Republicans relied upon the Protestant elite of bankers, businessmen, and fortune managers. The bagmen of earlier decades now were relegated to financing local races.

The extraordinary aspect of corruption in the United States is that it scandalizes and outrages public sensibilities, though in fact any generalization on the broad historical pattern of politics makes it inevitable to conclude that such corruption is predictable and systemic, and both the means and ends of politics as a vocation. The Nixon Administration scandals of 1973–1974 involved standard operating procedures well known to most of its more successful critics, and hence the artificiality of the entire Watergate crisis of confidence. If it were the mere discovery of corruption and kickbacks that justified the removal of Vice Presidents and Presidents from power, then hardly any of their detractors also in office would remain employed. A Congress that voted funds to drop 15 million tons of explosives on Indochina but reacted strongly only to the infinitesimally smaller crimes of Nixon Administration peculations in fact was an integral part of the entire political system which sustained press attention examined closely in only one of its more visible manifestations. Hence the instinctive, realistic public opinion, at the 1974 peak of Watergate controversy, which gave both Congress and the President an equally low rating of 29 percent who felt the two major institutions of national affairs were operating in an "excellent" manner.[18]

What was dangerous about the system on which such mass skepticism was registered, and from which the inherent organizational and financial rules of politics had excluded them, was the routine, systemic, and acceptable aspects of it, and the very purpose of the political structure of American capitalism at every level after the Civil War. While it does that politics a disservice to dismiss the chicanery, evil, and damage which some men can resort to, to reduce the causes of political failures to personalities rather than to the premises of a systematic politics that produces successions of men responsive to the same forces and interests in American life is the most common, naïve liberal error of all.

Politics in America, surely at the national level, had since the end of the nineteenth century become an arena in which competing power constituencies sought different solutions to problems and distinctive satisfactions for their desires—often at the expense of one another. Such a rivalry presumed conflict up to a point, but it was one in which only the wealthy and well-placed could participate, and it was this economic qualification that ultimately united them against those without property. In this fashion, the concept of "public interest" became a utilitarian justification for actions benefiting some, though usually not all, private ends. The history of the American political economy had amply proved that fact. That the two parties cultivated a certain minimal set of contrived distinctions which effectively channelized the votes of those masses who voted alone is sufficient justification for their claiming a genuine difference between the two. Yet what unites them, not merely in terms of "bipartisanship" or interchangeable officials, is immeasurably greater than that which divides, above all during the seasonal electoral charades. Indeed, as the shift of businessmen from one party to the other during the Presidential elections of 1896, 1932, and 1972 showed, or as with the critical assistance Truman gave Eisenhower in the effort to make him the 1952 Republican nominee and guarantee continuity in United States foreign policy, flexibility transcended ritual party allegiances whenever necessary. Yet beyond principles, which were common and profound regardless of the concrete ways specific constituencies wished them applied, were the similar organizational structures as they had developed in a parallel manner during a century's development. Oligarchic and premised on organized apathy, elite-led and financed, systematically and predictably corrupted, desirous of only carefully controlled and directed two- or four-year mass mobilizations, parties had become a critical reinforcement of the larger structure of power in America.

Local Reform and the Rise of the City

Not every urban community was based wholly on systematic corruption, and in this regard the picture became increasingly variegated after the rise of the "urban reform" movement with increasing momentum during the 1890s. The partial rationalization of national politics in the hands of businessmen after the inception of civil service reform was soon to reach numerous, mostly small, cities over the next two decades, but based on the premise that money would rule —presumably in the name of some technocratic criteria of administrative "efficiency" and the "public interest." The same removal of the masses from politics at a national level after 1896 was partially institutionalized locally over the same years.

To some extent, local elites desired a rationalization of municipal transport, services, and taxation which corrupt machines could not or would not provide. In any given locality elites were usually divided, and often pursued quite different strategies, including, it must be noted, paying no attention to municipal affairs. In Philadelphia, Cincinnati, or Manhattan they merely made deals with existing machines to service their needs, and such "reformers" were simply absorbed and served within a traditional framework. Bosses were generally not averse to such arrangements, since the ethnic-based machine was still evolving and most of the famous bosses were old Yankees themselves; and the ethnic coalition was not to attain truly national significance until the 1920s. The ethnic potential, which had already realized power in Boston and was self-evident everywhere in cities that immigrants and their children increasingly populated, required preventive measures, but the immediate problems of the community also prompted action via "reform." Still, the largest cities—which became the fairly consistent, though surely not invariable, backbone of Democratic Party successes nationally after 1928—were not so deeply touched by municipal reform experiments as smaller towns, and it was in the big cities that ethnics and their children formed majorities.

In a sense, however, organizational weapons were expedients selected to meet diverse local situations, and what was critical to many alleged reformers was the attainment of functional power which they could then use to resolve their needs and assuage their anxieties. Ward politics left the management of cities with the ward heelers, who were far from idealists but undoubtedly better informed about the needs and desires of their constituents—though no evidence exists that they possessed the will or means to systematically and successfully resolve them. Despite the nostalgia the ward politician evokes, with the memory of his Christmas baskets and such, the fact remains that ward politicians and officials were largely simply different types of entrepreneurs and oligarchs, in this case "rising on one suspender," as Edgar Lee Masters described the breed. There is no proof that services or education in any city were superior after reform, and both eventually proved typically mediocre. But with rising success after 1900, as James Weinstein and Samuel H. Hays proved conclusively, local business groups managed to transform hundreds of communities into organisms operated as corporations, directed by nominal efficiency experts who purged the ward form of administration and implemented the commission, manager, and comparable impersonal, nonelected directorships. Over 600 urban communities, mostly small and some new, had commission or manager forms of government by the 1920s. Water supplies were improved in some places, roads paved in others, taxes reduced or at least made less exploitative for private ends, and the urban structure rationalized, not out of some classless technological design—since the trend moved somewhat away from such forms after the 1920s—but to serve class needs more efficiently. Schools were centralized, but it is both naïve and unproven to argue, as some critics of this development have, that they were more class-oriented in the value inculcation than before. It is true that the city manager and commission forms of government were employed in certain communities to destroy the danger of the Socialist Party during its short-lived 1908–1917 upsurge, just as revisions of state election laws later became widely used means to interfere with radical successes at the polls, but that party's failure was due to far more significant forces which were national and international in scope. No less true, at the same time, is the fact that had such forces not defeated radicalism, ample obstacles to socialism's success via parliamentary means would have existed to inhibit its advancement.

In fact, what the widespread local reform movement did was to remove the masses from politics yet further and to satisfy business needs and desires for rationalized and efficient local administrative agencies. To describe this process as one passing from democracy to oligarchy is perhaps less accurate than suggesting that one traditional form of oligarchy, with a distinctive quasi-democratic rhetoric and style, was superseded by another with fewer pretensions and more overt class functions. That change in degree, if not kind, was but a bellwether to the direction of all American life. However structured and reformed, local and state politics in America had to a lesser or greater degree remained responsive to local economic interests that were influencing, if not wholly dominating, the political lives of their communities. The necessary change of favors this process required, including in towns made "efficient" with the reduction of the power of at least some elected officials, was always a fairly costly affair for those economic constituencies wishing to be served. In varying degrees, businessmen remained active in local affairs, increasingly during the 1950s with active corporate encouragement, though in fact both the importance and uncertainty of local politics to large corporations declined substantially after nearly a century of fairly predictable, controllable experience. To the extent it was necessary, local and state politics had become one more factor in the domination of business over American life.

The South and the Enigma of American Politics

With apathy and infantilism two of the main characteristics of American political campaigns, it is always a temptation to turn to the South's responsibility for this persistent enigma. If only because no region has been studied so carefully and candidly, we know far more about the overt racist totalitarianism of Southern politics and society than that of any other region. Yet however important the South as one of the major explanations of the condition of American political life, even as the South has changed—and since 1914 the alterations in its social and economic structure have been far more significant than in any region east of the Mississippi—the condition of politics elsewhere has remained as centralized and calculatedly immature as ever. It is true that the South has had more impostors and knaves, cynical comics and panderers to infantilism, than any region, but the persistence of the political success of movie stars and astronauts who are elected to high offices elsewhere indicates that the South never had a monopoly on underdevelopment in American politics but only revealed in more exaggerated form what was often the case elsewhere. With the advent of television and public relations agency–managed political campaigns after 1950, indeed, the meretricious, cynical effort to delude the public became an only somewhat more suave application of the country-music hucksterism and hokum that had long since become fairly widespread in the South. In essence, American politics and its leaders everywhere are cut out of one whole cloth whose Southern edges were only somewhat more coarse than all the rest.

Concern for the emphemeral rather than candid fundamentals is, in any case, a constant in American political dialogue; and it created a nationally underdeveloped politics that produced, in its turn, continuous turmoil and crisis when serious problems arose and relevant answers were sorely needed—of which the Watergate affair is the most recent manifestation only. For the fact is that apathy and infantilism aid political hegemony and the stability of machines, and hence their utility to politically dominant factions. By linking political issues to the extraneous concerns for race, glamour, religion, or experience, and avoiding central questions of power and purpose in society, the real intellectual and ideological questions of the social order have been wholly obscured and the mass capacity to respond to the problems of that order seriously reduced. For those in power, which is to say the oligarchs of the two parties, these truncated political perceptions have been a critical asset worth preserving, but it has by necessity left a mystified, ignorant, prejudiced, apolitical and potentially dangerous amorphous public opinion which has given the demagogue in the North as well as the South, even during prosperity, a far more fertile field than one finds in comparable Western capitalist nations save during periods of economic collapse.

The South, by virtue of its long history of economic underdevelopment, the institutional residue of a slave society, and its neocolonial relationship to the rest of the United States, has exhibited in more aggravated form the problems which plagued American politics since the Civil War; and after 1945, as its economic distance from the rest of the nation has closed, it has become more and more apparent that its differences with the country were those of degree rather than kind. McCarthy, MacArthur, and Nixon were not Southerners, and along with George Wallace's successes in the North as well as South they indicated how open to indigenous rascals and demagogues the entire nation had become.

Largely in response to the emergence of Populism and an incipient white-black coalition based on class, it was logical that Southern conservatives institutionalize the exclusion of the masses from politics after 1890. Given economic conditions, in no region was a politics based on class potentially more dangerous, and despite the racist attitudes of so many Populist and radical leaders, such sentiments were clearly in conflict with what proved temporarily to be a political formula that could bring power. Southern Populism not only momentarily subdued race as the center of politics, but had it succeeded on this initially fragile course the South would have had a party which transcended the pervasive social biases of the region. As it was, within the context of a unifying racism, class differences based on state and regional economic inequalities became important in the periodic redneck-led political campaigns after 1900 that managed to emerge from the jugular state political struggles; and far more often than not this meant that opposition within a usually single-party framework was liquidated by whatever organizational means were possible. The South pioneered the institutionalization of apathy, yet other regions in their own manner followed. The decline of voting after 1896, to a critical extent, was merely Southern-led.

By educational and property qualifications and grandfather clauses the blacks and poor whites were removed from politics. Mississippi disfranchised 70 percent of its electorate by 1892. The 130,000 registered black Louisiana voters in 1897 fell to barely 1000 by 1904, but so too did white registration decline from 164,000 to 92,000 over the same period—delivering the state safely to the oligarchy until Huey Long's triumph in 1928. Throughout the South between 1892 and 1906 the vote fell in a comparable manner—and remained that way for the next forty or more years. It is true that the emergence of the one-party state in the South made the Democratic primary the key contest, but even here voting fell enormously as a consequence of terror and institutional restrictions. In 1920–1944 Alabama registered the lowest white-citizen participation in Democratic Congressional primaries at 22.5 percent, but 14.5 percent when blacks are also calculated. New York general elections for Congress over the same period drew 55.4 percent, barely half of those qualified. This gap represented, perhaps, the approximate difference between institutionalized exclusion and the voluntary desire not to be involved. States like Alabama and Virginia, with their tight restrictions and yet tighter machines, were among the worst in the nation; but in 1920–1946 the percentage of white citizens over twenty-one voting in the Democratic primaries for governor in Mississippi, Louisiana, and South Carolina was greater than the percentages of all citizens voting in the general elections of Pennsylvania and almost equal to the share in Ohio and New York. Apathy and institutionalized exclusion, in brief, were the overriding collective national characteristics of American politics.[19]

The South's position in American politics was one of differences of degree in terms of state and local politics, though these distinctions were always important until the Supreme Court began eliminating them after World War Two—by which time the migration of blacks to the North had further reduced exclusion in American politics based on race only. The South's impact on the nation emerged most strikingly in its role as a vehicle of national capitalism and conservatism. The Southern middle class, with some degree of success, from 1880 onward sought to industrialize the economy and enter into what became a de facto neocolonial relationship with Northern capital investment. Modernization inevitably and slowly, without any dramatic shifts, brought it to oppose more psychotic racism as compared to the institutionalized variety, and with the demise of the Ku Klux Klan after the 1920s and lynchings in the 1940s the extent of racism in attitudes and social institutions and customs began to equalize at a very high level throughout the nation. True, transport and recreational segregation are lasting longer in the South, but after these barriers are smashed the institutionally more decisive job and housing discrimination in the North prove that structural racism is national rather than regional and transcends the social customs the South seeks to preserve. Violence against school integration in Boston in 1974 at least equaled any comparable Southern experience.

The South's greater significance is as the cutting edge of national conservatism. Woodrow Wilson installed Jim Crow more firmly in the federal civil service in part because of his racism, but also because the blacks were nominally Republicans, and no one has yet proved his Republican predecessors any less racist after exigencies forced them to settle political debts with patronage. In Congress the seniority the South accumulated meant that stability was assured that might otherwise have been attained by less customary means. The South has been politically utilitarian, therefore, in reinforcing a capitalism and consensus based on interest rather than party, standing for a security and continuity in American politics and foreign policy that are welcome to important national interests in the social order at virtually any given moment in modern historical development. A Congress that well-placed Southerners in key committees so cushioned against shock, in any case, was part and parcel of a national conservatism and oligarchical politics.[20]

With diminishing differences, therefore, the South played its critical role in a national political environment that continued to change with the nature and commitments of the South itself. Ultimately, the nation's politics was molded from the same clay, and was no less or more meretricious and totalitarian in Atlanta than in Boston—and perhaps less sanctimonious.

The main contours of American politics revealed a nation whose history had been far from democratic in practice, and whose rhetoric was scarcely more than an organizational weapon utilitarian in mobilizing votes and molding opinion. Elitist and oligarchical in fact and practice, politics had become another means for administering and securing capitalist power in America, a mechanism increasingly geared over time to access to money and acceptability in the eyes of those with funds to dispense—and interests to protect. In that large relationship between capitalism and politics, power and organizations, one can subsume the political history of the nation over the past century. If that evolution was based on a public consensus, the least that could be said is that the opinions of people were increasingly ignored or manipulated with time, and the basis on which that tailoring of attitudes occurred was anything but voluntarist and democratic. What explained the direction of political power, in the last instance, was its integral function in sustaining a larger social order of which it was inalterably a part.

9

The Structure of Political Capitalism, 1941–1975

All the problems that American capitalism could not solve before 1941 were seemingly swept away in the rush to rearm and do combat with the Axis. Resources which were unimaginable in 1937 were freely available just a few years later, and most of the Congressional political constraints of the preceding decades of national politics disappeared. The grave problem of insufficient demand and an over-supply of labor and capital within a year turned into shortages. The insoluble failures of the various economic sectors before 1941, and above all the inadequacy of earlier forms of political capitalism, now became irrevelant in the face of the onrushing state-guaranteed purchases of the economy's output. The dilemmas that had paralyzed the New Deal during 1937–1938 were now forgotten, save by a comparative handful who speculated about postwar adjustments, but so many new instrumentalities of action emerged that their specific anxieties were to prove largely misplaced, while they could not even imagine other potentially critical economic and social challenges.

The war economy resolved the long inter-war crisis of maturity and stagnation in the American economy, rupturing in vital ways the operational framework in which post-1877 American capitalism had sought to resolve its problems, and initiated a new era both for United States capitalism and also for the social order and world in which it now, by necessity, operated in a more comprehensive and integrative fashion. If it did so within the structural limits inherited from preceding decades, and with the same sympathetic merger of political and economic power which is the hallmark of all reform efforts, the American political economy was also to produce permanent new institutions. And within these, inevitably, there were also to be new as well as some older problems to resolve.

World War Two and the Organizational Foundations of the War Economy

Despite the internecine administrative and policy problems, which occupied the attention of both contemporaries and later historians, the main outcome of the war was not in the precise organizational structures it created but in the overriding development of the federal government's eventually enduring responsibility to provide a supply of capital and a level of economic demand hitherto unimaginable—but on behalf of arms procurement and appeals to "national security." This single most important innovation in the history of political capitalism grew by accretion, was only partially calculated, and quickly became too important to growing vested interests to abandon. The state was now free to spend according to rules of fiscal conduct previously unthinkable in the history of capitalism.

The manner in which the war organization and its successors were structured reflected the political and power context of American society as well as the needs and limits of the economy. These interrelations defined the war organization far more than the War Production Board and, after May 1943, the superior Office of War Mobilization. Suffice it to say, in the Roosevelt Administration's haste to garner the business community's favor and technical knowledge it largely transferred the war agencies to businessmen and appointed men such as James F. Byrnes to coordinate the conflicting agencies who were, preeminently, conservative and pro-business. If the big-business domination of these agencies determined reconversion planning and contract allocation, this fact was infinitely less surprising than if the reverse had been the case. Unquestionable is the fact that by 1944 many big-business leaders temporarily in government increasingly saw postwar cooperation among industry, government, and the military as the key to prosperity.

This emerging big-business domination over the wartime organizations and their later successors historians have mistakenly translated into a dispute significant only in terms of big versus small business, as if the latter were better able to reconcile public and private welfare. In fact, the wartime profits of the biggest firms, while very large by prewar standards, were also substantially less than those that firms with assets under $50 million were able to obtain. When it came to making money, there were no philanthropists anywhere in the business community.

The bulk of the war's economic gains still fell predominantly to big business and reinforced its relative control over the economy. Of the $175 billion in prime contracts placed from June 1940 through September 1944, thirty-three corporations received over one-half the total, while ten alone obtained almost one-third by value. This pattern of concentrated procurement was one that the state would follow over subsequent decades, though different firms were to figure among the privileged few. Yet more interesting to industry was the introduction of cost-plus-fixed-fee contracts which allowed companies to transfer all research and development costs to the state and provided a powerful incentive to increasing costs, as well as a basis for new industries. At the inception of the wartime buildup during 1940–1941, 42 percent of all significant army contracts were allocated in this manner, though the percentage fell to about one-third by the end of 1944. The unique principle of transferring all risk to the national government and subsequent profits to private hands was almost as original as the innovation of the state as not only the supplier of guaranteed markets with assured minimum profits but as the supplier of capital as well.

The government's share of the nation's capital goods, excluding roads and streets, land, and military assets, began growing significantly in percentage terms throughout the period after 1902, but was only one-tenth of the total in 1922 and 13 percent in 1939. By 1946 it was 21 percent, but larger yet if military holdings are added. It was the emergence of the federally funded defense plants that accounted for this important new growth of the government in the economy.

The government constructed $17 billion worth of new plant during the war period. This vast sum was equivalent to over one-third of the real net value of all manufacturing structures and equipment then installed in the United States—providing well over two-thirds of all the capital for military-related industrial expansion. But it would have spent far more had it not been for the vast unused productive capacity from the Depression, which the war once again made highly profitable. In addition, it spent many billions in research and development contracts to private industry, subsidies to stimulate the production of essential supplies, and the like—so that at the end of the war about $50 billion in war surplus property had accumulated. Controlled overwhelmingly by the 250 biggest manufacturing corporations, this sector—save in aluminum—was largely sold to the original wartime lessees at a price of less than one-quarter of the original cost, thereby consolidating the position of oligopoly in several key industries. If the United States emerged from the war without any firm economic program, save a desire for international economic integration, at least it had established some new, critical precedents which became the basis of a type of planning founded not on a coherent strategy but rather on incremental decisions which, taken together, seemed successful. Not the least of these was the role of government as capitalizer, subsidizer, and contractor to an extent imaginable only during a war that was from an economic viewpoint to continue, in varying degrees, until this day.

Apart from its material consequences, the World War Two interaction between big business and Washington led to important organizational developments which only further deepened the merger of key personnel in business and politics which began after the Civil War and which federal regulation had begun to institutionalize. A panoply of new federal agencies came into being after the war to deal with the greatly enhanced role of the national government, and these were largely manned with executives who interchangeably moved from corporate to government to big-law posts. The staffing of Washington with businessmen, which reached its apex during the war, was destined never to end, and despite occasional moments of tension the mutual confidence and working relations between big businessmen and the state were to become closer and more durable than at any time during the twentieth century.

Although big industrialists, bankers, and their lawyers could be found in the majority of key government posts dealing with military and foreign policy at virtually any time after 1946, in no way was this new integration of personnel more dramatically illustrated than in the creation of "without compensation" (WOC) executives in government to succeed the wartime "dollar-a-year" men. Almost all of the oil and gas officials in Washington after 1946 were drawn from the industry, and many were there on a no-compensation basis. During the Korean war, ten of twelve Petroleum Administration for Defense division heads were WOC's, while nearly 900 others filled key posts throughout government. In certain well-known cases, WOC's negotiated purchases on behalf of the government with their own firms, often at considerable extra cost to the nation, and in general they tended to improve the access that big business had to procurement contracting. On the other side of the coin, over 2000 former high-ranking military officers were by 1968 employed by the hundred largest contractors dealing with the Pentagon—nearly three times the number of a decade earlier—as loyalties became more indistinguishable than ever.

No less important than the WOC's were the assorted business advisory groups that existed in various forms, ranging from 184 committees in the Business and Defense Services Administration (BDSA) of the Department of Commerce in the period beginning 1953, to the older and more influential 160 heads of largely big corporations in the exclusive Business Advisory Council, the same department created during the New Deal regularly to advise and assist the government on matters of highest policy. Whether giving aid in passing tax legislation in 1962 or advice throughout the years to varying degrees of influence, the Council strengthened the role of businessmen as well as business values in government—efforts which the ideological consensus on capitalism made superfluous. Businessmen in agencies like the BDSA simply served themselves by serving government, making certain, for example, that the division of government purchases was one they approved or that Export-Import and World Bank loans did not create competitive industries overseas. In both cases, these typical mechanisms of the state as formulator of economic policy or provider of assured markets were but examples of an ongoing collaboration which took myriad forms, some new insofar as government contracts were concerned, and others old.

The distinctions within various industries by no means ended during the postwar era, as conflicts persisted, though even these tended to exist in a less exacerbated form—as with the petroleum industry—as high demand reduced differences that in earlier decades had been irreconcilable. So long as various sectors of each industry found markets and made profits, the economic and political struggles for mastery which had characterized the inter-war years were less common—though with each recession they would begin to reassert themselves in Congress or elsewhere. Oligopoly, too, was more integrative of industry conditions than had hitherto been the case. It was not because of the intended actions of the federal government, in any event, that various industries fell into difficulties—for as perhaps never before, the federal regulatory agencies sought to adopt, in the words of a cautious student of the process, "the approach and point of view . . . of those of business management."[1] In effect, the panoply of commissions—ICC, CAB, FCC, SEC, FPC—preeminently seek to rationalize the industries under their jurisdictions and, above all, protect them from new competition. In the case of the ICC this meant creating a transport cartel, and for the Civil Aeronautics Board protecting the aviation industry against new entrants seeking to carve out a share of the freight or passenger markets. Not a single trunk air carrier went bankrupt after the creation of the CAB in 1938, with mergers and higher rates and subsidies insulating any that fell on hard times for whatever reason. In surface transportation, the Council of Economic Advisers proclaimed the additional costs to consumers of the anti-competitive regulatory mechanism to be $4 to $9 billion in 1968 alone—and that much greater revenue to carriers. Largely because of the prevalence of well-placed laissez-faire ideologues in key government posts, President Ford in 1974–1975 began urging the deregulation of the transport sectors, at least, for a start. The immediate response of the leaders of the regulated industries was to attack the idea and unequivocally defend the existing system, and indeed the first concrete federal program consisted of making $6.4 billion in low-interest credit and outright grants available with which, effectively, to further subsidize the decrepit railroad structure. By 1976 it appeared certain that the historic system of regulation would remain fundamentally intact, despite verbiage and some streamlining, and even be strengthened.[2]

Partially due to the fact that because former industry employees and political appointees were pensioned off to cushy commissionerships few others could be found in key regulatory posts, the main explanation of the role of regulatory agencies in stabilizing and cartelizing their respective industries was that was what they were created to do. If the means of preferred business action have always been variable and flexible in the effort to attain the permanent goals of profit and stability, by the mid-1950s the organizational context in which the critical big-business community moved had become relatively durable with the seeming successes of postwar American capitalism. Those goals ultimately defined the economy, which therefore still possessed the capacity for future change, but the marriage of immensely high military expenditures, the government's economic strategy, regulation, and oligopolistic cooperation served as the main pillars to which an increasingly important and secure big business moored itself. If regulation of other industries remained ideologically distasteful to some, the appropriate government steps to ensure profits within their own sectors always found much favor within specific business circles, even as the ideologist capable of both describing and justifying this opportunistic merger of distinctive attitudes never appeared in either the world of affairs or of letters.

For the government itself, with its men of many and interchangeable occupations and an increasing supply of cunning and utterly responsive technicians, the relevance of each act to the attainment of a coherent system was a superfluous concern, for the important goal was that the economy work—which on its own terms meant profit—without undue political resistance at home and failures abroad. Hence the lack of discipline in calculating both the economic and political consequences of actions to future stability and crisis, and the growth of a type of unplanned, eclectic order, thereby laying the foundations of new problems beneath the seemingly successful solutions to old ones. Means for social management, even if temporarily utilitarian, could also build their own dysfunctions to challenge future decades.

The Government Sector and Capitalist Stability

The fact that the period after World War Two did not immediately experience a depression or even a serious economic downturn comparable to those of preceding decades touches on the precise nature of the new changes in the relation of the political structure to the economy. For the inequitable distribution of wealth and income in the American economy did not appreciably alter during or after the war. All of those prewar reform mechanisms which had failed to introduce stability, much less prosperity, into the capitalist system in fact now operated within a radically new context in which the state assumed responsibility for creating a level of effective demand sufficient to minimize, to an unprecedented extent, those economic crises which recurrently destabilized the United States from 1873 until 1941.

The two years after the termination of the Second World War in August 1945 did not witness a return of depression and mass unemployment for some quite simple reasons; and after 1948, spending overseas—detailed later in this chapter—also helped fill in the vacuum. The most important single factor was the immense reservoir of personal savings, amounting to $37 billion in 1944, which goods-starved Americans had amassed from near-zero Depression levels. By 1947 this sum had been trimmed down to less than $5 billion, and that which had been spent was about equal to the cut in military expenditures between fiscal 1946 and 1947. And with much lower corporate taxes, business began adding $18 billion to its inventories during 1945–1947, in addition to $68 billion in new investment in plant and equipment during 1946–1948. Moreover, despite immense reductions in military spending, the nearly $15 billion the government spent on the military in fiscal 1947 was still over $13 billion higher than in 1940, while total federal expenditures exceeded those of 1940 by over four times. The economy during the critical first two postwar years was still far short of a full-blown war capitalism, but in one vital sense it was living off the financial fat accumulated during the last war, and significant military-international innovations were beginning to mature.

Notwithstanding the demobilization of most of the military and reduction of wartime-inflated civilian employment, by 1949 the federal government's civilian payroll was over a million persons more than in 1940, while military personnel numbered nearly 1.3 million more than 1939, and the government sector was now a significant and growing cushion in keeping down unemployment. Permanent government workers, including military personnel, were but 6.5 percent of all employed workers in 1920, 7.4 percent in 1930, 9.5 percent in 1940, but 12.4 percent in 1949. By early 1949, however, as the backlogged wartime demand and spending nearly disappeared, the economy began to sink into new unemployment despite accelerated vast foreign grants after mid-1948. Unemployment, which had been under 4 percent during 1946–1948, by the third quarter of 1949 reached 6.6 percent; and as profits and orders began dropping, and production in industries like iron and steel fell as much as 30 percent, during the first quarter of 1950 7.9 percent of the wage and salary workers were unemployed. An impending period of economic troubles was publicly acknowledged by President Truman himself on July 13, 1949. Under the circumstances, Washington's growing difficulties in controlling military and political developments in Europe and Asia found expression in a vast increase in military spending, which the State Department, for political as well as explicitly economic reasons, had in any case desired since at least mid-1949. It would be unwarranted to suggest that the expansion of the military sector came only because of domestic economic needs, but had those needs not existed the resistance to deficit spending would have been far greater, and probably decisive. Moreover, the very existence of a domestic surplus productivity and labor force made the accumulation of arms, for whatever the reason, more plausible to its leading proponents. The Korean war itself cannot explain the emergence of the defense budget at just the propitious moment, since most of the increased spending from June 1950 until mid-1953 went to preparing for hypothetical, mainly unfought, wars elsewhere.

Between calendar 1950 and 1951, in any case, the military budget increased from $14 to $34 billion, and its share of the gross national product leaped from 5 percent to 10.3, and by 1953 reached the postwar high of 13.5 percent of the GNP. Despite a small decline in dollars during the post-Korean period, and a more significant drop in its share of the GNP, by 1957 the Pentagon budget began its inexorable annual dollar growth, and during the 1960s its share of the GNP hovered around 9 percent, or about twice the 1947–1950 average and alone about equal to the weight of peak government spending for all programs during the New Deal.

The military budget thereby became the sponge which absorbed much, if not always all, excess industrial capacity, thereby putting a floor under the capitalist economy. The Pentagon's annual 8 to 10 percent of the GNP provided that critical break-even point of economic stimulus which made much of the rest of the economy viable and far less perturbed by a crisis of demand. Its significance was qualitative rather than merely quantitative, lifting economic activity and capacity utilization to the point at which its seemingly relatively small increment to production provided a far larger share of profits. As a multiplier in stimulating business it greatly exceeded virtually all others. Until other difficulties arose—as they inevitably would—capitalism could at least resolve the problem of insufficient demand so troublesome during the inter-war years. Thereupon began a vast multifarious cornucopia which affected some industries, firms, and regions more than others, but spilled over with its multiplier effect to define the whole tempo of economic developments, with each major adjustment in military spending tending to have some concomitant impact on the level of employment. Private and public capital merged for defense contractors, who by 1967 were using $15 billion in government-owned property to realize some of the highest profits on their own investments in perhaps recorded United States history. Despite the fact that by 1968 fixed-price contracts made up about half the total, the opportunities for pyramiding profits offered firms astonishing and unprecedented possibilities for gains. At the extreme, the Pentagon filed suit against North American Aviation for in two successive years making 612 and 802 percent profits on their investment when the contract provided for only 8 percent. Less objectionable to it was the 43 percent return on investment the vast Minuteman missile program produced during 1958–1966.

On the whole, a hundred corporations received roughly two-thirds of the total defense contracts during the period after 1951, and although their precise identities changed, it was the big-business sector that benefited most from the new bonanza. California was by far the greatest recipient of contracts, but New York and eventually Texas were almost as dependent on the military demand. California in 1966 could calculate that 17 percent of its employment was directly defense generated, to which one would have to add the multiplier effect of consumer-oriented related jobs this key group had created with its higher incomes. In 1962 seven of the largest contractors were at least three-quarters dependent on military contracts, while another ten were at least one-half dependent and another eight at least one-quarter dependent. More important, as the B-36, F-111, and C-5A procurements showed, it was the Pentagon's capacity to award mammoth contracts and eventually even low-interest loans to ailing, less-competitive firms that repeatedly staved off major bankruptcies in the military-oriented industrial sector.

The government, citing military necessity, had now located new tools for stimulating the economy. Regions with higher than average unemployment received a preference for Pentagon contracts if all other factors were equal. During 1951–1959 the government granted over $23 billion in accelerated amortization to mainly big corporations, tantamount to granting interest-free loans via privileged tax write-offs as well as variable subsidies which ultimately will amount to billions. Its allocations to research and development, about 60 percent of which went to private business, by 1968 had surpassed $17 billion annually; and such federally financed research, while only 0.5 percent of the GNP in 1946, had reached 2.2 percent by 1966. Space and atomic research about equaled military "R and

D" by the mid-1960s, thereby opening a vast demand for new research- and labor-intensive industries as well as a pool of government-funded innovations virtually free to business. Government patent policy allowed contractors to retain exclusive patent rights, without charge, on inventions developed while fulfilling government contracts, though the Pentagon usually excludes itself from future royalty payments on such discoveries. Depletion allowances ended up giving oil and mining firms untold billions of dollars of additional profits. Rapid depreciation clauses, as in the 1954 Tax Act, offered other stipends, and the role of the government as subsidizer of the capitalist economy, employing not only the Defense but AEC, NASA, HEW, and numerous other budgets, as well as tax rulings, became a vast undertaking for which few, if any, pre-1941 precedents could be found.

Wherever one turned, the new federal economic policy had married economic growth with help to big business and upper-income groups, providing demand and contracts which covered every conceivable aspect of economic activity. In 1946 the relatively inefficient sector of mining, in the name of national defense, obtained the national stockpile act, which found in Washington a market for generally high-cost domestic output that no one else needed or could afford. Mainly buying minerals and certain agricultural raw materials, the program also built plants which it often sold at a minute fraction of cost, and by 1961 it had goods costing $9 billion on its hands—a figure almost matched in 1974. Large publications benefited most from the postal deficits that second-, third-, and fourth-class mails created, reaching anywhere from $403 to $726 million annually throughout the 1950s. Over $1 billion in direct subsidies went to United States shipowners during 1947–1960, not to mention far higher sums in guaranteed shipping contracts which the law that at least half of all government-financed cargoes must be carried in American-owned vessels required. All forms of farm subsidies, of which around one-half of the price-support component went to the richest tenth of the growers, amounted to over $22 billion during 1951–1961. Assorted services and subsidies to business (excluding tax decisions, Pentagon military functions, and strategic-raw-materials stockpiling) were estimated at over $11 billion during the same period.

In essence, concentrating on military spending and expenditures designed to serve business and big farmers, the postwar federal budget went far beyond anything known during the New Deal to more directly provide, in a manner the New Deal had not attempted, additional demand so essential to reasonably full production and employment. In 1936 the federal government's expenditures equaled 10 percent of the gross national product, a figure that dropped to 8 percent by 1938. In 1953, by contrast, federal expenditures were over 21 percent of the GNP, and during the budget-minded year of 1957 fell to almost 18 percent, with unemployment 4.3 percent in 1957 as opposed to 2.9 percent in 1953. But by 1975, with federal outlays 21 percent of the GNP, unemployment reached 8.5 percent. Unemployment, reflecting this central linkage of the economy to the military sector, proved exceedingly sensitive to federal expenditures until the 1970s, when other problems began reducing dramatically the efficacy of these anti-recessionary techniques. During fiscal 1958, when federal expenditures were cut back sharply to reduce what proved to be a $3 billion budget deficit, unemployment rose to 6.8 percent, an increase over the 1957 rate of more than one-half and a then postwar high until 1975. But a $13 billion deficit the following year and a 12 percent increase in federal outlays partially reversed the trend.

Overseeing this integration of politics and economics into a yet higher stage of political capitalism was a group of top officials drawn largely from the world of big business, top corporate law, and major finance. If this fact was not necessarily a cause of the new arrangement, and surely not a new precedent in United States history, it nevertheless simplified the administration of the machinery of state and guaranteed, along with much else, that the existing programs would not be significantly modified as had been many—though by no means all—earlier efforts in state integration of the economy. Of the 234 men who during 1944–1960 held the key positions in the State, Defense or War, Treasury, and Commerce departments, plus other relevant executive agencies dealing with foreign and military policy, their multiple government careers meant that they accounted for at least 678 posts, most of which were at the highest policymaking level. Those from big law, banking, and investment firms accounted for 36 percent of these key positions, while another 25 percent of the offices were occupied by those from industry, utilities, and miscellaneous business and commercial firms. In addition to these three-fifths of the key jobs falling to men of economic affairs, another 16 percent were held by career government officials who were subsequently to leave government—mainly for business.[3] Much more important than the WOC's, over whom they had ultimate control, this small elite sought to work within what was an inflexible framework of government-business relations which encompassed vast spending along with the enormous regulatory mechanisms inherited from earlier epochs.

More than ever, the merger of politics and economics had now produced the hybrid synthesis of political capitalism which, in the largest sense, became the foundation of capitalist power. The government was now financier and provider of capital as well as premium markets, and it could regulate the rate of economic activity, employment, and, to some measure, growth by a mixture of expenditures and policies which were overwhelmingly military both in form and consequence. Such a new power had not so much been planned after 1946 as grown by accretion, not the least because far fewer political constraints existed on spending for war than for other purposes. Hence there is a danger in automatically implying clarity to men who preferred merely to take the path of least resistance in solving the postwar political and economic dilemmas at one and the same time, just as it is unwarranted to impute too much innocence or stupidity to the men who directed the process. Each case must carefully be judged on its own merits.

The military sector largely resolved that portion of the problem of internal unemployment, demand, and profitability that the purely business economy could not cope with itself, and gave an added dynamism to it that otherwise indisputably would have evaporated by 1950. Still, the new arrangement did not plan so much on a specific war, especially after the emergence of the Soviet atomic bomb made conflict with Russia too dangerous, as on the function of war expenses in general. And because of the problem of "credibility," in which arms became useless if there was not also a willingness to employ them, and also because the stabilization of numerous Third World nations increasingly became the main focus for action as well as arms accumulation, the political logic of an arms economy encouraged impulses to act to accompany its economic utility. Precisely because America was counterrevolutionary it was ready to spend money even if it did not have an immediate beneficial economic outcome, and the fact that it did made that ideological-political role all the more attractive as well as essential. At the same time, the political and social justification that the perpetual arms spending the new economy required, lest it slip back into stagnation, contained its own imperatives in which everything from faulty logic to lies and sincerely believed false mystifications became integral to postwar American policies at home and abroad. And this too demanded not merely arms to sustain the economy but also to confront a world which the United States both accurately as well as falsely perceived—the former in terms of what was the larger revolutionary pattern of modern history and the latter as to how it might best control it. Its new economic strength also embodied, ultimately, new challenges and fatal traps which might yet undo the health of the economy it had helped to save. Much more slowly than during preceding decades the nation was again to learn that the political, economic, and organizational mechanisms for integrating America, along with the personalities directing them, were sorely inadequate for the magnitude of the problems that evolved.

Economic Policy: Accidental Designs

During the Second World War, economists, Congress, and the administration reflected on the possibility of a return to a depression after the war, and the outcome was a plethora of articles and debates which, after politics took its toll, was embodied in the Employment Act of 1946. Largely forgotten today, the Act embodied the quintessence of "Keynesian planning" for a peacetime society in which politics, as ever, also helped to define the limits of possibilities. Congress, which in 1944 feared "economic chaos" if the transition to peace were not carefully planned, was not of one mind as to what would work, nor could economists offer any convincing consensus to help guide them.[4] Strong on goals of full employment but weak on modalities—save for the reasonably vague one of greater federal and state spending whenever essential, the improvement of the old-age retirement program, and such—the final text was far more innocuous yet, and concretely produced only the Council of Economic Advisers to add to the nation's payroll. In either form, however, it left few specific mandates to direct the type of countercyclical, Keynesian economy that was later celebrated as a relatively full employment "welfare state." The economy that evolved, however, was almost wholly unanticipated by the society's social planners, men-of-power, and academic pundits, who were later to join in eulogizing it and implying that the outcome had been consciously planned all along. The desire to win elections often explained smaller variations in each administration's economic decisions. In fact, the dominant characteristic of government economic policy, especially in terms of manipulation of interest rates and using budgets and taxation to affect the level of economic activity, was vacillation. For when the negative consequences of each policy were attained, the economy was usually thrown into reverse gear.

The so-called welfare legislation of the first decade and a half after the war was almost wholly based on the New Deal foundations, and in hindsight we can see how peripheral these measures were, contrasted to the far larger employment and demand-creating forces of war spending, expanded federal employment in all its forms, and the factors considered below. And not until the 1960s did additional welfare legislation important enough to notice begin to appear, and even this scarcely altered the weight which the non-"welfare" components wielded in averting another economic crisis. Three celebrated examples show the vastly greater significance of warfare and inflation as opposed to welfare.

Unemployment compensation was intended to sustain consumer income during economic downturns, thereby braking declines as well as mitigating their human consequences. By the end of the first three decades of the postwar economy, which had periodically witnessed shorter recessions during 1948–1949, 1953–1954, 1957–1958, 1960–1961, 1969–1970, and from 1974 onward, the efficacy of the entire system from every point of view was in doubt; and the deficiencies in it which became plain by 1960 still existed in 1976. During the 1948–1949, early-1958, and post-1974 recessions, compensation offset only about one-fifth of the lost worker income, in part because weekly payments were well below average earnings of employed workers, and also because a large fraction of the labor force was not covered by the system or had exhausted the benefits, which lasted only twenty-six to thirty-nine weeks, depending on the state. At the beginning of 1975, with the highest unemployment since the Depression and over half those insured not qualified to obtain maximum benefits, emergency federal legislation extended the partial coverage to fifty-two weeks for a mere 3 percent of the unemployed. Nationally, during the 1950s through 1975, the weekly compensation check averaged from about one-third to two-fifths of the average weekly earnings for employed production workers; and at the end of 1975 fully 58 percent of the unemployed workers, for reasons of insufficient coverage or exhaustion of payment eligibility, were uninsured.

Even relatively minor, prolonged unemployment, as during 1957–1958, raised fundamental questions about the system's potential solvency in the event of a serious depression. Only in 1970 was the employee's annual income base on which an employer pays a variable payroll tax, depending on the state and extent of firm unemployment, increased from $3000 to $4200, but this cost in turn was transferred, to the extent of at least two-thirds, to consumers in terms of higher prices. States with protracted unemployment from 1957 onward quickly approached bankruptcy in their program reserves, forcing them to dip into the national reserve and accept emergency loans, which in turn lowered resources potentially available to other states—a pattern of stopgap transfusions which has continued to this day. National reserves in 1959 were barely 2 percent of employee compensation but far less yet in 1975 as the overall system was sorely strained. By that time, despite the obvious recurrent weaknesses of the system, nothing significant had been done to make it a serious countercyclical factor, much less better able to protect human lives from the shocks of unemployment.[5]

Minimum-wage legislation proved no exception to the rule, and consisted largely of fixing a figure well below the wages prevailing for the large majority of workers. Since 1939, in fact, the minimum wage's relationship to actual average wages has tended to drop, further reducing even the small significance it originally possessed in sustaining worker purchasing power. Moreover, those potentially able to benefit from it, above all in retail trades and farm labor, were generally not covered by the law. Perhaps most significant, the minimum wage was always far below the level necessary to maintain an adequate standard of living.

In 1956, when the minimum wage was raised to one dollar an hour, only 24 million out of 52 million nonagricultural workers were covered by the law, and of these only 2 million were earning less than the minimum wage, which was set far below the existing norm. The 1961 law, which increased the coverage of nonagricultural workers to half the total, raised the minimum to $1.25 on a sliding scale which took two to four years to attain, thereby leaving the real purchasing power of the new wage about where it had been at one dollar in 1956. In 1939 the minimum wage was two-thirds of the average manufacturing worker's hourly wage, but by 1961 it had fallen to no more than half. In 1966 the minimum wage was hiked to $1.60 hourly, almost three-fifths of the average manufacturing worker's hourly pay that year, but inflation quickly reduced it to barely one-third by May 1974—when yet another complicated annual incremental increase schedule was introduced which would get the minimum wage up to $2.30 by steps taking until January 1978 for some. The latest increase immediately affected only 4.2 million workers, a mere 6 percent of the nation's nonsupervisory total, in even the smallest degree, and still exempted one-fifth of the workers from any coverage at all. And adjusted for the rate of inflation, the new minimum wage meant it bought no more than one dollar did in 1956, and by 1977 would be slightly more than two-fifths of the average hourly pay in manufacturing, and less than that the following year. Belated and penurious at every turn and declining yet further in importance, the entire program was both irrelevant to human needs and surely did nothing to sustain the postwar prosperity celebrated as the triumph of the "welfare state."

Old-age and survivor insurance was but a part of the same Scroogian logic, perhaps more so by virtue of the fact that its payroll deduction base was increased from a flat 2.5 percent on an increasing income base of its participants in 1960 to 4.8 percent in 1969 and 5.85 percent in 1973, and thereby became a regressive tax taking a higher share of the income of the poor than any other income group. It provided only 22 percent of the income of the 65-and-over population in 1958, while public assistance provided another 7 percent in that year. By 1967 old-age insurance still accounted for only 26 percent of the income of this group, while public assistance had fallen to around 4 percent. In 1974, with the average old-age insurance payment for the retired a paltry $187 monthly, the larger part of the meager income of the aged, who formed one of the largest components of the population incorporated into the highly touted if short-lived "war on poverty," came from nongovernmental sources. And the little that came from Social Security was in fact but an aspect of the vast regressive system of self-supporting, forced savings wholly designed and intended to preserve the existing distribution of wealth. The introduction of Medicare in 1966, which insured 24 million elderly persons by 1973, was overexaggerated in its significance, while the later Medicaid for welfare and poverty cases assisted much more superficially the same number of persons in 1973. Medicare, in fact, in 1972 accounted for nearly 30 percent of all health insurance benefits paid—and, of course, all were actuarially self-financing in one manner or another.

The so-called war on poverty was cut from much the same penurious logic. By 1966, when this campaign was in full operation, the growth of per capita governmental expenditures for all forms of public welfare had grown 180 percent since 1950 compared to 257 percent for "national defense." Moreover, while federal, state, and local public welfare outlays were almost $7 billion in 1966, the tax burden on the two poorest tenths of the nation was somewhat higher than that sum—which meant that as a general class the lowest fifth of the nation was obtaining less than it was giving, and the redistributive effect of the war on poverty was nil. But if one added the more than $12 billion in taxes the third-poorest tenth paid, then the alleged effort to help lower-income Americans became a cruel farce, with the poorest third paying far more than they might be said to be receiving by even the most extravagant calculations.[6]

From a purely economic viewpoint, in which the sheer weight of dollars contributed most to demand, the federal budget for military purposes, aids to business and agriculture, and overseas grants and loans of arms and goods counted the most in sustaining the postwar economic dynamism, and the paltry so-called welfare measures were either inconsequential or self-financing in a manner that did nothing significant to alter overall consumer demand. Rather than being a welfare capitalism, the postwar economy had become heavily dependent on warfare—real or potential—and, perhaps as important, had introduced a debt economy which created a temporary stimulus along with an entirely new, potentially great weakness into the very structure of the system.

The federal debt itself was superficially not very different than had existed since 1931, when annual federal deficit spending became the rule rather than the exception and thereby produced a debt accumulation which, especially when connected with all other forms of credit, posed new dilemmas with which the state and private sectors both failed to cope as the potentially negative consequences of a credit capitalism began to emerge in the late 1950s. Indeed, it was only when the size and function of the federal budget fanned inflation and began competing against other economic sectors for money that it created new problems. Scarcely anything before World War One, and one-sixth of the GNP by 1929, the federal public debt equaled half of the GNP by 1957, and in 1973 it had stabilized at around 27 percent. The total federal budget, which was but 3.1 percent of the GNP in 1929 and 18.0 percent by 1957, by 1975 had grown to 20.9 percent. Beginning with the $25 billion 1968 budget deficit, by 1976 the federal government's deficit had grown to nearly three times that. But the greatest changes occurred in other areas of government debt. The federal housing mortgage and loan organizations that were created during the 1960s alone borrowed $74 billion in the decade before 1974, while the tax-starved state and local governments, cut by the federal war economy out of sufficient revenues, began borrowing to amass a debt which grew from $65 billion in 1960 to $206 billion in 1974, with potentially no end in sight to meet their urgent needs. In 1975, with the city of New York on the brink of default, urban and state access to loans began coming to an abrupt halt, carrying with it potentially great dangers for the entire financial system.

By the 1970s, in any case, the significance of these government deficits was not only in the demand they had sustained and the inflation they required to fulfill the military and economic objectives for which spending was essential, but especially the way in which they competed with the corporate sector and consumers for money, thereby introducing fragility and potential danger into the private economy which by 1974 greatly frightened knowledgeable businessmen and economists. Federal borrowing alone gobbled over two-fifths of the nation's total credit market by 1975–1976 compared to less than one-tenth during 1960–1961. Indeed, the federal government's budget policy had by the 1970s produced more inflation and expensive credit than the needs of the United States economy could bear, weakening its international as well as its domestic position in a fashion which contained untold potential repercussions. From a quite stable rate of inflation of 2 percent annually from 1950 to 1966, over the next eight years it leaped to 5.4 percent annually, and in 1974 had peaked at a dangerous 11 percent. The implications of this dilemma, quite new in modern American history, were multiple—and all ominous to the future of the economy.

A credit capitalism, wild by earlier standards, now came into existence as Washington sought to mitigate the pressures of relatively minor recessions and unemployment to stave off far worse. Federal war and overseas spending alone did not suffice for this purpose, and the logic of continuous, growing credit and inflation produced dangerous fragility and the threat of a liquidity crisis unlike any possible during the 1920s.

Nowhere was this danger greater than in the consumer sector, where families, with business encouragement, revolutionized their buying habits to make installment purchasing a way of life that defied poverty and unemployment. Installment credit debt in 1929 had been negligible—only 4.2 percent of the national personal income—and only about one-fifth of the families utilized this form of spending. In effect, the additional retrenchment and liquidation that Depression unemployment would have otherwise forced upon a high-credit economy was spared consumers, and their credit was certainly not a cause of the crash or its duration. It was in the comparable fantasy world of stock purchases on margin that catastrophic liquidations helped significantly to exacerbate the crash's impact. In 1947 the relative installment debt was less than 1929, but thereafter it began to grow until by 1957 it had reached $34 billion and 9.7 percent of personal income. One-half of all consumers, especially middle-income families, now were using installment credit. In that year the Federal Reserve Board took cognizance of the phenomenon in a monumental analysis which feebly tried to warn that "major depressions preceding World War Two were characterized by debt defaults and related difficulties. What started out to be a relatively modest problem of financial adjustment sometimes turned out to have vastly multiplied effects. . . . Even though the analogy of 1929 is of diminishing relevance, the possibility of an episode of drastic and spiraling liquidation should not be dismissed."[7] The Board's admonition went untranslated into policy as prosperity on time now moved to a stage that defied all predictions. Between 1957 and 1975 the consumer installment debt increased nearly five times and amounted now to 13 percent of personal income. Debt repayment as a percentage of disposable income had risen from less than 5 percent of disposable income in 1946 to 16 percent in 1974, and nearly four-fifths of the consumers were now in debt. Taking a long, careful look down the larger credit precipice in 1974, *Business Week* concluded that "The U.S. has tried to do too much with too little, and that cannot go on forever."[8]

For consumer-oriented companies, ranging from automobile manufacturers to giant retailers, this four-way rivalry for high-interest credit by 1974 was far greater than in the 1950s, when consumer debt defaults posed comparatively smaller dangers. To sustain demand, companies had to borrow and be prepared to take losses or else sharply restrict sales—which meant lower production and employment. And this dilemma in turn interacted with their borrowings for all purposes, which caused corporate debt to rise from $142 billion in 1950 to $1.3 trillion in 1974, with the debt-equity ratio of industrial corporations rising from 25 to 40 percent in the decade ending 1973. Internal sources of corporate capital after World War Two fell well below earlier norms, and by 1970–1974 one-half of nonfinancial corporate capital funds were borrowed. Banks themselves, in their eagerness to find customers, began taking unprecedented risks, and in 1975 had to write off at least $3 billion in bad loans—primarily to real estate and corporate borrowers. Forced to borrow to finance consumer credit, plant expansion, and much else, by 1974 the governments, consumers, and business were all competing for an ultimately limited and inadequate quantity of credit in an already overheated, unprecedentedly inflationary economy. This addiction to essential credit brought together innumerable critical economic forces in a common potential liquidity crisis which threatened to end the postwar expansion and bring a retrenchment which could eventually bring down the essentially convoluted, unnatural synthesis of war and credit which Washington's improvisation had created to make possible capitalism's successes in staving off the consequences of its structural limits. If no single one of these credit crises —public, corporate, or consumer—was alone necessarily sufficient to pose great new menace to the overheated, inflationary economy, collectively they created a danger that was insoluble and sooner or later sure to demand a reckoning. The deepest postwar economic downturn, which began in 1974, was proof that these problems could not indefinitely be avoided.

The Concentration of Economic Power

The concentration of economic power in the United States is not so much a question of statistical measurement as it is a question of comprehending the intangibles of operational, working relationships between economic forces and how often they seek to attain political solutions—often contradictory in nature—to their dilemmas. Throughout the twentieth century the trend toward big business was a constant factor in American economic history, yet its significance was usually wholly misperceived by contemporaries and historians alike. Data were only the starting point for dynamics which required much more sophisticated analysis than empiricism could provide. Superimposed on the question of concentration of ownership, control, assets, or directorates of corporations was the more central but elusive issue of what the figures signified for the real world. Historians, publicists, apologists, and economists, for the most part, tended to misunderstand the subtle dynamics in the concentration of economic power.

As an aggregate, it is unquestionable that by 1935 the 200 largest nonfinancial corporations had attained a preponderant position in the corporate sector and economy, with their percentage control increasing fairly steadily since that time. The share of the total manufacturing value added shared by the 200 largest companies increased from 30 percent in 1947 to 43 percent in 1972, in significant part because of the intensity of the merger movement during those years and a government contracting policy which favored the largest firms. Yet there was a certain artificiality in these, as all, statistics on concentration, interlocks, and control.

Apart from the fact that there was considerable turnover within this key group, so that of the fifty largest manufacturers in 1947 only twenty-five were still in that category in 1972, was the fact that not all industries were in the least concentrated in the same way, if at all, and that the pressures of competition and profit and their political as well as economic relationship to each other, the federal government, and the world economy might be radically different. And at the level of operational power, these distinctions can be crucial in how a class breaks up into rival elites at times capable of destabilizing the entire system. Moreover, firms in an industry might relate to each other in ways in which concentration was less important than more intangible techniques, and still not be able to solve their economic problems and attain profitable stabilization independent of economic conditions outside their particular branch of industrial activity. Concentration, as since the turn of the century, was not synonymous with control, which was far more dependent on how firms related to one another than purely statistical criteria.

One illustration of this in the postwar era was the electrical machinery industry, in which the four largest producers in many fields, and eight largest in most, accounted for anywhere from two-thirds to over 90 percent of the main products. But this simply did not produce effective controls of output or prices, which were only attained by communications and direct meetings between four companies beginning in 1951. Eventually it was essential for twenty-nine companies to be brought into a vast price-fixing and contract-allotment system which lasted a decade before anti-trust action destroyed it. In the case of selected pharmaceuticals, an industry in which the eight largest producers controlled less than half and a declining share of the output after 1947, collusion between only five firms sufficed to fix prices of major vaccines.[9] The fact is that the industrial concentration data which were used to explain the nature of the American economy ignored that they were heavily based on firms concentrated in relatively few industries—primary metals, autos, chemicals, electrical machinery, and the like. To the extent these industries had finally attained rationalization and stability via concentration rather than government regulation, a significant structural development had occurred in United States capitalism, though in fact concrete methods of applying oligopoly via private cooperation remained essential even here. But industries such as textiles, clothing, lumber, leather, or bituminous coal mining were spared most of the rigors of the prewar era of competition largely because high growth and demand of an artificially dynamic capitalism produced sufficient markets, though in fact these industries remained structurally more vulnerable than the concentrated sectors. But in 1963 two-thirds of the value of manufacturing was accounted for by industries in which the four largest companies in each accounted for less than half the value. Concentrated industries still could increase prices faster than competitive ones, and did so, but even these were compelled to take into account new forms of competition from outside their own product lines. Copper, steel, and lead producers—all highly concentrated—had to concern themselves with real and potential rivals in the plastics and aluminum fields, thereby complicating their problems of control. Unquestionably more able to regulate itself by virtue of concentration and the advantages of sheer size, it was still most doubtful whether a fundamentally major transformation of American capitalism had occurred to the extent it had overcome the problems of competition and its need for a politically based stabilizing mechanism.

Corporate control and coordination by other means might also be alleged to exist by virtue of interlocking directorates or stock ownership, yet proof by such means is intrinsically deductive, and the data are often inconclusive. Interlocking directorates among large corporations have existed since at least the beginning of the twentieth century, and though ostensibly greatly restricted by the 1914 Clayton Act, they have remained fairly widespread ever since. In 1939, 2500 men held the 3511 directorships of the 200 largest corporations, but also those of many smaller firms. Interlocks, if anything, declined after the war, and in 1968 over four-fifths of the directors of the 500 largest industrial corporations sat on only one board within that group, though, as always, interlocks increased substantially if one counts seats held outside the top firms. But certainly, by this standard alone, the commanding heights of industry were reasonably autonomous units. After the Second World War interlocks were more common among financially based directors who were not full-time officers of the companies they oversaw. But among the 1000 largest manufacturing firms at the beginning of the 1960s, the surprisingly small number of 317 directors sat on the boards of two or more firms making the same products. Interlocks to avoid competition existed, of course, but this was not the way common business strategies were attained in virtually any example one might find, and by necessity they had to employ more direct, efficient methods. Banks and common owners were in a position to dictate policy, if at all, for reasons far transcending the mere fact they held board seats: namely their control of finances or stock. Board membership, in fact, increasingly fell during the decades after 1937 to full-time officers within a firm, so that while 36 percent of the directors of the 200 top industrial companies then were also officers in their own firms, by 1957 it was exactly one-half, and officer-directors held absolute majorities of almost half these elite corporations. At this level of integration the largest corporations were officer-dominated, and although in fact that was more crucial to how corporations conducted their short- and middle-range affairs, it does not reveal the ultimate control of the company.[10]

Here evidence is more circumstantial. The question of the degree and location of concentration in private hands is less important than the mere fact that a relatively tiny group possesses this stock regardless of its precise identity. One Congressional study in 1968 argued that it was the commercial banking system that had become decisive, controlling over three-fifths of the more than $1 trillion in institutionally owned assets of every type, and holding interlocking directorates in many large corporations. Stated purely in terms of stock, another government-sponsored inquiry showed that the financial institutions' (excluding bank-administered personal trusts) and trusts' share of noninvestment company stock increased from 18 percent of the total in 1950 to 34 percent in 1973. But no less a fact was that most of this amount was being bought and sold for investment rather than control purposes, mainly for pension and mutual funds accounts.[11] To some extent, however, it was always possible to find industrial-financial interests in the economy who formed distinct groups on charts, and who unquestionably used their links for their own general gain. The existence of financial-banking centers that dominated the industrial economy has been a respectable theory during this century, but at best it was only partially accurate in attributing the origins of this hegemony to the power of finance rather than to industrial interests that later, as with the Rockefellers, Hannas, and Mellons, diversified into banking. In fact, because industry grew without significant dependence on a capital market, which was often employed only to pay off older entrepreneurs, and relied overwhelmingly on self-financing for most of the century, finance rarely attained the kind of control attributed to it, and much more competition and decentralization occurred than would have otherwise been possible. But in the world of reality no sharp dichotomy can easily be drawn between financial and industrial interests, since they are so often intertwined in so many ways.

The problem is whether finance and banking control introduced stability and order into the economy where none hitherto existed, and whether it was sufficient to eliminate the dangers both of competition and latent crises. And the answer is that despite possible increases in this concentration and linkage since the Depression, vast economic blocs could exist simultaneously with crisis, and in one critical sense might becomes its cause.

Surely the consolidated, largely finance-capital-inspired merger movement during 1897–1910 and then the 1920s sufficiently watered the corporate structure to create additional difficulties for it to master. And because the vast new holdings in the hands of commercial banks after 1955 increasingly represented pension fund and private assets that the banks did not own but were responsible only for profitably managing, it created an immense body of potentially fluid, even volatile, capital which might be a large fraction of the stock of one company at one time and might be abandoned to the market just as quickly as it was purchased. The dumping of stock in this form during the 1974 price downturn illustrated some of the least of the dangers of the growing commercial bank management of the savings of other institutions. What seemed to Congress a form of dangerous power and control was potentially a source of great instability to a capitalism already fragile after years of artificial, inflationary supports.

Within the corporate structure itself, in fact, it appeared that the almost universally accepted managerial theories of William Z. Ripley or Adolf Berle on the separation of corporate ownership from control and management explained little as to how and why the modern corporation was governed. In fact, the very definition of the problem set scholars off on the wrong track, as if the modern corporation was originally more synonymous with majority ownership than the skillful utilization of mainly other people's money along with sufficient mastery of the institution to optimize rewards and minimize risks. Even radicals fell victim to the notion by the late 1930s. Lack of data, in any case, created much of the illusion, as contrived stock diffusion and obscurity consistent with tax savings intensified it. But even in 1937–1939 it seemed as if a visible center of control did not exist in one-third of the 176 most important corporations, while various combinations sufficed to dominate the rest: large stockowners, family stockholding groups with seemingly as little as 4 percent of the stock but also in management, or the like. Four thousand shareholders, of whom individuals composed about one-half, held an average of 29 percent of the market value of the common stock in each of these 176 firms. Still, the notion of the divorce of management and ownership was even then very much in doubt, because in 1939 the officers and directors of the ninety-seven largest manufacturing corporations were known to possess at least 7 percent of the total stock of their own companies and in fact were also among the very rich.

The byzantine complexity of the data after World War Two need not delay us, but in 1957 the boards of directors of the hundred largest industrial corporations owned an average of at least 9.9 percent of the shares in their own companies, a figure that does not include concealed ownership. Yet in many of the corporations well below this average members of the families definitely once known to own large holdings in these firms still sit as directors. But since the majority of the directors of the key firms were also full-time officers, it was clear where operational control resided, and also that the motivation for action was not everything from ego to public service, as pundits ranging from David Lilienthal to John Kenneth Galbraith often asserted during the postwar era, but aggrandizement of profits and monetary returns in every form. Using a 4–5 percent minimum control and family representation on the board of directors over a sustained period, one meticulous scholar concluded that of the 300 largest corporations during the 1960s, 45 percent were under probable family control and another 15 percent under possible family control. Forty percent were management dominated, yet these men, it could justifiably be argued, by no means divorced themselves from stock ownership, since options on company stock at bargain prices became an established form of executive compensation after 1950, and any advocate of the separation of management from ownership thesis who closely examines executive conduct and holdings must conclude that their profit orientation was no less the primary motivator of their conduct than before.[12]

The corporate structure, then, was concentrated and inequitably owned and a minute elite managed it, but it was also full of complexities and problems which the continued growth of big firms had not eliminated. Its instabilities were endemic to a residue of competition which survived within even the most concentrated industries, and surely among the many still too decentralized to formulate a common policy. Prosperity after 1941 had deferred the most negative consequences of competition, so that the intense rivalries of the prewar era were not to reemerge in the same form, but yet other dangers to corporate capitalism had begun to arise to produce new challenges. In one critical sense, the greatest danger to the capitalist system was that it had used the last decades to systematically exhaust all the potential means—political and economic—for sustaining itself, thereby creating a new form of maturity and stagnation that inexorably evolved from the techniques used to resolve its protracted 1920–1940 dilemma. American capitalism now confronted a crisis of flexibility for which no potential new solutions existed. Stock ownership had changed in ways that made the stock market more volatile, and the growing dependence of the biggest corporations on a prosperous world economy and trade was beginning to match their needs for deficit-funded arms spending, tax and subsidy favors, and other benefits that had fanned high interest and inflation and led to a protracted war seemingly necessary to United States power in the world but ultimately also in contradiction with the strength of the American corporation in the world economy. Staving off these burgeoning, interacting, and insoluble economic dilemmas depended on demand; and how long it could be sustained by credit, guns, or prayers was by the nation's 200th anniversary gravely in doubt.

The Sinews of Profit

Profits are the sinews of capitalism, the goal of the system as well as the instrumentalities by which it grows. At no point in the history of the modern American economy, save 1931–1933, did profit ever fall to crisis proportions; but the way the economy was managed, the political and social problems it created, and its strategy at home and overseas reflected time and again the magnitude of domestic profitability. Despite the fact that crises often emerged for reasons quite independent of profitability, implications of profits both to national and foreign policy in all its dimensions were never less than large, and often immense. The condition of profit is one of the structural keystones influencing the course of American history in a capitalist society.

Profits are enormously difficult to calculate precisely, and no single adequate source of information exists. Seemingly small accounting changes will produce radically different figures, and very contradictory numbers for the same year are common. More intangibly, the point at which profits are insufficient for economic growth and the system's dynamism is often impossible to define, even by those receiving them. Different corporations, divided by both size and industry, experience quite distinctive profitability; and after 1941 the broadening of both the individual and corporate income tax created incentives to consume profits in nontaxable ways: expense accounts and perquisites, more complex forms of executive compensation, and such. This said, however, it appears likely that by any criterion the period since 1946 has probably been one of the most profitable in the history of American capitalism and about comparable to the 1920s—whose ample returns, however, did not prevent a subsequent depression. Considering the ratio of profits after federal income tax to stockholders' equity, manufacturing corporations during 1947–1959 averaged 12 percent annually, 11.2 percent over the next decade, and 11.5 percent during 1970–1974—virtually a consistent rate throughout the postwar period. Looking at profits per unit of output, there was no trend toward a falling rate of profit for nonfinancial corporations throughout the postwar period, with the business cycle being the key factor explaining annual variations. The dividend yield on common stocks fell sharply over the period, but, on the other hand, the price-earnings ratio was considerably higher in the period after 1960 than before, and the bulk of the evidence would support the contention that postwar profits were fairly constant and high. Needless to say, such averages included poorer years, and these naturally were closely correlated to recessions—making 1975 the worst year of the past decade. Banks were more profitable after 1946 than in any other peacetime period in United States history since 1876, and somewhat ahead of the 1920s. And with sharply increasing interest rates after 1968, bank net income moved to new highs.

Still, profits at any given time are unevenly distributed. Large corporations, with assets of at least $10 million after the war, tended to make far more on their equity before taxes than smaller firms, but companies among the 200 biggest manufacturers were much more profitable than the rest. The after-tax profits as a percentage of sales of the largest companies were at least two-fifths greater than the smaller firms during 1947–1956. This was due not merely to their economies in the scale of their production, which often were at best marginal, but also to their advantages in being able to use oligopoly to more effectively control prices and profit. Firms in industries with a high concentration ratio generally had a return on their net worth of anywhere from one-half to two-thirds greater than those more competitive. Both in terms of profits on equity before taxes or the always lower profits on sales before taxes, the 1961 profits of corporations with at least $250 million in assets were substantially greater than those in the $25–250 million asset range, and far greater than those below. Because of their monopolistic or oligopolistic control of prices, many of the giants could compensate for lower demand during economic downturns.

In the aggregate, with these critical distinctions in the data, United States capitalism prospered as never before throughout the period 1946–1959. But during the next decade, while some corporations did as well (as I shall discuss in greater detail in the next chapter), the outlets for profitable investment in the United States were exceeded abroad, so that during 1957–1973 the equivalent of over 12 percent of manufacturing expenditures at home for new plant and equipment went abroad as direct investments. United States capitalism became not so much saturated as spongy in terms of its domestic prospects, and investment abroad became more essential to many large firms. To be sure, many important exceptions, such as the petroleum industry, prospered throughout the decade after 1965, but this did not guarantee them a trouble-free political climate insulated against something far worse than just lower returns. Nor did it prevent their prosperity from greatly reducing that of other products, such as automobiles, which fell into a depression after 1973 as a consequence, among other things, of high oil costs and profits.

One index to the emerging contradictions in the capitalist economy after 1970 was the lower utilization of the productive capacity of manufacturing and major materials industries. Despite the business threats of that period of insufficient capital and profits to combat obsolescence, which were designed primarily to shock Congress into allocating yet more favorable tax provisions, the industrial plant far exceeded the domestic capacity to absorb its output. Industry, if anything, had overcapitalized during the postwar era. Five different indices all showed that 1970–1975 had the highest amount of unused capacity since World War Two, with late 1974 and 1975 marking the nadir. Taking the Federal Reserve Board's index, the manufacturing utilization rate was 77.2 percent during 1970–1975 compared to 91.9 percent in the postwar high period of 1950–1954. In brief, the capitalist economy's traditional nemesis of inadequate demand and overexpansion had reappeared in almost classic form despite all the vast means that had been employed to counteract them. And for that reason the dilemma was all the more dangerous, as the efficacy of the postwar economic measures proved all too finite—and no better ones remained to be employed.[13]

Wealth and Income Distribution

The distribution of income and wealth is the iron test of the outcome of years of alleged reform and the general trends in the economy, from profit rates to welfare payments. However debatable the dimensions or the motives of this or that issue or action, by looking at the distribution of the final benefits we can resolve all lesser problems. That decisive partition, indeed, was not only the culmination of all the legislative actions, strikes, and much else, but it created by itself a set of fundamental and quite inevitable and permanent structural challenges which not so much superseded the problems of the debt economy, rates of profit, and dilemmas of the world economy as paralleled and aggravated them all.

The distribution of income and wealth is not only a question of equity but also the determinant of a sufficient degree of demand and consumption to keep the economy in reasonably full employment and production. If adequate demand cannot be attained via consumer spending—a constant dilemma since the foundation of modern capitalism—then if other means are not found crises ensue. Underconsumption, while not the only structurally destabilizing force eroding the successes of the economy at any given time, is surely its most persistent, and quite able eventually to undo the compensatory achievements of such expenditures as federal spending, large armies, or credit. Aware of this possibility, since 1950 many celebrators of the status quo argued that the historically inequitable pattern of income and wealth distribution in the United States had been made more just as a part of the New Deal "welfare state," and that this explained the long postwar boom.

As debatable as the statistics may be—and after 1941 they grew worse—there was never any serious factual basis for the "income revolution" thesis, which was an ideological myth rather than a description of reality. During the period 1910–1941 the pretax share of the personal income received by the richest tenth of the recipients fluctuated, being somewhat higher during the 1920s than before or after, but in 1941 it was a fairly representative 34 percent. The share of the second-highest-income tenth increased substantially, raising the proportion of the top fifth from 46.2 percent in 1910 to 50 in 1941, but it was a gain largely at the expense of the poorest fifth, which dropped from 8.3 percent in 1910 to 3 percent in 1941. After 1941, when the alleged income revolution occurred, the complexity of the statistics increased with the advent of tax laws which placed an immense premium on the rich underreporting and deferring their income or devising covert ways of receiving it.

This new development led to the rise of innumerable techniques involving billions of dollars. The simplest and technically most illegal of these was nonreporting, which in 1941 alone was practiced by 35 percent of those receiving over $10,000 a year income opposed to 1 percent of those under $1000. In 1944–1946, 14 percent and in 1957 a full 9 percent of the national personal income was unreported on income tax forms—$28 billion in the latter year. By 1966, nearly one-fifth of the family income, valued at least at $100 billion, was hidden in this manner. Moreover, after 1941, closely held corporations radically altered their profit distributions so that during 1946–1959, 51 percent of all corporate profits—almost twice the 1923–1929 rate—were withheld. In any of those years, therefore, roughly $5 billion in potential income was withheld, mainly from upper-income families. Part of this money went overseas, opening new tax vistas along with new opportunities for gain; but in any given year it lopped one to four percentage points off the share of the top-income tenth, while non-reporting (conservatively assigning only half of it to the richest tenth) took off another three to five percentage points. Expense accounts, in addition, became a way of life for corporate executives and businessmen, amounting to $5 to $10 billion during 1957—another minimum of 1 percent to be added to the share of top-income categories. The most comprehensive study of this phenomenon merely confirmed this pattern when it documented that in 1966 the richest 1 percent of the families received 10.5 percent of the income rather than the 4.8 percent it reported, and the top 5 percent 22.1 rather than 16 percent—6.6 full points more than the usual statistics show.

Given such changes, which were merely a response to the income tax laws applied in comparative earnest after 1941, thereafter the statistically reported share of the upper-income tenth fell, hitting 29 percent in 1945, rising to 31.4 percent in 1953, falling as low as 27.1 percent in 1958 but climbing back to 30 percent in 1962 and 1968, and 27 percent in 1970. The reported share of the poorest fifth hovered around 4 to 5 percent, while the proportion that the second- and third-highest-income tenths obtained was higher than pre-1941. In fact, the most frequently cited postwar data meant little, for in any given year 5 to 10 percent of the total income that was concealed, deferred, or consumed otherwise had to be added to the share of the top tenth. When these were taken into account—as rarely happens—the share of the top tenth remained quite stable over the past sixty-five years, and the 47.9 percent of the income that the richest fifth received in 1966 was extremely close to the best figures we have for 1910 and 1929. Despite minor annual variations, therefore, the basic historic structure of income distribution in the United States had remained constant.[14]

The emergence of an extensive tax systems after 1941 was the cause of this unprecedented effort at income concealment, and therefore it could hardly make the after-tax income distribution more equitable. The number of taxable returns rose 10 million from the preceding year during 1941, and another 23 million over the next two years, and the main outcome of the permanent new system was to tax hitherto exempt lower- and middle-income groups. From 1944, the income tax replaced the corporation tax as the most important single source of federal revenue. The tax system that was to emerge after the war, both at the federal and state-local levels, meant that a vast amount of regressive taxation quickly offset the progressive income tax to fairly equally distribute the tax load to all income categories. After World War Two, the posttax income distribution was virtually identical to the pretax figures. In 1958, the share of total income of each income class below $15,000 going to every form of taxation was 20–21 percent. But in 1966, according to the most reliable estimate of the tax incidence, the poorest tenth paid 27 percent of its total income in all forms of taxes, while the other nine-tenths hovered around 25–26 percent. The most conservative calculation of the tax burden still has the poorest tenth paying out 17 percent of its income in taxes, and the richest only 30 percent. In fact, despite much discussion of tax evasion during 1962 and the revision of the tax laws, yet new loopholes were introduced into the system to protect the existing distribution from erosion. Innumerable special provisions and complexity now had become an institutionalized constant designed to create the illusion of equity while preserving inequality. By 1974, $58 billion worth of such special legal write-offs, euphemistically called "tax expenditures," were distributed among individual taxpayers with the excuse they stimulated some type of economic activity or action. Twenty-three percent of this amount went to individuals earning $50,000 or more, and another 30 percent went to those in the $20,000–$50,000 bracket—together, a mere 15 percent of the taxpayers.[15]

In one sense, the vast expansion of the tax base and new post-1941 structure of taxation in the United States had emerged as a means of subsidizing and sustaining an economy in which the rich obtained, by far, the largest material benefits of the postwar prosperity. Government expenditures for every form of "welfare" in the decade after the war, including half the outlays for farm parity payments, were always substantially less than the tax payments of the poorest third of the nation. Middle-income earners, therefore, were the main subsidizers of the government spending programs for arms and business benefits which consumed the larger fraction of the federal budget. After 1940 the rich were not taxed to give to the poor, but both were taxed together to sustain an economy which allocated but a small fraction of its total budget to the social needs of the larger bulk of the nation.

What was true of the constancy of the historic distribution of income was also valid for wealth—the ownership of all forms of stock, real estate, savings, and such—and despite the considerable problems of statistical measurement, all studies prove that inequality in income distribution naturally led to the same disparities in accumulated wealth.

This said, the fact that different analyses employ varying criteria and size of ownership groups makes comparisons more difficult. For example, the federally funded Survey Research Center used the richest 11 percent in 1953, but the top 14 percent in 1962, finding that these top groups owned 60 and 68 percent of the net private assets in those two years respectively—a share only slightly below the best data we have for the nineteenth century. Boiling it down to smaller groups, in 1953 the richest 5 percent possessed about 46 percent of the net worth, but a more conservatively calculated study of the same year allocated 24 percent of the wealth to the richest 1 percent of the population. Later, another analysis, based on quite debatable estate tax returns which greatly understate the degree of concentration, put this 1953 share of the 1 percent at 27.5 percent. Using this as the basis, a systematic inquiry of the post-1953 period showed that the richest 1 percent fluctuated in their concentration of wealth ownership, reaching a peak of 29.2 percent in 1965 and 24.9 percent in 1969. The richest 4.4 percent in 1969 owned 35.6 percent of the net worth. However controversial the methodology of competitive analyses, the fact remains they do not qualitatively differ, and no study of the postwar wealth structure or its components, such as stock, has challenged the factual basis of the proposition that the distribution of wealth remained highly concentrated in the hands of a relatively small elite during the postwar era, giving them mastery of the means and benefits of economic power.[16]

Translated into the real world, these statistics defined how people lived as well as the structural nature of capitalism and its problems. Despite the fashionable artificiality of the short-lived "war on poverty," which began in 1963 and was soon replaced by a much longer and immensely more expensive war against Indochina, it should always have been apparent after the Second World War that poverty was both widespread and persistent despite higher employment. The comprehensive, if ignored, technical studies the United States Bureau of Labor Statistics issued allowed an assessment which only euphoric self-congratulation and conventional wisdom kept from being employed as an analytic tool; and the same mood allowed the issue to return to obscurity after 1965. In fact, 51 percent of the nation's spending units, adjusted for family size, lived below the austere BLS maintenance level in 1947, and 44 percent in 1957, and by 1962 this figure was still a resistant 40 percent. Because of credit many families could transcend this frugal standard of living. Further down, at the 70 percent of the BLS level that was genuine poverty, 33, 27, and 25 percent of the nation's spending units during these respective years were living at a level well below the minimum necessary for health and decency. The durability of this group was due to the increase of both the very old and very young as a portion of the nation, the former living on inadequate retirement income, the latter earning less because of lower skills or experience.

In one regard, the economic consequences of sex, age, and race explained why poverty persisted throughout the alleged prosperity after 1946, and would continue into the future. The share of households headed by women, who were among the most exploited and discriminated against of all work force sectors, was 3.6 percent in 1935–1936, 9.3 percent in 1950, and 11.6 percent in 1972. The fact that women received one- to two-thirds less pay than men for the same task automatically inflated poverty statistics. The 65-and-over population was only 5.3 percent of the population in 1930, 8.4 percent in 1955, but 10.3 percent in 1974. Blacks, still the last hired and the first fired, and whose median male wages in 1947–1955 were slightly over one-half those of white male workers and 77 percent in 1974, were 9.7 percent of the population in 1930 but 11.1 percent in 1970.

Most important of all in preserving poverty and low incomes among all groups, after 1965 the level of workers' real earnings remained virtually stable, until the drop of 8 percent in weekly real income during 1973–1974 left the working class where it had been economically ten years earlier; and during 1975 it began to sink below that point. Given the interaction of demographic, sociological, and, above all, those economic factors intrinsic to modern capitalism, postwar poverty was inevitable and its persistence in the future no less likely.

Despite the credit, government deficits and orders, and artificially stimulated demand which had carried the economy along, with periods of unemployment culminating in the peak recession beginning in 1974, the relative boom could not obviate the consequences which inequality in income and wealth created for consumption. The problem of domestic underconsumption was partially resolved on the demand side when the federal government began spending on the war sector, though this too inevitably produced dangers from inflation, a negative balance of payments, social disintegration, and much else. It is superfluous to document once again the immense disparities in the consumption of health services, education, housing, and consumer goods of every sort, much less the tragic waste of human potential and resources this inequality automatically required.[17] Suffice it to say that in the fairly typical and exhaustively studied year of 1950 the average spending unit earning more than $10,000 annually on a per capita basis spent three and one-half times more than those receiving under $1000, and two and one-half times more than the $3000–$4000 category in which the median family could be found. In the spending unit consumption of household durable goods and operation, education, and automobiles, the disparity between the highest and lowest income category was sixteen to one, and anywhere from four to eight times greater than the median. This is not necessarily to argue that the physical material consumption of the lower-income categories was always insufficient, though in many cases this was indeed true, but the concentration of purchasing power followed quite closely the distribution of income, and this left, as well, a lack of demand and money alone necessary for sustaining full production without constant government spending for arms. Underconsumption was not the cause of the postwar American military capitalism, but the effect of a distribution of income and wealth that required palliatives which introduced economic complexity without durable solutions.

These surrogates essential to the sustenance of capitalism became increasingly dangerous with time—to the world immediately, but then to the American population and, ultimately, to the very health and viability of capitalism at home. If the mass' toleration of the mistakes of the status quo increased, as only the atavistic Right emerged in the form of the George Wallace movement as a durable, significant new factor on the political scene, capitalism's structural freedom to make further tragic as well as uneconomical errors appeared to be diminishing qualitatively after one century of American industrial capitalism. The social time that the population gave it could not forestall unprecedented new dangers to the system. The society of improvisations, composed at the economic policy level largely of responses designed to neutralize the consequences of past errors, and in which leaders neither truly planned nor could introduce a stable, permanent order, was finally beginning to produce an accumulation of ever-mounting problems. Hard-core unemployment, often rising to new levels; permanent inflation along with low growth; credit and deficits to and by all but still inadequate to assure sufficient industrial expansion and consumption by people; a greater dependence on an increasingly precarious international economy in which the United States was politically, militarily, and economically overextended; social chaos at home that made drugs, commercialized euphoria, and intensely violent and disintegrated communities and their disillusioned people the common present and dominant future—all this testified to the failure of American capitalism and the astonishingly fragile society it had created after one century. Though probably no single one was decisive, the conjunction between all the domestic and global frustrations and problems that continuous improvisations as well as structural imperatives produced had by the 1970s brought both the United States and world capitalism into a cycle of escalating crises for which no effective resolution could be found. Superficially rational, yet in fact half-managed in half-ignorance, the higher disorder of the system was coming home to rest, bringing with it the corrosive impact of a reality no longer capable of being deferred. The economic, political, and social limits of the postwar political economy were finally being approached—with what conclusion no one, from the system's managers and defenders to its strongest critics, could be certain.

In the end, the main lesson of the postwar political economy was surprisingly similar to that of earlier periods: that the problems of the society and economy eventually multiplied faster than its capacity to resolve them, that each new major effort produced its own destructive contradictions, and that merely to try to make the system work without fully, accurately gauging the consequences of each act was merely to court potential new crises. At no time was the effort to integrate and rationalize capitalism via political or economic instrumentalities to succeed, despite temporary accomplishments. The desire to stabilize capitalism is never independent of the political and structural capacity of the leadership to do so, and this it sought to accomplish mainly as a by-product to answering specific problems within the framework of the existing distribution of wealth and power. Controlling or reflecting such power scarcely qualified men in Washington to perceive the right course, which was much more defined by interest and exigency in the guise of disinterested insight. After 1945 it was politically easier to spend money on arms, especially if lavished properly among the Congressional districts, than on anything else, so that desire and political necessity were joined. By the time such fundamental policies decided in often capricious ways accumulated, an immense vested interest in the perpetuation of the postwar political economy, its ideological mystifications included, had come into being. And if the system could understandably not get off the well-worn track now fraught with limits and new dangers, circumstances would eventually run it off. After three decades, capitalism had become so fragile, so dependent on the health of so many seemingly small as well as immense variables, that no one could predict precisely which one—at home or abroad, involving inflation, credit, liquidity, war, peace, Presidents and their mellifluous men who lied as a way of life, and so much more—would intersect them all into a potential disaster.

At the end of the first century of American industrial capitalism the question was no longer if or how a new crisis would come but increasingly, even for the system's defenders, when it might arrive. Traumatized by the failures—Vietnam above all—of the three "successful" decades, more and more men-of-power doubted the efficacy of their own solutions. The economic and social malaise of contemporary capitalism could both be measured and felt, and the society was adrift, with its most dangerous challenges still before it. Capitalist America's power structure could not, because of ignorance and structural imperatives, resolve its crisis; but neither was the opposition capable of replacing it. Such an impasse condemned both the United States and the world to new, potentially endless, turmoil and misery yet to be inflicted at home and abroad. Despite the fact there was no serious opposition from a Left, that freedom from social challenge by no means solved the problems of the status quo. It merely implied that its inevitable need to confront its growing political and economic dilemmas, when it came, would be the inexorable consequence of capitalism's inherent contradictions.

10

The Perpetual Crisis: American Foreign Policy Since 1946

World War Two did not end with peace or a diplomatic settlement but only unleashed social, economic, and political forces which ultimately were not negotiatable and transcended the capacity of the United States or any other nation to control. One may define the postwar decades as being a "Cold War" of Soviet-American interaction, and it is from this perspective that postwar history is largely written. But that notion grossly misses the texture of a much larger, ultimately more decisive reality, bypasses the terror and virtually unlimited violence in which the United States was to engage and the revolutionary upheavals which repeatedly created disarray in Washington's priorities and strategy—and challenges to its ambitions and hegemony. And a myopic focus on Soviet-American affairs ignores, too, the fact that relations among capitalist states, and United States plans for their future, were ultimately to prove at least as decisive after the war as they had been before. The questions emerging from Washington's desire once and for all to create an integrated, cooperative world capitalism became inextricably linked to the manner in which the leaders of the United States confronted their problems with Russia and quite autonomous revolutionary struggles. If postwar American foreign policy therefore emerges as an indissoluble skein of events—in which the global framework is crucial, and priorities, crises, and needs are constantly mingling and clashing—the complexity of this picture to later viewers ultimately also gives them the sense of problems that confronted the American leaders who were ultimately to fail in imposing their essentially hegemonic goals on this bewildering diversity. It is true that to the men in Washington some questions were far more important than others, and they sought to stamp their priorities on what was to prove an uncontrollable world; but one cannot comprehend the final emergence of Vietnam as the most important war of the epoch—if not the century for the United States—save as an aspect of these universal ambitions and the intersection of its numerous and unattainable objectives touching every corner of the globe after 1945.

In a critical sense, the history of American foreign policy after World War Two is not merely one of how Washington sought to attain those main objectives it defined. More significant in the longer run was how a frustrating real world interacted with a myriad of the United States' seemingly lesser goals in a way that gradually evoked ever larger operational commitments, eventually dominating its foreign policy and greatly altering its priorities. Ultimately, the history of postwar foreign policy was to reveal that along with its increasingly bloody and expensive successes, the constraints of its resources and the uncontrollable nature of the international situation were to leave the nation in what has become a permanent and ever more frustrating crisis involving both its power and its confidence.

Nineteen seventy-six was a far cry from 1945, when the United States emerged from the war with real needs, and great ambitions, but no sense of its limits. Objectively the most powerful nation on earth amid the carnage that had gravely touched its past and future rivals, it possessed the initiative to define the rules of the diplomatic game but lacked mastery over socio-economic forces in fields, hills, and jungles, struggles even then evolving throughout Asia and Greece, which ultimately proved more critical to the course of postwar history than military power—at least as it is measured in classic terms—or diplomacy. The real forces of the next thirty years transcended any nation's control, eventually to shape America's destiny too when it threw itself against Indochina and thereby revealed and compounded all of its failures—altering irrevocably the United States' relative power on the world scene. In 1946, ironically, most of these realities were not so much dismissed as not perceived, as the impact of the war in weakening colonialism and capitalism was grossly underestimated, and the main focus of Washington's attention was on its relations to the USSR in Europe as well as the nations who were a part of the industrial capitalist world.

Building a World Power

The task of integrating the capitalist world into a cohesive, cooperative system under United States leadership was initially more critical to Washington's postwar objectives than the ancillary, intimately related problem of counterrevolution; but ultimately the efforts were in certain decisive ways to become mutually reinforcing. But capitalist integration was imaginable in part because American wartime planners looked upon the great world conflagrations as essentially exceptional events in the process of modern history, and scarcely as integral aspects of the disintegration of the century of colonialism and imperialism which had preceded them—a process that might create a multiplicity of revolutionary challenges too diverse for the United States to contain. No less significant were the war aims that Secretary of State Cordell Hull and his numerous associates had left indelibly planted in the minds of Washington's key foreign policy decision makers. These objectives were not merely ideological—an economic interpretation which maintained that the collapse of trade relations between states produced the causes of war—but also reflected the real need of the American economy to avoid the return of the prewar Depression which purely domestic New Deal efforts had ultimately failed to allay. This mixture of theory with interest made capitalist internationalism and cooperation with United States trade and financial goals the first major postwar challenge to Washington's foreign policy involving the mobilization of its power in some directed way. Relations with Russia and the confrontation with revolutionary movements were initially a less pressing and more slowly evolving concern, and eventually—to some critical though not exclusive degree—a way of coping with political reluctance in supporting "Hullian" objectives that arose both at home and in Western Europe. These economic goals were quite precise in 1945–1946, but the United States had only a vague notion of the political prerequisites for their attainment. Both to sustain and reform world capitalism, therefore, became the task confronting the United States. Such an undertaking required it to oppose the Left and revolutionary forces everywhere, whether or not they were pro-Soviet Communists. At least of equal importance was gaining the cooperation of a reticent Great Britain with its immense sterling bloc, above all, and then the other capitalist states. This meant, ultimately, resolving how Germany and Japan should be reintegrated into a world conforming to America's plans—a decision whose final form was held in abeyance until early 1947.

Germany, if not intentionally at least in fact, was eventually to provide the United States with critical leverage in dealing with the larger question of the increasingly troublesome movement within the capitalist states of Western Europe toward state economic control and autarky, a development which both the rise of socialist and Communist parties to power in Britain, France, and elsewhere, as well as the shortage of dollar and gold reserves, imposed on them. American political and business leaders worried about the reemergence of the prewar autarky in the relations between industrial nations that would again close off potential markets to United States trade and renew the specter of depression. Regardless of the problem of the historical Left, which included all the increasingly diverse traditional parties designating themselves socialists or revolutionaries of one type or another, it was a fact that the structural consequences of the war bequeathed the European nations few options but to sharply regulate foreign trade and, increasingly, during 1946–1947 encourage bilateral trade accords among themselves that conserved hard currencies. These improvisations were part of a generally successful beginning of economic recovery among the former allied nations of Europe, including Italy, but one which posed grave dangers by threatening to restrict the United States' future role in the world economy.

The United States had naïvely hoped during 1944 that the new organizational framework of postwar cooperation, beginning with the principles of Bretton Woods for financial policies and then the subsequent free-trade premises of the International Trade Organization proclaimed as an American goal the next year, would suffice to avert the return of the prewar autarky. But in fact it was not disagreement on principles that troubled United States relations with most nations so much as the simple exigencies that Europe's lack of dollars imposed. The creation of an International Monetary Fund and World Bank during 1946, both headquartered in Washington and United States–dominated by virtue of voting structures based on the size of capital donations, led neither to a resumption of currency convertibility nor to private investment. The ITO, which ultimately Congress itself rejected despite intensive State Department lobbying, even with its unintended permanent offspring in the weak form of the General Agreement on Tariffs and Trade, largely failed to remedy the trade dislocations the Depression and war had created. During spring 1946 the Truman Administration confronted two quite interrelated challenges to its plans to integrate the world economy under United States leadership. On the one hand Congress was reticent to supply Europe with credits; on the other the administration saw these tied grants and loans not merely as creating markets for American exports until "normal" trade was resumed but also as leverage by which to win hitherto elusive British and foreign support for United States plans. This crisis of domestic political mobilization was first to arise in the context of the reform of the capitalist world's economic structure, reassert itself after 1946 in continuous Congressional refusals to ratify the ITO charter the United States had both conceived and largely written, and pose the need to dissolve the inhibitions Congress was wont to impose on the State Department and the internationalist business constituency's desires.

Britain was the key to the attainment of America's objective of a structural reform of the world economy, since the sterling and dollar blocs accounted for one-half of prewar world trade, and their postwar share was destined to be higher yet. Britain was committed to the principles of laissez faire underlying the State Department's program, but was quite aware that the United States had yet to embody them in its world trade practice, which was full of exceptions: tariffs, agricultural export subsidies, preferential trading agreements with the Philippines and Cuba, and inconsistencies too numerous to mention. Moreover, to fight the war Britain had produced an immense debt to other sterling bloc members, a fact which also gave it a special market as well as excluding rival United States imports. Aware of British reluctance and weakness, Washington had tailored required wartime payments for Lend-Lease goods for the common struggle in such a way that London would have to ask the United States for a large postwar loan, and the termination of Lend-Lease in August 1945 produced exactly that intended result. After intensive bargaining, in which the British were forced to concede opening the sterling bloc to dollar purchases by its members within one year as well as free currency convertibility, the Truman Administration in January 1946 asked Congress for a $3.75 billion loan to England, citing the need for reform of world trading relations, stopping the trend toward British socialism, greater United States access to colonial raw materials, and full employment at home as the initial, valid reasons.

Congress, with a large pro-Zionist, pro-Irish, and Midwestern isolationist membership, was both unimpressed and slow; and the less cautious Senate, after unusually intensive lobbying from business and agricultural circles favoring the loan, approved it 46 to 34. The Senate vote was barely swung to passage with the additional argument of anti-Communism and the need to maintain a strong ally and buffer against the Soviet Union, the justification that proved decisive in the 219 to 155 House vote in July. Merging American global economic ambitions with anti-Communism thereby became the key to political mobilization of a hesitant Congress. This often cynical form of the expansion of American capitalism overseas was in due course to become a partially sincere mystification of the objectives of its hegemony.

That United States foreign economic policy was also genuinely concerned about the threat of socialism and Communism in Western Europe, above all in Germany, was a fact that during 1947 caused Washington to give up its ambiguous flirtation with reform and revenge to gerrymander West German political and economic life to keep the temporarily radicalized Social Democrats out of power and make West Germany's recovery the heart of the reintegration of Western European capitalism into what was designed to be a new Western capitalist trading bloc. For apparent from the British loan experience was that anti-Communism was the precondition of obtaining the vast sums of money from Congress—eventually to reach over $20 billion in loans or grants during 1946–1949—essential to Western Europe's cooperation with American goals as well as immediate United States exports.

Given the now critical role that loans and grants would have to play both as a means of providing a market for United States exports as well as integrating diffident Western European nations into cooperation with American economic and political strategy, in reality the two main motivations to the declaration of the Marshall Plan the following June, the fear of Communism was to become a well-worn technique of political mobilization at home—one that was to last, with diminishing efficiency after 1963, until our own day. Yet it was the British loan of 1946 that was to begin that strategy as well as most clearly reveal its intent. This process did not involve secrecy as to real intentions, which anyone could read in the State Department's public declarations, but only added a disingenuousness for those whom they did not persuade and who had to be convinced with arguments oriented to their loyalty, chauvinism, or courage. Hence the beginning of the red scare overseas, a campaign which Truman's 1947 loyalty program and, in cruder form, Senator Joseph McCarthy were to bring home.[1]

The Question of Russia

The problem of deteriorating relations with the USSR can only partially be linked to the Truman Administration's decision to embark on a massive foreign aid program in 1947, but in 1946 the question of Russia had no connection with the British loan. Without exception, any issue between the United States and Russia was a source of the most intense aggravation to American leaders, but their military experts repeatedly assured them that their monopoly of the A-bomb gave them overwhelming superiority over the large Soviet army. Materially, a Soviet Union which had witnessed almost half its economy occupied and destroyed, and with at least 20 million dead, United States authorities saw as no match for the indefinite future, and hence the risk of war was considered small.

Since the First World War, America had planned its military policy on the assumption, traditional to all industrial nations, that military power consisted of physical plant, economic resources, and the capacity to destroy them; and in 1946 through most of 1949 the United States was indisputably the most powerful nation on earth in this regard. This premise was also a definition of the nature of world conflict, which after 1945 designated Russia as the main enemy. Such a belief, which did not so much discount as ignore the potential of guerrilla and liberation movements, revolutionary ideologies and military techniques, left the United States with supreme confidence in the efficacy and strategic doctrines of its own military arm. This military force was designed almost wholly to operate against centralized industrial societies, a posture the Truman Administration thought the diplomatic and political realities warranted. And since it had finite targets it had a predictable, fairly low cost compatible with the larger budgetary assumptions that prevailed in Washington until the end of 1949.

More dangerous was the emergence of a radicalized Left and

important Communist parties everywhere in Western and Southern Europe and Asia, and because of the USSR's ideological proclamations the United States saw it behind the increasingly diverse and autonomous revolutionary movements of the world long after the evidence proved that Russia, if anything, was an inhibitor to decisive revolutionary action wherever it controlled local Communist parties. Indeed, independence from Soviet direction became the precondition of success everywhere, a fact that was not effectively to shape United States strategy and ideas for another two decades.

In Eastern Europe the United States ignored the wartime political precedents it and Britain had imposed in Italy and Greece, its overt limits on a resurgent Left in its own zone in Germany, and its explicit willingness after 1946 to use its own troops if necessary to prevent a Communist victory via the polls in France or Italy. No less important, it slighted the immense diversity among the political parties of Czechoslovakia and Hungary as well as the critical fact that the USSR was not yet married to a fixed strategy in Eastern Europe. At every opportunity, from the United Nations discussions of atomic disarmament or Iran, to the immensely complicated negotiations over Germany's reparations and political future and at Council of Foreign Ministers meetings and the 1946 Paris Peace Conference, the American leaders waxed self-righteous and excoriated Russia. They refused to negotiate in any serious way simply because as self-confident master of economic and military power the United States felt it could ultimately define the world order. It had the greatest amount of force in the world as well as the readiness to employ it. Containing the USSR within its bloc, and then integrating the vast remainder of the world, was not so much a new policy but rather a continuation of the quarantine strategy of the United States and its allies after 1918. It is this process of integration of the capitalist and former colonial spheres, and the American encounter with the Asian revolution and upheavals in Greece, Latin America, and elsewhere, that formed the main pattern of postwar history and so confounded the United States priorities of the 1946–1949 period. If we now are fully aware of the autonomous character of the successful revolutionary movements in China, Yugoslavia, Vietnam, and Cuba, which surprised the cautious Russians almost as much as the Americans, the formidable evidence for the indigenous and independent nature of the forces that existed at the time never colored the ideology that the United States was to articulate in the form of Dean Acheson's simplistic anti-Communism. The Russians, at the time and to this day, never ceased to proclaim their devotion to "peaceful coexistence," even at the sacrifice of socialism in China, Germany, Greece, or elsewhere, as they relegated ideology to a place far behind state interests in their own priorities.

American leaders increasingly defined the world in a manner that dissociated reality's inhibitions from their own desires and needs, reinforcing an often amazingly simplistic paranoid perceptual thread that runs throughout postwar American foreign policy and which men from Truman to Forrestal to Dulles shared; and from this the heightening of a sense of danger from Communism and Russia became one of the more critical United States organizational mechanisms in integrating states prone to pursue an autonomous capitalist and conservative strategy. The "internationalism" which Washington evoked for its dominated "collective security" structures by hazard provided whatever superficial ideological underpinnings the Americans could conjure for their vast enterprise, a theoretical warrant that a few key leaders, such as Defense Secretary James Forrestal, thought was sorely needed. For the remainder of the postwar epoch, such an American-controlled "internationalism" became an increasingly less efficacious pillar of argument and justification as other nations followed the United States in their instinctive pursuits of national interest. NATO became the model for numerous regional mechanisms, from SEATO to CENTO, designed to deal with alleged military threats but in fact utilitarian to the American effort to use political hegemony parallel to economic integration to avoid the reemergence of nationalism. Never, of course, did the United States abandon a strategy based on its own forces to depend more than tangentially on these alliances, which at best it saw as a means for coping with internal rebellions. Given the conservative nature of the leadership of so many of the members of these blocs, as well as the growing financial incentives the United States attached to belonging to them, that effort was surprisingly successful in Europe, until the rise of DeGaulle after 1958 and then the Greek-Turkish dispute that made NATO a shambles, while elsewhere the instability of local dictators made the "collective security" pacts wholly ephemeral.

The Priorities Dilemma

What was significant about the format of contrived crises into which United States foreign policy was plunged from mid-1946 onward was not the way in which American leaders rationalized the vast sums spent to help the American economy or integrate Western Europe in the name of the struggle against Russia—for they offered both truth and falsity simultaneously—but the manner by which the complexity of the world, the limits of American power, and the ignorance, myopia, and naïveté of its most sophisticated leaders led to a confusion of priorities and their loss of mastery over events. With each failure the range of their possible action and options altered, often imperceptibly and at times in dramatic ways, as America's ability to define the course of world history diminished over time. This was true in its dealings with the capitalist world, however temporary its quite costly successes in stabilizing West German politics and gaining a modicum of Western European obeisance, and above all in its relationship to the non-European world. It was only in regard to the USSR, ironically, that a predictable understanding evolved, even if it was based on reciprocal fear that was gradually allowed to accommodate mutual trade as well. An equilibrium also emerged because, while ideologically revolutionary, in terms of state conduct the Russians consistently pursued a primary devotion to national security and interests at the sacrifice of destabilizing revolutionary actions.

What appears "accidental" in American foreign policy after 1946 was essentially a result of the dilemmas and superficially unpredictable crises intrinsic in a foreign policy that set before itself no less a goal than the economic reconstruction and integration of world capitalism, along with the political and military protection of the venal and repressive regimes whose retention in a neocolonial status became a precondition for their incorporation into a world under American direction. And given the possibility of altered priorities which the world and its inherently uncontrollable qualities repeatedly presented to a United States which reacted to one crisis after another as if its resources were inexhaustible, the American leaders' seemingly improvised responses to reality cannot be appreciated save as a function of a set of objectives sooner or later preordained to create frustrations and, with the changing balance of world power, failures. Even if its exact actions are not always predictable, one may in principle anticipate the nature, if not the precise time and place, of the difficulties that imperialist powers will encounter. After 1946, this process becomes the defining experience of United States foreign policy.

Like a slowly, inexorably unfolding plant, revolutions and upheavals that far exceeded the aftermath of World War One had begun or were incipient throughout the world. With Japanese, French, and British colonialism defeated or weakened, the world now saw immense vacuums which the tides of revolutionary forces would fill in due course. The interaction of these alterations in the balance of world forces, the impact of revolutionary ideologies and nationalism of socialist as well bourgeois varieties, meant that a new epoch of continuous struggle had begun. China, Indochina, Korea, Greece, the Philippines, Malaya, Algeria, Angola, Indonesia, Cuba, Chile, Portugal, to mention but a few, were beginning in a vast elliptical fashion, including losses and terrible tragedies, to wholly transform the world. The United States now sought to relate to this world with its theories of expansive national power defined as "internationalism," its increasingly irrelevant fascination with a technology oriented only to mastery over other technological societies, and an increasingly objective need to operate abroad. Given the collapse of European imperialisms, it was only the existence of the United States as the aspiring surrogate of them all that held up the leaking walls of the old order and reaction, and thereby defined the terrible main violence of modern history. America's guns, money, and men created the central experience of the post-1945 epoch.

Viewing the world and American goals, Washington's global priorities at the end of the Second World War naturally oriented it toward Europe, for it was not only there that the control of industrial plant and the existence of developed economies would define the distribution of world power, but it was in the European environment that United States military power was indisputably supreme. Both in terms of objective interests and America's armed resources, the European emphasis was logical.

Asia was of far lesser significance, and that ranking was to prevail until the 1960s, though in fact the relationship of one portion of the world to another was after 1950 merged in such a manner as to make priorities less and less distinct and the logic of commitments more convoluted and even dialectically metaphysical. Latin America, until 1959, was so integrated that it was not to pose an option to a dominant stress on Europe. It was in its preference of Europe over Asia that Washington's world view was most explicit. It scarcely appreciated the fact that priorities are defined by action as well as calculation, and that reality led to the confusions in the pursuit of national policy that colored the later course of United States history.

Given the task of sustaining decadent old orders against revolution, the United States began applying its resources in China to the extent of more than $2.8 billion and thousands of advisers until 1949, when the social and economic collapse of the Chiang regime made further arms futile, and the vast size of the nation made any direct intervention unthinkable. The loss of China seemed to men such as Dean Acheson likely to lead only to perpetuation of chaos and decentralization there, with a weak nation remaining. The alternative anchor for American power in the Far East, one which had been considered for five or more years, was a Japan revived and integrated into an American-led international trading system. Purged of its atavistic feudal class, the main backer of prewar Japanese imperialism, the "liberal" industrialists were installed to rule Japan under the tight control of the State Department and the military occupation, which became the final arbiter of Japan's restoration. After 1947, as in West Germany, the policy of penalizing Japan was replaced by a strategy of its controlled integration into a United States–led bloc, though in fact it was not to recover economically until the Korean war gave it the necessary environment for its "economic miracle."

The liberation of China led to the private, and later famous, July 1949 Acheson order to Philip Jessup to begin a review of United States policy in Asia on the "assumption that it is a fundamental decision of American policy that the United States does not intend to permit further extension of Communist domination on the continent of Asia or in the southeast Asia area."[2] But in fact much the same resolution had been made in early 1947 regarding Greece and Western and Southern Europe. Indeed, from November 1948 onward the National Security Council was secretly on record in favor of the elimination of Soviet control in Eastern Europe. The context which such earlier decisions had created provided the suitable pretext for a vast expansion of economic-tied credits to Western Europe in the form of the Marshall Plan, West Germany's final partition and reconstruction, and later the reshaping of the Brussels Pact into NATO and an anti-Soviet rather than anti-German military alliance. The willingness of the United States to engage its power in potentially unlimited ways almost everywhere in the world depended no longer on the existence of priorities, but the sheer amount of resources it was willing to expend as well as the capacity and need of the economy to absorb arms budgets. Before the Korean war, the United States had made a commitment to fighting wherever necessary against the further expansion of "Communism" and to sustain counterrevolution, a decision that left it not to Washington to define its priorities but to the will and capacities of the revolutionary leadership, peasants in villages taking spontaneous action successfully, and external forces that Moscow's fear and caution could not inhibit. Priorities were defined where the shooting was, a reality which only America's unlimited funds and resources and patience could seemingly absorb—and Vietnam proved it did not have them. After the Soviet explosion of its own atomic bomb in August 1949, the readiness of the United States to vastly increase its arms outlays was foreordained when the administration, under Acheson's guidance, began assessing its need to greatly enlarge the military budget—culminating in the secret NSC-68 policy paper. Proposed during a downturn in the economy and greatly increased unemployment, the up to $35 billion more on arms the NSC-68 group proposed was the logic not of the Korean war, which came afterward, but the enormous and growing disparity between United States objectives and the military and political resources at its command. Moreover, given their detailed comprehension of the 1948–1949 recession and their prediction of "a decline in economic activity of serious proportions" in the near future, the NSC-68 planners explicitly regarded greater arms spending also as a way of heading off a depression.[3] As the percentage of the gross national product going to arms more than doubled between 1950 and 1951, the United States was to begin its futile, increasingly costly and violent effort to relate its power and ambitions to a world ever more difficult for it to master. What it did accomplish, at least for a time, was to dampen the risk of a depression at home.

The Permanent Strategy Crisis

At the beginning of 1950 the foreign policy of the United States was at an impasse. China had been "lost" to communism and the USSR had developed an atomic bomb and created the beginning of a balance of military terror which the January 1950 decision in Washington to construct the hydrogen bomb was never to alter. America's economic integration of Western Europe was increasingly in doubt as Marshall Plan credits began dropping, and most of the turbulence in the world seemed to be present in the Far East. The Korean war greatly intensified a crisis of strategic confidence, and it marked the inception of a long and ultimately futile American effort to make its technological might credible, perhaps as much to itself as anyone else. For the weaknesses of United States power became immediately apparent in Korea.

The Korean war was essentially the internationalization of a civil conflict that had begun in 1945 immediately after Korea's liberation from Japan and the artificial partition, which the United States imposed in August 1945, of the nation into what was to become two permanent sectors. The totalitarian regime that United States funds and, until June 1949, troops kept alive in the south left the nation in constant turmoil, with guerrilla warfare within the south itself and increasingly large scale combat between the two sections along the 38th parallel in the year before the north autonomously made the decision to reunify the nation in June 1950. Divorced from the preceding five years of history, theories on the origins of the Korean war merely become a part of the Cold War's mythology. In June 1950, despite its sincere belief in Soviet responsibility for the conflict's outbreak, Washington was fully aware of the deeper internal origins of the conflict and not wholly surprised by the event. And it was also quite confident its participation in keeping the Right in power in the south would not involve much of its resources for too long. By the late fall, as well, the Korean war gave the Truman Administration the otherwise unavailable means for mobilizing vast new Congressional appropriations sufficient to implement NSC-68 and deal with myriad expensive needs in Europe—programs far exceeding the cost of the Korean war itself. What indeed was likely to have been a short war lasted until July 1953, requiring 33,600 American lives and $18 billion, only to end in a total military stalemate along the 38th parallel where it had first begun. Despite the fact that by mid-1951 Major General Emmett O'Donnell, Jr., could report that "almost the entire Korean Peninsula is just a terrible mess. Everything is destroyed," a vast United States air, naval, and artillery superiority could not produce military victory over a dedicated enemy using high mobility, decentralization, tunnel defenses, and movement at night.[4] Massive firepower produced barbarism, killing over a million South Korean civilians and at least an equal number in the north, but not victory. Korea proved there was no relationship between the expenditure of industrial power and the political and military results obtained. The dilemma of adjusting its power to reality was now a permanent frustration for United States foreign and military policy, with its goals far exceeding its means.

In overt warfare, the limits of violence were now publicly exposed. In covert warfare, however, and in aid to reactionary comprador regimes such as the Philippines or in suppressing weak local guerrilla movements, a whole new world of techniques—from the jailer's key and the torturer's interrogation, to repression at every level of violence and instigating coups—opened itself to the United States in ways essentially unknown before World War Two. Those who assert that the application of American power is entirely open and known to the careful observer are just as naïve as those who argue that the functioning of its foreign policy is wholly conspiratorial in means and ends rather than the flexible effort to attain prescribed objectives and needs. America's private armies, police agents, cultural apparatuses with kept ideologists, and so much else begin at this time as a permanent, heavily funded means of combating still fragile revolutionary movements or even, as with Iran in 1954, eliminating the domination of nominal allies over oil supplies and introducing United States control. Guatemala in 1954, Indonesia in 1957, the Bay of Pigs in 1961, private armies in Laos and Vietnam beginning in the 1960s, Indonesia again in 1965—the United States after 1948, operating through the CIA and the Pentagon, recorded numerous successes as well as failures in its often barely clandestine campaign of persuasion, bribes, assassinations, torture, and repression. Against revolutionary movements operating in a propitious structural environment, and with an adequate mass base and free of putschist, legalist, or similar errors, police repression rarely succeeded. At best it could only gain time, which in Greece, the Philippines, or South Korea only produced the restoration of the old corruption and, sooner or later, the return of new struggles and, for the United States, new challenges and losses.

Still, the existence of covert warfare as an evolving technique was never in fact or conception a sufficient substitute for the failure of America's limited warfare capacities in Korea. That war left a gnawing insecurity among its leaders, and the "New Look" and "massive retaliation" debate of 1953–1954 was less a new strategy than a part of a continuous search for one. The ambiguous threat to use total strategic air power against Russia in the event of local war on the Asian rimland was irrelevant to the specific realities then evolving in the jungles of Indochina, as it was later in the hills of Cuba; and the Soviet development of its own hydrogen bomb in August 1953 only deprived United States threats of all credibility with each passing month. The erroneous thesis that behind local revolutions lay, somehow, the hand of Russia or China wholly minimized the origins of the periodic transformations of nations into anti-capitalist social systems, for it was not to the interest of the United States or the normal thought of any ambitious state to believe that the system of which it had become the keystone contained within its own shortcomings the seeds of self-destruction. Any illusion was superior to the loss of self-confidence such an admission implied.

In effect, rather than resolve the strategy debate which followed the Korean bloodletting, the United States drifted into a de facto policy of responding to specific events in seemingly minimal ways, resolved never again to fight a war with its massed land armies in Asia but also quite unclear about the relevance of each seemingly small commitment or problem to its overall priorities, resources, and needs. The rational administration of its finite resources to optimize results thereby became impossible, and it was for events to define for the United States where or with what type of arms it was to respond, and virtual chance to dictate the depth to which it might get mired in the inherently unpredictable task of what was reflexive and self-interested counterrevolutionary violence. However superficially sophisticated and respected the publicized academic debates over strategy which flourished after the mid-1950s, giving rise to a whole generation of military intellectuals from the Rostows to Kissinger who were to have their turns with power, no one was able to formulate the intrinsically elusive policies which could lead to the coveted United States mastery over the world's direction. Instead of mastery, indeed, there was only strategic, if not tactical, failure and drift. The operational limits that the immensely diverse real world imposed on neat blueprints made virtually every conflict raise questions of America's "credibility" as the limits of its capacities were increasingly exposed. The application of tactics that could not work but were acceptable to a power structure dedicated to dominating the contours of world social and economic institutions only pointed to those self-destructive contradictions in all expansive capitalist nations which since 1914 produced the three major wars that profoundly altered the distribution of power among states and the direction of the history of this century.

During the 1950s Vietnam became an issue linked to so many other questions—from France's role in Europe and the efficacy of American weaponry and the New Look to the need to insulate the raw-materials producers against the tides of revolution—that it is now scarcely any surprise that the increasing successes of the Vietminh in mobilizing the masses for the revolution and protracted struggle should have become the major postwar conjunction of America's effort to relate to the dominant if not unilinear trends of history and resolve its gnawing self-doubts about its ability to protect the larger world socio-economic matrix in which its interests could survive and prosper. Vietnam was, over time and with increasing intensity, the inevitable, transcendent test of the entire world system the United States aspired to create; it was the fusion of all its past frustrations as an imperialist nation, and a test in which the United States was to fail totally. It revealed, as none others would, the virtually unlimited violence and terrorism to which American foreign policy could resort—as well as its motivations and limits—and thereby became the most important revolutionary event in at least a quarter-century.

The domino theory was first articulated in the context of the Middle East during the 1947 Truman Doctrine "crisis," and even before its first Indochina challenge Washington had defined a concept of political-military overhead charges as integral to the realization of its economic goals. In effect, just as the United States in the 1920s learned it had to make economic investments in the Third World to control raw materials, so in the revolutionary world context of the postwar epoch it increasingly understood it had to make political and military investments to sustain the specific environment in which the neocolonial economic system could operate. The domino theory was simply an articulation of this counterrevolutionary assumption, yet its cost was one American leaders could never estimate in advance, thereby laying the seeds of their undoing.

After the final triumph of the Chinese revolution, the struggle in Vietnam was initially a question of Acheson's resolve to stem the further advance of revolution, and in May 1950 the United States began to give economic and military aid to the Indochina puppet regimes. Had Korea not immediately thereafter absorbed Washington's attention in Asia, it is likely that far more yet would have been done to assist the French cause. As it was, from 1950 through June 1954 and the signing of the Geneva Accords, the United States supplied the French with at least $3.5 billion in military aid, paying for over half of the war by 1953. Diverse reasons lay behind this large commitment.

Two vital American considerations were France's ability to block West German rearmament so long as it was bogged down in Indochina, and the future of Japan in Asia and the world economy. As for France, its quick victory would mean its return to European problems and an army at home sufficiently powerful to guarantee that a remilitarized Germany posed no threat. And for Japan, a Communist Southeast Asia meant the loss of its most logical markets and raw-materials suppliers as well as a possible dependence on Leftist states which might thereby affect Japan's social system. In the global integrated economy which American leaders planned, the Japan–East Asia axis was the logical structure for cooperation with the metropolis.

The "New Look" strategy debate, which came at the time France was losing the major battles of the war as well as the period the United States sought totally to isolate China, further intensified the resolve of men in Washington to apply their force in Vietnam. If the United States did not come nearly so close to entering the war with its air and atomic power as some have supposed on the basis of the statements of John Foster Dulles, Admiral Arthur Radford, and others, it still made certain that the Geneva Accords would be ignored in the south in its desire that the nation remain permanently partitioned.

By far the most important reason for America's mounting involvement in Indochina, however, was the strategic economic argument the Joint Chiefs of Staff first articulated in April 1950 and which American leaders shared consistently thereafter. The fall of Indochina would cause Thailand and Burma to follow, "major sources of certain strategic materials" would be lost, and the balance of world power would shift in a significant way against the United States. The "critical psychological, political and economic consequences," the National Security Council decided in a formal policy paper in June

1952, could even "endanger the stability and security of Europe." After Southeast Asia's fall, India and the Middle East might follow, and the situation of the Pacific offshore chain might become "precarious."[5] Rubber, tin, and oil would be lost in Southeast Asia, which alone could endanger Japan; and the loss of Thai and Burmese rice exports might force Japan to accommodate to Communism. References to tin, rubber, copra, iron ore, tungsten, and oil were integral to all major United States evaluations of the war for the next decades. The domino concept, in which the fate of an entire region became contingent on the survival of its weakest member, also became a major theme along with the test of the military effectiveness of the Pentagon's arsenal—"credibility."[6] However variable the emphasis on any of these points in the period after 1950, all remained important in explaining the motives which made Indochina the conjunction of all the unresolved frustrations of military power, economic integration, and leadership against counterrevolution which was to inspire American foreign policy after World War Two. When Dulles in 1954 resolved to impose the violent, corrupt, and moribund Diem regime on South Vietnam, little did he realize that by frustrating the implementation of the Geneva Accords, and given the continuing American aspirations and fears in Southeast Asia, he would lay the foundations for the most important defeat of his nation's power in its modern history. But that event was the logic of the frustrations inherent in the vast objectives for world hegemony under American guidance that had motivated its foreign policy after 1945.

The Fragile Hegemony

Indochina as the culmination of the generalized crisis in United States power in the world was not quick to come, and that crisis unfolded both slowly and irresistibly over the next two decades. Meanwhile, other frustrations of the attainment of America's overweening world goals were emerging elsewhere, particularly in Western Europe, also to lay the basis for subsequent crises with which we live today.

The restoration of normal world trade which the United States hoped would follow the Marshall Plan period did not occur immediately for numerous reasons, including the policies of the United States itself. American business failed to invest outside the hemisphere to any significant extent, save in Middle East petroleum.

Europe's loss of the formerly large Latin American market for its exports, which the United States had captured to an unprecedented extent during the 1940s, blocked a key channel to the restoration of normal trade, while agricultural protectionism within the United States, and the subsidized exports of American agricultural commodities, closed others. In fact, the Hullian principles of the ITO which Congress had consistently refused to ratify, as well as the numerous exceptions the United States had insisted upon in the GATT trade agreements, meant, in effect, that if the market for its exports in the world was going to be sustained before the accumulation problems of the Depression and the war were resolved, something more than the Marshall Plan would be required. With the decline of Marshall Plan aid after 1949, and the rise of domestic unemployment to postwar highs from mid-1949 onward, the need of Western European nations that were still plagued by currency problems, spreading economic stagnation, and unemployment to conserve foreign exchange challenged directly prosperity within the United States and its aspiration for economic integration via larger trade. The key foreign policy leaders in Washington were keenly aware of the need to sustain European imports of American goods, yet they lacked a way to mobilize Congress to allocate yet more grants, and the Truman Administration by 1950 was in a quandary. As it was, exports as a share of the gross national product that year fell by one-quarter to become the lowest postwar year on record. With Congress unwilling to expand Marshall Plan aid, and coming within a few votes of cutting it substantially, Acheson and his associates hoped that Congress might be more willing to give Europe economic aid on behalf of the struggle against "Communism," and with the outbreak of the Korean war this now became the new means of sustaining exports. If Congress insisted that arms replace economic aid, a policy which many Western European leaders justifiably worried might cause more harm than good to their already wobbling economies still in need of peace to recover, their reluctance was overwhelmed as United States military grants increased from $211 million in 1949 to $4.2 billion in 1953, fueling the American economy to new heights of prosperity even as it caused significant damage to Britain and other nations hit hard by the impact of the Korean war on their essential raw-materials imports. For the French, however, it meant a new opportunity to intensify their struggle to win in Indochina and, later, to hold on to a portion of it long enough to transfer that responsibility to the United States. And for the Japanese and West Germans, not permitted to rearm to any significant extent, the Korean war and the rest of the industrial capitalist world's preoccupation with rearmament gave them the context in which their economic "take-offs" could occur.

To some critical extent the new cornucopia of arms, as well as common obsessions over the dangers of a new war, bound the Western European nations to United States direction, and thereby allowed America the integration via political and military means it had otherwise failed to attain through the medium of trade and investment, as Hull and his peers once thought possible. Yet the world had become so politicized, and the global economy along with it, that normal economic intercourse conducted in conventional ways now became less viable and attainable given the problems in the European economy, the hesitancy of Congress, and the real impact of revolution in making smaller capitalism's area of operation. In this context, with the United States now prosperously in the new political economy that war was seemingly to make enduring, with 12 percent of the gross national product in 1952 and 1953 going into the Pentagon budget alone, plus foreign arms aid, and a budget deficit of over $9 billion in 1953, it was clear that the Hullian world system would be sharply modified, that new rules were being written for sustaining world capitalism, and that along with new strength the system might also in due course develop new weaknesses for which no one could concoct a permanent cure.

The Will to Prevail

Indochina unintentionally became the testing ground for all the assumptions and mechanisms by which the United States hoped to retain the Third World for its larger political-economic system, yet in the end it only succeeded in bringing to a head all the stresses and structural crises inherent in that effort to impose hegemony. The priorities dilemma of Europe versus Asia, of limited versus general war, of perpetual counterrevolution versus balanced budgets, all emerged despite repeated American desires not to lose control over the extent of its commitment to the ever-growing quagmire. "Accidental" only in that in the National Liberation Front the United States met its master in a force that could mobilize the political, economic, and material factors of the terrain to fight a protracted resistance, the war was the logic of the necessity to prove that America's imperialist aspirations had the will as well as material capacity to stop revolutionary advances and retain the world for itself. The counterrevolutionary impulse, which continued elsewhere simultaneously with the evolving commitment to fighting in Indochina, would have eventually produced its "Vietnam" somewhere else if not Indochina. For Vietnam only brought permanently to the surface the inherent weaknesses in America's conservative social role and military tactics which its repeated efforts to sustain reactionary comprador regimes and the Korean war had also exposed in somewhat less stark form. Precisely because the regime in Saigon was so dependent, venal, and—ultimately—ephemeral, the Vietnam war was an international intervention and the destiny of its puppet was wholly dependent on the presence of large American forces.

Vietnam was in one sense all the more essential as a testing ground for the efficacy of the United States counterrevolutionary capacities because of the trauma of the Cuban revolution on Washington's self-confidence. Cuba was unquestionably an exceptional situation in the hemisphere, and its very proximity to the mainland and the extent of United States domination made it both more galling to Washington and riper for revolution. The Cuban elite failed to resist what was initially a small revolutionary military challenge because of that movement's still unclarified nature. And at least as important was the elite's relative physical mobility made possible by the proximity of a safe haven ninety miles away and the liquid nature of its capital and functions as a consequence of its symbiotic and marginal economic role in servicing the United States investment and tourism which controlled the island's economy. No ruling class was as weak or disloyal as Havana's, while at the same time the revolution's absence of a definite ideological and economic commitment left the United States uncertain as to whether it was essential to act. This unintentional protective indecision gave the revolution two critical years during which to consolidate its power and to evolve politically. In large part it was to do so in response to Washington's boycotts, pressures, and other assaults on its national self-determination, which made resistance to Yankee imperialism and the creation of an anti-imperialist ideology the precondition of genuine independence.

It was its stunning defeats in Cuba, and particularly the failure of the CIA's "Bay of Pigs" invasion in April 1961, that humiliated the

Kennedy Administration, with its bevy of limited war theorists so influential on the instinctively combative President, into making Indochina the proof of "credibility," "the various techniques and gadgets now available" both doctrinally and in terms of weapons, and turning Indochina into a symbolic test of strength between the major power of the West and the Communist bloc.[7] And just as the still keen remembrance of the Korean war, the Berlin crisis of 1961, and the failures of Cuba encouraged this confrontation in Vietnam that would reiterate the efficacy of United States strength, each American success at counterrevolution elsewhere primed Washington to believe that it could attain the same triumph imminently in Indochina, as its experts there always saw the victory at the end of the tunnel —if only more were done to grasp it. The Brazilian coup in 1964, the terrible Indonesian massacres and reactionary coup of 1965, the short, effective United States invasion of the Dominican Republic with 21,000 of its troops the same year—each success as well as each failure spurred on men in Washington who were increasingly confident of the efficacy of their "techniques and gadgets." Just as the United States had responded to Korea with the frustration of China ever present in its calculations, Kennedy and his circle reacted to the Indochinese crisis after 1961 with the failures of Cuba hanging over them—in that larger global and contextual linkage which was the natural reflection of the world view which had guided United States foreign policy since 1945. The merger of accumulated frustrations and failures, Vietnam was the optimum possible American effort to make its military power, economic integration, and leadership decisive against the tides of revolutionary change which have all too slowly but quite irresistibly transformed the world since 1917. The crucifixion of Indochina that was then to begin to unfold in the second Indochina war was directed toward Southeast Asia and the dominoes, but also against all the rest of revolutionary mankind, leaving the people of Indochina to confront the vindictive, increasingly desperate barbarism postwar American imperialism's defeats produced—and to win complete victory. Yet their total triumph out of the terrible period to follow was not merely testimony to America's weakness but a lesson to others as to the potential and means for future revolutionary successes.

References to the dominoes in the region persisted during this time and until the final debacle, and a consciousness of the raw materials involved and the economic element continued throughout the period until 1968 for which relatively full documentation exists, though less strongly after 1962 than before. The strategic explanation, and the need to resist the alleged expansionist designs of China against all of Asia, became the most prominent, though surely not exclusive, justification of all. The war was one of a world conflict, "the testing ground" for wars of liberation, as Secretary of State Dean Rusk put it in March 1966; "part of a continuing struggle to prevent the Communists from upsetting the fragile balance of power," Undersecretary of State George Ball explained.[8] Once committed, Defense Secretary Robert McNamara told President Johnson in January 1964 that "we cannot disengage U.S. prestige to any significant degree."[9] "If we leave Vietnam with our tail between our legs," General Maxwell Taylor argued the following September, "the consequences of this defeat in the rest of Asia, Africa, and Latin America would be disastrous."[10] American leaders made similar justifications repeatedly in internal as well as public policy discussions. This synthesis of credibility and the domino theory profoundly influenced the commitment to fight on. Yet neither challenge was new to Vietnam, nor would they end with the final American defeat there.

Both unable and unwilling to confront the triumph of the National Liberation Front with the Vietnamese people as successions of its own venal puppets moved from crisis to failure in Saigon, the United States prepared to compensate for the acknowledged influence and recuperative powers of the revolutionary cause with a sheer quantity of arms and funds that was not only to make Vietnam a test of credibility but also of the limits of technology and firepower. A kind of Maginot Line psychology which assumed that military hardware solved socio-economic and political as well as military problems spawned a technological fetishism which, while immensely destructive, was never decisive against high mobility, decentralization, revolutionary elan, and organization. The NLF mastered the objective conditions, even creating a symbiotic relationship with the enemy-occupied territories from which it could at least also extract some strength. Ultimately, its resourcefulness as well as devotion, combined with the trauma that the United States was to impose on South Vietnam's society and economy, provided it with the ingredients for complete victory. And in combat, American officers morosely concluded by mid-1967 that the NLF controlled the timing and terms of combat in almost four-fifths of the engagements. Technological fetishism was to fail, and the United States military machine could perform barbarous acts but not victorious ones. Indeed, precisely because the United States had put its forces on the testing line of battle, some American leaders correctly appreciated, the NLF's immense triumph might inspire others to follow its example, and the dominoes might fall yet more quickly than had the United States stayed out of Indochina altogether.

Over a million Vietnamese were killed, over 10 million were driven from their homes, fighting lasted a decade and a half, 46,000 Americans died, at the peak of the war about three-quarters of a million American men were stationed in or around Indochina in war-related tasks, and at least $200 billion was spent on the war. The continuing and now far deeper crisis of the limits of United States power since World War Two, the conflict over priorities, and the transformation of its position from global preeminence into decline were the main outcomes of the Vietnam test. For Vietnam was not just a total defeat for the United States. It was also an ignominious humiliation of its erstwhile power that was greater than anything it imagined possible. In May 1975, after it occurred, Washington could only lamely assert that the gargantuan quarter-century effort in Vietnam had not, after all, been so crucial to American power. In any case, President Ford then argued, it would be best to forget about Vietnam and not allow it to be "rehashed. . . . The lessons of Vietnam have all been learned."[11] On the contrary, the Vietnam experience was permanently seared into the American dilemma, and the crisis of United States power was now all the more grave regardless of the readiness of virtually all of the nation's leaders to dismiss the immense significance of Vietnam to oblivion.

Objectively, the United States had a smaller stake in Southeast Asia before its intervention than virtually anyplace else in the world. It simply grossly misjudged the costs of preserving the capitalist bloc and its freedom to expand into a region should it wish to do so. Vietnam was scarcely atypical, since so many small United States interventions elsewhere had, and have, easily and quickly succeeded. It was an error only insofar as the United States understandably minimized the extent of the effort it might have to expend; and one could find no better case for the utter futility of "rational" planning and foresight in the effort to apply a foreign policy against a tide of objective forces. What began as a consensus among foreign policy leaders and factions of the function of intervention, and the need to prove "credibility" and stop falling dominoes, by 1967 became a source of deepening division among those who shared an agreement on abstract principles of the uses of American power but disputed where to apply it once Vietnam embarrassingly exposed its limits.

Vietnam further imbalanced the budget and fanned inflation seriously, weakened the dollar in world trade, alienated more citizens and created more internal divisions than any event of the past half-century, gave a critical respite to Cuba to consolidate power and Chile to move Left, made Western Europe far more independent politically as well as economically, diminished the military challenges to the USSR by reducing United States funds available for missiles, and in almost every conceivable manner shifted the balance of world economic, political, and military power against the United States. Never did any great imperialism diminish in its global strength so quickly. By 1968 that fact was so clear that the pressure within the United States to reduce the commitment to the war, if only for economic and pragmatic rather than principled reasons, had become too great for both Johnson and Nixon to ignore.

The consensus and "bipartisanship" among the elite broke down because short of unifying principles they had a real conflict of concrete interests, and reality is not just a question of agreement on ultimate rhetoric but whose pocketbook is being filled. For the first time since the end of the Second World War, the decisive foreign policy constituencies separated on a key issue largely because the war had become too expensive and was leading to the serious neglect of other aspects of global expansion. Unable to do everything and satisfy all interests, the struggle over foreign policy priorities began. Even the Pentagon, whose strategic air and naval power factions had seen their prestige and budgets fall as the conventional land army became temporarily supreme, split on the cost of the war. To all of these factions total United States withdrawal from Indochina was unthinkable, and not even nominally anti-war Presidential aspirants like Eugene McCarthy and George McGovern advocated it. When the ideologues like W.W. Rostow and Dean Rusk, and army generals like William Westmoreland, in early 1968 advocated a massive escalation of the war to exceed the already great strain it was imposing on the dollar abroad and budget at home, the men from big business and big law who had earlier hoped for cheap, quick victory in the Vietnam test case—personalities such as Acheson, George Ball, McGeorge Bundy, Douglas Dillon, Cyrus Vance, Arthur Dean, and John J. McCloy—persuaded Johnson to stop the escalation and thereby shattered his own self-confidence. It was for Richard Nixon now to resolve the pressures from those who wished to fight as well as those who sought to direct foreign policy elsewhere and save the economy at home and abroad from the consequences of a Pentagon budget which far exceeded the capacity of the economy to absorb.

The process by which escalation of costs and manpower in Vietnam ended, as distinct from the cheaper war that later disturbed none of the men at the top, proved that powerful leaders in the United States still responded only to their peers, seeking to reach mutually satisfactory compromises once differences emerged. Obeisance to the public's will, which voted overwhelmingly against Goldwater's threats of escalation in 1964, occurred only when it confirmed their own conclusions. Now the dynamics of bureaucratic interaction became critical, but not because of any "accidental" qualities in the conduct of foreign policy or a rupture of the consensus of the uses of power, but only because of disputes as to how and where America should apply that violence and repression. The crisis of "credibility" into which the United States entered was the wholly predictable outcome of the deepening failures of American foreign policy after World War Two and only its time and place were unknown. Once the limits of that "bipartisan" vision became so bald that it could no longer be denied, differences emerged with an intensity that could not only cost the careers of hawks like Rostow and Rusk, but later contribute significantly to the demise of Spiro Agnew, Richard Nixon, and their vast entourage as well.

More important, however, was to explain the contradictions, dilemmas, and dysfunctions that persistence with ideologies of credibility, dominoes, and such produced, and their more enduring economic and social consequences. So many respectable and official paranoid and conspiracy theories as to the origins of the world's turmoil had been concocted after 1946 that quite autonomous mystifications in the conduct of foreign relations became self-evident truths, with violence and war crimes sanctioned as the diffusion of the blessings of freedom. Once Vietnam proved them quite dangerous to the rational conservation of America's power in the world, modifications were inevitable; but changes came unevenly, for diverse and often devious reasons, and could not easily dissolve what generations had learned as the righteousness of counterrevolution. The process of undoing the analytic failures of the Cold War involved not only overcoming the impact of fiction on reason, but also the fact that whether justified by truth or falsity, the objective interests of the United States still left it a counterrevolutionary nation. And that fact alone imposed certain commitments and duties intrinsic in its global imperialist role. Whatever else occurred, the United States was going to remain the most violent nation on earth, the one most likely to create wars and threats of future crises. And in that role it would prove not only a danger to the world, but increasingly to itself as well.

Détente and Counterrevolution

By 1969 it was undeniably self-evident that while all the Cold War myths about the USSR and China might make functional doctrine for the schools and press, they were inaccurate descriptions of their conduct as states as well as irrelevant to the way the emergence of polycentric communism was affecting their foreign policies. In Vietnam it was perfectly clear that the revolution followed its own principles and was successful precisely because it was indigenous and independent. The aid that both the USSR and China gave it after 1965 was in part the consequence of their mutual rivalry as well as practical economics, for had the United States not been so deeply mired in the Indochina war the increased strategic arms directed toward Russia and China would have been far more costly for them to neutralize than the paltry aid they gave Indochina. The Vietnamese thereby gave those two nations incomparably more in terms of the absence of military and economic pressures than they could ever receive in turn. As it was, far more and better arms went from Russia to Egypt, where Communists are jailed, than to Vietnam, and Moscow never supported the revolutionary struggle in Cambodia until its victory was imminent.

"Détente" originated largely as a consequence of the Nixon Administration's belief that it needed Soviet cooperation to attain a diplomatic victory out of a Vietnam military stalemate that threatened to become a defeat. The economic motivations behind this strategy emerged later as the Soviet market gained interest, but there were at least a few important "Establishment" elements anxious to normalize relations with China and Russia, and they assumed that more trade and less conflict would evolve from such stabilization. And given the demoralization of the United States leadership over its failure in Vietnam, reflected in the curious, vast retrospective pessimistic history later called *The Pentagon Papers,* it was clear that diplomacy would have to succeed where guns had failed or the United States would lose the major war of at least a quarter-century. Nixon, before selecting Henry Kissinger as his adviser, had become converted to such an approach. By linking Vietnam to arms control, trade, and European security issues, the Nixon Administration hoped to reach a quid pro quo with Russia—the "linkage" to make Soviet pressures on the Vietnamese rewarding. Since the Russians candidly admitted they did not have the influence over the Vietnamese the Americans required, the matter of obtaining their participation in the "détente" effort remained in the background until Nixon decided to exploit the Sino-Soviet mutual obsession to "triangulate" the picture and compel them to cooperate on Vietnam as the United States threatened to ally with one against the other in some fashion. From the viewpoint of those two nations, keeping their socialist enemy from uniting with their capitalist enemy thereby became a main focus of their foreign policies, a tension which the Vietnamese themselves could also try to use to maintain their independent line and sustain the necessary minimum aid.

In its essence, despite tactical gains for the United States, the strategy of détente did not succeed in Indochina, nor did it lead to decisive or permanent shifts in United States diplomacy. Despite all its proclamations of a new era of good feelings, with the peak of summit diplomacy came only a vast increase in the quantity of air war and terror the United States employed against Indochina, as if to make clear to Russia that with détente it also had to tolerate greater counterrevolutionary warfare. Indeed, in the end the effort to bring détente to bear on the boundaries which reality imposed in Indochina permitted the decisive events in those countries to further bypass the United States and leave it even less able to impose its will there or in the rest of the world. Unable to comprehend the immense limits of foreign policy in the context of the durable constraints that social and economic events imposed, diplomacy for Washington became far more a comforting escape from the inhibitions of structural frustrations than a means for mastering them.

The promise of trade that détente engendered became increasingly important in relations with the USSR as the United States balance-of-payments crisis deepened after 1969, and a significant big-business constituency quite anxious to sell to the Russians as well as to the Pentagon emerged with no particular philosophy but to trade and profit thereby. In the administration itself there was now a material interest, backed by important industrial and banking constituencies, but also a persistent, quite traditional interpretation of the origins of Soviet conduct and intentions—dualistic, inconsistent, but also convenient. In the framework of the public explorations of United States policy then taking place, which in mid-1971 led Nixon and Kissinger to speculate aloud on the creation of trade blocs and a five-cornered world of implicit spheres of influence—an undeveloped conceptualization the United States neither believed nor had the power to implement—China's place was largely strategic and only secondarily economic. In fact China was economically too small to offer the United States a large market but mainly useful as a leverage to extract Soviet cooperation and as an aid, it was hoped, in sustaining the status quo in East Asia.

Never did the United States interpretation of Soviet or Chinese motives alter. "The commitment of the two Communist powers to leftward movements in the world will remain an important factor in international relations," Undersecretary of State John N. Irwin II argued in June 1972, justifying the maintenance of existing alliances and high arms spending.[12] In the wake of its lower expenditures in Vietnam the United States returned to building more sophisticated strategic arms aimed at the USSR and China, and in fact arms control remained as much a chimera after the tentative agreements on vague principles in Geneva, Helsinki, or Vladivostok as before. In the Middle East and Africa the United States and Russia were further apart in 1976 than they had been in 1971. Even trade relations remained too nominal to prove decisive except to a few corporations, who in the last instance had less influence when it came to mobilizing Congress on the passage of credits than an alliance of pro-Israel elements and such traditional arms race advocates as Senator Henry Jackson. "Détente," preeminently, was a question of counterrevolution and the maintenance of the status quo in Southeast Asia and wherever else the United States could buy or blackmail Chinese or Soviet cooperation.

The vague Nixon Doctrine of July 1969, with its promise to replace American manpower with aid to regimes willing to use Asians to fight their own people, in no way excluded the dominant future role the United States would play along with Japan in the East Asian economy. Quite explicitly the United States wished to preserve the neocolonial economies, a position which refused to accede to the irresistible social dynamics that had marked East Asia for twenty-five years and could not be undone save at the potentially unlimited cost of the United States militarily reversing them. So too, as United States Ambassador to the Philippines William H. Sullivan put it in September 1973, "There will be certain areas . . . where we think it essential for the United States to retain military presence precisely so that it can be seen that we are not abandoning our friends and not leaving the area."[13] "A network of mutual understanding and mutual restraint among the major powers in Asia," Undersecretary of State Kenneth Rush declared as the United States goal in January 1974, linking détente to the Nixon Doctrine's fulfillment; yet at the same time he argued that "both Moscow and Peking continue to view their relationships with us and our allies as fundamentally competitive—politically, strategically, economically, and ideologically."[14] The "equilibrium" in East Asia the United States explicitly sought postulated a status quo that was even then dying. The Indochina revolution's triumph in the spring of 1975 guaranteed, as never before, the United States' failure in Asia.

Contradictory in conception, openly not believed by those proclaiming it, incapable of being applied to reality, and with neither Russia nor China able or willing to produce the coveted victory in Vietnam, the desire to use détente as an arm of counterrevolution proved to be a short interlude and experiment in United States diplomacy that failed to resolve the quarter-century of frustrations in the conduct of American foreign policy. Washington could not transcend politically the limits of its military power. It was ordained to fall back into drift, increasing conflict, and adventures in a world now far more mercurial and with rival states far stronger, to evoke "The American Destiny" against inexorable forces which were prevailing, and to fail.[15] For the dynamics of social transformation in the nations of the world—Vietnam one time, Cuba another, Portugal later—made the fundamental problems of economic and military integration confronting American ambitions ones that no great power could resolve or end. In that primordial context the next epoch of its foreign policy will evolve.

Structural Foundations of Foreign Policy

Any study of post-1945 prosperity and the American political economy must assign some critical importance to the government's function in sustaining the export of the nation's products, for while the relative magnitude of this commerce was not greater than in most prewar decades, it is certain that without Washington's intercession the export of goods, and at least some capital, would have been far lower. It was the government's role artifically to restore the channels of exports by virtue of the unique social and political conditions existing throughout the world immediately after the war, and then for normal trade to supplement this foundation and to become a significant pillar of postwar economic growth as well as a guidepost for the application of foreign policy. Washington immediately after the war set out on this task of economic expansion, for however difficult its problem in defining political and military priorities and applying them, in economic matters it had none. The United States always sought markets, as well as the construction of economic ties that provided American firms access to needed raw materials and opportunities for profitable investment and exports.

Given the variety of statistical calculations that exists, the precise magnitude of postwar exports is open to debate, but at the least the nonmilitary export trade as a percentage of the gross national product during the 1950s—6.6 percent—was about equal to the 1920s and at least a fifth greater than the 1930s. But government-funded grants, loans, and subsidies initially sustained much of this trade. In 1948–1950, when United States exports equaled about $35 billion, Marshall Plan and other forms of economic aid amounted to more than $14 billion; and over the next decade more than $31 billion in nonmilitary grants and loans helped sustain the demand for United States goods. In addition, during 1950–1963, military grants amounted to almost $30 billion, with at the very least another $14 billion in grants and credits over the next eleven years—most of which were tied to the purchase of American arms and equipment. Officially subsidized agricultural exports amounted to $2 to $3 billion annually between 1957 and 1967, accounting for anywhere from one- to two-thirds of all agricultural exports during that time, explaining the sharply rising United States share of the total world trade for agricultural goods after 1953 from 12 percent to 19 percent in 1966. As late as 1962, 11 percent of all exports were government financed. While no longer large in percentage terms, such government-financed exports were critical in opening and creating markets, as John F. Kennedy put it in September 1963, "where they would have no entry and no experience and which has traditionally been European."[16] Washington thereby preserved future markets and waged counterrevolution at one and the same time.

Alone, by whatever criterion, the export of goods could not make postwar United States capitalism prosperous, but by artificially buoying it up, and in conjunction with other steps, it ranks as one of the major causes of the postwar boom. Without it, the United States economy's crisis would have come much earlier. By the 1960s, the export of goods was 5.9 percent of the GNP for the entire decade, but it leaped to 9.4 percent the following decade. The ratio of United States manufactured-goods exports to gross domestic production in the manufacturing sector rose from 6.4 percent in the unusually poor year of 1950 to 11.7 percent in 1972. High technology, over which America had a temporary lead because of enormous Pentagon subsidies to private research, accounted for much of this expansion. The integration of United States prosperity with the world economy was finally sufficiently established in ways that were critical both to American capitalism's welfare as well as decisive to the motives and conduct of its foreign relations. No less important, the creation of the more and more interrelated world economy was to pose altogether new problems and dangers both to United States power and prosperity—of which more will be said later.

It was in the private export of capital that the postwar American economy failed wholly to restore, much less exceed, the peak levels of the 1920s, which as a fraction of capital accumulation was possibly twice as high as the period after 1957. But postwar capital export was nevertheless important, and took the equivalent of 12 percent of the total United States business investment in new plant and equipment during 1957–1973 and reduced the amount of capital available to the domestic sector, thereby accelerating the growth of obsolescent plant within the American economy, raising the cost of domestic goods, and also reducing their competitiveness abroad. In addition to indirectly adding yet another cause of the negative United States balance of trade after 1971, it eventually helped produce the highly touted "capital shortage" of the 1970s.[17] Low overseas investment until 1957 was in part the result of more profitable markets at home or political uncertainty in Europe and Asia, and after 1949 it became almost immediately apparent that if United States capital investment were going to be made abroad the government would have to assume the major responsibility for doing so. Because of American industry's dependence on imported raw materials it did invest to some extent in these foreign sectors, particularly in seemingly absolutely safe Canada and Latin America. What private investors had done during the 1920s the government did after World War Two, with $18 billion in long-term capital loans between 1946 and 1960, a sum greater than the historical accumulation of all United States direct investments abroad until 1955. During 1945–1948, indeed, private sources accounted for only 15 percent of the vast United States capital exports. But even after the maturation of high private investment in 1957, the use of governmental funds for foreign loans became a new, permanent feature of the postwar economy as the politically based export of capital at first replaced and then paralleled the private market.

After 1955, however, the importance of foreign capital export to the health of United States capitalism increased significantly, and by 1966 the book value of direct United States private investment abroad had increased five times over 1950, reaching $55 billion, and by 1981 it had attained $227 billion—with the market value as opposed to the book value of this amount being about twice as great. Yet the larger part of this sum represented overseas borrowing and reinvested earnings rather than the shipment of United States funds abroad. The annual yields on these investments during 1950–1974 ranged from 11.5 to 23 percent, but in Third World regions like Latin America 20 to 25 percent after taxes was more common. But despite this generally far higher profit in the less developed nations, the potential there declined with capital saturation, and after 1957 the flow of United States private capital shifted toward the other industrial nations, particularly Western Europe.[18]

More critical, in 1966 the sales of the foreign subsidiaries of American corporations were equivalent to 13 percent of their sales within America, but by 1973 it was 23 percent. No less important, such investments in raw-materials industries abroad guaranteed American firms cheaper supplies of the indispensable ingredients of production, and they provided the nation with about two-thirds of its own imports of raw materials in 1973. Despite the seeming modesty of these data to the entire economy, to the top United States corporations they were now critical, and to many the foundations of their present and future prosperity. Already by 1961 the number of the largest American corporations dependent on their foreign subsidiaries for a significant share of their net income numbered forty-four of the top hundred, but by 1972 it had become far more widespread. By that year over two-thirds of the 178 large corporations operating overseas—of which only seventy accounted for around half of total United States investment in the Third World—were receiving a higher rate of profit on their foreign than domestic investments. In 1964 only slightly more than one-fifth of them had found their foreign operations so advantageous. Over half of this group earned at least one-quarter of their profits abroad, while thirty-eight earned at least one-half. In the aggregate, foreign earnings of all United States corporations as a percentage of their total corporate profits after taxes were but 11 percent in 1966 but climbed consistently thereafter to reach 30 percent in 1974. Foreign operations of these corporations produced a significantly higher share of their profits than of their sales—and that is what counted most.

For the seven largest United States banks, in 1971 their foreign operations produced 28 percent of their total profits. Some of the largest New York banks earned as much as one-half of their net income after taxes overseas. This trend reflected the astonishing post-1965 explosion of branch banking abroad. In 1966 only thirteen United States banks had foreign branches, and these had total assets of about $9 billion. By 1974 the number of American banks in these operations had increased tenfold and their assets by seventeen times, with increasingly risky loans amounting in the billions becoming commonplace. This internationalization of the corporate and banking sectors added temporary profit and dynamism to United States capitalism and staved off possible problems that a purely domestic-based capitalism would have engendered, but it also integrated it far more closely to a world economic structure which was simultaneously weakening for numerous reasons, not the least of which was the inflationary impact of United States military and economic policy discussed later in this chapter. Early in 1976 the United States Comptroller of Currency revealed that twenty-eight banks, including some of the nation's largest, were in serious and even critical financial difficulties because of their many billions of marginal foreign loans. Insufficient to save the system at home, the internationalization of American banks added only a potential permanent weakness along with temporary success, setting the stage for later crises.[19]

Above all, the reemergence of a large trade and investment market gave the United States both an orientation and a responsibility for conducting foreign policy along lines which interested United States firms advocated, though the creation of this constituency merely reinforced natural preferences. America's political and strategic interventions, however costly, increasingly became the necessary overhead charge for its present and future freedom to expand and prosper. Capitalism in one country having become impossible, the necessary cost of insulating the vast Third World from revolution became imperialism's responsibility for saving its future. Hence the logic of Vietnam and stopping the fall of dominoes, of insisting since the end of 1945, to quote a typical 1954 formulation of the proposition, that "foreign investment is one of the factors which contributes to the objective of winning the great masses of people of Asia, Africa, and Latin America for the free-world cause."[20]

That determination to equate the "free world" cause with that of America's profit became the foundation of numerous actions—from troop interventions and CIA covert aid, to counterrevolution in Chile and Indonesia—and the wellspring of the postwar crisis which the United States response to Third World change had created. World economic integration, not on the basis of equality but of domination, became the essential prerequisite for the American economy, and the political and military obligations and immense costs this objective imposed were never-ending. Where local compradors and oligarchies buttressed with arms, money, and advisers would not suffice, more direct United States power was essential; and hence began a long succession of interventions into the domestic social orders of numerous areas of the globe. The stakes involved in that struggle to establish American hegemony were increasingly great, for the United States and above all for the national independence movements committed to economic growth for their own rather than America's welfare. Ironically, it was the effort to attain its hegemonic objectives that was to weaken the United States as a world economic power far more profoundly than its important successes in preserving the status quo, with its prisons, violence, and stagnation, and eventually create the very trap in which the relatively short-lived United States–dominated capitalist world was to produce its own crisis and internal contradictions.

Raw Materials and Industrial Power

The role of raw materials in any industrial economy is qualitative rather than quantitative, and analyses which focus simply on their volume and price ignore wholly the intricate nature of modern economies, where the lack of even small amounts of resources can produce major dislocations. The same relationship exists between industrial capitalist and so-called developing nations: The Third World countries may be poor, but in the last analysis the industrial countries need access to their resources far more than impoverished nations need foreign markets that in any case never eliminated their poverty. This larger dependence became a foundation and motivation of United States foreign policy after World War Two that has only grown with time.

The United States raw-materials deficit began during the 1920s, and specific industries became concerned with the economic accessibility and political nature of every nation in which some of their essential imports were located. In the Middle East, of course, securing oil became the keystone around which United States conduct was at least initially founded, and in Chile and Africa raw materials assumed decisive proportions. Academics who argue that alternate sources to the supplies of any country or for any product could be found, or even that the United States might become self-sufficient in either oil or copper if ready to pay the higher costs, ignore entirely how operational foreign policy was conducted in response to specific pressures as well as objective needs.

With the Korean war, when the United States and European demand for raw materials greatly increased both prices and absolute quantities imported, the raw-materials orientation in the conduct of American foreign policy became an obsession, among others, that time has only increased along with growing United States dependence. The domino concept, both in Greece and Indochina, was but another expression of what was to a large extent a theory of the accessibility of raw materials to America and its allied nations, thereby giving a concrete material basis to counterrevolution. Despite the large United States domestic output of raw materials, its share of almost half the world's total consumption of copper, lead, zinc, aluminum, and steel in 1948–1950 made it early in the postwar era much more dependent on foreign suppliers, many of which were increasingly found in the nations of a Third World which the tides of revolution and nationalism were profoundly changing. The creation of the President's Raw Materials Policy Commission in 1950, the Paley Commission, deepened this awareness when it predicted a growing United States deficit of essential materials and an increasing dependence on the Third World. The Commission, which largely reflected the collective opinion of the businessmen it interviewed, oriented United States policy toward expanding production abroad rather than becoming self-sufficient on diminishing, high-cost domestic mines, a policy that merely reinforced the practice of United States industry at the time and thereafter. Such United States foreign investment as there was until the late 1950s was directed largely to the Third World, with American companies abroad supplying their nation with one-quarter of their imports—overwhelmingly raw materials—during 1946–1950 alone. Enlarging raw-materials production in the Third World became the function of both government loan and aid policy, with the Export-Import Bank and "Point Four" during the four years after the Korean war lending well over a half-billion dollars for the development of raw materials in "secure" nations. "Our purpose," a semi-official Council on Foreign Relations report on the topic proposed in 1958, "should be to encourage the expansion of low-cost production and to make sure that neither nationalistic policies nor Communist influences deny American industries access on reasonable terms to the basic materials necessary to the continued growth of the American economy."[21] "Development diplomacy" that the United States–dominated World Bank sponsored thereafter was geared no less to increasing the exports of the Third World and preserving it within the capitalist sphere, regardless of the fact that fluctuating and generally declining prices for these goods guaranteed poverty and dependence—thereby increasing the problems "to make sure" United States access could be guaranteed.

By 1956–1960 the United States was importing over half of all its required metallic ores and almost 60 percent of its wool. It is irrelevant that after 1959 United States investments and imports shifted toward developed nations and manufactured products, for the absolute dependence on imported raw materials grew throughout the 1960s until, with the outbreak of the 1973 oil price war between the Organization of Petroleum Exporting Countries (OPEC) producers and industrial world, it was an obsession based on objective needs. More important was the trend of United States imports of raw materials to grow far more rapidly than its exports of goods. And while many of its essential needs came from a Canada, which was largely United States–dominated economically and politically, it is no less a fact that global reserves for numerous vital minerals were found in the Third World. Manganese, chromium, nickel, copper, tin, bauxite, and so much else were still largely located in areas of political and social upheaval. Importing at least half of fifty-four essential commodities in 1956–1960, by the beginning of the 1970s the United States was realizing a 1954 Senate report's prediction that "to a very dangerous extent, the vital security of this Nation is in serious jeopardy" without free access to imported raw materials.[22]

The United States consumed about two-fifths of the entire world's nonrenewable resources in 1971, utilizing 42 percent of the aluminum production, 38 percent of its nickel, and 32 percent of its cobalt—minerals in which its own reserves were less than 2 percent of the world's total. In 1950 the United States relied on imports for more than half its supplies of only four of the thirteen basic raw materials, reached six by the early 1970s, and projected a deficiency of nine by 1985. In 1974 its raw-materials balance of payments was $16 billion in the red, and while dire predictions of yet greater dependency in the future are partially contingent on the extent of economic activity, it was still clear that America's integration into the world raw-materials system was a question of fundamental significance to it. However variable the predictions of future United States deficiencies, by 1974 it was the indisputable consensus that the United States, along with the remainder of the capitalist world, was confronting greater shortages and increasing dependency on the rest of the world, including that portion of it in upheaval. With the United States importing over one-third of its oil by 1973, and scheduled to reach one-half by 1985, "Even a brief interruption of this supply," a 1972 Chase Manhattan Bank report noted, "can have a severely damaging impact."[23] "Petroleum is a finite commodity that is essential, to an extent unequaled by any other commodity, to a country's well-being," Undersecretary of State John N. Irwin noted in April 1972, "and . . . it is the most political of all commodities."[24]

By late 1974, as the highest United States officials were implying that the United States might invade the most reactionary Middle East states unless they were more cooperative on matters which, in the last analysis, involved the price and control of petroleum, the vital significance of raw materials, as well as their profits for comprehending the motives of United States diplomacy, was no longer debatable. Having skillfully pushed Britain out of dominance in the Middle East in the decade after 1945, the United States was not passively going to tolerate its own elimination, even in the hands of regimes whose conservatism it had always admired. "It is also important that we do not undermine the role of the international oil companies," the Undersecretary of State for Economic Affairs stressed in July 1973; and when the Arab states moved to eliminate them from the region in which two-thirds of the world's oil reserves could be found, the possibility of a United States–promoted new world conflict became an additional source of danger to the international community during late 1974 and 1975.[25]

Vietnam, Iran, Indonesia, Brazil, Chile, and a list of United States–sponsored coups and direct interventions too numerous to mention stood as disproof to those who argued against the fact, to quote one official prognostication of the future that was scarcely less valid for the past, that "economic relationships will also become a more prominent aspect of our foreign policy in the future because of our constantly increasing consumption of energy and nonrenewable resources."[26] That structural imperative had always existed in the conduct of postwar foreign policy, both in creating a desire and need for the integration of the Third World into a United States–led capitalist hegemony and in preventing the reemergence of Japan and other states as rivals "falling back," to quote Undersecretary of State U. Alexis Johnson in February 1970, "on the outworn shibboleths and practices of national autarky and protectionism."[27] The integration of the world's raw-materials structure was essential not only to stymie the spread of nationalism and revolution—of whatever type—and thereby create dangers to the free expansion and high profitability of the United States economy, but to avoid the "increasing opportunity for international conflict" of which the scientific panel of the United States National Commission on Materials Policy warned in late 1972—long after that conflict was too far advanced to reverse.[28] But by the 1970s the full economic, political, and human costs of the vast postwar United States enterprise to integrate a capitalist world under its own direction had already produced a grave crisis, the development of which will be the hallmark of future American history.

The Eclipse of United States Economic Power

While the origins of the eclipse of United States economic power in the world are complex, the crisis in its international position was a fact that the events of the 1970s made common newspaper fare.[29] Intimately linked with the very nature of postwar United States foreign policy, it was ironic that the measures which were essential to that policy's fulfillment and which prevented the return of the dangers of maturity and stagnation of the post-1918 period also produced a new set of challenges to the stability of American capitalism, challenges perhaps ultimately more serious than those it had acted to avoid. But in an integrated fashion, the political-military overhead charges of implementing American foreign goals and sustaining the new war economy merged with the shift in the balance of power between capitalist states as it slowly evolved after 1950, and the Vietnam war brought to a head all the latent weaknesses within United States capitalism's position in the world.

To some critical degree, United States economic supremacy after 1918, and especially after 1945, was based on the consequences to Europe of its two major internecine wars while America avoided extended, large-scale combat. With increasing intensity after 1950, the United States reversed its earlier role of making business while avoiding the protracted costs of war, and Europe and Japan emerged relatively far stronger. For perpetual war and preparations for it imposed a debilitating political context on the purely economic aspects of capitalist power—in part supporting the economy at one level while weakening it in a deeper, more fundamental way—and upset all efforts to sustain the much celebrated new era of domestic and global prosperity. The accumulated costs of militarism and successive administrations had turned a series of improvised policies and global adventures into a firm system for which no better logic could be found than that it seemingly solved immediate problems. By the late 1960s the capacity of American imperialism to sustain such an incremental foreign policy had ended despite Washington's inability to acknowledge that fact.

The capacity of the United States economy to sustain the global military-political costs—from military budgets to foreign economic and military grants—essential to world economic integration and political stability was not initially in doubt until Europe and Japan emerged as the collective economic superior to the United States. Throughout the period until the 1960s the United States balance of trade and exports were always favorable, but in the critical consumer goods sector this positive balance existed until the mid-1960s only because of automobile exports. In 1954–1956 the United States accounted for 30.5 percent of the world export trade for principal manufactures, but by 1966 it was down to 22.7 percent, and then slipped to 16.9 percent in 1973. When the Vietnam war's peak demand absorbed America's industrial capacity, numerous traditional exporters neglected their foreign customers, and this greatly accelerated the natural loss of world trade markets in the critical, rapidly growing manufactured and processed goods field. In this as well as numerous other crucial areas, Vietnam structurally undermined and accelerated the United States' ability to dominate the capitalist world, thereby producing a qualitative, historic defeat in its global power.

This was all the more important because despite its favorable trade balances, in part achieved through high government spending for everything from military aid grants to agricultural export subsidies, they were insufficient to pay for the overall impact of the political-military overhead charges, which became the most important single cause of the United States balance-of-payments deficits. Beginning in 1950, with a net deficit of almost $2 billion, in every year but two (which produced small surpluses) after 1950 the United States negative payments balances created immense foreign claims on the dollar. By 1960, when United States investments overseas began rapidly expanding, in large part because of the willingness of foreigners to accept overvalued dollars in return for their economic resources, Washington's gold reserves were far less than the potential claims on the dollar. While high United States officials worried about this no later than 1958, the fact remains that the compulsions of American imperialism committed it to an extravagant course whose price the Vietnam war forced it to pay.

Superimposed on this exceedingly unfavorable structural situation for the United States was an extremely convoluted and astonishingly complicated world capitalist system that gave it a temporary respite while it added new dangers. The creation of a mercurial Eurodollar market added instability to the world economy, as did the world loan and interest structure that encouraged vast international capital movements which exceeded anything known in the 1920s. At the same time—and raising grave doubts about the liquidity and security of enormous sums—came a further weakening of a dollar whose strongest defense was the fact that so many were in foreign hands that those Europeans with power hesitated to compel the United States to follow rules of discipline essential to a restoration of the dollar's future health. Yet in March 1968 the leading European central bankers were able to restrain a further escalation in the cost of the Vietnam war, and despite a policy of "benign neglect," which consisted mainly of a United States threat to destroy Europe along with itself unless it proved more cooperative, the dollar crisis merely persevered in the context of the objective weakening of United States power over the world economy—save via political and military means and outright bullying.

Intimidation became the last refuge of United States capitalism when the oil-producing states after October 1973 merged to form a cohesive bloc able to threaten the dollar's already tottering position. While the dynamics of this relationship have yet to be exhausted, it was the context of the world economic crisis and already immense divisions among the major capitalist nations that gave the oil countries the opportunity to ignore American pressures. At the same time, the oil nations further intensified the rivalry among capitalist states for economic spheres of influence as Japan and most of the Western European nations scrambled to fill in the vacuum that the growing removal of United States oil majors created. At the end of the postwar epoch, most of the greatest gains the United States had achieved, especially in its supplanting of British power in the Middle East, were back on the carving board of intra-capitalist rivalries.

Vietnam absorbed the resources of United States industry, fanned inflation that only allowed the value of the dollar to lose attractiveness; and after the war's expenses declined, the United States found itself no longer competitive in numerous fields which it had once dominated—autos among others. The United States, which produced 47 percent of the world's steel in 1950, when it was abnormally strong and able to impose the rules on the world economy that were to last until 1968, by 1973 accounted for less than one-fifth. Only in highly advanced products was it able to rival Europe and Japan, and by 1971 its trade deficit was $2 billion, with more than three times that amount the following year. Beginning in 1969, its officially recorded payments deficits reached unprecedented heights, with $22 billion for 1971 only—or almost $93 billion in payments deficits from 1950 to 1973. United States liabilities to foreign official agencies by then vastly exceeded its gold reserves. The dollar, in brief, was based only on its purchasing power in an American economy plagued by a sustained and growing inflation, and by the capacity of the United States to impose it on others—if only by the threat of mutual economic destruction. On August 15, 1971, the United States withdrew the official gold backing of the dollar, which it de facto had long ceased to have, and in December devalued the dollar only to try again in February 1973, and then the following month permitted it to float along its generally downward course. With these gestures the limits of American power were again acknowledged and the world once more embarked on a new period of crises, instability, and doubt in the relations among capitalist nations. For whatever solutions to its problems successive United States administrations tried to apply after 1968 failed to produce a permanent cure.

In part these sharply emerging rivalries among the capitalist nations were intrinsic in their mutual needs and desires to resolve their domestic economic problems—many of which touched the political stability of states in a way unknown in the United States—at the expense of another country, and the United States was the major target. But apart from trade and tariff structures, interest rates, the valuation of currencies and monetary policies, and so much else was the dangerous reemergence of rival neocolonialisms in numerous nations as a way for capitalist nations to guarantee themselves raw-materials resources as well as markets and work forces. Japan, particularly, tightened its grip over the Far Eastern economy, dominating the trade sector and coming increasingly into conflict with the United States over control of investments. Repeated American efforts to smooth over these irreversible structural differences with reassuring joint communiqués produced only more of the cosmetic diplomacy which was Henry Kissinger's speciality, but underneath the conflicts still remained. Indeed, its desire to reduce its dependence on United States imports, particularly foods, naturally forced Japan to turn to Asian sources on a vast and ever-growing scale. And because of its total reliance on United States–controlled oil imports, the key to its economy, it inevitably moved to create new relations with the oil-producing states where once only the United States had been master of the situation. "It will be inevitable," the prestigious *Nihon Keizai Shimbun* observed in mid-1972, "that confrontation and friction between the two countries over resources will intensify in the future."[30] By 1975 that prediction was being realized. Able temporarily to checkmate Japan because of the political infrastructure that years of sponsoring counterrevolution gave it in Indonesia, Taiwan, and the Philippines, by the end of the United States–dominated epoch in world affairs the renewed contest with Japan for dominance in Asia was only again beginning, but this time in a radically different situation in which revolutionary states and struggles paralleled divisions within the ranks of expansionary capitalist nations and made increasingly successful social transformation in Asia the alternative to a divided neocolonialism's failures.

By 1972 the world capitalist economy, with increasing risks and dangers, began a process of stumbling from crisis to crisis involving the weakness and volatility of the dollar which the Americans had imposed upon it, inflation and payments deficits, along with rising unemployment, excess currency flows while the liquidity of numerous American and world banks was in doubt, the saturation of markets which intensified new rivalries, and a larger integration of problems that accompanied the stage to which world capitalism had developed. Cooperation among capitalist states was now far less natural than conflict. By 1975 it was a situation whose closest, yet inadequate, parallel was the end of the 1920s, for which no solution could be proposed or found, and which guaranteed new tribulations as the next stage of the United States in the world began to unfold.

Ironically, it was the very process of using the means of an enormous federal budget, military and overseas expansion, and credit to avert the return of the pre-1941 economic stagnation that was to set the stage for the next crisis in United States development. In fact, the dissipation of all the post-1945 means for sustaining both domestic full production and international expansion and counterrevolution left United States capitalism adrift at the conclusion of its first century as an industrial power. The world order and institutions Washington had formulated during World War Two simply had no utility in coping with the consequences which the vast political-military overhead had imposed on the economy. Compared to Britain's former mastery, United States imperialism's period of hegemony had been indeed brief. Its symbolic end came with the final humiliating scramble of Americans onto evacuation helicopters in Saigon during April 1975.

The exhaustion and contradictions of the postwar political economy meant the return of structural unemployment even as the military budget was so high as to offer no hope for resolving that dilemma without creating other problems the United States could not risk in the global context in which the dollar was so vulnerable. The scale of international economic integration was already too vast and precarious to accept more of the same, and the very emergence of capitalist rivals reduced the space into which United States capitalism could move to solve its problems. Others, too, were waiting their turn, and possessed the power to exercise their desires. And the very enormity and intricacy of the existing world economy produced the interacting mechanisms that created dangers on every hand, so that size and complexity, in the context of structural fragility, itself became one of the system's greatest sources of weakness. By a process of accretion, all the political, economic, and military premises of American postwar ambitions began failing with increasing frequency, so that by the 1970s it was plain that all of the problems and risks inherent in the postwar system since its inception had finally fully ripened. Size, maturity, and integration all combined amounted to a formula for troubles in a system that had exhausted its flexibility as the solutions of the first postwar decade now imposed a debilitating context which removed optional responses that had both solved problems and created others at one and the same time.

In the end, all that the new stage of the failure of capitalist integration made certain was uncertainty itself, presenting only the prospect of a destiny of many and frequent crises. If radical critics cannot predict a timetable or the exact magnitude of future difficulties, men-of-power have no viable and durable means for avoiding them. For those ruling America's political and economic institutions, the challenges were theirs to inherit and resolve, and their past incapacity to do so without generating turmoil for the rest of American society and war for Third World nations bequeathed the opening of the second century of modern American history a tortuous future.

The Crisis of American Foreign Policy

By the end of its first century as a modern nation the United States was deeply enmeshed in a profound crisis of priorities and power which its leaders freely acknowledged but for which they had no cure. "I feel we are at a watershed," Henry Kissinger admitted in January 1975. "We are at a period which in retrospect is either going to be seen as a period of extraordinary creativity or a period when really the international order came apart—politically, economically, and morally. . . . If we miss the opportunity, I think there is going to be chaos."[31] And since it had disintegrated more quickly with Kissinger at the helm than during any other period in recent American history, which option would be realized was a foregone conclusion.

That tortured recognition began with Washington's hesitant, partial awareness after 1971 that its vast investment of resources in

Vietnam was the most important overcommitment of American power of the past century, and the very success of technicians like Kissinger and Schlesinger reflected the failure of traditional strategies and leaders, and the hope that the academic high priests could accomplish with their verbalism and presumed insights what the professionals and Wall Street lawyers had not. That the failure was structural, and the mandarins could do no more about it than others, was a reality Washington and purveyors of conventional wisdom would not so readily admit, but America's increasing difficulties made it evident nonetheless.

The collapse of confidence in the efficacy and mechanisms of United States foreign policy was very much a part of the greater dilemma of the limits of social knowledge in managing American capitalism. The vastly increased complexity that the American domestic and international political economy had created only made control over the application and stabilization of United States power at home and abroad that much more difficult. And because solutions to challenges now had to become more comprehensive and costly, they also became more dangerous and politically impossible—and thereby more elusive. In fact, long before 1976 remedial actions had become insufficient to cope with the vast accumulation of new structural problems along with more traditional dilemmas, with the post-1945 society of improvisation and gargantuan spending now largely adrift. Capitalism was an always changing order, full of new configurations that upset established patterns and made irrelevant past solutions. Yet there were more than structural constraints on saving the system. Given the limits of their social knowledge, both in defining answers, as well as in applying them correctly on a global scale, the directors of the system were bewildered and had lost one vital capacity for mastery, virtually guaranteeing that modern America's second century from its inception would be quite unlike the first, with hubris a mood that repeated failures would hardly long sustain.

America's disastrous fascination in Vietnam with its technology and the symbolism of its purposes there led to a fatal myopia which some in Washington during 1970–1971 vainly attempted to alter. In the spring of 1971 Secretary of State William Rogers, who had little responsibility for the overall management of foreign affairs, announced that the United States would impose formal priorities to guide foreign policy. Yet no sooner were guidelines defined than American leaders ignored them, as the unanticipated consequences of past economic and military failures created new concrete challenges and diversions. And given the universal objectives of United States foreign policy, with its 370 treaties on every conceivable topic by the 1970s, its over 300 major bases abroad, and adventures and interests everywhere, the imposition of rationality and control on the inherently mercurial became just another chimera. Most of the crises to which America was to respond for the next five years were unanticipated and, more important, unwanted.

The so-called Watergate scandal alone sufficed to send the leaders of the nation off on new distractions quite unlike those that are predictable in principle, if not detail. Watergate was an outcome of the general loss of confidence in only a man among the leaders of American society, and although Nixon also believed in the traditional ends of United States foreign policy, he had badly abused, largely by excluding them, many of the constituencies that traditionally gave it guidance. In terms of actual legal violations, the administration's peculations were no more than customary, and the bald lies and criminality which Nixon's Indochina policy involved caused the offenses of Watergate to pale to insignificance by contrast. This process, which Kissinger's systematic concentration of foreign policy decision-making in his own hands reinforced, ended by leaving the Secretary of State far more powerful. It stimulated the reemergence of Congress as a vehicle for the inhibition of those foreign policies displeasing to powerful constituencies, and placed at least a momentary brake on Executive authority. It did not, however, alter the goals of United States policy or those fundamental shared commitments and interests which bound the President and his critics together, much less reduce America's already massive existing dilemmas. Perhaps more than anything else, Watergate showed the strains that the frustrations as well as the abuse of the prerogatives of foreign policy had created, thereby further intensifying a disunity within the power structure that had once been traditional to it on the level of practice if not ultimate purposes.[32] The Watergate crisis was a symptom of battle fatigue in the face of past and future failures in the conduct of American power.

Perhaps no less consequential was the fact that the originally often cynical symbolism and means employed in foreign policy after 1946, at least in the noneconomic fields, increasingly over time became ends and introduced grave dysfunctions—both in terms of expenses and commitments of time—that further undermined all attempts to redeem a thirty-year foreign policy that had only managed in the end to reduce United States power and prestige drastically. Ideology was essential, of course, to mask the functional means inherent in the application of United States foreign policy in Third World decentralized societies, where the vast use of munitions and firepower, as in Indochina, made war against an entire population and war crimes intrinsic to the very process. The technological fetishism this mode of warfare reflected was both good for business as well as a genuine article of belief in a society in which machinery is alleged to be omnipotent for every problem. And citing the defense of "order" and "law" was a more convenient justification for its support of police, jails, and torture than their simple effectiveness in stamping out opponents to the will of its numerous client police states from Brazil to Vietnam.

National "credibility," "dominoes," or "treaty obligations" caused the United States to persist with the Indochina debacle long after it was plainly apparent it had irrevocably lost that war and would lose much more elsewhere if it continued with its folly. However rationally motivated the origins of these doctrines were in terms of rationalizing the expansion of imperialism, by 1976 they became a menace insofar as they forced objectives on the United States that far exceeded its capacities to attain. "The American Destiny" "dominoes," and "credibility" which the Secretaries of State and Defense and the President continued to cite at the beginning of 1975, despite the fact that they could no longer always convince either Congress or the press with such verbiage, revealed only how reified earlier rationalizations had become, and how inflexible the system was before the fluid and enormous challenges it now confronted.[33] The conventional wisdom of thirty years was acceptable, but it had become increasingly self-destructive to a system that was structurally incapable of veering from its collision course.

In fact, despite its abortive efforts at imposing priorities and constraints on its conduct, it was plain by 1976 after the Angola debacle that Washington had not learned enough from its monumental Indochina defeat to make a difference in the way it related to challenges to its power in the world both from the Left and its nominal allies. Its half-hearted search after May 1975 for a new global doctrine which would bring its definition of goals, interests, and resources together to master a world of certain surprises was exactly like all earlier postwar efforts to unify priorities and actions—and to somehow overcome the increasingly great limits on American power. "The phrase that the United States cannot be the world's policeman is one of those generalities that needs some refinement," Kissinger could state at the end of 1975 with the same compulsive rationale that had made possible three decades of unrelenting aggression—and guaranteed its continuation. "The fact of the matter is that security and progress in most parts of the world depend on some American commitment."[34] While there were cruder reasons beneath the purposes of its actions in terms of its ultimate objectives, experience had shown that to impute excess rationality to the routine formulation and conduct of United States foreign policy was not only an error but slighted the manner by which Washington itself undermined the attainment of its structural goals. American capitalism, both at home and abroad, was always changing, always full of new alignments within its power structure, continuously facing new problems to produce new dysfunctions at a tactical level: a Vietnam, a Nixon, oil firms nearly pricing out of its market an auto industry, and a sequence of seemingly never-ending crises that were now a predictable part of a century which had been full of them. The very existence of divisions among power constituencies, each proposing strategies to advance its own goals but usually necessarily damaging those of other factions within the power structure, meant that a tactically coherent foreign policy direction was impossible, with free traders opposing protectionists, a pro-Israel bloc and the oil majors in conflict, arms producers and advocates of détente at loggerheads, and so much more.

To a critical and dysfunctional degree, to repeat, the law of capitalist society and its foreign policy was that it had no rules or trends sufficiently precise for administrative control, and hence instability from many different domestic and global sources—economic, political, social—continuously plagued it. It could not formulate a consistent reflective ideology adequate to guide a practice too diverse to be codified, and the feeble efforts to do so usually consisted of the fatal error, which Cordell Hull personified, of advancing into the future on the basis of the lessons learned in the past—thereby limiting perceptions, yet having no viable alternatives short of the application of such leverage as sheer power affords. Rather than guiding it, America's ideological mystifications merely reflected the absence of clarity among leaders and the led. The vast distance between social reality and social analysis and responses that had historically characterized the system both at home and abroad continued to intensify, even accelerate, capitalism's weaknesses. Yet this void was not simply a consequence of a lack of competence among men-of-power, but reflected the truth that one could not regulate or redeem such a system.

11

Epilogue: The Continuity of Past and Present

The legacies of the past rest heavily on the present, and despite the distinctive problems that emerged after 1976, continuity between past and present is still the dominant characteristic of contemporary American history. The unique promises and sincere intentions of both Presidents Carter and Reagan notwithstanding, inertia and the enormous residues of earlier ambitions and failures persistently intruded on them, frustrating their domestic and foreign policies.

The line between domestic and foreign affairs and interests became increasingly blurred after 1976, particularly when economic questions were involved, and their growing mutual contradictions prevented a coherent policy in either area. This dilemma also accelerated the decline of American influence over the political and economic direction of the world. The extent to which successive administrations merely responded to problems which arose faster than solutions for them could be found became increasingly apparent by the end of the first Reagan Administration. A now disquieted American people, uncertain about the government's conventional wisdom yet still unwilling to transcend it, watched as their nation drifted to a destiny increasingly determined by events and forces beyond the control of those at the helm.

The tension between domestic and international needs and priorities recurs over and over in modern American history, beginning with Wilson and culminating with the Johnson Administration's Great Society program, which the Vietnam War dissipated. Presidents have usually chosen to stress domestic issues because of the political imperatives of obtaining supporters or votes and satisfying those powerful elements in the social order that have been able to impose their priorities on the federal government's agenda for action. In reality, of course, each administration was compelled to deal with domestic and foreign issues simultaneously. Although the Carter and Reagan Administrations had clear differences in tone, image, and proclaimed intentions, they ultimately groped primarily with the same traditional dilemmas both at home and abroad. And while it is important not to minimize their dissimilarities, it is also essential to a comprehension of the modern American historical experience to appreciate both the origins of their distinctions and the forces which so quickly eroded them.

The Evolving Domestic Context: Changing the Regulatory System

Every President is elected with practical or moral debts to those who supported him, and Jimmy Carter in 1977 was no exception. While Carter, unlike Reagan, immediately sought to stress foreign rather than domestic affairs, both his accumulated political obligations and events themselves forced national questions into his purview. Favorable economic conditions during the first half of his term allowed him some discretion, but slow growth after 1979 and then the recession and sharply increased unemployment that began in 1980 rudely intruded on both Carter and his successor. More important was the persistently high inflation which began with the Vietnam War in 1966 and which became a new structural aspect and destabilizing threat to the American economy, reaching an unprecedented 13.5 percent in 1980. Inflationary pressures are highly corrosive to existing economic relationships and upset numerous powerful economic interests as well as the entire population. The result was a growing cacophony of demands to resolve the perplexing economic and social problems inflation brought with it. Such economic challenges as well as regulation quickly intruded themselves upon the Carter Administration, and Reagan promised to make them his principal concern.

As I discussed in chapter one, federal intervention into all phases of the economy was from its inception largely pragmatic in origin, and was designed to meet the economic needs of the politically most powerful sector of the regulated industry. Regulation and social legislation can be defined as arenas in which various interests and constituencies seek to obtain through political means what they cannot otherwise, making political competition quite as crucial as economic in determining the nature of power and profit in American society. As the distribution of political power within an industry as well as its objective requirements changed, so too did the nature of regulation. By the time the Carter Administration came to office the future of federal regulation was very much on the business community's agenda as various interests sought major changes. Ironically, while Reagan was to say far more about removing regulation than his predecessor, it was the Democratic administration that was to move most aggressively to do so.

Passage of a spate of environmental and safety laws during the late 1960s had by 1977 vastly expanded the variety of issues involved in the future of regulation. Moreover, the market structure as well as the desires of various regulated industries had changed greatly over the decades. The best example of this was in banking, where the major commercial banks—most of which had earlier campaigned for the law—at the end of the 1960s began quietly to lobby for a change in the Glass-Steagall Act of 1933 which had required them to stay out of underwriting stocks and bonds. Securities firms and investment bankers, on the other hand, began fighting in the name of financial prudence to protect their lucrative monopoly while seeking themselves to diversify into some commercial bank services. By 1984 the equally matched struggle between enormously powerful financial interests had reached an advanced legislative stage in Congress. Even if the regulatory forms the industry advocated had altered, its desire for profit had not, and that was the key to change.

The deregulation of natural gas was more straightforward since the Sunbelt's natural gas industry was Carter's earliest and single most important source of funding in his campaign for the Presidency. Here decisive action was required notwithstanding the resistance of utilities and industrial consumers to any price increases. The sums involved in gas price deregulation were embarrassingly large, so much so that modest compromises proved essential, and passage of the Natural Gas Policy Act at the end of 1977 remains the speediest deregulation of any economic sector in the decade after 1975. A phased deregulation scheme which removed the majority of gas price constraints by 1985, the Act meant untold billions to Southwest producers whose main asset was that they had supported an ambitious but unknown Georgia politician in his race for the Presidency.[1]

Precisely because no other issue of deregulation involved a

group so well placed politically, most other phases of the problem persisted from the mid-1970s onwards, spilling over to the Reagan Administration. Reagan had pledged to reduce regulation but in reality arrived in office when the main contours of the struggle for changes were already fully defined. Save for reducing environmental and safety protection, he was to remain essentially passive before the forces that had already drawn themselves up against each other in Congress.

The most classic regulatory problems involved the railroads, which transferred all passenger services to the federal government in 1971 and received a $2 billion subsidy in return over the next five years. In 1976, with the projected subsidy three times that and the freight sector sorely in need of yet more, the extent to which the function of federal regulation was to keep alive obsolete and inefficient industries became a serious issue. A 1976 Railroad Act promised another $1.6 billion subsidy, but failed to solve the reality that less than half of the existing rail mileage was now profitable. Backed by enormously powerful local political and industrial interests, railroads had become the main beneficiary of the regulatory system, stoutly resisting its dismantling. Indeed, federal intervention in this case was merely a concealed transfer of the financial losses of sick industries to the general public. This same principle was now extended to ailing industrial firms, and beginning with Lockheed in 1971, the specialty steel industry in 1977, and Chrysler in 1979, guaranteed loans of $250 million to $1.5 billion were given to firms able to rally the votes in Congress.

In the case of trucking, whose organizations since 1948 had been allowed to fix rates and have the ICC enforce them, obsolescence or losses did not becloud the issue. The Carter Administration in 1977 sought to introduce a mild degree of price flexibility for individual shippers in what has become a high-profit industry. Small truckers and shippers also favored it, but the large truckers' association as well as the Teamsters blocked it in Congress until 1980, when, unable to prevent legislation which was quickly to hurt them, they threw their forces behind Reagan's candidacy despite his anti-regulation campaign rhetoric. They were rewarded with the selection of their candidate for the chairmanship of the ICC. When in mid-1983 more deregulation legislation finally reached Congress, Teamster and trucking-interest promises to support the President's reelection bid convinced the White House to withhold backing for what was clearly a step to implement its public commitment to free competition.[2]

With the profitable airline industry, it was again the Carter Administration that pushed through deregulation in 1978, backed by one large carrier and many smaller ones eager to grab a greater share of the market. Most big carriers and all the unions opposed it, arguing that the industry would lose money—which was indeed correct. By 1980 it was in the red, with successively larger losses in each of the following years.

Experiences with deregulation revealed much about regulation's role and development from the inception. Originally, regulation sought to protect the larger firms within the industry, maintaining income by restricting competition. The exact form deregulation took after 1976 depended, as regulation had earlier, on the political power of the various interests involved and the nature of the industries affected, with abstract ideological notions playing a minor role even when the President was nominally an ideologue. Regulation was essentially a struggle for economic gains between economic constituencies whose problems and needs changed with time, and while its form altered, its goal did not. For inflation was eroding regulation's central role in the modern American economy, compelling many firms to seek new solutions, including a temporary return to more competitive forms of doing business. Yet as these too failed, the dilemma grew in more and more of the critical industries: how could the economy resolve its own growing contradictions?

The Reagan Economic Program and the Constraints of Reality

Ronald Reagan's election in 1980 revealed both the possibilities and constraints on the Presidency and the enigmas of contemporary politics. He campaigned on a platform merging nostalgia and self-interest with utopian competitive capitalist theory which the self-made California entrepreneurs who were his main backers defined. Yet most who voted for Reagan were really protesting against Carter's failures. And while Reagan's advocacy of less economic regulation, more competition, lower taxes, and a balanced budget along with far greater military spending was an inconsistent program designed mainly to win votes and campaign funds, it also revealed those deep ideological legacies that have persisted in confusing American political dialogue for generations.

The Reagan Administration did plan to make the domestic economy and social order its first priority, a commitment its most active supporters enthusiastically shared. What surprised the President and his followers most in their first confrontation with reality was both the persistence of past economic policies and interests in inhibiting new action and the fundamental conflict between a tax reduction, a budget-balancing program, and an expansive foreign policy.

Aside from the fact that the "supply-side" economics of Reagan's campaign and first year in office was merely an assertion of the classic conservative faith that removal of government from the economy automatically solves all problems, it was inherently impossible to cut taxes 10 percent a year for three years and balance the budget by 1984. Throughout 1981 the Budget director, David A. Stockman, saw the debacle of Reaganomics coming, admitting, ". . . we [had] to get a program out fast . . . in a 20- or 25-day time frame, and we didn't think it all the way through. We didn't add up all the numbers."[3]

By summer 1981 Congress began stoutly resisting the President's proposals and defending their constituencies' immense interests in their favorite subsidies and spending programs. As the President tried to raise military spending and cut taxes simultaneously the economy fell even more deeply into a malaise which quickly alienated his initial supporters and made his policies appear both confused and adventurist. The highest interest rates in American history in 1981, the biggest post-1946 drop in the gross national product in 1982, the greatest and longest postwar unemployment during 1982–83 along with sharply reduced profits and the lowest capacity utilization rate in manufacturing since the 1930s . . . all the results destroyed Reagan's domestic dreams. Most of his supply-side advocates were gone by the summer of 1982, but not before the damage had been done. With a federal budget deficit in 1981 of $58 billion, the following year it grew to $111 billion, and in 1983 it was $195 billion, with predictions of even higher amounts for the following years.

Reagan did not invent the nation's basic postwar structural problems; he only exacerbated them. Just as changes in the regulatory system had begun under Carter and gone much further under him, so too there was a direct continuity between the fate of the social welfare system under both Presidencies, revealing that not even the most audacious men could easily transform basic problems and patterns confronting the nation. After the Vietnam War, inflation persistently undermined the entire Social Security system, from old-age benefits to unemployment compensation, making constant and increasingly costly changes in them a rising dilemma. In 1977, hoping to cope with a decade's accumulating problems, Congress made a major revision in the Social Security Act, projecting a rate of inflation and unemployment that quickly proved wholly unrealistic. It failed to address its fundamental weakness—the pay-as-you-go structure—and by 1982 the system was in deficit and, depending on trends in the economy, losses were projected to reach $19 to $85 billion by 1986. Early Reagan Administration efforts to reduce retirement benefits met a stone wall of opposition in Congress, forcing a compromise law in April 1983 which essentially kept the existing system intact but still left open the possibility of another actuarial crisis should the economy perform worse than anticipated.

But inflation and unemployment also began creating myriad new economic problems. Household indebtedness rose sharply after 1976 to unprecedented postwar levels, only to plunge after 1980 in a manner which protracted the recession. Combined with unemployment, which hit 8.5 percent in 1975 and after dropping over the next four years was 9.6 percent in 1983, the results appeared in an exceptional new trend in modern American history: real wages of workers in the entire private, nonfarm sector began a sharp long-term decline after 1972, dropping 15 percent by 1983.

By late 1982 the Reagan Administration's self-confidence in domestic matters had fallen precipitously and it contented itself with patching up a program that was both less exotic and more attuned to its own reelection prospects and to the enormous vested interests in Congress and the business community who were successfully resisting all efforts to impinge on their favorite programs. A $98 billion tax increase in August 1982 neutralized the cut of the preceding year as administration spokesmen admitted the supply-side program had failed, and with the election of twenty-six more Democrats to the House the following November the President further lost his ability to control his own Party. From that point onward his effort to increase military expenditures, which had grown from 24 percent of the budget in 1981 and was originally scheduled to be 32 percent in 1984, was subjected to stout and growing Congressional and business resistance, compelling the administration to significantly reduce its ambitions. Political exigencies and the economy had quite quickly managed to wear down the most ideological President in modern American history, leaving his administration adrift and subject to uncontrollable forces to which it responded with growing perplexity.

The Growing Integration of the American and World Economies

In part this loss of mastery was due to the analytic myopia which has increasingly plagued the national government since Franklin Roosevelt: it has simply been unable to understand the nature of American society, its problems and their solutions, quickly enough to head them off. Social reform, regulation, and economic management in a highly dynamic, fluid nation increasingly involved in a yet far more uncontrollable world had by the mid-1970s reached a point where persistent failures were exhausting the social order's abilities to cope with such a diverse reality.

The trends were clear, the problems also. America's exports as a proportion of the GNP doubled between 1970 and 1980, and over the same time the share of United States corporate profits coming from direct overseas investments increased from 12 to 33 percent. Nearly five million jobs in 1980 were linked to the export of manufactures, and by the early 1980s well over one quarter of the value of all farm products, double the share of a decade earlier, was being exported. Four-fifths of the new jobs in manufacturing between 1977 and 1980 were linked in some way to exports. At the same time, the sharp post-1971 fluctuations in the value of the United States dollar by 1976 had begun to erode the American balance of trade, which hit a record deficit of $43 billion in 1982, climbed to well over $70 million in 1983, and was projected to be $110 billion in 1984. Temporarily spared resolving this crisis because of the enormous flow of foreign capital into the United States in search of high interest, the American economy was on the horns of an irreconcilable dilemma. The moment it resorted to more protectionist measures to balance its trade, other nations would reduce their imports of its goods; either way the American economy would suffer, and frequent international conferences to prevent a world trade war failed to alter its growing imminence.

Even more ominous was the spiralling world debt structure that banks, led by United States firms, created after 1970. In 1971 the non–oil-developing countries held $50 billion in external debts, but it increased to $400 billion in 1980, half held by private banks. By

1984 it had reached an estimated $700 billion. With it came insoluble debt service difficulties for these nations, which merely kept borrowing without any solutions to reverse their indebtedness. So long as banks could continue the borrowing cycle they made fabulous profits, but by the end of 1982 the ten largest United States banks had sums equal to 169 percent of their entire equity tied up in the most troubled countries. The problem of how to resolve this paradoxical outcome of universal greed and naiveté became the topic of endless meetings and conferences seeking to head off the collapse of the world capitalist economy.

This astonishing vulnerability of the American to the world economy was by the 1980s the main structural outcome of its sustained effort to integrate the global order along Wilsonian lines. Rather than attaining a stable and prosperous international system it had managed to stimulate high economic growth in the context of structural changes that also produced enormously perplexing challenges. Its fate was directly dependent on increasingly uncontrollable trends beyond its borders.

American Global Ambitions and Reality: The Carter Administration

The world the United States had sought to remold after 1945 has become increasingly diverse both politically and economically, and the passage of time and shifting distribution of world military and economic power added to its difficulties as America's resources became more discernibly finite even as its goals remained constant. And since reducing its global objectives exceeded the willingness and ability of either the Carter or Reagan Administrations, in a fundamental sense American efforts since the Vietnam debacle have been composed of increasingly futile and dangerous attempts to transcend the limits of its own power.

Despite the historic importance of the Vietnam War, no foreign policy leader reflected seriously on its meaning to future action, and when Carter became President he surrounded himself with men drawn from the tiny circle of the foreign policy Establishment: men who had worked for Johnson, Nixon, and Ford and who shared core assumptions and styles of operation. Such men are not partisan in the American political sense and generally regard foreign policy problems as technical issues within the framework of a binding consensus.

Kissinger helped Cyrus Vance during the State Department transition, and Vance kept four of Kissinger's advisors. Carter himself, when he initiated his race for the nomination in 1973, joined the newly formed Trilateral Commission of key American, Japanese, and Western European business and foreign policy leaders seeking to prevent the emergence of exclusive trade and political alliances in the wake of growing world economic problems. Linked to numerous other equally influential groups, the Trilateral supplied him with many classically bipartisan advisors, including his National Security assistant, Zbigniew Brzezinski.

While such men were interchangable with those in any postwar administration, Carter during his first one hundred days in office sought to create a distinctive image of himself as someone "bold, imaginative and skeptical—in short, refreshing."[4] This posture was also an attempt to preempt future political challenges from both wings of his Party. From the inception, therefore, he emerged with the reputation of being an unorthodox innovator on a number of key foreign policy questions, but since he never intended to reject inherited wisdom he eventually also appeared confused and inconsistent.

Tackling the human rights question was the first of his errors, and while largely conceived as a part of image building it was also a reflection of a more serious dilemma in American foreign policy. As Washington has learned repeatedly since 1946, the most repressive dictatorships are the most easily overthrown and also provide Leftist parties with the best environment for growth. America has searched continuously since 1945 for honest, reasonably democratic men who are ready to act as willing collaborators—with no success. When compelled to choose between sycophancy and obedience or independence and honesty in foreign political leaders, the United States has invariably opted for the former. It has often done so reluctantly, for both its own ideology and practical considerations make it a dubious choice, and after the fall of Saigon even Kissinger doubted the wisdom of such expediency. At the end of 1976 both CIA and State Department officials were questioning American support for the brutally repressive Park Chung Hee regime in South Korea for precisely such reasons.

Since both the public and Congress were concerned with human rights the new administration created the proper image by mildly complaining about South Korea, Uganda, Argentina, Uruguay, and Ethiopia, with modest military aid cuts to the last three. Yet when an American diplomat in early March 1977 publicly linked the United States to the overthrow of Allende in Chile and the subsequent reign of terror the President personally chastised him, and by April, the one hundred days over, the administration was in full retreat on the issue.

Important nations capable of surviving without United States support, such as Iran, Brazil, and Indonesia, were from the inception of this policy exempted from Washington's barbs on repression and terror. This decision reached the heart of America's foreign policy dilemma and revealed its own dependency and weaknesses in relying on surrogates. Iran proved the greatest challenge to the Carter Administration, epitomizing the dysfunction of its reliance on decadent regimes as well as American economic vulnerability and military weakness in the face of its allies' collapse.

Iran and the Dilemma of American Power

Washington installed the Shah of Iran after the CIA organized the overthrow of the nationalist Mossadegh government in 1953. Seeking to build a modern army, the Shah spent a large part of the nation's wealth to buy $18 billion in arms from the United States by 1977, absorbing one-quarter of all American arms sales after 1950. Washington saw Iran, its key link in the Gulf region, as crucial to the global economics and geopolitics of oil as well as the military control of the area. Visiting Teheran at the end of 1977, President Carter feted Iran as "an island of stability" in the region.[5] Within months a growing opposition under the direction of mainly religious leaders, fully aware of America's role as the Shah's major supporter, began leading the first effective opposition since 1953 to the astonishingly corrupt and notoriously repressive regime. In the last months of 1978, as resistance reached vast proportions and the Shah's police and army shot thousands of protestors, Carter stood loyally by him. When elements of his own military forced him finally to go into exile in January 1979, fundamentalist Islamic forces bent on destroying American influence in the country quickly triumphed. In the months that followed American power looked pathetic, and when the Ayatollah Khomeini in November ordered the seizure of the American embassy and kept fifty-three of its employees hostage all of the problems of contemporary foreign policy crystallized around the sustained crisis. By the time he left office, the President could count Iran as his major foreign policy disaster.

After Vietnam, concern over the "credibility" of American power became the dominant theme in Washington's responses to foreign policy crises. Yet it was more aware than ever that the mere application of power to prove American might could very well entangle it in protracted conflicts that would lead to a loss of control over its priorities. In the combination of support for unstable regimes, credibility, and fear of the domino, the Carter Administration maintained all the dilemmas that have plagued United States foreign policy before and since. To break out of this contradictory and repeatedly uncontrollable crisis-producing context became Carter's main preoccupation.

The Carter Administration responded to this problem primarily by attempting triangular diplomacy and by developing a military capability appropriate for a limited war that it knew could break out anywhere in the world. Despite this administration's "human rights" campaign it instinctively staked American interests on pliant undemocratic and corrupt regimes in the Third World. Washington's primary objective was to neutralize Soviet power and free American forces for the vast areas of instability and crisis in the rest of the world.

Creating military power was the least complex aspect of this strategy, and it no more occurred to Carter's advisors that arms would fail them as it had their predecessors than did the notion of reducing American globalism's unlimited goals. Within months of coming to office the Carter Administration decided to create a 100,000-man "rapid deployment force" (RDF), able, as the President later described it, "to protect our own interest and to act in response to requests for help from our allies and friends."[6] Authorizing the expansion of advance bases, such as Diego Garcia in the Indian Ocean, the real impetus to the RDF came with the Shah's fall and the collapse of the dictatorial 46-year-old Somoza regime in Nicaragua in July 1979. When Central America thus intruded itself into Washington's focus, the administration concluded that its other right-wing allies in the region were also in danger. In October 1979, after Brzezinski pressed for action, top priority was given to procuring the equipment the RDF needed to airlift itself and its heavy equipment anywhere in the world. It was also at this time that the Carter Administration went on record for a substantially larger increase in military spending through 1984, and the 1980 defense budget grew 15 percent over the preceding year. Crucial to its assumptions was that America would be able and willing to intervene decisively and efficiently anywhere in the world to prove the credibility of American power.

Diplomacy was directly linked to the administration's arms policy and plans for local interventions, notwithstanding a bitter dispute among Carter's advisors over whether it should take an anti-Soviet direction or attempt to press for détente and arms control. Even before the new President came to office a growing number of strategists, Brzezinski included, decided that China was no longer an expansionist power and that Washington could employ it as leverage to obtain Soviet cooperation outside of Asia. "Triangulation," first attempted successfully to obtain Chinese assistance in reaching the 1973 Vietnam peace settlement, now could be used to stabilize Southeast Asia, where Chinese influence seemed crucial, and penalize the Russians should they persist in helping countries the United States opposed. Secretary of State Cyrus R. Vance thought the strategy might provoke the Soviets in Europe, and would fail in any case. But Brzezinski prevailed and in the spring of 1978 traveled to China and publicly linked Soviet policy in Africa to American aid to China. Although the Chinese were delighted to cooperate and thought a strategic alliance with Washington might become the basis of their foreign policy, too many reservations existed among influential policymakers outside the White House. By 1980, after full diplomatic relations were established, the triangulation policy stalled, not the least because China still had ambitions in Taiwan and other regions which many of America's older allies thought dangerous. Still, as a potential if not a real threat, playing the "China card" was a new factor in Washington's global strategy.

The success of triangulation encouraged the White House to its next major move: confronting the implications of xenophobic theocracy in Iran to America's position in the whole crucial Persian Gulf region. That the new regime was also anti-Communist made slight difference, for it was destabilizing to the feudal societies in the area and it was in a position to control, and even cut off, vast petroleum resources. While credibility was also an important consideration, mastery of the region's oil was now crucial to the entire world capitalist system. That preoccupation was very much on the Carter Administration's mind when the Russians invaded Afghanistan in January 1980, even though the Persian Gulf itself was not directly menaced and a pro-Soviet regime had existed in Kabul since mid-1978.

On January 23, 1980, the President proclaimed the "Carter Doctrine," the most ambitious, open-ended commitment of American power in the world since the 1947 Truman Doctrine. But unlike the Truman Doctrine, Carter's was hastily improvised without consultation with the State Department and Congress, and it was not clear, whatever else it might mean elsewhere, just what it could accomplish in a region where the major threat now came from a militant and expansive Islam and a nationalism that was, ironically, also anti-Marxist. For what the United States was now opposing was not merely Communism but change itself, and even its friends in the region were increasingly unsure if they wanted American help.

The Carter Doctrine warned any "outside force" seeking "to gain control of the Persian Gulf region" that it would be attacking the "vital interests" of the United States, which would use all of its means to repel it. Such intervention was no longer dependent on a request for help from a specific nation, and it ignored the fact that the War Powers Act of 1973 reaffirmed Congress's right to prohibit American troops from fighting longer than sixty days. Worse yet, senior State Department officials argued, there was no security framework to support American intervention, nor was there yet a rapid deployment force capable of acting unilaterally. The following month both Carter and Defense Secretary Harold Brown went one step further, enunciating a concept comparable to Dulles's "by means and at places of our choosing" in his warnings to the Russians and Chinese in January 1954. Should the Russians invade the Gulf region, the President stated, "We cannot afford to let the Soviets choose either the terrain or the tactics." "The Soviets couldn't count on it being confined there," Brown added, and both the weapons, forces, and location of the American response were to remain its discretion.

The Carter Doctrine placed the President on the defensive, from which he never recovered. "If the industrial democracies are deprived of access to those resources," Brown tried to argue against a wave of domestic criticism, "there would almost certainly be a worldwide economic collapse of the kind that hasn't been seen for almost fifty years, probably worse."[7] Now the problem of economic power merged with credibility, for at the beginning of 1980 the

Carter Administration looked both confused and weak, and its impotence goaded it into action to refurbish America's image in the world by attempting to rescue the fifty-three hostages in Teheran. On the night of April 24, the most modern American technology was sent to rescue them and also restore the national psyche. Eight ultra-modern helicopters with one hundred commandos took off on the mission, but three developed mechanical problems and the effort was cancelled. As it tried to withdraw, one helicopter collided with a United States C-130 airplane, killing eight men. "The mission was complex and difficult," a humiliated Harold Brown told a press conference the next morning.[8] American technology had ruined it!

Despite its obsessive struggle to master events in Iran, the United States suffered a major defeat at the hands of militant Islam. But if the failure of American resources taught nothing more to those in power than it had to its predecessors, it did convince the American public that it wanted no more of Jimmy Carter. What is surprising is that any differences between the Georgian and the Californian, despite Reagan's bellicose rhetoric, were clearly going to be of degree rather than of kind. Both hoped to reverse the deepening failures of American globalism, and they were ready, at least verbally, to intervene virtually anywhere in order to do so. Money would not prove an obstacle to either, and their means and goals proved remarkably similar. So too did the sheer magnitude of the challenges facing them.

Reagan and the Dilemma of Foreign Policy

Although Reagan had gone on record for greatly increased military spending for both strategic and local war, the sagging state of the economy as well as difficulties with Congress over his domestic economic policies, particularly his huge budget deficits, soon entangled his military and foreign policies in a web of insoluble contradictory problems. During the first two years, the Reagan Administration sought to avoid any major foreign policy decisions or crises that might erode further its shaky Congressional coalition. The strong-willed Secretary of State, Alexander Haig, articulated an aggressive rhetorical stance on numerous issues, but opposition from the Pentagon to a variety of plans for military intervention in Central America or the Middle East and the inhibiting White House preoccupation with domestic problems revealed the complex difficulties of managing American world ambitions in a period of economic stagnation both at home and abroad.

Also, events quickly disclosed the extent to which personalities could temporarily confound the already immensely complex task of applying the President's foreign policy campaign pledges of taking a tougher line to the USSR and defending Taiwan against China. As Kissinger's protegé, Haig was very much in favor of continuing the de facto alliance with China, yet he was unable to overcome the White House's commitment to Taiwan or its basic skepticism toward "triangulation." Relations with China cooled very quickly to the lowest point since 1972, recovering somewhat during 1983–84. The Reagan Administration's decision to deploy cruise and Pershing missiles in Western Europe starting in 1983 as well as to build MX and other sophisticated strategic weapons was about as much of a challenge to the Soviets as hard-line advisors thought necessary.

Reagan's abrupt removal of Haig in June 1982 failed to have any beneficial impact on the overwhelming difficulties facing the United States throughout the world. Despite differences in emphasis, the Reagan Administration was soon forced to adapt variations of its predecessor's main policies as it began to look and act, if not talk, like just another traditional postwar government. By 1983, with its domestic economic plans in tatters and gigantic budget deficits projected into the indefinite future, the White House's concerns shifted increasingly to foreign affairs as its policies became more and more assertive.

The years 1982 and 1983 were unusually troubled ones for the world. Crises in Lebanon and the Gulf region, mounting upheaval in Central America, war between Britain and Argentina over the Falklands, and rising Western European opposition to the installation of American missiles all forced Washington to try more actively to regulate a turbulent, swirling world challenging its hegemony and guidance. In attempting to allocate increasingly finite American power in the 1980s, however, the vastly more threatening and precarious domestic and international economic situation made such a rational ordering of commitments at once all the more imperative and all the more difficult.

The first major effort to resolve the priorities riddle came in February 1982 with the Pentagon's 1983 budget request, part of a four-year plan to spend $200 billion more over a five-year period than the Carter Administration had proposed. Apart from upgrading strategic missile delivery systems, the Pentagon began to indicate how it ranked regions in its own planning for future wars, stressing first the critical position of Western Europe, followed by the need to keep open the oil routes leading from the Persian Gulf. But it then left open the possibility of action in Africa, East Asia, and Latin America, without attaching specific priorities. The following April, Defense Secretary Caspar Weinberger made it clear that the United States would not forego intervening anywhere in the world lest the USSR enter the vacuum, leaving the Pentagon again with the need to be able to fight everywhere.

Because effective military responses to any and every local conflict are a technical and economic impossibility, the Reagan Administration endorsed a doctrine of "horizontal escalation" very much like that in the Carter Doctrine or in Dulles's 1953 statement on "massive retaliation." Should the USSR attack a nation the United States considered vital, American forces "may also have to launch counter-offensives elsewhere, . . ." where Soviet interests are vulnerable.[9] For example, a conflict in South Asia might see the United States attack Cuba. The most obvious military and geopolitical limit of "horizontal escalation" is that it did not seem at first to deal with autonomous revolutionary forces taking orders from no one, yet willing to accept Soviet aid. During late 1983 the Reagan Administration sought to answer this dilemma by suggesting that in Central America, Lebanon, and elsewhere, Moscow could be seen as somehow goading Salvadoran peasants, Druse militiamen, or Grenadans to action, a vision of diabolical Russian power that did not solve the problems of American priorities and finite power but only aggravated them by threatening to spread a local war in one part of the world elsewhere.

Such threats were explicitly intended, at the very least, to push the USSR to increase its arms spending, further weakening its ability to deal with its pressing internal economic problems. Reagan's strategy revived the confrontational rhetoric of the Cold War's worst days, raised economic costs to America and her allies at a time they were least able to afford it, and thereby helped to galvanize a growing opposition to the arms race and the world's endless political tensions both at home and in Western Europe that was unique in the post-1945 era. Fear of nuclear war grew to the extent that the solidity of the NATO alliance was seriously eroded and a vast number of people in the world made themselves a significant political force as they became unwilling to live passively with the reality of constant local wars, including the ultimate risk of global nuclear destruction.

Apart from the enormous anti-bomb movement which spread throughout Europe and Japan after 1981 was the further decline of a consensus on foreign policy questions within the United States which had begun with the Vietnam War. A gradual alienation of the American people towards politics and politicians since then showed up in the proportion of qualified voters casting a Presidential vote: what was 63 percent in 1960 fell to 56 percent in 1972, with the right of 18-year-olds to vote, and declined to 53 percent in 1980, when Reagan was elected with the votes of only 28 percent of those eligible to cast a ballot. Public apathy masked a very real reservoir of mass political alienation. Congress too began to emerge as more of an obstacle to an administration's military and foreign policies than any time since 1947. Apart from threatening to evoke the War Powers Act of 1973 in Central America, it immediately created other obstacles, forcing the administration through numerous ordeals and compromises to obtain the MX intercontinental missile after the House in December 1982, in the first such vote on a major weapons system since 1946, refused to give the President funds. The growth of a large and very respectable nuclear freeze and anti-bomb movement, which mobilized over 750,000 people in a New York City demonstration in June 1982, forced Congress to look carefully at the articulate minority willing to work for its goals and therefore far more potent politically than those who remained silent. By April 1983 polls showed that Americans were six to one opposed to a United States-backed invasion of Nicaragua and a far greater number opposed involvement in El Salvador than favored it. Congress was to some lesser degree ready to follow the public climate and sharply cut military aid to El Salvador as well as block funds for "covert" CIA operations to overthrow the Sandinistas in Nicaragua. Although the public's mood varied with successes and failures, and it endorsed the quick and essentially bloodless invasion of Grenada in October 1983, public opinion polls indicated that the protracted tensions and failures produced hostility to Reagan's foreign policy that Congress finally could not ignore. At the end of September 1983, after 1,600 Marines landed in Lebanon, growing threats of United States invasions in Central America, and the Soviet downing of a South Korean airliner, the public disapproved of Reagan's foreign policy by a majority of 47 to 38 percent.

Having shifted his focus from domestic to foreign policies, the President was meeting with the same hostility to his failures—and indeed, no less an impasse. The attempt to buy answers with new technology had repeatedly failed since 1945, but what was startling was the refusal of a significant and growing portion of the population to live passively with the tension and risks inherent in the very conduct and premises of American goals in a diverse, pluralistic world. Indeed, given the new conflict between domestic social and economic needs and military spending, it was now more than simply the threat of war that was beginning to exact a toll on the public. Whether the emergence of such an articulate, broadly based opposition would be a transitional event remained to be seen, but given the permanence of the crises and the challenges to American imperialism the likelihood of more and more such resistance in the future appeared much greater.

The other constraint on Reagan was the state of the postwar American-led alliance. Economically, of course, trade and financial rivalries had begun to reach critical levels that had spilled over to East-West relations well before Reagan. The new administration immediately sought to obtain Japanese cooperation in spending more on arms and regional security as well as cutting their exports to the world and reducing their protection against imports. By 1983 Washington was hoping Japan would agree to become its main partner in the future in regulating the entire Pacific Basin on behalf of their joint interest, an ambition to which the Japanese, as usual, responded politely and evasively while assiduously consolidating their own interests. Yet the failure to attain this goal, all Americans understood, would once again make Japan potentially the most powerful barrier to American ambitions in the entire Asian region, and objectively a formidable economic and political rival.

Equally challenging was the deterioration of American relations with its NATO allies over economic, military, and political issues. Washington's failure to support England unequivocally during its Falkland Islands war with Argentina in April 1982, and the subsequent dispute over whether the United States should sell arms to Argentina, was exacerbated when the Americans invaded Grenada in October 1983 despite London's objections. Compounding this was the American effort from the summer of 1982 onwards to stop European Economic Community trade with the USSR in order to penalize the Soviets and hinder their economic development. Combined with bitter disagreements over EEC steel exports to the United States and a whole range of financial and economic issues, including high American interest rates, Washington's unsuccessful effort to stop the construction of a USSR-West European gas pipeline deeply alienated the Europeans. They also resented the installation of new missiles which disaffected large groups of Europeans who began making the issue the main item on the West German, Dutch, and other governments' political agenda.

By the 1980s the centrifugal forces of world economic problems and rivalries, the growing political burdens of membership in NATO, and the disquieting specter of possible war were seriously eroding the Western Alliance. By its very ambition, ironically, America was now beginning to become isolated in the world, less and less able to call upon its allies for a cooperation that also evokes their confidence or basic interests. If the speed with which the laboriously constructed United States-led system would come apart was uncertain, Europe's growing autonomy was nonetheless increasingly a major challenge to American power.

The Problem of Local Wars

Like all of its predecessors since 1950, the Reagan Administration still had to obtain the military power essential to its foreign policy priorities in the various regions of the world and to make this power look "credible" to America's enemies. Its first response was to continue Carter's RDF program, also concentrating its use in the Middle East. But this administration realized that airlifting the RDF's equipment 8,000 miles would prove difficult and it began considering storing heavy arms in the region in advance, permanently stationing American forces there also, as well as relying more on its local allies' manpower. After the Israeli invasion of Lebanon in 1982, Washington's Middle East strategy became confused, particularly after Israel rejected the President's short-lived plan for settling the Palestinian question. The Reagan Administration, like most of its predecessors since 1945, split publicly on which Middle East nation to support, and Haig's endorsement of Israel was one critical factor in his being pushed aside for George Shultz. That American-supplied arms to

Israel were being used for an aggression the United States strongly condemned clearly illustrated the problem of military aid to nations at war with neighbors. Meanwhile, by the spring of 1983 the Pentagon was looking forward to 1986 as the year it would have its RDF in the Gulf ready to fight, although against whom and with whose assistance remained obscure.

It did not take the Reagan Administration long to realize that the complexities of the world made its RDF in the Gulf appear a bit quixotic. Global political events were not evolving to conform to the carefully planned advance locations of its arms or troops, much less to its elaborately calculated priorities, as indeed they had not since 1945. CIA efforts in Central America had failed. Its growing efforts to destabilize Nicaragua as well as save the repressive right-wing El Salvador regime were still bearing little fruit, and its contemplated 1981 covert operation against Grenada had been stopped in the Senate. Yet Washington concluded in July 1983 that maintaining the chain of corrupt conservative governments in El Salvador, Guatemala, and Honduras now required eliminating the Sandinistas in Nicaragua. Not only were counterrevolutionary forces armed despite initial House votes against it, but American technicians began to provide key services for them, using CIA equipment. Most importantly, the United States in the summer of 1983 initiated a vast base complex in Honduras as periodic military maneuvers were inaugurated for an indefinite period and threatened a naval blockade of Nicaragua. The National Security Council on July 8 endorsed the domino theory for Central America, and several months later senior administration spokesmen made it plain that the overthrow of the Sandinistas was official policy. Yet the decisive inhibition to any single military action remained the basic dilemma also plaguing its general commitment to interventions everywhere in the world: the United States knew that it did not have either the political or military strength to fight successfully a protracted war in Central America, yet it had no assurance that once intervening it could avoid it. Sponsoring harassment from neighboring governments and various right-wing elements still seemed its only alternative, yet it, too, was not likely to succeed.

True to past experiences, American priorities tend to be determined by where the nation's direct combat involvement is greatest —this meant that the world's problems exceeded the Pentagon's capacity to cope with them and undermined the RDF concept. In

Washington, the Pentagon alone during 1983 doubted the feasibility of fighting in Central America without Congressional approval, and since it admitted that the United States-backed regimes were losing the conflict, it knew that large-scale intervention was essential to save them. By the summer of 1983 military spokesmen publicly stated that the armed forces were spread too thinly throughout the world, with fleets off Nicaragua, Iran, and Lebanon. In addition to Nicaragua the Reagan Administration threatened Libya, which invaded Chad in the summer of 1983, but Washington was unable to control either government. When an unknown man in a truck blew up 240 Marines in Beirut in October 1983 the United States looked helpless, dangerously menacing Syria with a retaliation that could have quickly escalated. Then, only days later, the President sent 6,000 soldiers to take the tiny Caribbean island of Grenada away from a leftist government that had first destroyed itself in an internecine struggle.

The problem of global crisis management at the very time that internal economic and political problems subverted the country's freedom and resources for dealing with foreign military challenges did not change with American success in Grenada, but it was inevitable that after three years of sustained foreign policy losses and menacing rhetoric the United States would attempt to make its "credibility" seem real. In speedily conquering an island of fewer than 100,000 people the Reagan Administration managed, however, to alienate further its European allies and increase suspicion of it in Congress and among the critical public able to see the larger world scene.

Hubris and Dependency in a World of Upheaval

From the end of the Korean War to the end of the first Reagan Administration the Soviet-led world had in certain crucial regards become far weaker. The Sino-Soviet split moved from ideological differences to military confrontation, and within Eastern Europe the Hungarian, Czech, and Polish upheavals were neutralized only by force or threat of arms, while Rumania pursued an independent foreign policy. Failures of economic planning mired Soviet-bloc economies in domestic troubles, while in Afghanistan the Russians had committed themselves to a war that dragged on futilely. China, politically and economically unstable as well as ideologically demoralized, was pursuing a policy of military pressure on Vietnam after its terribly destructive invasion of it in January 1979.

Despite the profound turmoil within the Communist bloc, the United States was still far less able to control the remainder of the globe than it was in 1949, when it confronted a united enemy and was at the peak of its own hegemony over Europe, atomic arms, and the world economy. While its Communist enemies languished, thereby fulfilling one of the main American goals, United States power in the world declined even more quickly.

The United States in the mid-1980s stood alone among all nations in its readiness to intervene with its own overt and covert military power virtually everywhere in the world. Counting the number of American threats of military intervention since 1945, a 1978 Brookings Institution study itemized over 200 cases.[10] But it was now increasingly clear that despite Washington's profound effect on the forces of change throughout the globe, the entire world was still changing and the United States had failed in the large majority of cases to control its direction. Nor had Moscow done any better, as movements from the Right to the Left exploited it for their own purposes. In a pluralistic world no nation could realistically aspire to lead or guide mankind's course, and the price of attempting to do so would increasingly become a loss of control over its own destiny.

Ironically, while Washington gained much from the problems within the Communist world it lost far more from the sheer magnitude and diversity of global pluralism. And because of Washington's desire to block the development of radical and nationalist states everywhere, the emergence of uncontrollable and unpredictable political and social dynamics integral to modern history increasingly defied it. Corrupt and self-serving economic and military elites in so many nations of the world alone guaranteed that movements would inevitably arise to resist the social systems such regimes fostered. And the very nature of the social, demographic, and economic problems of vast areas demanded radical responses that only the Left could provide, making its leadership inevitable. The increasingly independent nature of that Left in most countries made it more rather than less dangerous to the United States, for both China and the Soviet Union had repeatedly shown that liberation movements heeding their advice were far less militant than those which did not. Indeed, just as both world capitalism and Marxism-Leninism had become far more internally nuanced and diverse than any theorist would have conceived during the first half of this century, so too had Third World and even radical movements in industrial nations evolved in ways that seemed unimaginable. From ecologists and churches opposing the nuclear bomb in Western Europe, to Solidarity resisting the pro-Soviet state from a radical position in Poland, to militant Islam in Iran and peasant movements in Central America, the nature and origins of forces of change in the world no longer conformed to neat, simple models.

The Carter and Reagan Administrations never confronted the nature of this real world and its relevance to its far-flung objectives, nor did any great debates emerge among those who have responsibility for governing. The United States was now paying a growing price for its ideological underdevelopment as well as the fathomless hubris of inherited American values. By failing to define and lower its goals the successive Carter and Reagan Administrations only deepened America's postwar crisis.

The quickening integration of the world economy that occurred after 1970 was rooted in the earlier ambitions of an American-led world capitalism. Although creating vast profits for American business, the economic integration of world capitalism was now independent of any one nation's control. It had produced a structure of growth and prosperity vulnerable to debt defaults, currency fluctuations, and political upheavals that were hopelessly entangling and were by 1984 growing in intensity and perplexity. For what integration did not bring was economic or political stability. Nations such as Brazil, Mexico, and even Communist Poland found that an alliance of the International Monetary Fund and private bankers was telling them how to run their internal social systems—something that workers refused to accept voluntarily in any of those places. The economic fate of capitalism in the world, the United States included, was to some degree now bound up with political events in a relatively few poor but large countries, a situation which no one imagined possible when Hull first articulated his vision of a postwar world order.

And while the postwar search for equilibrium through nuclear and conventional arms was surely one of the ostensible justifications for the arms race after 1954, by the 1980s that race was more precarious than ever. The spread of nuclear weapons had shattered the Soviet and American monopolies, and apart from the increasing technological sophistication of their own arsenals, the expected proliferation of nuclear arms to a dozen or more states by 1990 was making the Soviet-American role in the world arms balance less and less important. The world was moving beyond the balance of terror as bombs became increasingly accessible to political leaders and regimes of the most diverse nature. Also beyond control was the economic and even the political cost of weapons of all kinds as increasingly stark economic realities merged with political resistance within America and its alliance to pose new and growing challenges unique in the postwar period. The implications of this new enigma to Washington were still not clear. Yet it loomed larger as a central issue for the rest of the century for a growing proportion of the people in many nations who inchoately sought a new definition of the goals of their society in a troubled world whose problems American actions had so gravely aggravated. This articulate minority was no longer impressed by the undeniable argument that the USSR had interfered unconscionably in the affairs of Eastern Europe. Anti-Communism was losing its potency for a growing sector of Americans who could see plainly that Central American or Vietnamese peasants were anything but the victims of Moscow's machinations, as all postwar administrations had continuously alleged.

Increasingly crucial to the crisis of American power, both militarily and economically, was the unavoidable weakness intrinsic in its own ironic dependency on regimes it was trying to keep in office. With Washington generally unwilling and often unable to modify and reform them, their internal weaknesses rose logically from those very qualities that made them such willing allies of the United States in the first place. Beginning with China after 1945, then South Vietnam from 1954 until its fall in 1975, and most recently El Salvador and much of Latin America, the political systems Washington attempted to preserve were virtually all self-destructive and incapable of being reformed without losing their very purpose to those in power. Unwilling to change, the United States invariably supported such regimes because they easily played on Washington's fears of independent, Left alternatives, so that the viability of the American effort to lead nations and regions as part of its ideal world order was no stronger than its weakest links. And when those links broke, as they inevitably did, Washington's choice was to try to save them directly with its own forces or oppose those who came to power justly convinced that the Americans were the ultimate bastion of the corrupt old regimes. Anti-Americanism thereby became a necessary political precondition for movements of social change and progress everywhere.

The only certainty about the future is change, and change produces economic and political instabilities. America's ambition to control and regulate change in the world, much less prevent it, is a formula for perpetual turbulence at home and violence abroad, for it is futile and has by the end of the twentieth century become the main source of instability and crises in the American experience. The causes and consequences of this monumental dilemma were fully evident by 1976, and experiences since then have only deepened and aggravated the trends that were quite obvious much earlier. Less clear was how long American society could afford the economic and military costs of its obsessions overseas, costs which even after Vietnam rose to unprecedented levels. Least certain of all was the role of the American people in seeking to reverse the crisis of their social order for better or worse, and it was this reaction, perhaps above all, that would determine their own fates as well as the destiny of much of mankind. Indeed, given the increasing risks of an already dangerous world drifting amidst ever more destructive weaponry, their response might also decide the ultimate nature of the modern historical experience.

Notes

Chapter 1. The Foundations of the Political Economy, 1876–1920

1. The economic history which follows is a much abbreviated version of an analysis I published in 1963 in *The Triumph of Conservatism* (New York, 1963). With the unimportant exception of a few conservatives who ignored everything which undermined their case, no one paid much attention to my economic exposition, preferring to focus on my political narrative—which generated considerable attention and dispute—rather than its integral economic context. My position now remains the same: political events followed from the economic conditions and were a response to them, and scarcely from some self-generated effort motivated by socially displaced elite groups or intellectually alienated individuals—as earlier historians argued.

2. The geographic and capital mobility of the period are outlined in Harvey S. Perloff et al., *Regions, Resources, and Economic Growth* (Baltimore, 1960), 50–51, 252–253; Carter Goodrich et al., *Migration and Economic Opportunity: The Report of the Study of Population Distribution* (Philadelphia, 1936), 252ff.; Simon Kuznets et al., *Population Redistribution and Economic Growth: United States, 1870–1950—Analysis of Economic Change* (Philadelphia, 1960), **II**, 112ff., 126, 136ff.; Daniel Creamer et al., *Capital in Manufacturing and Mining: Its Formation and Financing* (New York, 1960), 25.

3. I have discussed these issues in detail in my *Railroads and Regulation, 1877–1916* (Princeton, 1965). The "public interest" thesis is ably assessed by Robert B. Carson, "Railroads and Regulation Revisited: A Note on Problems of Historiography and Ideology," *The Historian,* **34** (1972), 437–446.

4. U.S. House, Committee on Banking and Currency, *Hearings: Money Trust Investigation: Investigation of Financial and Monetary Conditions in the United States,* 62:2, May 1912–February 1913 (Washington, 1913), **III**, 1879. Valuable insight into the banking dilemma may be found in Milton

Friedman and Anna J. Schwartz, *A Monetary History of the United States, 1867–1960* (New York, 1963), 149–171.

5. *Congressional Record,* 64:1, January 27, 1916, vol. 53, p. 187 of appendix.

6. The best account of the war period is Robert D. Cuff, *The War Industries Board: Business-Government Relations During World War I* (Baltimore, 1973), *passim.* Also important are Paul A. C. Koistinen, "The 'Industrial-Military Complex' in Historical Perspective: World War I," *Business History Review,* **41** (1967), 376–403; Melvin I. Urofsky, *Big Steel and the Wilson Administration: A Study in Business-Government Relations* (Columbus, 1969), chap. 8; Robert F. Himmelberg, "The War Industries Board and the Antitrust Question in November 1918," *Journal of American History,* **52** (1965), 59–74; and Himmelberg, "Business, Antitrust Policy, and the Industrial Board of the Department of Commerce, 1919," *Business History Review,* **42** (1968), 1–23.

7. The structural aspects of Populism's demise were analyzed decades ago in James C. Malin, "The Turnover of Farm Population in Kansas," *Kansas Historical Quarterly,* **4** (1935), 339–372; Gerald K. Aistrup, "An Investigation of the Relationship Between Climatic Conditions and Population Changes in Western Kansas, 1885–1900" (unpublished M.S. thesis, Fort Hays, Kansas State College, 1956), *passim;* Goodrich, *Migration and Economic Opportunity,* 210–215.

8. This migration to Canada is fully discussed in Paul F. Sharp, "The American Farmer and the 'Last Best West,'" *Agricultural History,* **21** (1947), 65–75; Sharp, "When Our West Moved North," *American Historical Review,* **55** (1950), 286–300; Karel D. Bicha, "Canadian Immigration Policy and the American Farmer, 1896–1914" (unpublished Ph.D. thesis, Minneapolis, University of Minnesota, 1963).

9. Ray S. Baker and William E. Dodd, eds., *The Public Papers of Woodrow Wilson* (New York, 1925), **III**, 423.

Chapter 2. **The Foundations of the United States as a World Power, 1880–1919**

1. Though far from definitive, the only real effort to analyze the economics of this period's contradictions is the much neglected work by J. Steindl, *Maturity and Stagnation in American Capitalism* (Oxford, 1952).

2. The major statistical dimensions of these trends are to be found in Robert E. Lipsey, *Price and Quantity Trends in the Foreign Trade of the United States* (New York, 1963), 148, 430–431; Donald R. Sherk, *The United States and the Pacific Trade Basin* (Federal Reserve Bank of San Francisco, n.d. [1971]), 41.

3. U.S. Department of State, *Papers Relating to the Foreign Relations of the United States, 1900* (Washington, 1902), 385.

4. *Ibid.,* 290.

5. Howard K. Beale, *Theodore Roosevelt and the Rise of America to World Power* (New York, 1956), 270.

6. Huntington Wilson, "The Relation of Government to Foreign Investment," *Annals of the American Academy of Political and Social Science,* **68** (1916), 302.

7. Joan Hoff Wilson, *American Business and Foreign Policy, 1920–1933* (Lexington, Mass., 1971), *passim.*

8. U.S. Department of State, *Papers Relating to the Foreign Relations of the United States: The Lansing Papers, 1914–1920* (Washington, 1940), **II**, 462–464, 470.

9. Margaret Leech, *In the Days of McKinley* (New York, 1959), 345.

10. Quoted in William Diamond's realistic work, *The Economic Thought of Woodrow Wilson* (Baltimore, 1943), 132.

11. Ray S. Baker and William E. Dodd, eds., *The Public Papers of Woodrow Wilson* (New York, 1925), **IV**, 314.

12. Diamond, *Economic Thought of Woodrow Wilson,* 138.

13. James T. Shotwell, *At the Paris Peace Conference* (New York, 1937), 39.

14. The immense importance of the war for the remainder of this century is superbly discussed in Arno J. Mayer's *The Political Origins of the New Diplomacy, 1917–1918* (New Haven, 1959), and *Politics and Diplomacy of Peacemaking* (New York, 1967); and N. Gordon Levin, Jr., *Woodrow Wilson and World Politics* (New York, 1968).

15. Roy Watson Curry, *Woodrow Wilson and Far Eastern Policy, 1913–1921* (New York, 1957), 185.

16. Diamond, *Economic Thought of Woodrow Wilson,* 178.

17. John Maynard Keynes, *The Economic Consequences of the Peace* (London, 1919), 2.

18. Diamond, *Economic Thought of Woodrow Wilson,* 187.

19. Shotwell, *At the Paris Peace Conference,* 39.

20. Diamond, *Economic Thought of Woodrow Wilson,* 136.

21. Curry, *Wilson and Far Eastern Policy,* 241.

22. This mobilization for postwar expansion is detailed in Burton I. Kaufman, *Efficiency and Expansion: Foreign Trade Organization in the Wilson Administration, 1913–1921* (Westport, Conn., 1974); and Carl P. Parrini, *Heir to Empire: United States Economic Diplomacy, 1916–1923* (Pittsburgh, 1969).

Chapter 3. The American Working Class: Immigrant Foundations

1. International working-class migration is a topic of great significance, and while the analytical assessments of it are still thin, the data with which to begin major studies are first-class. Particularly good are Imre Ferenczi, ed., *International Migrations* (New York, 1929), **I**; Walter F. Willcox, ed., *International Migrations* (New York, 1931), **II**; Edith Abbott, ed., *Historical Aspects of the Immigration Problem: Select Documents* (Chicago, 1926).

2. Aaron Antonovsky, ed., *The Early Jewish Labor Movement in the United States,* a revision of the Yiddish original edited by Elias Tcherikower (New York, 1961), 54–55, 73–74; Willcox, *International Migrations,* 536–543,

556; Ferenczi, *International Migrations,* 82–87; Abbott, *Historical Aspects,* 160; William I. Thomas and Florian Znaniecki, *The Polish Peasant in Europe and America* (New York, 1958, 2d ed.), 1496–1497; Victor R. Greene, *The Slavic Community on Strike: Immigrant Labor in Pennsylvania Anthracite* (Notre Dame, 1968), 30–31; Frank J. Sheridan, "Italian, Slavic, and Hungarian Unskilled Immigrant Laborers in the United States," *Bulletin of the* [U.S.] *Bureau of Labor,* **72** (1907), 481.

3. Harry Jerome's *Migration and Business Cycles* (New York, 1926), 44–45, 151, *passim,* is the fundamental work on the returnee phenomenon; that it was the intent of most migrants to remain temporarily is shown in Thomas and Znaniecki, *The Polish Peasant,* 1504–1510; W. Lloyd Warner and Leo Srole, *The Social Systems of American Ethnic Groups* (New Haven, 1945), 99, 106; Herman L. Lantz, *People of Coal Town* (New York, 1958), 61–63; Greene, *Slavic Community on Strike,* 30–31; Joshua A. Fishman, *Hungarian Language Maintenance in the United States* (Bloomington, 1966), 3–5; George J. Prpic, *The Croatian Immigrants in America* (New York, 1971), 110–111; Silvano M. Tomasi and Madeline H. Engel, eds., *The Italian Experience in the United States* (Staten Island, 1970), 164–165; David Brody, *Steelworkers in America: The Nonunion Era* (Cambridge, 1960), 96–101; see also Willcox, *International Migrations,* 89, 477.

4. Tomasi and Engel, *The Italian Experience,* 164. See also *ibid.,* 223; Jerome, *Migration and Business Cycles,* 144–145; Willcox, *International Migrations,* 483; Warner and Srole, *Social Systems of American Ethnic Groups,* 99; Sheridan, "Unskilled Immigrant Laborers," 477; Prpic, *Croatian Immigrants,* 152; Greene, *Slavic Community on Strike,* 30–31; Lantz, *People of Coal Town,* 61–63.

5. John Palmer Gavit, *Americans By Choice* (New York, 1922), 207, 240–241; U.S. Immigration Commission, *Immigrants in Cities* (Reports of the Immigration Commission, vol. 26), 61:2 (Washington, 1911), 155–156.

6. Brinley Thomas, *Migration and Economic Growth: A Study of Great Britain and the Atlantic Economy* (Cambridge, 1954); H. J. Habakkuk, *American and British Technology in the Nineteenth Century: The Search for Labour-Saving Inventions* (Cambridge, 1962); Daniel Creamer et al., *Capital in Manufacturing and Mining: Its Formation and Financing* (New York, 1960), 25, 40–43, 65, 95; Israel Borenstein, *Capital and Output Trends in Mining Industries, 1870–1948* (New York, 1954), 30–34; J. Steindl, *Maturity and Stagnation in American Capitalism* (Oxford, 1952), 76, 160, 184–185; Harry Jerome, *Mechanization in Industry* (New York, 1934), 227.

7. Habakkuk, *American and British Technology, passim;* Thomas, *Migration and Economic Growth, passim;* Abbott, *Historical Aspects of the Immigration Problem,* 352–354, 370–382; Simon Kuznets and Ernest Rubin, *Immigration and the Foreign Born* (New York, 1954), 45; Charlotte Erickson, *American Industry and the European Immigrant, 1860–1885* (Cambridge, 1957), 33–34, 63, chap. 7; Victor S. Clark, *History of Manufactures in the United States* (Washington, 1929), **II**, 87–88, 96–97, chap. 30; **III**, 212–213; Vera Shlakman, *Economic History of a Factory Town: A Study of Chicopee, Massachusetts* (Northampton, 1935), 206–207; John H. M. Laslett,

Labor and the Left: A Study of Socialist and Radical Influences in the American Labor Movement, 1881–1924 (New York, 1970), 152–153; W. Lloyd Warner and J. O. Low, *The Social System of the Modern Factory: The Strike: A Social Analysis* (New Haven, 1947), 60–70; Clyde Griffen article in Stephen Thernstrom and Richard Sennett, eds., *Nineteenth-Century Cities: Essays in the New Urban History* (New Haven, 1969), 51; Jerold S. Auerbach, ed., *American Labor: The Twentieth Century* (Indianapolis, 1969), 50–55.

8. William M. Leiserson, *Adjusting Immigrant and Industry* (New York, 1924), 13; Gerald Rosenblum, *Immigrant Workers: Their Impact on American Labor Radicalism* (New York, 1973), 77; U.S. Immigration Commission, *Statistical Review of Immigration, 1820–1910—Distribution of Immigrants, 1850–1900* (Washington, 1911), 96–97, 441; Isaac M. Hourwich, *Immigration and Labor: The Economic Aspects of European Immigration to the United States* (New York, 1922), 402; E. P. Hutchinson, *Immigrants and Their Children, 1850–1950* (New York, 1956), 3; U.S. Immigration Commission, *Immigrants in Industries,* (Washington, 1911), **VIII**, 33, 176; **X**, 208.

9. Shlakman, *Economic History of a Factory Town,* 215–217; Auerbach, *American Labor,* 38–39; Donald B. Cole, *Immigrant City: Lawrence, Massachusetts, 1845–1921* (Chapel Hill, 1963), 116; Gerd Korman, *Industrialization, Immigrants, and Americanizers: The View from Milwaukee, 1866–1921* (Madison, 1967), 66–69, 112; Rowland Berthoff, "The Social Order of the Anthracite Region, 1825–1902," *Pennsylvania Magazine of History and Biography,* **89** (1965), 226; Lantz, *People of Coal Town,* 84–85; Emily Greene Balch, *Our Slavic Fellow Citizens* (New York, 1910), 367; David Montgomery, *Beyond Equality: Labor and the Radical Republicans, 1862–1872* (New York, 1967), 42–43.

10. Hourwich, *Immigration and Labor,* 402, 424–429; U.S. Immigration Commission, *Immigrants in Industries,* **VIII**, 386–387, 442; Don D. Lescohier and Elizabeth Brandeis, *History of Labor in the United States,* John R. Commons, ed. (New York, 1935), **III**, xxv; Peter Roberts, *Anthracite Coal Communities* (New York, 1940), 10, 24; Raymond A. Mohl and Neil Betten, "Ethnic Adjustment in the Industrial City: The International Institute of Gary, 1919–1940," *International Migration Review,* **6** (1972), 364–365; Oscar Handlin, ed., *Immigration as a Factor in American History* (Englewood Cliffs, 1959), 66–69; Cole, *Immigrant City,* 116; Korman, *Industrialization, Immigrants, and Americanizers,* 66–69, 112; Erickson, *American Industry and the European Immigrant,* 88; Christine Avghi Galitzi, *A Study of Assimilation Among the Roumanians in the United States* (New York, 1929), 64; Warner and Low, *Social System of the Modern Factory,* 92–98.

11. Jerome, *Migration and Business Cycles,* 104; Shlakman, *Economic History of a Factory Town,* 213; Rowland T. Berthoff, *British Immigrants in Industrial America, 1870–1950* (Cambridge, 1953), 33, chap. 7; Clark, *History of Manufacturers,* **II**, 88; Laslett, *Labor and the Left,* 196–205; Samuel L. Baily article in Tomasi and Engel, *The Italian Experience,* 122–123; Antonovsky, *Early Jewish Labor Movement,* 336–338; U.S. Immigration Commission, *Immigrants in Industries,* (Washington, 1911), **VI**, 101; **VIII**, 91, 279; **X**, 121. I use union membership data for iron and steel, bituminous coal,

and cotton goods workers only. Aggregate Immigration Commission data on union membership in all industries were nearly twice as high as unionism's share of the nonagricultural work force in fact was at this time, and therefore of doubtful validity.

12. Wayne G. Broehl, Jr., *The Molly Maguires* (Cambridge, 1964), *passim;* Leiserson, *Adjusting Immigrant and Industry,* 186–187, 194, 286–288; Antonovsky, *Early Jewish Labor Movement,* chaps. 14, 15; Shlakman, *Economic History of a Factory Town,* 214–215; Cole, *Immigrant City,* 185–188; Auerbach, *American Labor,* 35; Greene, *Slavic Community on Strike,* chap. 9; Lantz, *People of Coal Town,* 75; and, above all, Laslett, *Labor and the Left, passim,* for a valuable survey of the socialists, ethnics, and unions.

13. Hutchinson, *Immigrants and Their Children,* 3; Hope T. Eldridge and Dorothy Swaine Thomas, *Demographic Analyses and Interrelations* (Philadelphia, 1964), 90, 119; Robert Coles, *The South Goes North* (Boston, 1971), 313ff.; Warner and Low, *Social System of the Modern Factory,* 29.

14. U.S. Immigration Commission, *Immigrants in Industries,* **VIII**, 400–401; **X**, 178–179; Brody, *Steelworkers in America,* 86; Oscar Handlin, *Boston's Immigrants: A Study in Acculturation* (Cambridge, 1959), 82–84; Berthoff, "Social Order of the Anthracite Region," 264; Hourwich, *Immigration and Labor,* 422.

15. Warner and Low, *Social System of the Modern Factory,* 29; Immigration Commission, *Statistical Review of Immigration,* 96; Lantz, *People of Coal Town,* 229; Berthoff, *British Immigrants in Industrial America, passim;* Thomas, *Migration and Economic Growth,* 144–151.

16. U.S. Immigration Commission, *Immigrants in Industries,* (Washington, 1911), **XIX**, 119–120; *Statistical Review of Immigration, passim;* Hutchinson, *Immigrants and Their Children,* 204–206; Thomas, *Migration and Economic Growth,* 114ff.; Joseph Schachter, "Net Immigration of Gainful Workers into the United States, 1870–1930," *Demography,* 9 (1972), 89–92; Stephan Thernstrom article in Thernstrom and Sennett, *Nineteenth-Century Cities,* 129ff.; Cole, *Immigrant City,* 122–129.

17. U.S. Immigration Commission, *Immigrants in Industries,* **VIII**, 329 facepiece; *Statistical Review of Immigration,* 420–423; David Ward, *Cities and Immigrants: A Geography of Change in Nineteenth-Century America* (New York, 1971), 52–53, 71–80; Willcox, *International Migrations,* 108; Hutchinson, *Immigrants and Their Children,* 26–27; Robert E. Park and Herbert A. Miller, *Old World Traits Transplanted* (New York, 1921), 45, 129, 146–147, 198–202; Evangelos C. Vlachos, *The Assimilation of Greeks in the United States* (Athens, 1968), 75–80; Charlotte Erickson, *Invisible Immigrants: The Adaption of English and Scottish Immigrants in Nineteenth-Century America* (London, 1972), 70–73; Berthoff, *British Immigrants in Industrial America,* chap. 10; Fishman, *Hungarian Language Maintenance,* 6; Herbert J. Gans, *The Urban Villagers: Group and Class in the Life of Italian-Americans* (New York, 1962), 7–11; Rudolph J. Vecoli, "*Contadini* in Chicago: A Critique of *The Uprooted,*" *Journal of American History,* **51** (1964), 404–417; Wilbur S. Shepperson, *Emigration and Disenchantment:*

Portraits of Englishmen Repatriated from the United States (Norman, 1965), 182–184; William Foote Whyte, *Street Corner Society: The Social Structure of an Italian Slum* (Chicago, 1955), xvii, 269–271; Tomasi and Engel, *The Italian Experience, passim;* Humbert S. Nelli, *Italians in Chicago, 1880–1930: A Study in Ethnic Mobility* (New York, 1970), *passim;* Broehl, *The Molly Maguires,* 165; Antonovsky, *Early Jewish Labor Movement,* 133; Otto Feinstein, ed., *Ethnic Groups in the City: Culture, Institutions, and Power* (Lexington, Mass., 1971), 129–133; Lantz, *People of Coal Town,* 61–63; Cole, *Immigrant City, passim;* Gilbert Osofsky, *Harlem: The Making of a Ghetto* (New York, 1966), *passim;* Philip Taylor, *The Distant Magnet: European Emigration to the U.S.A.* (New York, 1971), chap. 10.

18. Thomas and Znaniecki, *The Polish Peasant,* 1537–1541, 1650–1651; Park and Miller, *Old World Traits Transplanted,* 198–202; Warner and Low, *Social System of the Modern Factory,* 226.

19. U.S. Immigration Commission, *Immigrants in Industries,* **VIII**, 161; *Immigrants in Cities,* 144–145; Roberts, *Anthracite Coal Communities,* 41–43; Balch, *Our Slavic Fellow Citizens,* 305–306; Cole, *Immigrant City,* 130–131; Warner and Srole, *Social Systems of American Ethnic Groups,* 80; Galitzi, *Assimilation Among Roumanians,* 84.

20. Antonovsky, *Early Jewish Labor Movement,* 128–129; *New York Sun,* July 8, 1882; Herbert Asbury, *The Gangs of New York* (Garden City, 1927), 119, chap. 12; Park and Miller, *Old World Traits Transplanted,* 49–50; Balch, *Our Slavic Fellow Citizens,* 366–367; Lantz, *People of Coal Town,* 92–101; Berthoff, "Social Order of the Anthracite Region," 264–267; Michael Novak, *The Rise of the Unmeltable Ethnic: Politics and Culture in the Seventies* (New York, 1972), 11–12; John C. Leggett, *Class, Race, and Labor: Working-Class Consciousness in Detroit* (New York, 1968), 126–127.

21. Roberts, *Anthracite Coal Communities,* 210, 215; Gans, *The Urban Villagers,* 111–113; Nicholas J. Russo article in Tomasi and Engel, *The Italian Experience,* 195–209; Thomas and Znaniecki, *The Polish Peasant,* 1525–1529, 1650–1651; Lydio F. Tomasi, *The Italian American Family: The Southern Italian Family's Process of Adjustment to an Urban America* (Staten Island, 1972), 8–33; Park and Miller, *Old World Traits Transplanted,* 48–51, 60–61; Nelli, *Italians in Chicago,* 121–123, 146–147, 211–215; Daniel Bell, *The End of Ideology* (New York, 1960), 128–148; Oscar Handlin, *The Uprooted* (Boston, 1951), *passim;* Whyte, *Street Corner Society,* 123–124, 138, 273; Cole, *Immigrant City,* 27–52, 69, 78, 89, 92, 109–112.

22. Luciano J. Iorizzo article in Tomasi and Engel, *The Italian Experience,* 43–75; Novak, *Rise of the Unmeltable Ethnic,* 26; J. David Greenstone, *Labor in American Politics* (New York, 1969), 286; Park and Miller, *Old World Traits Transplanted,* 97; Milton M. Gordon, *Assimilation in American Life: The Role of Race, Religion, and National Origins* (New York, 1964), 34.

23. M. Heald, "Business Attitudes Toward European Immigration, 1880–1900," *Journal of Economic History,* **13** (1953), 291–304; Hourwich, *Immigration and Labor,* iii–v, for a good explanation of the origins of restric-

tion; Edward George Hartmann, *The Movement to Americanize the Immigrant* (New York, 1948), chaps. 2, 3; Brody, *Steelworkers in America,* 186–191.

24. U.S. Immigration Commission, *Immigrants in Industries,* **VI**, 209, 213–215, 234–235; Leiserson, *Adjusting Immigrant and Industry,* 100–101, 107–108, 118–119, 134–136; Hartmann, *Movement to Americanize the Immigrant,* chaps. 2, 3; Frank H. Streightoff, *The Standard of Living Among Industrial People of America* (Boston, 1911), 127; Korman, *Industrialization, Immigrants, and Americanizers,* chaps, 5, 6; Balch, *Our Slavic Fellow Citizens,* 301.

25. Park and Miller, *Old World Traits Transplanted,* 60–61, 104–109; Thomas and Znaniecki, *The Polish Peasant,* 1537, 1650–1651; U.S. Immigration Commission, *Abstracts of Reports,* vol. II of series (Washington, 1911), 165–170; Tomasi, *Italian American Family,* 8–27; Rowland T. Berthoff, *An Unsettled People: Social Order and Disorder in American History* (New York, 1971), 372ff.; Whyte, *Street Corner Society,* 272–273; Prpic, *Croatian Immigrants,* 223–227; Berthoff, *British Immigrants in Industrial America,* 136–141; Erickson, *Invisible Immigrants,* 5; Abraham Menes article in Herbert G. Gutman and Gregory S. Kealey, eds., *Many Pasts* (Englewood Cliffs, 1973), **II**, 227–237; Geno Baroni article in Michael Wenk et al., eds., *Pieces of a Dream: The Ethnic Worker's Crisis with America* (Staten Island, 1972), 4ff.; Vlachos, *Assimilation of Greeks,* 99–105; Fishman, *Hungarian Language Maintenance,* 31ff.; H. L. Mencken, *The American Language* (New York, 1948), *passim.*

26. Benjamin Malzberg and Everett S. Lee, *Migration and Mental Disease: A Study of First Admissions to Hospitals for Mental Disease, New York, 1939–1941* (New York, 1956), 26. See also *ibid.,* 18–23, 58, 116, *passim;* Eldridge and Thomas, *Demographic Analyses,* xxxii–xxxiii; U.S. Immigration Commission, *Abstracts of Reports,* 234–236; Henry Wechsler, "Community Growth, Depressive Disorders, and Suicide," *American Journal of Sociology,* **67** (1961), 13–14.

27. Theodore Saloutos, *They Remember America: The Story of Repatriated Greek-Americans* (Berkeley, 1956), *passim;* Prpic, *Croatian Immigrants,* 162–165; George R. Gilkey article in Franklin D. Scott, ed., *World Migrations in Modern Times* (Englewood Cliffs, 1968), 44–50; Francesco Cerase article in Tomasi and Engel, *The Italian Experience,* 217–238.

Chapter 4. The Political Economy of Capitalism in Crisis, 1920–1940

1. Daniel Creamer et al., *Capital in Manufacturing and Mining: Its Formation and Financing* (New York, 1960), 25, 95; John W. Kendrick, *Productivity Trends in the United States* (New York, 1961), 148, 152, 396, 464; U.S. Congress, Joint Economic Committee, *Productivity, Prices, and Incomes,* 85:1 (Washington, 1957), 59, 89, 116, 150–151; Richard A. Easterlin, *Population, Labor Force, and Long Swings in Economic Growth: The American Experience* (New York, 1968), 84; U.S. Senate, Committee on Labor and Public Welfare, *History of Employment and Manpower Policy in*

the United States, 88:2 (Washington, 1965), V, 1592–1593; J. Steindl, *Maturity and Stagnation in American Capitalism* (Oxford, 1952), 173; U.S. Council of Economic Advisers, *Economic Report of the President, 1975* (Washington, 1975), 337.

2. Simon Kuznets, *Capital in the American Economy: Its Formation and Financing* (New York, 1961), 209; Harold G. Moulton, *The Formation of Capital* (Washington, 1935), 143–145; Kendrick, *Productivity Trends in the United States,* 396, 464; Senate Committee on Labor and Public Welfare, *History of Employment and Manpower Policy,* V, 1589, 1594, 1635, 1646; Gabriel Kolko, *Wealth and Power in America* (New York, 1962), 14, 99; U.S. Bureau of the Census, *Historical Statistics of the United States, Colonial Times to 1957* (Washington, 1960), 73, 283, 286; Alvin S. Tostlebe, *Capital in Agriculture: Its Formation and Financing Since 1870* (New York, 1957), 19, 48; Christiana McFadyen Campbell, *The Farm Bureau and the New Deal: A Study of the Making of National Farm Policy, 1933–40* (Urbana, 1962), 3ff.; Grant McConnell, *The Decline of Agrarian Democracy* (Berkeley, 1953), 57.

3. Herbert Hoover, *The Memoirs of Herbert Hoover: The Cabinet and the Presidency, 1920–1933* (New York, 1952), 301. See also *ibid.,* 28ff., 62ff.; Senate Committee on Labor and Public Welfare, *History of Employment and Manpower Policy,* V, 1735–1739.

4. For the general dilemma of trade associationism and competition, see Hoover, *Memoirs,* 169–170; John Perry Miller, *Unfair Competition: A Study in Criteria for the Control of Trade Practices* (Cambridge, 1941), 89–94, 285–287; Louis Galambos, *Competition and Cooperation: The Emergence of a National Trade Association* (Baltimore, 1966), chaps. 1–6; Arden J. Lea, "Cotton Textiles and the Federal Child Labor Act of 1916," *Labor History,* **16** (1975), 485–494; Jesse Thomas Carpenter, *Competition and Collective Bargaining in the Needle Trades, 1910–1967* (Ithaca, 1972), 522–523; Ellis W. Hawley, "Secretary Hoover and the Bituminous Coal Problem, 1921–1928," *Business History Review,* **42** (1968), 247–270. The oil difficulty is outlined in Gerald D. Nash, *United States Oil Policy, 1890–1964: Business and Government in Twentieth-Century America* (Pittsburgh, 1968), 85–111; Harold F. Williamson et al., *The American Petroleum Industry, 1899–1959* (Evanston, 1959), 504ff. The investment problems are presented in Michael E. Parrish, *Securities Regulation and the New Deal* (New Haven, 1970), 8–9, 20–21, 30–31; Vincent P. Carosso, *Investment Banking in America: A History* (Cambridge, 1970), 96–97, 104–109, 170–171, 258–279; Stephen V. O. Clarke, *Central Bank Cooperation, 1924–31* (New York, 1967), 149–157; Milton Friedman and Anna Jacobson Schwartz, *A Monetary History of the United States, 1867–1960* (New York, 1963), 240–241, 255, 298.

5. William Starr Myers and Walter H. Newton, *The Hoover Administration: A Documented Narrative* (New York, 1936), 4.

6. *Ibid.,* 119. See also Nash, *United States Oil Policy,* 112–120.

7. Myers and Newton, *The Hoover Administration,* 155. See also the excellent and unconscionably ignored study by Grant N. Farr, *The Origins of Recent Labor Policy* (Boulder, 1959), 21–29.

8. Hoover, *Memoirs,* 300. See also *ibid.,* 335; Farr, *Origins of Recent Labor Policy,* 24–25; Myers and Newton, *The Hoover Administration,* 155; Daniel Nelson, *Unemployment Insurance: The American Experience, 1915–1935* (Madison, 1969), 144; Barry Karl, "Presidential Planning and Social Science Research: Mr. Hoover's Experts," *Perspectives in American History,* 3 (1969), 361, 364, 403.

9. Jordan A. Schwarz, *The Interregnum of Despair: Hoover, Congress, and the Depression* (Urbana, Ill., 1970), 89–105, 176–177; Myers and Newton, *The Hoover Administration,* 26–27, 126–129; Gerald D. Nash, "Herbert Hoover and the Origins of the Reconstruction Finance Corporation," *Mississippi Valley Historical Review,* **46** (1959), 455–468.

10. Frances Perkins, *The Roosevelt I Knew* (New York, 1946), 328.

11. Raymond Moley, *The First New Deal* (New York, 1966), 6.

12. *Ibid.,* 228. See also *ibid.,* 4–7, 223; Daniel R. Fusfeld, *The Economic Thought of Franklin D. Roosevelt and the Origins of the New Deal* (New York, 1956), 107, 247–253; Schwarz, *Interregnum of Despair,* chap. 5, 228n.; Farr, *Origins of Recent Labor Policy,* 35; Galambos, *Competition and Cooperation,* 187ff.

13. Farr, *Origins of Recent Labor Policy,* 71–72. See also *ibid.,* 62–64; Moley, *The First New Deal,* 228, 286–289; Galambos, *Competition and Cooperation,* 190–196; Perkins, *The Roosevelt I Knew,* 194; Ellis W. Hawley, *The New Deal and the Problem of Monopoly: A Study in Economic Ambivalence* (Princeton, 1966), 24–25.

14. Nash, *United States Oil Policy,* 134–135; Moley, *The First New Deal,* 288–289, 291; Galambos, *Competition and Cooperation,* 196–199; Farr, *Origins of Recent Labor Policy,* 65; Hawley, *New Deal and the Problem of Monopoly,* 24–26.

15. Moley, *The First New Deal,* 291.

16. Farr, *Origins of Recent Labor Policy,* 73. See also Grace Abbott memo, May 25, 1933, to Felix Frankfurter, Frankfurter Papers, Library of Congress.

17. Farr, *Origins of Recent Labor Policy,* 30. See also *ibid.,* 29, 75, 92–95; Hawley, *New Deal and the Problem of Monopoly,* 54–64, 67, 213–223, 232–234; Galambos, *Competition and Cooperation,* 204, 226, 240–256, 268–271, chap. 12; William E. Leuchtenburg, *Franklin D. Roosevelt and the New Deal* (New York, 1963), 261–263; James T. Patterson, "A Conservative Coalition Forms in Congress, 1933–1939," *Journal of American History,* **52** (1966), 761; Meyer Fishbein, "The Trucking Industry and the National Recovery Administration," *Social Forces,* **34** (1955), 171–179; Nash, *United States Oil Policy,* 128–156; Williamson, *American Petroleum Industry,* 548–551; Sidney Fine, *The Automobile Under the Blue Eagle: Labor, Management, and the Automobile Manufacturing Code* (Ann Arbor, 1963), 37–38, 57, 70–73; Joint Economic Committee, *Productivity, Prices, and Incomes,* 265; Grace Abbott, May 25, 1933, memo, Frankfurter Papers; Carpenter, *Competition and Collective Bargaining,* 591–595, 614–615, 628–629, 652–653, 768–771, 814–815; James P. Johnson, "Drafting the NRA Code of Fair

Competition for the Bituminous Coal Industry," *Journal of American History,* 53 (1966), 521–554.

18. Moley, *The First New Deal,* 312. See also Parrish, *Securities Regulation,* 46–53; Carosso, *Investment Banking in America,* 348–351; Arthur M. Johnson, *Winthrop W. Aldrich: Lawyer, Banker, Diplomat* (Boston, 1968), 138–151.

19. Parrish, *Securities Regulation,* 42. See also Moley, *The First New Deal,* 312–313; Carosso, *Investment Banking in America,* 352; Felix Frankfurter to Eustice Seligman, April 25, 1933; Seligman to Frankfurter, May 15, 1933; George S. Stevenson to Frankfurter, June 10, 1933; Bernard Flexner to Frankfurter, August 8, 1933, Frankfurter Papers.

20. Johnson, *Winthrop W. Aldrich,* 206. See also *ibid.,* 156–157, 178–179, 198–199; Carosso, *Investment Banking in America,* 362–363, 372–384; Parrish, *Securities Regulation,* 108–111, 153, chap. 5; Counsel for Investment Bankers Association to Senator Joseph T. Robinson, May 5, 1933, in Frankfurter Papers; Helen M. Burns, *The American Banking Community and the New Deal Banking Reforms, 1933–1935* (Westport, Conn., 1974), 49–50, 68, 74, 86–87, 158–161, 173–175.

21. Parrish, *Securities Regulation,* 179. See also *ibid.,* 162–178; Leuchtenburg, *Roosevelt and the New Deal,* 159–161; Johnson, *Winthrop W. Aldrich,* 206–208; Samuel P. Huntington, "Clientalism: A Study in Administrative Politics" (unpublished Ph.D. thesis, Harvard University, 1950), *passim.*

22. Parrish, *Securities Regulation,* 230. See also *ibid.,* 228–229; Carosso, *Investment Banking in America,* 384–385.

23. Johnson, *Winthrop W. Aldrich,* 213. See also Parrish, *Securities Regulation,* 230.

24. U.S. Bureau of Labor Statistics, *Handbook of Labor Statistics,* Bulletin No. 694 (Washington, 1942), I, 97. See also Creamer, *Capital in Manufacturing and Mining,* 95; Kendrick, *Productivity Trends in the United States,* 396, 464; Joint Economic Committee, *Productivity, Prices, and Incomes,* 151; Gladys L. Palmer and Katherine D. Wood, *Urban Workers on Relief,* WPA Research Monograph IV (Washington, 1936), 37, 67; Leuchtenburg, *Roosevelt and the New Deal,* 120–125, 131–132, 152–154; Arthur M. Schlesinger, Jr., *The Age of Roosevelt: The Politics of Upheaval* (Boston, 1960), 326–328, 334; Hawley, *New Deal and the Problem of Monopoly,* 348–350; Roy G. and Gladys C. Blakey, *The Federal Income Tax* (New York, 1940), 366–373; Johnson, *Winthrop W. Aldrich,* 209; Kolko, *Wealth and Power in America,* 14, 32–33, 80–81, 89–90, 99–100; Nelson, *Unemployment Insurance,* 213–217; Roy Lubove, *The Struggle for Social Security, 1900–1935* (Cambridge, 1968), 53–61, chap. 4; Senate Committee on Labor and Public Welfare, *History of Employment and Manpower Policy,* V, 2018–2021; Tostlebe, *Capital in Agriculture,* 48–51; Carter Goodrich et al., *Migration and Economic Opportunity: The Report of the Study of Population Redistribution* (Philadelphia, 1936), 73–74; *Historical Statistics,* 283; Campbell, *The Farm Bureau and the New Deal,* 48–49, chap. 7; McConnell, *Decline of Agrarian Democracy,* 70, 149, 185; Theodore Saloutos and John D. Hicks,

Agricultural Discontent in the Middle West, 1900–1939 (Madison, 1951), chaps. 8–12.

25. Joint Economic Committee, *Productivity, Prices, and Incomes,* 109; Howard J. Sherman, *Profits in the United States: An Introduction to a Study of Economic Concentration and Business Cycles* (Ithaca, 1968), 41; William L. Crum, *Corporate Size and Earning Power* (Cambridge, 1939), 31, 45.

26. Johnson, *Winthrop W. Aldrich,* 197, 230–239; *Business Week,* October 6, 1934; Hawley, *New Deal and the Problem of Monopoly,* 397; Harmon Zeigler, *The Politics of Small Business* (Washington, 1961), 17; Moley, *The First New Deal,* 200–203; Leuchtenburg, *Roosevelt and the New Deal,* 243–249, 263; Perkins, *The Roosevelt I Knew,* 321.

27. Felix Frankfurter to Franklin D. Roosevelt, June 4, 1940, Frankfurter Papers. See also Leuchtenburg, *Roosevelt and the New Deal,* 272; Hawley, *New Deal and the Problem of Monopoly,* 411, 418–419, chap. 20; Gabriel Kolko, "American Business and Germany, 1930–1941," *Western Political Quarterly,* **15** (1962), 716–717; Johnson, *Winthrop W. Aldrich,* 210, 241.

Chapter 5. **The American Working Class: Structure and Limits**

1. Some of the more important studies of these trends are Harold M. Levinson, *Unionism, Wage Trends, and Income Distribution, 1914–1947* (Ann Arbor, 1951), 111, *passim;* Levinson, *Determining Forces in Collective Wage Bargaining* (New York, 1966), 12–18; Joseph Garbarino, "A Theory of Interindustry Wage Structure Variation," *Quarterly Journal of Economics,* **64** (1950), 282–305; M. W. Reder, "The Theory of Union Wage Policy," *Review of Economics and Statistics,* **34** (1952), 34–45; Paul M. Schieble, "Changes in Employee Compensation, 1966 to 1972," *Monthly Labor Review,* March 1975, 15.

2. John W. Kendrick, *Productivity Trends in the United States* (New York, 1961), 197; Gabriel Kolko, *Wealth and Power in America* (New York, 1962), 85; Dixie Sommers, "Occupational Rankings for Men and Women by Earnings," *Monthly Labor Review,* August 1974, 34–51.

3. *New York Times,* February 9, 1958. See also John H. M. Laslett, *Labor and the Left: A Study of Socialist and Radical Influences in the American Labor Movement, 1881–1924* (New York, 1970), 84–85, 90–91, 111; George B. Tindall, *The Emergence of the New South, 1913–1945* (Baton Rouge, 1967), 347–351, 511–512, 520–521; Lloyd Ulman, "The Development of Trades and Labor Unions," *American Economic History,* Seymour E. Harris, ed. (New York, 1961), 388–389; Levinson, *Determining Forces,* 274–275.

4. *Wall Street Journal,* March 31, 1958.

5. *Wall Street Journal,* February 14, March 3, May 6, September 11, 1958; Everett G. Martin, "Walter Reuther Makes a Big Bid in a Bad Year," *The Reporter,* April 3, 1958, 24–30; Reder, "Theory of Union Wage Policy," 45; Levinson, *Unionism, Wage Trends,* 112–124; Kolko, *Wealth and Power in America, passim;* Clark Kerr, "Trade-Unionism and Distributive Shares,"

American Economic Review, **44** (1954), 288ff.

6. This critical issue of labor costs and technology is assessed in Kendrick, *Productivity Trends,* 148, 197; J. Steindl, *Maturity and Stagnation in American Capitalism* (Oxford, 1952), 76–77; W. Paul Strassmann, *Risk and Technological Innovation: American Manufacturing Methods in the Nineteenth Century* (Ithaca, 1959), 111–113; Joseph A. Litterer, "Systematic Management: The Search for Order and Integration," *Business History Review,* **35** (1961), 464–467; U.S. Congress, Joint Economic Committee, *Productivity, Prices, and Incomes,* 85:1 (Washington, 1957), 150–151; Harry Jerome, *Mechanization in Industry* (New York, 1934), 227. Using a broader definition of all wages paid relative to the value of manufactures, Jerome fixes this drop from 48.1 percent in 1879 to 36.4 percent in 1929.

7. Lloyd Ulman, *The Rise of the National Trade Union* (Cambridge, 1966), 519–521; Jesse Thomas Carpenter, *Competition and Collective Bargaining in the Needle Trades, 1910–1967* (Ithaca, 1972), xix–xxi, 20–21, 42–43, 492–493, 502–505; Irving Bernstein, *Turbulent Years: A History of the American Worker, 1933–1941* (Boston, 1970), 21–22; Stanley Vittoz, "American Industrial Economy and the Political Origins of Federal Labor Policy Between the World Wars" (unpublished Ph.D. thesis, Toronto, York University, 1976), *passim.*

8. Abraham Berglund et al., *Labor in the Industrial South* (Charlottesville, 1930), 16–18; Hope T. Eldridge and Dorothy Swaine Thomas, *Demographic Analyses and Interrelations* (Philadelphia, 1964), 23, 118–119, 125; Clarence D. Long, *Wages and Earnings in the United States, 1860–1890* (New York, 1960), 80, 109; Kolko, *Wealth and Power in America,* 77, 92–93; Carpenter, *Competition and Collective Bargaining,* 460–461, 474–477, 549–551, 614–615, 628; Lloyd Ulman, "The Development of Trades and Labor Unions," 368; E.H.P. Brown, *A Century of Pay* (London, 1968), 116–117, 301; Everett J. Burtt, Jr., *Labor Markets, Unions, and Government Policies* (New York 1963), 313; Don D. Lescohier and Elizabeth Brandeis, *History of Labor in the United States* (New York, 1935), 56–57, 61, 83; Paul H. Douglas, *Real Wages in the United States, 1890–1926* (New York, 1930), chaps. 6, 13; Kendrick, *Productivity Trends,* 84; Richard A. Easterlin, *Population, Labor Force, and Long Swings in Economic Growth: The American Experience* (New York, 1968), 256; Albert Rees, *Real Wages in Manufacturing, 1890–1914* (New York, 1961), *passim;* Irving Bernstein, *The Lean Years: A History of the American Worker, 1920–1933* (Boston, 1960), 65; Joint Economic Committee, *Productivity,* 137; U.S. Department of Labor 1976 release 76–45.

9. Kendrick, *Productivity Trends,* 89; Conrad and Irene B. Taeuber, *The Changing Population of the United States* (New York, 1958), 155, 207–208, 224; U.S. Bureau of the Census, *Statistical Abstracts* for various years; Seymour Melman, "The Rise of Administrative Overhead in the Manufacturing Industries of the United States, 1899–1947," *Oxford Economic Papers,* **3** (1951), 66; Industrial Union Department, AFL-CIO, *Automation and Technological Change* (IUD, April 22, 1958), 6; Clarence D. Long, *The Labor*

Force Under Changing Income and Employment (New York, 1958), 7, 112; Kolko, *Wealth and Power in America,* 91–92, 104; Department of Labor 1975 releases 75–136, 75–323.

10. Philip Taft and Philip Ross in Hugh Davis Graham and Ted Robert Gurr, eds., *The History of Violence in America* (New York, 1970), 281.

11. New York *Tribune,* July 24, 1877.

12. U.S. President's Conference on Unemployment, Committee on Recent Economic Changes, *Recent Economic Changes in the United States* (New York, 1929), xxii. See also Vittoz, "American Industrial Economy," *passim;* Arden J. Lea, "Cotton Textiles and the Federal Child Labor Act of 1916," *Labor History,* **16** (1975), 485–494; Bernstein, *The Lean Years,* chap. 11.

13. Bernstein, *Turbulent Years,* 783. See also Laslett, *Labor and the Left,* introduction and conclusion; Ira Kipnis, *The American Socialist Movement, 1897–1912* (New York, 1952), 129–133, 245–278, 347, 397; Carpenter, *Competition and Collective Bargaining, passim;* Harold D. Lasswell and Dorothy Blumenstock, *World Revolutionary Propaganda: A Chicago Study* (New York, 1939), 261.

14. Brotherhood of Locomotive Engineers, *Minutes of Proceedings . . . Boston, 1866* (Rochester, 1866), 6. See also David Montgomery, *Beyond Equality: Labor and the Radical Republicans, 1862–1872* (New York, 1967), 208–209; Warren R. Van Tine, *The Making of the Labor Bureaucrat: Union Leadership in the United States* (Amherst, 1973), 9–18, 184–185; David Brody, *Steelworkers in America: The Nonunion Era* (Cambridge, 1960), 86; Terence V. Powderly, *The Path I Trod* (New York, 1940), *passim;* Norman J. Ware, *The Labor Movement in the United States, 1860–1895* (New York, 1929), chap. 7.

15. Brotherhood of Locomotive Firemen, *Journal of Proceedings . . . Buffalo, 1878* (Terre Haute?, 1878), 7; *Journal of Proceedings . . . Chicago, 1880* (Terre Haute?, 1880), 15–16.

16. American Civil Liberties Union, *Democracy in Labor Unions* (New York, June, 1952), 3. See also Van Tine, *The Making of the Labor Bureaucrat,* chaps. 4–5.

17. *New York Times,* October 25, 1953; *Wall Street Journal,* December 17, 1957, January 28, May 16, September 16, 18, October 10, 1958.

18. Walter H. Uphoff and Marvin D. Dunnette, *Understanding the Union Member* (Minneapolis, 1956), *passim;* Ruth Alice Hudson and Hjalmar Rosen, "Union Political Action: The Member Speaks," *Industrial and Labor Relations Review,* 7 (1954), 404–418; *Wall Street Journal,* January 17, June 6, 1958; J. David Greenstone, *Labor in American Politics* (New York, 1969), *passim; New Republic,* July 21, 1958, 13–18.

19. John I. Snyder, Jr., *Address Before Second Annual Industrial Relations Conference, Industrial Union Department, AFL-CIO,* June 17, 1958 (Washington, 1958), 9. See also *ibid.,* 5; Carpenter, *Competition and Collective Bargaining,* 192–193; David Brody article in John Braeman et al., eds., *Change and Continuity in Twentieth-Century America: The 1920's* (Columbus, 1968), 150.

20. *Wall Street Journal,* October 10, 1958. See also Van Tine, *The Making of the Labor Bureaucrat,* 80–81.; and especially William Serrin, *The Company and the Union* (New York, 1973), for the auto industry.

Chapter 6. The United States and the World Crisis, 1920–1945

1. J. Steindl, *Maturity and Stagnation in American Capitalism* (Oxford, 1952), 5–7, 151, 160, 173, 225; U.S. Congress, Joint Economic Committee, *Productivity, Prices, and Incomes,* 85:1 (Washington, 1957), 116; Harold G. Moulton, *The Formation of Capital* (Washington, 1935), 144–145; Simon Kuznets, *Capital in the American Economy: Its Formation and Financing* (New York, 1961), 95; Daniel Creamer et al., *Capital in Manufacturing and Mining: Its Formation and Financing* (New York, 1960), 25; Edwin G. Nourse, *America's Capacity to Produce* (Washington, 1934), 416–417, 560, 582–585.

2. Robert E. Lipsey, *Price and Quantity Trends in the Foreign Trade of the United States* (New York, 1963), 148–149, 154–155, 430–431; Jaroslav Vanek, *The Natural Resource Content of United States Foreign Trade, 1870–1955* (Cambridge, 1963), 46, 59–60, 69; Stephen V. O. Clarke, *Central Bank Cooperation: 1924–31* (New York, 1967), 20; Donald R. Sherk, *The United States and the Pacific Trade Basin* (Federal Reserve Bank of San Francisco, n.d. [1971]), 41.

3. Harold Nicolson, *Dwight Morrow* (New York, 1935), 242. See also Clarke, *Central Bank Cooperation,* 20–21; Joan Hoff Wilson, *American Business and Foreign Policy, 1920–1933* (Lexington, Mass., 1971), 16–23; Kuznets, *Capital in the American Economy,* 132, 573.

4. Benjamin Shwadran, *The Middle East, Oil, and the Great Powers* (New York, 1955), 223.

5. Nicolson, *Morrow,* 243. See also Joseph Brandes, *Herbert Hoover and Economic Diplomacy: Department of Commerce Policy, 1921–1928* (Pittsburgh, 1962), *passim.*

6. Clarke, *Central Bank Cooperation,* 22–23, 47–48; Carl P. Parrini, *Heir to Empire: United States Economic Diplomacy, 1916–1923* (Pittsburgh, 1969), chap. 4; Wilson, *American Business and Foreign Policy,* chaps. 4, 5; Paul P. Abrahams, "American Bankers and the Economic Tactics of Peace: 1919," *Journal of American History,* **56** (1969), 583; Gabriel Kolko, "American Business and Germany, 1930–1941," *Western Political Quarterly,* **15** (1962), 718.

7. Jules R. Benjamin, *The United States and Cuba: Hegemony and Dependent Development* (Pittsburgh, 1977), chaps. 6–10. See also Charles P. Kindleberger, *The World in Depression, 1929–1939* (Berkeley, 1973), 172ff.; Clarke, *Central Bank Cooperation,* 202–218; Robert F. Smith, *The United States and Cuba: Business and Diplomacy, 1917–1960* (New York, 1960), 155.

8. Cordell Hull, *Memoirs* (New York, 1948), 344.

9. William L. Neumann article in Alexander DeConde, ed., *Isolation and Security* (Durham, 1957), 147. See also Wilson, *America's Business and*

Foreign Policy, 202–211; Roy Watson Curry, *Woodrow Wilson and Far Eastern Policy, 1913–1921* (New York, 1957), 297–302; Herbert Feis, *The Diplomacy of the Dollar: First Era, 1919–1932* (Baltimore, 1950), 34–35.

10. A. Whitney Griswold, *The Far Eastern Policy of the United States* (New York, 1938), 422. See also Wilson, *American Business and Foreign Policy,* chap. 8; Dorothy Borg, *The United States and the Far Eastern Crisis of 1933–1938* (Cambridge, 1964), 31–32.

11. Hull, *Memoirs,* 538. See also *ibid.,* 280ff.; Borg, *United States and the Far Eastern Crisis,* 80ff.; Wilson, *American Business and Foreign Policy,* chap. 12.

12. Hull, *Memoirs,* 554.

13. *Ibid.,* 591–592. See also Robert Divine, *The Illusion of Neutrality* (Chicago, 1962), 162; Wayne S. Cole, *Senator Gerald P. Nye and American Foreign Relations* (Minneapolis, 1962), *passim.*

14. Hull, *Memoirs,* 81.

15. *Ibid.,* 391.

16. *Ibid.,* 518.

17. *Ibid.,* 594.

18. *Ibid.,* 746.

19. The discussion which follows is based on my *The Politics of War: The World and United States Foreign Policy, 1943–1945* (New York, 1968), where further details and documentation may be found.

20. *Ibid.,* 148.

21. *Ibid.,* 167.

22. *Ibid.,* 249.

23. *Ibid.,* 268.

Chapter 7. The Accumulation of Power

1. Bliss Perry, *Richard Henry Dana, 1851–1931* (Boston, 1933), 118. I have amplified this concept of a "head start" in "Brahmins and Business, 1870–1914," in Barrington Moore, Jr., and Kurt H. Wolff, eds., *The Critical Spirit: Essays in Honor of Herbert Marcuse* (Boston, 1967), 343–363.

2. Bliss Perry, *Life and Letters of Henry Lee Higginson* (Boston, 1921), 272. Also see E. Digby Baltzell, *Philadelphia Gentlemen: The Making of a National Upper Class* (Glencoe, 1958), 71ff.

3. Perry, *Higginson,* 271.

4. Edward C. Kirkland, *Charles Francis Adams, Jr., 1835–1915: The Patrician at Bay* (Cambridge, 1965), 95.

5. Barry E. Supple, "A Business Elite: German-Jewish Financiers in Nineteenth-Century New York," *Business History Review,* 31 (1957), 143–178; Arthur M. Johnson and Barry E. Supple, *Boston Capitalists and Western Railroads: A Study in the Nineteenth-Century Railroad Investment Process* (Cambridge, 1967), *passim;* Baltzell, *Philadelphia Gentlemen,* 20, 365.

6. David T. Stanley et al., *Men Who Govern: A Biographical Profile of Federal Political Executives* (Washington, 1967), *passim.*

7. William Endicott, Jr., to Richard Olney, April 23, 1893, Olney Papers, vol. 5, Library of Congress.

8. Eugene Staley, *War and the Private Investor* (Chicago, 1935), 219.

9. Gabriel Kolko, *The Roots of American Foreign Policy* (Boston, 1969), chap. 2.

10. Gen. Dwight D. Eisenhower, Memo, "Scientific and Technological Resources as Military Assets," April 27, 1946, Henry L. Stimson Papers, Yale University Library.

11. U.S. Senate, Committee on Government Operations, *Hearings: Organizing for National Security,* 87:1 (Washington, 1961), I, 1190. See also Kolko, *Roots of American Foreign Policy,* 20ff.

Chapter 8. **Politics and the Foundations of Power**

1. Philip H. Burch, Jr., "The NAM as an Interest Group," *Politics and Society,* 3 (1973), 97–130; Charles Francis Adams, Jr., to W. P. Gorman, November 12, 1910; Charles Francis Adams, Jr., to Charles W. Eliot, May 6, 1914, Adams Papers, Massachusetts Historical Society; *New York Times,* January 30, 1974.

2. Otto Kirchheimer, *Political Justice: The Use of Legal Procedure for Political Ends* (Princeton, 1961), 6. See also Walter Dean Burnham, "The Changing Shape of the American Political Universe," *American Political Science Review,* 59 (1965), 7–28; C. Vann Woodward, *The Origins of the New South, 1877–1913* (Baton Rouge, 1951), *passim;* Jerome M. Clubb and Howard W. Allen article in Clubb and Allen, eds., *Electoral Change and Stability in American Political History* (New York, 1971), 248; Robert D. Marcus, *Grand Old Party: Political Structure in the Gilded Age, 1880–1896* (New York, 1971), 5, 253; J. David Greenstone, *Labor in American Politics* (New York, 1969), 76; Donald K. Pickens, *Eugenics and the Progressives* (Nashville, 1968), *passim.*

3. Gerald G. Eggert, *Railroad Labor Disputes: The Beginnings of Federal Strike Policy* (Ann Arbor, 1967), *passim;* Arnold M. Paul, *Conservative Crisis and the Rule of Law: Attitudes of Bar and Bench, 1887–1895* (Ithaca, 1960), 35–37, chap. 4; Ray S. Baker and William E. Dodd, eds., *The Public Papers of Woodrow Wilson* (New York, 1925), IV, 35–45.

4. Robert K. Murray, *Red Scare: A Study in National Hysteria, 1919–1920* (Minneapolis, 1955), 251, states there were 3000 arrests during November 1919–January 1920 and about 600 deportations. See also H. C. Peterson and Gilbert C. Fite, *Opponents of War, 1917–1918* (Madison, 1957), *passim;* William Preston, Jr., *Aliens and Dissenters: Federal Suppression of Radicals, 1903–1933* (Cambridge, 1963), chap. 1.

5. Henry Lee Higginson to Andrew J. Peters, December 16, 1912, Higginson Papers, vol. 3, Baker Library, Harvard Business School. See also Edward N. Saveth, *American Historians and European Immigrants* (New York, 1948), *passim;* John Higham, *Strangers in the Land: Patterns of American Nativism, 1860–1925* (New Brunswick, 1955), *passim.*

6. Norton E. Long, "Public Relations Policies of the Bell System," *Public Opinion Quarterly,* 1 (1937), 20–21.

7. Angie Debo, *A History of the Indians of the United States* (Norman, 1970), *passim;* Daniel B. Schirmer, *Republic or Empire: American Resistance to the Philippine War* (Cambridge, 1972), 142–143; Renato Constantino, *The Philippines: A Past Revisited* (Manila, 1975), 242–245.

8. Philip Taft and Philip Ross article in Hugh Davis Graham and Ted Robert Gurr, eds., *The History of Violence in America* (New York, 1970), 281. See also *ibid.,* 69.

9. *Ibid.,* 93, 490–492; Sheldon Hackney, "Southern Violence," *American Historical Review,* 74 (1969), 910, 913, 919.

10. Thomas D. Clark to members of the Organization of American Historians, February 1, 1973.

11. Gabriel Kolko, *The Triumph of Conservatism* (New York, 1963), 207.

12. Herbert Croly, *Marcus Alonzo Hanna: His Life and Work* (New York, 1912), 317. See also *ibid.,* 114–115; David J. Rothman, *Politics and Power: The United States Senate, 1869–1901* (Cambridge, 1966), 114–115, 122–133, 186–198, 210–211; Matthew Josephson, *The Politicos, 1865–1896* (New York, 1938), *passim;* Marcus, *Grand Old Party, passim.*

13. Gabriel Kolko, "Max Weber and America: Theory and Evidence," *History and Theory,* 1 (1961), 243–260; Josephson, *The Politicos, passim;* Marcus, *Grand Old Party, passim;* Ari Hoogenboom and R. Hal Williams articles in H. Wayne Morgan, ed., *The Gilded Age,* revised edition (Syracuse, 1970), 78–79, 144–145. For a defense of the Senate, see Rothman, *Politics and Power,* 197–201; but for an example of its corruption, involving $4857 sent by a railroad president to a key Senator well placed to influence U.S. policy on mail-service contracts, land grants, or rights-of-way on Indian lands, see Senator John H. Mitchell's acknowledgments of receipts in his letters to Henry Villard, December 8, 1882, June 12, 1883, August 3, 1883, in Villard Papers, box 95, Harvard College Library.

14. Leonard D. White, *The Republican Era: 1869–1901—A Study in Administrative History* (New York, 1958), chap. 17; Marcus, *Grand Old Party,* 12–13; Louise Overacker, *Money in Elections* (New York, 1932), 32–33.

15. Croly, *Hanna,* 469. See also *ibid.,* 145.

16. Kolko, *The Triumph of Conservatism,* 121.

17. *Ibid.,* 123–124, 143, 202; U.S. Senate, Committee on Privileges and Elections, *Hearings: Campaign Contributions,* 62:3, June 1912–February 1913 (Washington, 1913), I, 123, 152–155, 173, 386–400, 641–642, 736–741; Marcus, *Grand Old Party,* 25; Overacker, *Money in Elections,* 73, 100–101; C. K. Yearley, *The Money Machines: The Breakdown and Reform of Governmental and Party Finance in the North, 1860–1920* (Albany, 1970), 114–115, *passim; New York Times,* September 19, 1973; David A. Pollock, *Methods of Electronic Audio Surveillance* (Springfield, 1973), 324–329; Donald R. Cressey, *Theft of the Nation: The Structure and Operations of Organized Crime in America* (New York, 1969), 197–199, chap. 11.

18. *New York Times,* August 7, 1974. See also Overacker, *Money in*

Elections, 133, 162; David Nichols, *Financing Elections: The Politics of an American Ruling Class* (New York, 1974), 56–59, 64, 178; Greenstone, *Labor in American Politics,* 10.

19. Woodward, *Origins of the New South,* 341–346; V. O. Key, Jr., *Southern Politics: In State and Nation* (New York, 1949), 496, 501.

20. See also Key, *Southern Politics, passim;* George B. Tindall, *The Emergence of the New South, 1913–1945* (Baton Rouge, 1967), *passim;* Harvey S. Perloff et al., *Regions, Resources, and Economic Growth* (Baltimore, 1960), 252–253; Nancy J. Weiss, "The Negro and the New Freedom: Fighting Wilsonian Segregation," *Political Science Quarterly,* **84** (1969), 61–79.

Chapter **9. The Structure of Political Capitalism, 1941–1975**

1. Marver H. Bernstein, *Regulating Business by Independent Commission* (Princeton, 1955), 87. See also U.S. Senate, Special Committee to Study Problems of American Small Business, *Economic Concentration and World War II,* 79:2, June 14, 1946 (Washington, 1946), 30–31 and *passim;* Solomon Fabricant, *The Trend of Government Activity in the United States Since 1900* (New York, 1952), 14–19; Walter Adams and Horace M. Gray, *Monopoly in America: The Government as Promoter* (New York, 1955), 106–107, 203–205, chap. 6; U.S. Congress, Joint Economic Committee, *Subsidy and Subsidylike Programs of the U.S. Government,* 86:2 (Washington, 1960), 74; Gabriel Kolko, *The Roots of American Foreign Policy* (Boston, 1969), 25.

2. Adams and Gray, *Monopoly in America,* 65–67; U.S. Council of Economic Advisers, *Economic Report of the President, 1975* (Washington, 1975), 149–159; U.S. Senate, Committee on the Judiciary, *Report on Regulatory Agencies to the President-Elect, December 1960,* 86:2 (Washington, 1960), 71–72; *Business Week,* May 12, 1975, 74–80.

3. U.S. Congress, Joint Economic Committee, *Report: The Economics of Military Procurement,* 91:1, May 1969 (Washington, 1969), 5–7, 15–17; Joint Economic Committee, *Subsidy and Subsidylike Programs,* 20–21, 44–51, 61–63; *Business Week,* January 19, 1976, 51–52; Clarence H. Danhof, *Government Contracting and Technological Change* (Washington, 1968), 75, 94; Adams and Gray, *Monopoly in America,* 79–88; U.S. Senate, Committee on Armed Services, *Draft Report: Inquiry Into the Strategic and Critical Materials Stockpiles of the United States,* 88:1, October 24, 1963 (Washington, 1963), 4–8; *New York Times,* November 17, 1974; Kolko, *Roots of American Foreign Policy,* 16–23, 140–141.

4. U.S. Senate, Committee on Labor and Public Welfare, *History of Employment and Manpower Policy in the United States,* 88:2 (Washington, 1965), **VI**, 2136. See also *ibid.,* 2449ff.

5. *Ibid.,* 2390ff., 2438–2442; *Economic Report of the President, 1975,* 26, 120–122; U.S. Department of Labor releases 74–677 and 76–17; *Business Week,* October 5, 1974, 29–30; Gabriel Kolko, *Wealth and Power in America* (New York, 1962), 79–81.

6. U.S. Social Security Administration, Office of Research and Statistics, *Demographic and Economic Characteristics of the Aged: 1968 Social Secu-*

rity Survey, Research Report No. 45 (Washington, 1975), 17–18; *Monthly Labor Review,* July 1974, 33–37; *Social Security Bulletin,* August 1974, 3; January 1975, 6; U.S. Congress, Joint Economic Committee, *Studies in Public Welfare,* Paper No. 14, 93:2, April 15, 1974 (Washington, 1974), 45–49. The comparison of tax burdens and welfare is calculated from Joseph A. Pechman and Benjamin A. Okner, *Who Bears the Tax Burden?* (Washington, 1974), 56, 61; *Statistical Abstract of the United States,* 1967 (Washington, 1967), 390–391, 421; *Economic Report of the President, 1975,* 268.

7. Kolko, *Wealth and Power in America,* 107.

8. *Business Week,* October 12, 1974, 120. See also *ibid.,* 94–96; *Economic Report of the President, 1976,* 187, 240–241.

9. U.S. Senate, Committee on the Judiciary, *Report: Concentration Ratios in Manufacturing Industry: 1963,* 89:2 (Washington, 1966), 2–3, 19, 31–32; *Wall Street Journal,* January 9, April 13, 1961; *New York Times,* October 14, 1959; NICB *Conference Board Record,* March 1976, 19.

10. John M. Blair, *Economic Concentration* (New York, 1972), *passim;* Kolko, *Wealth and Power in America,* 57–60; U.S. House, Committee on the Judiciary, *Report: Interlocks in Corporate Management,* 89:1, March 12, 1965 (Washington, 1965), *passim.*

11. *Survey of Current Business,* November 1974, 25ff.

12. Joyce Kolko, *America and the Crisis of World Capitalism* (Boston, 1974), 71; Kolko, *Wealth and Power in America,* 41, 61–67; Philip H. Burch, Jr., *The Managerial Revolution Reassessed: Family Control in America's Large Corporations* (Lexington, Mass., 1972), 29–30, 70; Wilbur G. Lewellen, *The Ownership Income of Management* (New York, 1971), *passim.*

13. U.S. Congress, Joint Economic Committee, *Productivity, Prices, and Incomes,* 85:1 (Washington, 1957), 101, 117, 120; *Federal Reserve Bulletin,* June 1974, 424; *Statistical Abstract—1974,* 453; *Economic Report of the President, 1975,* 296, 342; *1976,* 211, 261; National Bureau of Economic Research, *54th Annual Report, September 1974* (New York, 1974), 39, 42; First National City Bank *Monthly Economic Letter,* May 1975, 7–9; July 1975, 6; *Survey of Current Business,* May 1974, 19ff.; July 1974, 48–50; Howard J. Sherman, *Profits in the United States: An Introduction to a Study of Economic Concentration and Business Cycles* (Ithaca, 1968), 41–47, 64–67, 88–93; Industrial Union Department, AFL-CIO, *Labor, Big Business, and Inflation* (Washington, 1958), 28–31, and September 2, 1958, United Automobile Workers report on finances of 30 leading corporations; Chase Manhattan Bank *Business in Brief,* December 1974, n.p.

14. Kolko, *Wealth and Power in America,* 20, chap. 1; Pechman and Okner, *Who Bears the Tax Burden?,* 45–46; Lewis Mandell et al., *Surveys of Consumers, 1971–72: Contributions to Behavioral Economics* (Ann Arbor, 1973), 72.

15. Kolko, *Wealth and Power in America,* 34; Pechman and Okner, *Who Bears the Tax Burden?,* 51, 56, 61, 64; Senator Walter F. Mondale, May 26, 1975, press release and accompanying report.

16. Kolko, *Wealth and Power in America,* x, chap. 3, 149–150; James D. Smith et al., "The Distribution of Financial Assets" (unpublished study,

1973), *passim;* James D. Smith and Stephen D. Franklin, "The Concentration of Personal Wealth, 1922–1969" (1973), *passim,* (a version of this research appeared in *American Economic Review,* **64** [1974], 162–167); *Survey of Current Business,* November 1974, 25–27; Robert E. Gallman in Lee Soltow, ed., *Six Papers on the Size Distribution of Wealth and Income* (New York, 1969), 5–11.

17. U.S. Department of Labor 1974–1975 releases 74-502, 74-620, 75-159; *Statistical Abstract—1973,* 46; Kolko, *Wealth and Power in America,* 140–141, chap. 7.

Chapter **10. The Perpetual Crisis: American Foreign Policy Since 1946**

1. The preceding discussion, and much that follows, is detailed in Joyce and Gabriel Kolko, *The Limits of Power: The World and United States Foreign Policy, 1945–1954* (New York, 1972), *passim.* Throughout this book I refer to the "Left." By Left I mean all parties in the historic socialist tradition—from Social Democrats to Communists—as well as new national liberation forces with radical social programs. Self-identification is sufficient to qualify for the appellation, though in fact it occurred that many of these parties lacked the capacity or will to decisively alter the status quo.

2. Gabriel Kolko, *The Roots of American Foreign Policy* (Boston, 1969), 95.

3. U.S. National Security Council, Report NSC-68, "United States Objectives and Programs for National Security," April 14, 1950, 31. See also *ibid.,* 28, 57–58, regarding the economic rationale for greater military spending, and 21, 56–57, and 61–62 on the rollback of Communism in Eastern Europe and even the USSR. Declassified April 8, 1975, my copy of NSC-68 came from the President's Secretary's File, Harry S. Truman Papers, Truman Library, Independence, Mo.

4. Kolko, *The Limits of Power,* 616.

5. The Senator Gravel Edition, *The Pentagon Papers: The Defense Department History of United States Decisionmaking on Vietnam* (Boston, 1971), **I**, 83–84, 187.

6. I have explored this theme and the causes of Vietnam in much greater detail in Noam Chomsky and Howard Zinn, eds., *The Pentagon Papers: Critical Essays* (Boston, 1972), 4–5.

7. *Ibid.,* 6. See also Maurice Zeitlin and Robert Scheer, *Cuba: Tragedy in Our Hemisphere* (New York, 1963), and Joyce Kolko et al., eds., "A Press Digest on United States–Cuba Relations, 1957–1961" (Cambridge, 1961), copies in Harvard and Princeton Libraries.

8. Kolko, *Roots of American Foreign Policy,* 131.

9. *Pentagon Papers,* **II**, 193.

10. *Ibid.,* 336.

11. *New York Times,* July 20, 1975.

12. *Department of State Bulletin,* July 3, 1972, 18. See also Richard Whalen, *Catch the Falling Flag* (Boston, 1972), 27–32, 128–144, 236–240, 248–293; Marvin Kalb and Bernard Kalb, *Kissinger* (Boston, 1974), *passim.*

13. William H. Sullivan, "The United States and the Pacific Region," *Rotary Balita* (Manila), September 20, 1973.

14. *Department of State Bulletin,* February 25, 1974, 187–188.

15. James Schlesinger in *Wall Street Journal,* January 27, 1975.

16. Kolko, *Roots of American Foreign Policy,* 70. See also U.S. Department of Agriculture, *Handbook of Agricultural Charts, 1967* (Washington, 1967), 42.

17. U.S. Council of Economic Advisers, *Economic Report of the President, 1975* (Washington, 1975), 249, 259; *1983*, 163; Department of Commerce, Office of Business Economics, *Fixed Nonresidential Business Capital in the United States, 1925–1970* (COM–71–01111) (Washington, 1971), 427; U.S. National Advisory Council on International Monetary and Financial Policies, *Annual Report, 1972–1973* (Washington, 1973?), 9; Robert E. Lipsey, *Price and Quantity Trends in the Foreign Trade of the United States* (New York, 1963), 144–145, 431; *Business Week,* November 30, 1974, 27.

18. *Survey of Current Business,* October 1975, 32, 48; *Department of State Bulletin,* April 1, 1974, 339; Richard Rosecrance and Arthur Stein, "Interdependence: Myth or Reality?," *World Politics,* **26** (1973), 24.

19. Joyce Kolko, *America and the Crisis of World Capitalism* (Boston, 1974), 33–37; *Survey of Current Business,* August 1975, 23–24; October 1975, 48; *Economic Report of the President, 1975,* 256, 335, 352; Kolko, *Roots of American Foreign Policy,* 74, 76; Federal Reserve Bank of New York *Monthly Bulletin,* June 1975, 124; *New York Times,* February 6, 1976.

20. U.S. Commission on Foreign Economic Policy, *Staff Papers* (Washington, 1954), 88.

21. Kolko, *Roots of American Foreign Policy,* 79. See also United Nations, Department of Economic Affairs, *The International Flow of Private Capital, 1946–1952* (New York, 1954), 34; Lipsey, *Price and Quantity Trends,* 149; Commission on Foreign Economic Policy, *Staff Papers,* 88–91, 138–139, 221; Rosecrance and Stein, "Interdependence: Myth or Reality?," 24.

22. Kolko, *Roots of American Foreign Policy,* 51. See also *ibid.,* 79; *Department of State Bulletin,* June 9, 1975, 775–776.

23. Energy Economics Division, Chase Manhattan Bank, *Outlook for Energy in the United States to 1985* (New York, June 1972), 45. See also *Department of State Bulletin,* October 2, 1972, 374–375; March 25, 1974, 293; U.S. House, Committee on Foreign Affairs, *Hearings: Global Scarcities in an Interdependent World,* 93:2, May 1974 (Washington, 1974), 95, 101, 121–122, 139, 247; *New York Times,* November 17, 1974; *International Herald Tribune,* February 13, 1975.

24. *Department of State Bulletin,* May 1, 1972, 630.

25. *Ibid.,* July 30, 1973, 194.

26. *Ibid.,* October 2, 1972, 374.

27. *Ibid.,* March 23, 1970, 386.

28. *New York Times,* October 5, 1972.

29. For all aspects of this crisis, see Kolko, *America and the Crisis of World Capitalism, passim.*

30. Cited in *Pacific Basin Reports,* August 1, 1972, 234. See also National Advisory Council, *Annual Report, 1972–1973,* 9–10, 120; U.S. House, Committee on Appropriations, *Hearings: Foreign Assistance and Related Agencies Appropriations for 1975,* 93:2 (Washington, 1974), I, 837.

31. Department of State, January 16, 1975, release.

32. These issues I have discussed in greater detail in Richard Falk et al., eds., *Crimes of War* (New York, 1971), 403–415; and in Donald W. Harward, ed., *Crisis in Confidence: The Impact of Watergate* (Boston, 1974), 113–126. See also Michael Klare, "Operation Phoenix and the Failure of Pacification in South Vietnam," *Liberation,* May 1973, 21–27. For the exclusion of traditional elites by Nixon, see U.S. Senate, Committee on Foreign Relations, *The Role of Advisory Committees in U.S. Foreign Policy,* 94:1, April 1975 (Washington, 1975), 1–2, 54.

33. *Wall Street Journal,* January 27, 1975; *International Herald Tribune,* February 25, 26, 1975.

34. *Department of State Bulletin,* January 19, 1976, 71.

Chapter 11. Epilogue: The Continuity of Past and Present

1. *Business Week,* March 21, 1977, 128; April 11, 1977, 88; U.S. Council of Economic Advisers, *Economic Report of the President, 1983* (Washington, 1983), 103–122.

2. *Economic Report of the President, 1977,* 150; *1983,* 111; *New York Times,* January 23, 25, April 15, 1979; *Business Week,* March 5, 1979, 25; March 16, 1981, 27; July 4, 1983, 97; November 28, 1983, 80.

3. *International Herald Tribune,* November 12, 1981.

4. *Ibid.,* May 5, 1977.

5. *New York Times,* January 17, 1979.

6. *Ibid.,* October 4, 1979.

7. *International Herald Tribune,* February 16–17, 1980.

8. Department of State release, April 25, 1980.

9. Text of April 20, 1982, speech, Defense Department press release.

10. Barry M. Blechman and Stephen S. Kaplan, *Force Without War: U.S. Armed Forces as a Political Instrument* (Washington, 1978).

Index

About the Author

GABRIEL KOLKO is the author of *The Roots of American Foreign Policy, The Politics of War, Railroads and Regulation, The Triumph of Conservatism. Wealth and Power in America,* and, with Joyce Kolko, *The Limits of Power.* He received a doctorate from Harvard University and is currently professor of history at York University in Toronto. He is in the process of completing a book on the Vietnam War, which Pantheon will publish in 1986.